TOP 10 OF EVERYTHING 2004

NOVOTEL
palm
BEST
MUSICAL
NYC

TOP 10 OF EVERYTHING 2004

RUSSELL ASH

Contents

Senior Editor Nicki Lampon
Senior Art Editor Kevin Ryan
DTP Designers Rajen Shah
Production Heather Hughes

Managing Editor Adèle Hayward
Managing Art Editor Karen Self
Category Publisher Stephanie Jackson

Author's Project Manager Aylla Macphail

Canadian edition produced by
International Book Productions Inc.,
25A Morrow Avenue, Suite 202,
Toronto, ON M6R 2H9, Canada

Project editor Barbara Hopkinson
Researcher Terri Rothman
Editors Sheila Hall, Judy Phillips
DTP designer Dietmar Kokemohr

Dorling Kindersley is represented in Canada by
Tourmaline Editions Inc.,
662 King St. West, Suite 304, Toronto, ON M5V 1M7

Canadian Cataloguing in Publication Data
Ash, Russell
The top 10 of everything / Russell Ash
Annual.
Began publication with issue for 1996 (produced 1995).
Issues for 2002- published: Toronto : Dorling Kindersley, 2001- .
Includes index.
ISSN 1209-3882
ISBN 1-55363-018-1 (2004 edition)
1. World records. 2. Curiosities and wonders.
I. Title. II. Title: Top ten of everything.
AG243.A75 031.02'05 0 C97-301371-0

Reproduction by Colourscan, Singapore
Printed and bound in Germany by
GGP Media GmbH
03 04 05 3 2 1

See our complete catalogue at
www.dk.com

Introduction

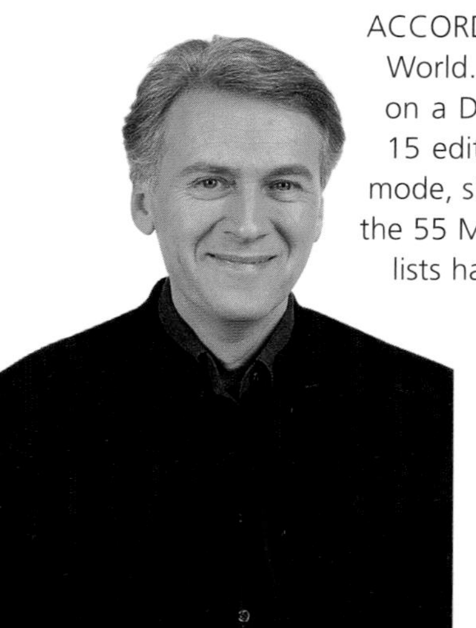

ACCORDING TO HISTORIAN Edward Creasy, there were Fifteen Decisive Battles of the World. The planet Uranus has 15 moons, while in *Treasure Island* there are "15 Men on a Dead Man's Chest." Now, with the publication of this book, there have been 15 editions of *The Top 10 of Everything*. It's all too easy to slip into this list-geared mode, since we are constantly assailed with lists: from the 100 Greatest Film Stars and the 55 Most Wanted Iraqis to the bestselling DVDs and the most-visited Internet sites, lists have become a part of our world view.

A SENSE OF PERSPECTIVE

One function of *The Top 10 of Everything* is to distill down a wealth of data by drawing together a diversity of quantitative superlatives. They are not anyone's "10 bests" (which are qualitative judgments), but there are some "10 worsts" in the case of accidents and disasters, since, sadly, these can be gauged by numbers of victims. The only "bests" are bestsellers, because sales can be measured. There are the results of major polls and also some "firsts" and "latests," which recognize pioneers, most recent achievers and award-winners.

SOURCE MATERIAL

My data sources include "official" and government departments, from the United Nations and sports governing bodies to commercial organizations and research groups, every one of whom have granted me privileged access to their databases. Among the most rewarding sources of all are the private individuals who are specialists in everything from poisonous creatures to the world's tallest buildings, and who have been generous enough to share with me the results of their researches.

AS TIME GOES BY...

Entry levels for Top 10 lists have changed, often dramatically, over the 15 annual publications of *The Top 10 of Everything*: the richest American of 15 years ago had a mere $6.7 billion, while Bill Gates is today more than six times wealthier. We have ever-bigger cruise liners, spiraling transfer fees for sports superstars, and increasing levels of worldwide box office income—the criterion on which the film lists are mostly based—which means that *Star Wars*, the highest-earning film in 1990, is now ranked tenth.

A COMEDY OF ERRORS

I endeavor to ensure that the information in *The Top 10 of Everything* is as up to date and as accurate as possible, but arguments continue to rage over the precise lengths of rivers, how many
ces
disagree with each other, some may disagree with me. But then at least I don't claim—as certain respected reference books have—that Mt. Pico in the Azores is 20,639 m (67,713 ft) high (more than twice the height of Everest), that Iceland has 1,754 tractors per hectare (hence a total of 180 billion tractors), or that Manila has a population of 21 people per square foot...

KEEP IN CONTACT

Do please send me your comments and any corrections or ideas for new lists by writing to me c/o the publishers or by e-mailing me direct at ash@pavilion.co.uk

Other Dorling Kindersley books by Russell Ash:
The Factastic Book of 1,001 Lists
The Factastic Book of Comparisons
Great Wonders of the World
The Top 10 of Sports (with Ian Morrison)
The Top 10 of Film

SPECIAL FEATURES

- Over 700 lists on everything under—and beyond—the Sun
- Completely updated with many innovative lists, from pop star film debuts and films from song titles, to the strongest men and the most valuable comics
- "First Fact" features throughout on such diverse subjects as the first in-flight wedding and the first radio broadcast, to the first newspaper in Canada and the first 200-mph car
- Further Information—a valuable guide to the Top 10 websites to explore for each of the principal themes in *The Top 10 of Everything*

THE UNIVERSE & THE EARTH

Heavenly Bodies

TOP 10 COMETS COMING CLOSEST TO THE EARTH

	COMET	DATE*	(AU)#	DISTANCE (MILES)	(KM)
1	**Comet of 1491**	Feb 20, 1491	0.0094	873,784	1,406,220
2	**Lexell**	July 1, 1770	0.0151	1,403,633	2,258,928
3	**Tempel-Tuttle**	Oct 26, 1366	0.0229	2,128,688	3,425,791
4	**IRAS-Araki-Alcock**	May 11, 1983	0.0313	2,909,516	4,682,413
5	**Halley**	Apr 10, 837	0.0334	3,104,724	4,996,569
6	**Biela**	Dec 9, 1805	0.0366	3,402,182	5,475,282
7	**Grischow**	Feb 8, 1743	0.0390	3,625,276	5,834,317
8	**Pons-Winnecke**	June 26, 1927	0.0394	3,662,458	5,894,156
9	**Comet of 1014**	Feb 24, 1014	0.0407	3,783,301	6,088,633
10	**La Hire**	Apr 20, 1702	0.0437	4,062,168	6,537,427

* *Of closest approach to the Earth*

\# *Astronomical Units: 1 AU = mean distance from the Earth to the Sun (149,597,870 km/92,955,793 miles)*

TOP 10 LARGEST METEORITES EVER FOUND

	LOCATION	ESTIMATED WEIGHT (TONNES)
1	**Hoba West, Grootfontein, Namibia**	more than 60.0
2	**Ahnighito ("The Tent"), Cape York, West Greenland**	57.3
3	**Campo del Cielo, Argentina**	41.4
4	**Canyon Diablo*, Arizona**	30.0
5	**Sikhote-Alin, Russia**	27.0
6	**Chupaderos, Mexico**	24.2
7	**Bacuberito, Mexico**	22.0
8	**Armanty, Western Mongolia**	20.0
9	**Mundrabilla#, Western Australia**	17.0
10	**Mbosi, Tanzania**	16.0

* *Formed Meteor Crater; fragmented; total in public collections is around 11.5 tonnes*

\# *In two parts*

ASTEROID DISCOVERED!

FIRST FACT

ON NEW YEAR'S DAY, 1801, at the observatory at Palermo, Sicily, Giuseppe Piazzi (1746–1826), a monk, astronomer, and professor of mathematics, was working on what was later published as a catalog of 7,646 stars when he observed an object in the constellation of Taurus. Having recorded its location, he noted over the next six weeks that it had moved, thus demonstrating the existence of asteroids—rocks orbiting between Mars and Jupiter. Named Ceres, the asteroid has been examined by the Hubble Space Telescope, and NASA's *Dawn* mission, scheduled to be launched in 2006, will make a close study of Ceres in 2014.

TOP 10 LARGEST ASTEROIDS

	ASTEROID	YEAR DISCOVERED	DIAMETER (MILES)	(KM)
1	**Ceres**	1801	582	936
2	**Pallas**	1802	377	607
3	**Vesta**	1807	322	519
4	**Hygeia**	1849	279	450
5	**Euphrosyne**	1854	229	370
6	**Interamnia**	1910	217	349
7	**Davida**	1903	200	322
8	**Cybele**	1861	192	308
9	**Europa**	1858	179	288
10	**Patientia**	1899	171	275

NASA's NEO (Near Earth Object) program monitors close approaches of asteroids and other space objects to Earth. "Near" in this context means within 45 million km (28 million miles) of Earth's orbit.

TOP 10 LARGEST PLANETARY MOONS

	MOON	PLANET	DIAMETER (MILES)	(KM)
1	**Ganymede**	Jupiter	3,274	5,269
2	**Titan**	Saturn	3,200	5,150
3	**Callisto**	Jupiter	2,986	4,806
4	**Io**	Jupiter	2,263	3,642
5	**Moon**	Earth	2,159	3,475
6	**Europa**	Jupiter	1,945	3,130
7	**Triton**	Neptune	1,680	2,704
8	**Titania**	Uranus	980	1,578
9	**Rhea**	Saturn	949	1,528
10	**Oberon**	Uranus	946	1,522

► Galileo and Ganymede
The cratered surface of Ganymede, the largest of Jupiter's moons and larger than the planet Mercury. Ganymede was discovered by Italian astronomer Galileo on January 7, 1610, and investigated by NASA's aptly named *Galileo* probe, which reached it in 1996.

TOP 10 GALAXIES CLOSEST TO THE EARTH

	GALAXY	DISTANCE (LIGHT-YEARS)
1	Large Cloud of Magellan	169,000
2	Small Cloud of Magellan	190,000
3	Ursa Minor dwarf	250,000
4	Draco dwarf	260,000
5	Sculptor dwarf	280,000
6	Fornax dwarf	420,000
7	= Leo I dwarf	750,000
	= Leo II dwarf	750,000
9	Barnard's Galaxy	1,700,000
10	Andromeda Spiral	2,200,000

These and other galaxies are members of the so-called "Local Group," although with vast distances such as these, "local" is clearly a relative term.

► By Jupiter!
The Solar System's largest planet is more massive than all the other eight planets combined. The prominent Great Red Spot, seen here on the right, turns counterclockwise and is easily large enough to swallow Earth.

TOP 10 LARGEST BODIES IN THE SOLAR SYSTEM

	BODY	MAXIMUM DIAMETER (KM)	(MILES)
1	Sun	1,392,140	865,036
2	Jupiter	142,984	88,846
3	Saturn	120,536	74,898
4	Uranus	51,118	31,763
5	Neptune	49,532	30,778
6	Earth	12,756	7,926
7	Venus	12,103	7,520
8	Mars	6,794	4,222
9	Ganymede	5,269	3,274
10	Titan	5,150	3,200

Most of the planets are visible to the naked eye and have been the object of systematic study since ancient times. The planets that are too small to be seen unaided are Uranus, discovered on March 13, 1781, by British astronomer William Herschel; Neptune, found by German astronomer Johann Galle, who announced his discovery on September 23, 1846; and, outside the Top 10, Pluto, located by US astronomer Clyde Tombaugh on March 13, 1930.

TOP 10 LARGEST AND HEAVIEST METEORITES FOUND IN CANADA

	SITE/PROVINCE	YEAR DISCOVERED	ESTIMATED WEIGHT (LB)	(KG)
1	Madoc, Ontario	1864	369.3	167.5
2	Iron Creek, Alberta	1869	321.9	146.0
3	Albee, Alberta	1952	235.9	107.0
4	Osseo, Ontario	1931	102.1	46.3
5	Dresden*, Ontario	1939	88.0	39.9
6	Manitouwabing, Ontario	1962	86.0	39.0
7	Springwater#, Saskatchewan	1931	85.1	38.6
8	Bruderheim, Alberta	1930	68.8	31.2
9	Hagersville†, Ontario	1999	66.1	30.0
10	Vulcan, Alberta	1962	41.9	19.0

** Greatest mass*

 # Greatest mass of three masses

† An iron meteorite, single mass, not yet officially accepted and named

Geological Survey of Canada

TOP 10 LONGEST SPACE MISSIONS*

	NAME#	MISSION DATES	DURATION DAYS:HR:MIN
1	**Valeri V. Polyakov**	Jan 8, 1994–Mar 22, 1995	437:17:59
2	**Sergei V. Avdeyev**	Aug 13, 1998–Aug 28, 1999	379:14:52
3	**= Musa K. Manarov**	Dec 21, 1987–Dec 21, 1988	365:22:39
	= Vladimir G. Titov	Dec 21, 1987–Dec 21, 1988	365:22:39
5	**Yuri V. Romanenko**	Feb 5–Dec 5, 1987	326:11:38
6	**Sergei K. Krikalyov**	May 18, 1991–Mar 25, 1992	311:20:01
7	**Valeri V. Polyakov**	Aug 31, 1988–Apr 27, 1989	240:22:35
8	**= Oleg Y. Atkov**	Feb 8–Oct 2, 1984	236:22:50
	= Leonid D. Kizim	Feb 8–Oct 2, 1984	236:22:50
	= Anatoli Y. Solovyov	Feb 8–Oct 2, 1984	236:22:50

To January 1, 2003

All Soviet/Russian

)ace-medicine specialist Valeri Vladimirovich Polyakov (born April 27, 1942))ent his 52nd birthday in space during his record-breaking mission aboard the *ir* space station. One of its purposes was to study the effects on the human body long-duration spaceflight.

TOP 10 LARGEST REFLECTING TELESCOPES

	TELESCOPE NAME	LOCATION	APERTURE (FT)	(M)
1	**= Keck I Telescope***	Mauna Kea, Hawaii	32.8	10.0
	= Keck II Telescope*	Mauna Kea, Hawaii	32.8	10.0
3	**Hobby-Eberly Telescope**	Mount Fowlkes, Texas	30.9	9.2
4	**Subaru Telescope**	Mauna Kea, Hawaii	27.2	8.3
5	**= Antu Telescope**	Cerro Paranal, Chile	26.9	8.2
	= Kueyen Telescope	Cerro Paranal, Chile	26.9	8.2
	= Melipal Telescope	Cerro Paranal, Chile	26.9	8.2
	= Yepun Telescope	Cerro Paranal, Chile	26.9	8.2
9	**= Gemini North Telescope***	Mauna Kea, Hawaii	26.5	8.1
	= Gemini South Telescope*	Cerro Pachon, Chile	26.5	8.1

* *Twins*

Antu, Kueyen, Melipal, and Yepun are soon to be combined to form the appropriately named Very Large Telescope, which will take first place in this list with an aperture of 16.4 m (53.8 ft). The Keck telescopes work in tandem to produce the largest reflecting surface. They are to be combined with several smaller scopes to form the 14.6-m (47.9-ft) Keck Interferometer.

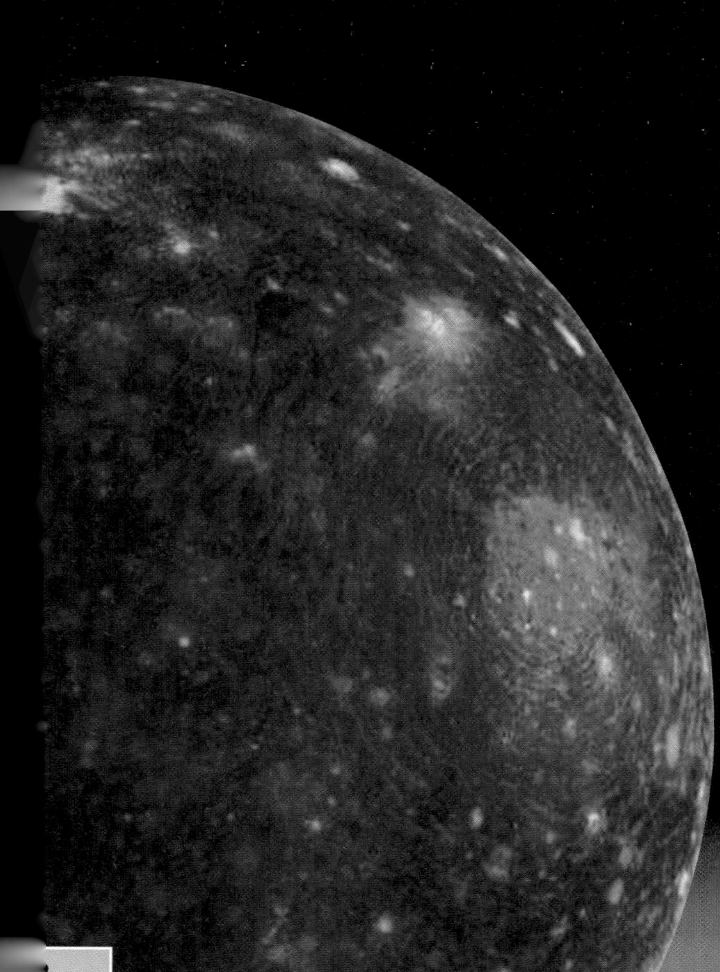

◀ Callisto's Craters
First observed by Galileo, Callisto, the second largest of Jupiter's satellites, has the most heavily cratered surface of any body in the solar system: Valhalla, the crater seen here on the right-hand side of Callisto, is 600 km (373 miles) in diameter.

THE 10 FIRST PLANETARY MOONS TO BE DISCOVERED

	MOON	PLANET	DISCOVERER	YEAR
1	**Moon**	Earth	—	Ancient
2	**Io**	Jupiter	Galileo Galilei (Italian)	1610
3	**Europa**	Jupiter	Galileo Galilei	1610
4	**Ganymede**	Jupiter	Galileo Galilei	1610
5	**Callisto**	Jupiter	Galileo Galilei	1610
6	**Titan**	Saturn	Christian Huygens (Dutch)	1655
7	**Iapetus**	Saturn	Giovanni Cassini (Italian/French)	1671
8	**Rhea**	Saturn	Giovanni Cassini	1672
9	**Tethys**	Saturn	Giovanni Cassini	1684
10	**Dione**	Saturn	Giovanni Cassini	1684

While Earth's Moon has been observed since ancient times, it was not until the development of the telescope that Galileo was first able to discover (on January 7, 1610) the moons of another planet.

TOP 10 COUNTRIES WITH MOST SPACEFLIGHT EXPERIENCE*

	COUNTRY	ASTRONAUTS	DURATION OF MISSION (DAYS)	(HR)	(MIN)	(SEC)
1	USSR/Russia#	96	15,806	1[illegible]	16	36
2	US	271	8,509	08	48	22
3	France	9	384	23	38	00
4	Kazakhstan	2	349	14	59	03
5	Germany	10	309	17	08	56
6	Canada	8	122	13	30	58
7	Japan	5	88	06	00	40
8	Italy	4	76	06	34	09
9	Switzerland	1	42	12	05	32
10	South Africa	1	24	22	28	22

* *To January 1, 2003*

\# *Russia became a separate independent state on December 25, 1991*

The USSR, and now Russia, has clocked up its considerable lead on the rest of the world (with 61 percent of the total time spent by humans in space) largely through the long-duration stays of its cosmonauts on board the *Mir* space station. The US has had almost three times as many astronauts in space—principally aboard the Space Shuttle—but its missions have been of shorter duration. Up to January 1, 2003, the USSR/Russia and the US had hosted representatives of 28 further countries. Of these, Mexico's space experience is the shortest: a single six-day mission. Canada has participated in eight shuttle missions. On April 22, 2001, Chris Hadfield became the first Canadian to walk in space.

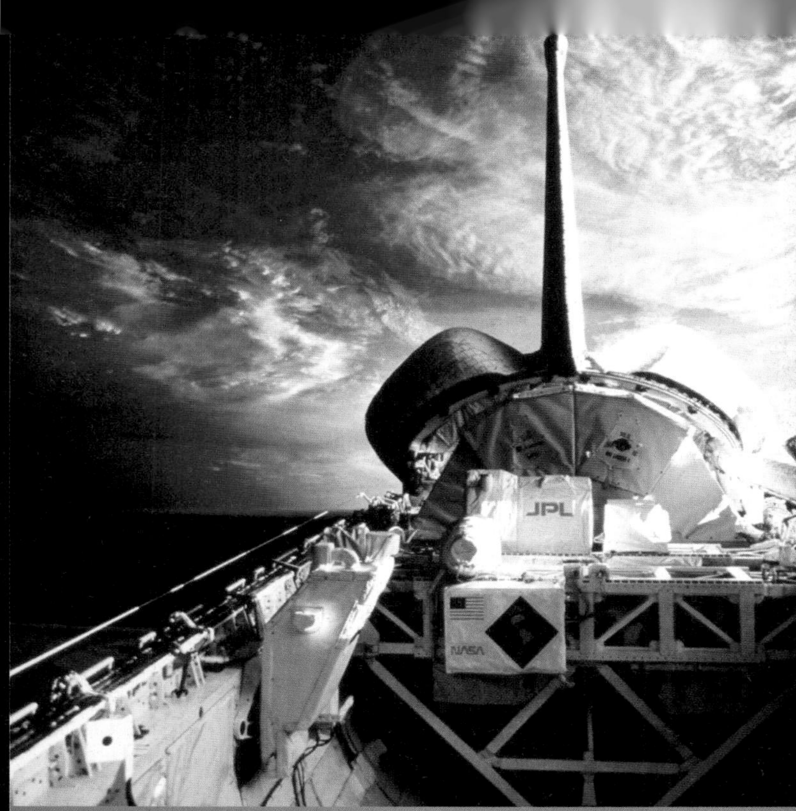

▲ Space Shuttle
The Space Shuttle's cargo bay is 18.3 m (60 ft) long and 4.6 m (15 ft) in diameter. The bay has a Remote Manipulator System arm (the Canadarm2 built by SPAR Aerospace in Canada) to maneuver and deploy the shuttle's cargo, and also contains the docking systems that are used during missions to the International Space Station.

THE 10 FIRST UNMANNED MOON LANDINGS

	NAME	COUNTRY	DATE (LAUNCH/IMPACT)
1	Lunik 2	USSR	Sept 12/14, 1959
2	Ranger 4*	US	Apr 23/26, 1962
3	Ranger 6	US	Jan 30/Feb 2, 1964
4	Ranger 7	US	July 28/31, 1964
5	Ranger 8	US	Feb 17/20, 1965
6	Ranger 9	US	Mar 21/24, 1965
7	Luna 5*	USSR	May 9/12, 1965
8	Luna 7*	USSR	Oct 4/8, 1965
9	Luna 8*	USSR	Dec 3/7, 1965
10	Luna 9	USSR	Jan 31/Feb 3, 1966

* *Crash-landing*

TOP 10 LONGEST SPACE SHUTTLE FLIGHTS*

	FLIGHT	DATES	DURATION OF MISSION (DAYS)	(HR)	(MIN)	(SEC)
1	STS-80 Columbia	Nov 19–Dec 7, 1996	17	08	53	18
2	STS-78 Columbia	June 20–July 7, 1996	16	21	48	30
3	STS-67 Endeavour	Mar 2–18, 1995	16	15	09	46
4	STS-73 Columbia	Oct 20–Nov 5, 1995	15	21	53	16
5	STS-90 Columbia	Apr 17–May 3, 1998	15	21	15	58
6	STS-75 Columbia	Feb 22–Mar 9, 1996	15	17	41	25
7	STS-94 Columbia	July 1–17, 1997	15	16	46	01
8	STS-87 Atlantis	Sept 25–Oct 6, 1997	15	16	35	01
9	STS-65 Columbia	July 8–23, 1994	14	17	55	00
10	STS-58 Columbia	Oct 18–Nov 1, 1993	14	00	12	32

* *To January 1, 2003*

Waterworld

TOP 10 LARGEST OCEANS AND SEAS

	OCEAN/SEA	APPROXIMATE AREA* (SQ MILES)	(SQ KM)
1	**Pacific Ocean**	64,186,600	166,242,500
2	**Atlantic Ocean**	33,420,160	86,557,800
3	**Indian Ocean**	28,350,640	73,427,800
4	**Arctic Ocean**	5,105,740	13,223,800
5	**South China Sea**	1,148,499	2,974,600
6	**Caribbean Sea**	971,400	2,515,900
7	**Mediterranean Sea**	969,120	2,510,000
8	**Bering Sea**	873,020	2,261,100
9	**Sea of Okhotsk**	589,800	1,527,570
10	**Gulf of Mexico**	582,100	1,507,600

* *Excluding tributary seas*

The Coral, Weddell, and Tasman Seas would be eligible for this list, but most authorities consider them part of the Pacific Ocean. However, the Bering Sea is more commonly identified as an independent sea, rather than part of the Pacific.

TOP 10 LONGEST RIVERS

	RIVER	LOCATION	LENGTH (MILES)	(KM)
1	**Nile**	Burundi/Dem. Rep. of Congo/Egypt/Eritrea/ Ethiopia/Kenya/Rwanda/Sudan/Tanzania/Uganda	4,158	6,695
2	**Amazon**	Peru/Brazil	4,007	6,448
3	**Chang Jiang (Yangtze)**	China	3,964	6,378
4	**Huang He (Yellow)**	China	3,395	5,464
5	**Amur**	China/Russia	2,744	4,415
6	**Lena**	Russia	2,734	4,400
7	**Congo**	Angola/Dem. Rep. of Congo	2,718	4,373
8	**Irtysh**	China/Kazakhstan/Mongolia/Russia	2,640	4,248
9	**Mackenzie**	Canada	2,635	4,241
10	**Mekong**	Tibet/China/Myanmar/Laos/ Cambodia/Vietnam	2,600	4,183

TOP 10 DEEPEST DEEP-SEA TRENCHES

	TRENCH*	DEEPEST POINT (FT)	(M)
1	**Marianas**	35,837	10,924
2	**Tonga**#	35,430	10,800
3	**Philippine**	34,436	10,497
4	**Kermadec**#	32,960	10,047
5	**Bonin**	32,786	9,994
6	**New Britain**	32,609	9,940
7	**Kuril**	31,985	9,750
8	**Izu**	31,805	9,695
9	**Puerto Rico**	28,229	8,605
10	**Yap**	27,973	8,527

* *With the exception of the Puerto Rico (Atlantic), all the trenches are in the Pacific*

\# *Some authorities consider these parts of the same feature*

TOP 10 HIGHEST WATERFALLS

	WATERFALL	RIVER	LOCATION	TOTAL DROP (FT)	(M)
1	**Angel**	Carrao	Venezuela	3,212*	979
2	**Tugela**	Tugela	South Africa	3,107	947
3	**Utigård**	Jostedal Glacier	Nesdale, Norway	2,625	800
4	**Mongefossen**	Monge	Mongebekk, Norway	2,540	774
5	**Yosemite**	Yosemite Creek	California	2,425	739
6	**Østre Mardøla Foss**	Mardals	Eikisdal, Norway	2,152	656
7	**Tyssestrengane**	Tysso	Hardanger, Norway	2,120	646
8	**Cuquenán**	Arabopo	Venezuela	2,000	610
9	**Sutherland**	Arthur	South Island, New Zealand	1,904	580
10	**Kjellfossen**	Naero	Gudvangen, Norway	1,841	561

* *Longest single drop 807 m (2,648 ft)*

TOP 10 COUNTRIES WITH THE LARGEST AREAS OF CORAL REEF

	COUNTRY	REEF AREA (SQ MILES)	PERCENTAGE OF WORLD TOTAL
1	**Indonesia**	19,699	17.95
2	**Australia**	18,903	17.22
3	**Philippines**	9,676	8.81
4	**France** – overseas territories	5,514	5.02
5	**Papua New Guinea**	5,344	4.87
6	**Fiji**	3,869	3.52
7	**Maldives**	3,444	3.14
8	**Saudi Arabia**	2,571	2.34
9	**Marshall Islands**	2,539	2.15
10	**India**	2,305	2.04
	World total (including those not in Top 10)	*109,768*	*100.00*

Source: *World Atlas of Coral Reefs*

◀ Beneath the Waves
Coral reefs have taken millions of years to form and, as habitats for a huge variety of sea life, are subject to stringent controls.

TOP 10 DEEPEST LAKES

	LAKE	LOCATION	GREATEST DEPTH (FT)	(M)
1	**Baikal**	Russia	5,371	1,637
2	**Tanganyika**	Burundi/Tanzania/Dem. Rep. of Congo/Zambia	4,825	1,471
3	**Caspian Sea**	Azerbaijan/Iran/Kazakhstan/Russia/Turkmenistan	3,363	1,025
4	**Malawi**	Malawi/Mozambique/Tanzania	2,316	706
5	**Issyk-kul**	Kyrgyzstan	2,257	688
6	**Great Slave**	Canada	2,015	614
7	**Crater**	Oregon	1,932	589
8	**Toba**	Sumatra, Indonesia	1,736	529
9	**Hornindals**	Norway	1,686	514
10 =	**Sarez**	Tajikistan	1,657	505
=	**Tahoe**	California/Nevada	1,657	505

Lake Baikal contains some 20 percent of the world's unfrozen fresh water, a volume of 23,000 km^3 (5,518 cubic miles).

Island Treasure

TOP 10 LARGEST ISLANDS

	ISLAND	AREA* (SQ MILES)	(SQ KM)
1	**Greenland (Kalaatllit Nunaat)**	840,003.9	2,175,600.0
2	**New Guinea**	303,381.0	785,753.0
3	**Borneo** (Indonesia/Malaysia/Brunei)	288,869.3	748,168.1
4	**Madagascar** (Malagasy Republic)	226,917.3	587,713.1
5	**Baffin Island,** Canada	194,573.9	503,944.0
6	**Sumatra,** Indonesia	171,068.7	443,065.8
7	**Great Britain**	88,786.9	229,957.0
8	**Honshu,** Japan	87,182.0	225,800.3
9	**Victoria Island,** Canada	85,154.2	220,548.2
10	**Ellesmere Island,** Canada	71,029.1	183,964.6

* *Mainlands, including areas of inland water, but excluding offshore islands*

Australia is regarded as a continental landmass rather than an island; otherwise it would rank first, at 7,618,493 sq km (2,941,517 sq miles), or 35 times the size of Great Britain. The largest US island is Hawaii, which measures 10,456 sq km (4,037 sq miles), and the largest off mainland US is Kodiak, Alaska, at 9,510 sq km (3,672 sq miles).

TOP 10 LARGEST ISLAND COUNTRIES

	COUNTRY	AREA (SQ MILES)	(SQ KM)
1	**Indonesia**	705,192	1,826,440
2	**Madagascar**	224,534	581,540
3	**Papua New Guinea**	174,406	451,709
4	**Japan**	152,411	394,744
5	**Malaysia**	126,853	328,549
6	**Philippines**	115,124	298,171
7	**New Zealand**	103,734	268,671
8	**Cuba**	42,803	110,860
9	**Iceland**	38,707	100,251
10	**Sri Lanka**	24,996	64,740

Source: *US Census Bureau, International Data Base*

All of the countries on this list are completely self-contained island countries. Because Ireland and Northern Ireland share an island, the UK and Ireland are both excluded from this list. Had it been included, the UK would take eighth place with an area of 241,590 sq km (93,278 sq miles).

TOP 10 MOST IMPORTANT ISLANDS FOR CONSERVATION

	ISLAND/LOCATION	ENDEMIC SPECIES	THREATENED SPECIES	CONSERVATION IMPORTANCE INDEX
1	**New Caledonia,** Southwest Pacific	2,688	172	115
2	**Mauritius,** Indian Ocean	316	223	85
3	**Malta,** Mediterranean Sea	32	230	63
4	**Lord Howe Island,** Australia	130	79	58
5	**St. Helena,** South Atlantic	62	54	50
6	**Rapa Iti,** South West Pacific	225	51	49
7	**Madeira,** Atlantic Ocean	230	136	48
8	**Henderson,** Pitcairn Islands, South Pacific	21	2	47
9	**Viti Levu,** Fiji, Southwest Pacific	9	4	44
10 =	**Jamaica,** Caribbean Sea	1,020	13	42
=	**Vanua Levu,** Fiji Southwest Pacific	2	3	42

Source: *United Nations System-wide Earthwatch*

The United Nations' Conservation Importance Index ranks islands according to terrestrial and marine conservation importance, endemic and threatened species, vulnerability, and features, such as seabird rookeries and sea turtle nesting areas.

TOP 10 SMALLEST ISLAND COUNTRIES

	COUNTRY/LOCATION	AREA (SQ MILES)	(SQ KM)
1	**Nauru,** Pacific Ocean	8	21
2	**Tuvalu,** Pacific Ocean	10	26
3	**Marshall Islands,** Pacific Ocean	70	181
4	**Maldives,** Indian Ocean	116	300
5	**Malta,** Mediterranean Sea	124	321
6 =	**Grenada,** Caribbean Sea	131	339
=	**St. Vincent and the Grenadines,** Caribbean Sea	131	339
8	**St. Kitts and Nevis,** Caribbean Sea	139	360
9	**Barbados,** Caribbean Sea	166	430
10	**Antigua and Barbuda,** Caribbean Sea	170	440

Source: *US Census Bureau, International Data Base*

▶ Easter Island

Guarded by over 600 giant statues, or "moais," of mysterious origin, Easter Island was discovered by Jacob Roggeveen on Easter Day, 1722. It lies more than 3,200 km (2,000 miles) from the nearest population centers in Tahiti and Chile, making it the world's most isolated inhabited island.

TOP 10 MOST ISOLATED ISLANDS

	ISLAND/LOCATION	ISOLATION INDEX
1	**Easter Island,** South Pacific	149
2	**Rapa Iti,** Southwest Pacific	130
3	**Kiritimati,** Line Islands, Central Pacific	129
4	**Jarvis Island,** Central Pacific	128
5	= **Kosrae,** Micronesia, Pacific	126
	= **Malden,** Line Islands, Central Pacific	126
	= **Starbuck,** Line Islands, Central Pacific	126
	= **Vostok,** Line Islands, Central Pacific	126
9	= **Bouvet Island,** South Atlantic	125
	= **Gough Island,** South Atlantic	125
	= **Palmyra Island,** Central Pacific	125

Source: *United Nations*

The United Nation's isolation index is calculated by adding together the square roots of the distances to the nearest island, group of islands, and continent.

TOP 10 LARGEST VOLCANIC ISLANDS

			AREA	
	ISLAND/LOCATION	TYPE	(SQ MILES)	(SQ KM)
1	**Sumatra,** Indonesia	Active volcanic	171,068.7	443,065.8
2	**Honshu,** Japan	Volcanic	87,182.0	225,800.3
3	**Java,** Indonesia	Volcanic	53,588.5	138,793.6
4	**North Island,** New Zealand	Volcanic	43,082.4	111,582.8
5	**Luzon,** Philippines	Active volcanic	42,457.7	109,964.9
6	**Iceland**	Active volcanic	39,315.2	101,826.0
7	**Mindanao,** Philippines	Active volcanic	37,656.5	97,530.0
8	**Hokkaido,** Japan	Active volcanic	30,394.7	78,719.4
9	**New Britain,** Papua New Guinea	Volcanic	13,569.4	35,144.6
10	**Halmahera,** Indonesia	Active volcanic	6,965.1	18,039.6

Source: *United Nations*

High & Mighty

TOP 10 HIGHEST MOUNTAINS

	MOUNTAIN/LOCATION	FIRST ASCENT	TEAM LEADER(S) NATIONALITY	HEIGHT* (FT)	(M)
1	**Everest,** Nepal/China	May 29, 1953	British/ New Zealander	29,035	8,850
2	**K2 (Chogori),** Pakistan/China	July 31, 1954	Italian	28,238	8,607
3	**Kangchenjunga,** Nepal/India	May 25,1955	British	28,208	8,598
4	**Lhotse,** Nepal/China	May 18, 1956	Swiss	27,923	8,511
5	**Makalu I,** Nepal/China	May 15, 1955	French	27,824	8,481
6	**Lhotse Shar II,** Nepal/China	May 12, 1970	Austrian	27,504	8,383
7	**Dhaulagiri I,** Nepal	May 13, 1960	Swiss/Austrian	26,810	8,172
8	**Manaslu I (Kutang I),** Nepal	May 9, 1956	Japanese	26,760	8,156
9	**Cho Oyu,** Nepal	Oct 19, 1954	Austrian	26,750	8,153
10	**Nanga Parbat (Diamir),** Kashmir	July 3, 1953	German/ Austrian	26,660	8,126

* *Height of principal peak; lower peaks of the same mountain are excluded*

The current "official" height of Everest was announced in November 1999 following analysis of data beamed from sensors on Everest's summit to GPS (Global Positioning System) satellites. This superseded the previous "official" measurement of 8,848 m (29,028 ft), recorded on April 20, 1993.

TOP 10 HIGHEST ACTIVE VOLCANOS

	VOLCANO/LOCATION	LATEST ACTIVITY	HEIGHT (FT)	(M)
1	**Cerro Pular,** Chile	1990	20,449	6,233
2	**San Pedro,** Chile	1960	20,161	6,145
3	**Antofallar,** Argentina	1911	20,013	6,100
4	**Aracar,** Argentina	1993	19,954	6,082
5	**Guallatiri,** Chile	1985	19,918	6,071
6	**Tupungatito,** Chile	1986	19,685	6,000
7	**Tacora,** Chile	1937	19,619	5,980
8	**Sabancaya,** Peru	2000	19,577	5,967
9	**Cotopaxi,** Ecuador	1942	19,393	5,911
10	**Putana,** Chile	1972	19,324	5,890

This list includes only volcanoes that were active at some time during the 20th century. The most active volcanic region in Canada is the Stikine Volcanic Belt, located in northwestern British Columbia. It contains more than 100 volcanoes, including Lava Fork, which is believed to be the latest active volcano in Canada, having erupted approximately 150 years ago. At 2,786 m (9,140 ft), Mt. Edziza, in the same area, is the tallest volcano in Canada.

TOP 10 HIGHEST MOUNTAINS IN NORTH AMERICA

	MOUNTAIN	COUNTRY	HEIGHT* (FT)	(M)
1	**McKinley**	US (Alaska)	20,320	6,194
2	**Logan**	Canada	19,545	5,959
3	**Citlaltépetl** (Orizaba)	Mexico	18,409	5,611
4	**St. Elias**	US (Alaska)/Canada	18,008	5,489
5	**Popocatépetl**	Mexico	17,887	5,452
6	**Foraker**	US (Alaska)	17,400	5,304
7	**Ixtaccihuatl**	Mexico	17,343	5,286
8	**Lucania**	Canada	17,147	5,226
9	**King**	Canada	16,971	5,173
10	**Steele**	Canada	16,644	5,073

* *Height of principal peak; lower peaks of the same mountain are excluded*

Peak Performance
The Andes, the world's longest mountain range, stretches the length of South America, from Lago de Maracaibo in the north to Tierra del Fuego in the south.

TOP 10 HIGHEST MOUNTAINS IN EUROPE

	MOUNTAIN/COUNTRY	HEIGHT* (FT)	(M)
1	**Mont Blanc,** France/Italy	15,771	4,807
2	**Monte Rosa,** Switzerland	15,203	4,634
3	**Zumsteinspitze,** Italy/Switzerland	14,970	4,564
4	**Signalkuppe,** Italy/Switzerland	14,941	4,555
5	**Dom,** Switzerland	14,911	4,545
6	**Liskamm,** Italy/Switzerland	14,853	4,527
7	**Weisshorn,** Switzerland	14,780	4,505
8	**Täschorn,** Switzerland	14,733	4,491
9	**Matterhorn,** Italy/Switzerland	14,688	4,477
10	**Mont Maudit,** France/Italy	14,649	4,466

** Height of principal peak; lower peaks of the same mountain are excluded*

TOP 10 LONGEST MOUNTAIN RANGES

	RANGE/LOCATION	LENGTH (MILES)	(KM)
1	**Andes,** South America	4,500	7,242
2	**Rocky Mountains,** North America	3,750	6,035
3	**Himalayas/Karakoram/Hindu Kush,** Asia	2,400	3,862
4	**Great Dividing Range,** Australia	2,250	3,621
5	**Trans-Antarctic Mountains,** Antarctica	2,200	3,541
6	**Brazilian East Coast Range,** Brazil	1,900	3,058
7	**Sumatran/Javan Range,** Sumatra, Java	1,800	2,897
8	**Tien Shan,** China	1,400	2,253
9	**Eastern Ghats,** India	1,300	2,092
10 =	**Altai,** Asia	1,250	2,012
=	**Central New Guinean Range,** Papua New Guinea	1,250	2,012
=	**Urals,** Russia	1,250	2,012

THE 10 FIRST MOUNTAINEERS TO CLIMB EVEREST

	MOUNTAINEER/COUNTRY	DATE
1	**Edmund Hillary,** New Zealand	May 29, 1953
2	**Tenzing Norgay,** Nepal	May 29, 1953
3	**Jürg Marmet,** Switzerland	May 23, 1956
4	**Ernst Schmied,** Switzerland	May 23, 1956
5	**Hans-Rudolf von Gunten,** Switzerland	May 24, 1956
6	**Adolf Reist,** Switzerland	May 24, 1956
7	**Wang Fu-chou,** China	May 25, 1960
8	**Chu Ying-hua,** China	May 25, 1960
9	**Konbu,** Tibet	May 25, 1960
10 =	**Nawang Gombu,** India	May 1, 1963
=	**James Whittaker,** US	May 1, 1963

Hillary and Tenzing's conquest of Everest followed at least 16 unsuccessful expeditions from 1921 to 1952. Whether George Leigh Mallory and Andrew Irvine, the British climbers who died on the 1924 expedition, reached the summit is still controversial. Mallory's body was discovered in 1999 at an elevation of 8,230 m (27,000 ft). Nawang Gombu and James Whittaker are 10th equal as neither wished to deny the other the privilege of being first, so they ascended the last steps to the summit side by side.

Face of the Earth

TOP 10 LONGEST CAVES

	CAVE/LOCATION	TOTAL KNOWN LENGTH (MILES)	(KM)
1	**Mammoth Cave System,** Kentucky, US	346	557
2	**Optimisticheskaya,** Ukraine	131	212
3	**Jewel Cave,** South Dakota, US	128	206
4	**Hölloch,** Switzerland	114	184
5	**Lechuguilla Cave,** New Mexico, US	109	176
6	**Wind Cave,** South Dakota, US	106	171
7	**Fisher Ridge System,** Kentucky, US	105	169
8	**Siebenhengstehohle,** Switzerland	90	145
9	**Ozernaya,** Ukraine	73	117
10	**Gua Air Jernih,** Malaysia	68	109

Source: *Tony Waltham, BCRA*

Castleguard Caves in Banff National Park, Alberta, is the longest cave system in Canada at 16.2 km (10 miles) in length and 350 m (1,148 ft) in depth.

TOP 10 LARGEST METEORITE CRATERS

	CRATER/LOCATION	DIAMETER (KM)	(MILES)
1	**Vredefort,** South Africa	300	186
2	**Sudbury,** Ontario, Canada	250	155
3	**Chicxulub,** Yucatan, Mexico	170	107
4=	**Manicouagan,** Quebec, Canada	100	62
=	**Popigai,** Russia	100	62
6	**Acraman,** Australia	90	56
7	**Chesapeake Bay,** Virginia, US	85	53
8	**Puchezh-Katunki,** Russia	80	50
9	**Morokweng,** South Africa	70	43
10	**Kara,** Russia	65	40

Source: *Geological Survey of Canada, Continental Geoscience Division*

One of the ongoing debates in geology is whether certain crater-like structures are of meteoric origin or are the remnants of extinct volcanoes. Recently, photographs taken from space have revealed a 320-km (199-mile) diameter site centered on Prague, Czech Republic. If caused by a meteor, the object would have been 80 km (50 miles) in diameter. Besides those listed above, other large meteorite craters in Canada are located in Newfoundland, Nova Scotia, Saskatchewan, and Manitoba.

▼ An Immense and Ancient Land
The Sahara's boundaries are the Atlantic Ocean to the west, the Atlas Mountains and the Mediterranean Sea to the north, the Red Sea and Egypt to the east, and the Sudan and the Niger River to the south. Over 8,000 years ago, the Sahara was a fertile area where millet and other crops were cultivated. However, as conditions gradually became drier and the desert began to form, the farmers abandoned their land.

TOP 10 LAND MASSES WITH THE LOWEST ELEVATIONS

	LAND MASS/LOCATION/POSSESSION	HIGHEST POINT (FT)	(M)
1	**Kingman Reef,** North Pacific Ocean (US)	3.2	1
2	**Palmyra Atoll,** North Pacific Ocean (US)	6.5	2
3	= **Bassas da India,** Mozambique Channel (France)	7.8	2.4
	= **Wingili Island in the Addu Atoll,** Indian Ocean (Maldives)	7.8	2.4
5	= **Ashmore and Cartier Islands,** Indian Ocean (Australia)	9.8	3
	= **Howland Island,** North Pacific Ocean (US)	9.8	3
7	**Spratly Islands,** South China Sea (claimed by China, Taiwan, Vietnam, Malaysia, and Philippines)	13.1	4
8	= **Cocos (Keeling) Islands,** Indian Ocean (Australia)	16.4	5
	= **Johnston Atoll,** North Pacific Ocean (US)	16.4	5
	= **Tokelau,** South Pacific Ocean (New Zealand)	16.4	5
	= **Tuvalu,** South Pacific Ocean	16.4	5

Source: *CIA,* The World Factbook 2001

These 10 locations are definitely off the agenda if you are planning a climbing vacation, none of them possessing a single elevation taller than a small house. Beyond these exceptionally low-lying places, several countries, including Gambia and the Marshall Islands, lack a rise greater than 10 m (33 ft). Compared with these, even the Netherlands' 321-m (1,050-ft) Vaalserberg hill makes the country's appellation as one of the "Low Countries" seem almost unfair.

TOP 10 LARGEST DESERTS

	DESERT/LOCATION	APPROX. AREA (SQ MILES)	(SQ KM)
1	**Sahara,** Northern Africa	3,500,000	9,100,000
2	**Australian,** Australia*	1,300,000	3,400,000
3	**Arabian Peninsula,** Southwest Asia#	1,000,000	2,600,000
4	**Turkestan,** Central Asia†	750,000	1,900,000
5	= **Gobi,** Central Asia	500,000	1,300,000
	= **North American Desert,** US/Mexico⋆	500,000	1,300,000
7	**Patagonia,** Southern Argentina	260,000	670,000
8	**Thar,** Northwest India/Pakistan	230,000	600,000
9	**Kalahari,** Southwestern Africa	220,000	570,000
10	**Takla Makan,** Northwestern China	185,000	480,000

* *Includes Gibson, Great Sandy, Great Victoria, and Simpson*

\# *Includes an-Nafud and Rub al-Khali*

† *Includes Kara-Kum and Kyzylkum*

⋆ *Includes Great Basin, Mojave, Sonorah, and Chihuahuan*

This Top 10 presents the approximate areas and ranking of the world's great deserts, which are often broken down into smaller desert regions—the Australian Desert into the Gibson, Great Sandy, Great Victoria, and Simpson, for example. The world total is more than double that of the Top 10 at some 35,264,000 sq km (13,616,000 sq miles), or about one-quarter of the world's land area. However, deserts may range from the extremely arid and typical barren sandy desert (about four percent of the total land surface of the globe), through arid (15 percent) to semiarid (almost 15 percent), and most exhibit features that encompass all these degrees of aridity, with one zone merging almost imperceptibly into the next.

Elementary Matters

MOST COMMON ELEMENTS IN THE EARTH'S CRUST

	ELEMENT	PARTS PER MILLION*
1	Oxygen	460,000
2	Silicon	270,000
3	Aluminum	82,000
4	Iron	63,000
5	Calcium	50,000
6	Magnesium	29,000
7	Sodium	23,000
8	Potassium	15,000
9	Titanium	6,600
10	Hydrogen	1,500

* *mg per kg*

This is based on the average percentages of the elements in igneous rock. Of every million atoms, some 200,000 are silicon, 63,000 aluminum, and 31,000 hydrogen—although in the Universe as a whole, hydrogen is by far the most common element, comprising some 930,000 out of every million atoms.

HEAVIEST ELEMENTS

	ELEMENT	DISCOVERER/ COUNTRY	YEAR DISCOVERED	DENSITY*
1	Osmium	Smithson Tennant, UK	1804	22.59
2	Iridium	Smithson Tennant, UK	1804	22.56
3	Platinum	Julius Caesar Scaliger, Italy/France#; Charles Wood, UK†	1557 1741	21.45
4	Rhenium	Walter K. Noddack et al., Germany	1925	21.01
5	Neptunium	Edwin Mattison McMillan/Philip H. Abelson, US	1940	20.47
6	Plutonium	Glenn Theodore Seaborg et al., US	1940	20.26
7	Gold	Prehistoric		19.29
8	Tungsten	Juan José and Fausto de Elhuijar, Spain	1783	19.26
9	Uranium	Martin Heinrich Klaproth, Germany	1789	19.05
10	Tantalum	Anders Gustav Ekeberg, Sweden	1802	16.67

* *Grams per cubic centimeter at 20°C*

\# *Earliest reference to*

† *Discovered*

The two heaviest elements, the metals osmium and iridium, were discovered at the same time by the British chemist Smithson Tennant (1761–1815), who was also the first to prove that diamonds are made of carbon. A cubic foot (0.028317 m^3) of osmium weighs 1,410 lb (640 kg).

MOST COMMON ELEMENTS ON THE MOON

	ELEMENT	PERCENTAGE
1	Oxygen	40.0
2	Silicon	19.2
3	Iron	14.3
4	Calcium	8.0
5	Titanium	5.9
6	Aluminum	5.6
7	Magnesium	4.5
8	Sodium	0.33
9	Potassium	0.14
10	Chromium	0.002

This Top 10 is based on the analysis of the 20.77 kg (45.8 lb) of rock samples brought back to Earth by the crew of the 1969 *Apollo 11* lunar mission. One of the minerals they discovered was named Armalcolite in honor of the three astronauts—Armstrong, Aldrin, and Collins.

HYDROGEN DISCOVERED

FIRST FACT

THE EXISTENCE OF hydrogen, the lightest and most abundant element in the Universe, was first demonstrated in 1766 by British scientist Henry Cavendish (1731–1810). He called it "inflammable air," but because it produces water when it burns in oxygen, it was given a name that means "water-forming." Soon after Cavendish's discovery, techniques for extracting hydrogen were developed, which led to one of its earliest practical uses by enabling the first hydrogen balloon flight, by Jacques Charles and Nicholas-Louis Robert, to take place in France on December 1, 1783.

MOST COMMON ELEMENTS IN THE SUN

	ELEMENT	PARTS PER MILLION*
1	Hydrogen	750,000
2	Helium	230,000
3	Oxygen	9,000
4	Carbon	3,000
5	= Iron	1,000
	= Neon	1,000
	= Nitrogen	1,000
8	Silicon	900
9	Magnesium	700
10	Sulfur	400

* *mg per kg*

More than 70 elements have been detected in the Sun, the most common of which correspond closely to those found in the Universe as a whole, but with some variations in their ratios, including a greater proportion of the principal element, hydrogen. The atoms of hydrogen in the Universe outnumber those of all the other elements combined.

TOP 10 MOST COMMON ELEMENTS IN THE UNIVERSE

	ELEMENT	PARTS PER MILLION*
1	Hydrogen	750,000
2	Helium	230,000
3	Oxygen	10,000
4	Carbon	5,000
5	Neon	1,300
6	Iron	1,100
7	Nitrogen	1,000
8	Silicon	700
9	Magnesium	600
10	Sulfur	500

* *mg per kg*

Hydrogen is the simplest atom—a single proton circled by a single electron. The atoms of hydrogen in the Universe outnumber those of all the other elements combined.

TOP 10 PRINCIPAL COMPONENTS OF AIR

	COMPONENT	PERCENTAGE BY VOLUME
1	Nitrogen	78.110
2	Oxygen	20.953
3	Argon	0.934
4	Carbon dioxide	0.01–0.10
5	Neon	0.001818
6	Helium	0.000524
7	Methane	0.0002
8	Krypton	0.000114
9	= Hydrogen	0.00005
	= Nitrous oxide	0.00005

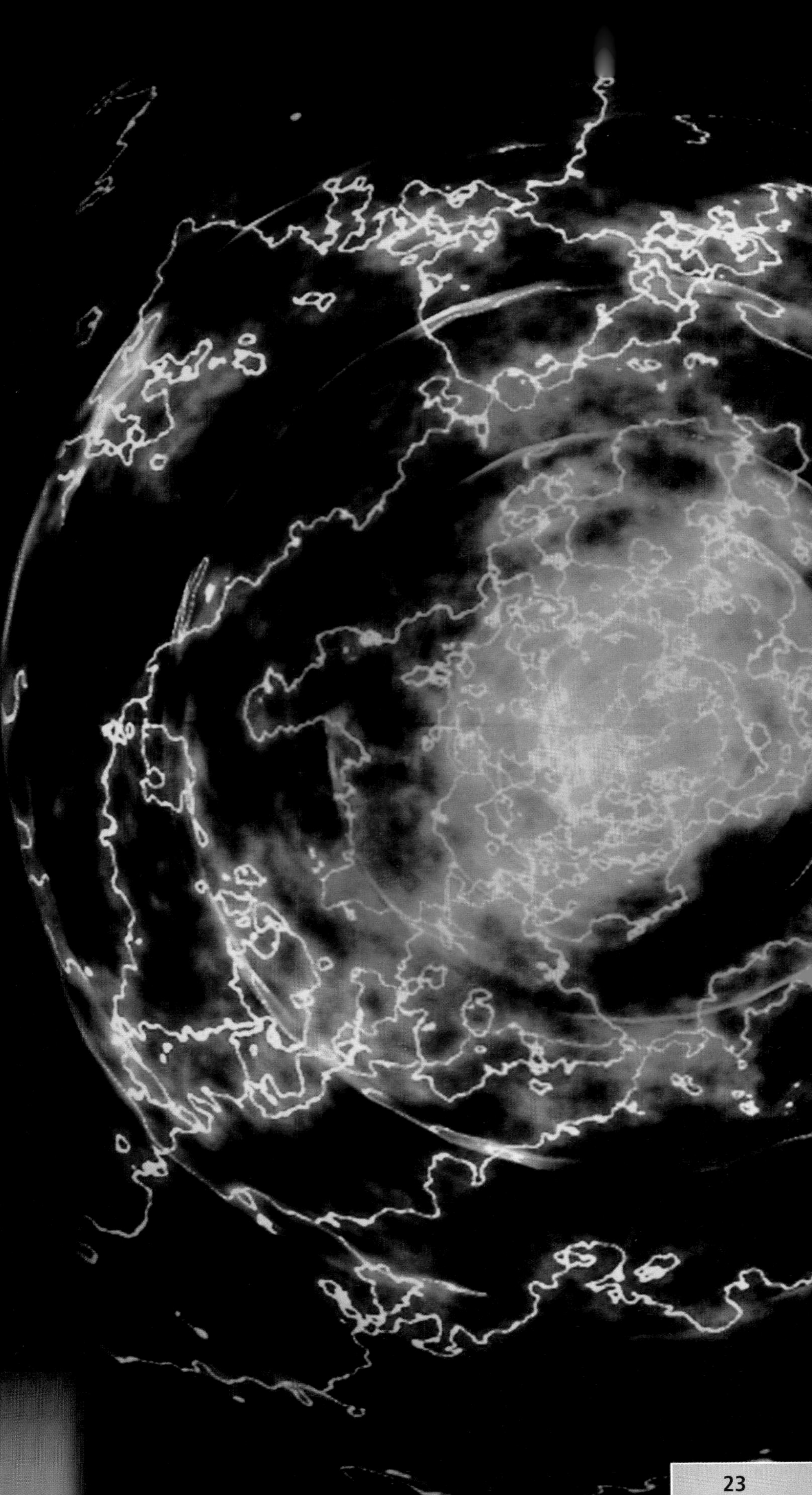

Gas Light
A cloud of electrons whirls around an atom of helium, the lightest and most abundant element after hydrogen. Helium was discovered in the Sun's spectrum during an eclipse in 1868, and isolated on Earth in 1895.

Weather Extremes

TOP 10 HOTTEST PLACES—EXTREMES

	LOCATION	HIGHEST TEMPERATURE (°F)	(°C)
1	**Al'Azīzīyah,** Libya	136.4	58.0
2	**Greenland Ranch,** Death Valley, California	134.0	56.7
3	= **Ghudamis,** Libya	131.0	55.0
	= **Kebili,** Tunisia	131.0	55.0
5	**Tombouctou,** Mali	130.1	54.5
6	**Araouane,** Mali	130.0	54.4
7	**Tirat Tavi,** Israel	129.0	53.9
8	**Ahwāz,** Iran	128.3	53.5
9	**Agha Jārī,** Iran	128.0	53.3
10	**Wadi Halfa,** Sudan	127.0	52.8

Maximum of two places per country listed

Source: *Philip Eden*

The hottest temperature on Earth was that recorded by meteorologists from the National Geographic Society at Al'Aziziyah, 40 km (25 miles) south of Tripoli, Libya, on September 13, 1922.

TOP 10 COLDEST PLACES—EXTREMES

	LOCATION	LOWEST RECORDED TEMPERATURE (°F)	(°C)
1	**Vostok*,** Antarctica	-138.6	-89.2
2	**Plateau Station*,** Antarctica	-129.2	-84.0
3	**Oymyakon,** Russia	-96.0	-71.1
4	**Verkhoyansk,** Russia	-90.0	-67.7
5	**Northice*,** Greenland	-87.0	-66.0
6	**Eismitte*,** Greenland	-85.0	-64.9
7	**Snag,** Yukon, Canada	-81.4	-63.0
8	**Prospect Creek,** Alaska	-79.8	-62.1
9	**Fort Selkirk,** Yukon, Canada	-74.0	-58.9
10	**Rogers Pass,** Montana	-69.7	-56.5

Maximum of two places per country listed

* *Present or former scientific research base*

Source: *Philip Eden*

▼ Freezing Point
The Martin A. Pomerantz Observatory at the Amundsen-Scott base at the South Pole. The American scientific research facility is located in almost the coldest place on Earth.

TOP 10 PLACES WITH THE MOST CONTRASTING SEASONS*

	LOCATION	WINTER (°F)	WINTER (°C)	SUMMER (°F)	SUMMER (°C)	DIFFERENCE (°F)	DIFFERENCE (°C)
1	**Verkhoyansk,** Russia	-58.5	-50.3	56.5	13.6	115.0	63.9
2	**Yakutsk,** Russia	-49.0	-45.0	63.5	17.5	112.5	62.5
3	**Manzhouli,** China	-15.0	-26.1	69.0	20.6	84.0	46.7
4	**Fort Yukon,** Alaska	-20.2	-29.0	61.4	16.3	81.6	45.3
5	**Fort Good Hope,** Northwest Territories, Canada	-21.8	-29.9	59.5	15.3	81.3	45.2
6	**Brochet,** Manitoba, Canada	-20.5	-29.2	59.7	15.4	80.2	44.6
7	**Tunka,** Mongolia	-16.0	-26.7	61.0	16.1	77.0	42.8
8	**Fairbanks,** Alaska	-11.2	-24.0	60.1	15.6	71.3	39.6
9	**Semipalatinsk,** Kazakhstan	0.5	-17.7	69.0	20.6	68.5	38.3
10	**Jorgen Bronlund Fjørd,** Greenland	-23.6	-30.9	43.5	6.4	67.1	37.3

Maximum of two places per country listed

* *Biggest differences between mean monthly temperatures in summer and winter*

Source: *Philip Eden*

Whether based on the differences in its mean winter and summer temperatures, or on its extremes, having recorded a winter temperature as low as -68°C (-90°F) and summer temperatures as high as 37°C (98°F), Verkhoyansk, a river port in northeast Siberia, has the most extreme climate on the planet.

TOP 10 PLACES WITH THE LEAST CONTRASTING SEASONS*

	LOCATION	COOLEST (°F)	COOLEST (°C)	WARMEST (°F)	WARMEST (°C)	DIFFERENCE (°F)	DIFFERENCE (°C)
1	= **Lorengau,** New Guinea	80.0	26.7	81.0	27.2	1.0	0.5
	= **Malacca,** Malaysia	80.0	26.7	81.0	27.2	1.0	0.5
	= **Malden Island,** Kiribati	82.0	27.8	83.0	28.3	1.0	0.5
	= **Ocean Island,** Kiribati	82.0	27.8	83.0	28.3	1.0	0.5
5	= **Kavieng,** New Guinea	81.0	27.2	82.0	27.8	1.0	0.6
	= **Quito,** Ecuador	58.0	14.4	59.0	15.0	1.0	0.6
7	= **Andagoya,** Colombia	81.0	27.2	82.4	28.0	1.4	0.8
	= **Labuhan,** Indonesia	81.0	27.2	82.4	28.0	1.4	0.8
	= **Mwanza,** Tanzania	72.7	22.6	74.1	23.4	1.4	0.8
10	**Belém,** Brazil	79.0	26.1	80.5	26.9	1.5	0.8

Maximum of two places per country listed

* *Smallest differences between mean monthly temperature of warmest and coolest months*

Source: *Philip Eden*

TOP 10 WETTEST CITIES IN CANADA

	LOCATION	ANNUAL AVERAGE* (MM)
1	**St. John's,** Newfoundland	1,482
2	**Halifax,** Nova Scotia	1,474
3	**Quebec City,** Quebec	1,208
4	**Charlottetown,** Prince Edward Island	1,201
5	**Vancouver,** British Columbia	1,167
6	**Fredericton,** New Brunswick	1,131
7	**Montreal,** Quebec	940
8	**Ottawa,** Ontario	911
9	**Victoria,** British Columbia	858
10	**Toronto,** Ontario	819

* *Total precipitation in major cities*

Source: Climate Normals 1961–1990, *Climate Information Branch, Canadian Meteorological Centre, Environment Canada; Statistics Canada*

The wettest place in Canada, and the eighth wettest place in the world, is Henderson Lake, BC, with an annual average rainfall of 6,502 mm (256 in).

TOP 10 COLDEST PLACES—AVERAGE

	LOCATION	AVERAGE TEMPERATURE* (°F)	(°C)
1	**Plateau#,** Antarctica	-70.0	-56.7
2	**Amundsen-Scott#,** Antarctica	-56.2	-49.0
3	**Northice#,** Greenland	-22.0	-30.0
4	**Eismitte#,** Greenland	-20.5	-29.2
5	**Resolute,** NWT, Canada	-11.6	-24.2
6	**Eureka,** NWT, Canada	-3.5	-19.7
7	**Ostrov Bol'shoy,** Lyakhovskiy, Russia	5.5	-14.7
8	**Barrow Point,** Alaska	9.8	-12.3
9	**Barter Island,** Alaska	10.2	-12.1
10	**Ostrov Vrangela,** Russia	11.0	-11.7

Maximum of two places per country listed

* *Lowest long-term temperature averaged throughout the year*

\# *Present or former scientific research base*

Source: *Philip Eden*

TOP 10 HOTTEST PLACES—AVERAGE

	LOCATION	AVERAGE TEMPERATURE* (°F)	(°C)
1	**Dallol,** Ethiopia	94.3	34.6
2	**Assab,** Eritrea	86.8	30.4
3	**Néma,** Mauritania	86.5	30.3
4	**Berbera,** Somalia	86.2	30.1
5	**Hombori,** Mali	86.1	30.1
6	**Perm Island,** South Yemen	86.0	30.0
7	**Djibouti,** Djibouti	85.8	29.9
8	**Atbara,** Sudan	85.7	29.8
9	= **Bender Qaasim,** Somalia	85.5	29.7
	= **Kamarān Island,** North Yemen	85.5	29.7

Maximum of two places per country listed

* *Highest long-term temperature averaged throughout the year*

Source: *Philip Eden*

Natural Disasters

WORST EARTHQUAKES

	LOCATION	DATE	ESTIMATED NO. KILLED
1	**Near East/Mediterranean**	May 20, 1202	1,100,000
2	**Shenshi,** China	Feb 2, 1556	820,000
3	**Calcutta,** India	Oct 11, 1737	300,000
4	**Antioch,** Syria	May 20, 526	250,000
5	**Tang-shan,** China	July 28, 1976	242,419
6	**Nan-Shan,** China	May 22, 1927	200,000
7	**Yeddo,** Japan	Dec 30, 1703	190,000
8	**Kansu,** China	Dec 16, 1920	180,000
9	**Messina,** Italy	Dec 28, 1908	160,000
10	**Tokyo/Yokohama,** Japan	Sept 1, 1923	142,807

There are discrepancies between the "official" death tolls in many earthquakes and the estimates of other authorities: a figure of 750,000 is sometimes quoted for the 1976 Tang-shan earthquake, for example, and totals ranging from 58,000 to 250,000 for the quake that devastated Messina in 1908. In more recent times, the Armenian earthquake of December 7, 1988, killed over 55,000 (28,854 officially), and that in Iran on June 21, 1990, killed over 55,000 (50,000 officially).

THE 10 WORST FLOODS IN CANADA*

	LOCATIONS AFFECTED	YEAR	TOTAL COSTS ($)#
1	**Saguenay,** Quebec	1996	1,598,068,072
2	**Winnipeg,** Manitoba	1950	1,093,495,890
3	**Southern Manitoba**	1997	815,036,745
4	**Fraser River,** British Columbia	1948	427,458,803
5	**Winnipeg,** Manitoba	1993	406,203,746
6	**Maniwaki,** Quebec	1974	359,413,362
7	**Montreal,** Quebec	1987	356,022,806
8	**Southern Alberta**	1995	156,038,635
9	**Gaspesie,** Quebec	1983	141,979,918
10	**Saint John River Basin,** New Brunswick	1973	127,168,364

* *For the period 1900–2000*

\# *Numbers are subject to updates and may not be exhaustive*

Source: *OCIPEP, 2001.* OCIPEP Disaster Database vers. 3.2. *Office of Critical Infrastructure Protection and Emergency Preparedness*

In 1950, heavy rain and snowmelt flooded the Red River in Manitoba for 51 days, resulting in the death of one person and the evacuation of 107,000 people.

THE 10 WORST VOLCANIC ERUPTIONS

	LOCATION	DATE	ESTIMATED NO. KILLED
1	**Tambora,** Indonesia	Apr 5–12, 1815	92,000

The eruption of Tambora on the island of Sumbawa killed about 10,000 islanders immediately, with a further 82,000 dying subsequently from disease and famine resulting from crops being destroyed. An estimated 1,700,000 metric tons (1,840,000 tons) of ash were hurled into the atmosphere. This blocked out the sunlight and affected the weather over the globe during the following year. An effect of this was to produce brilliantly colored sunsets, depicted strikingly in paintings from the period.

2	**Unsen,** Japan	Apr 1, 1793	53,000

During a period of intense volcanic activity in the area, the island of Unsen, or Unzen, completely disappeared, killing all its inhabitants.

3	**Mont Pelée,** Martinique	May 8, 1902	40,000

After lying dormant for centuries, Mont Pelée began to erupt in April 1902. Assured that there was no danger, the 30,000 residents of the main city, St. Pierre, stayed in their homes and were there when, at 7:30 a.m. on May 8, the volcano burst apart and showered the port with molten lava, ash, and gas, destroying virtually all life and property.

4	**Krakatoa,** Sumatra/Java	Aug 26–27, 1883	36,380

The uninhabited island of Krakatoa exploded after a series of eruptions over the course of several days, and was audible up to 4,800 km (3,000 miles) away. Some sources put the fatalities as high as 200,000, most of them killed by subsequent tsunamis that reached 30 m (100 ft) high. The events were portrayed in the 1969 film *Krakatoa, East of Java*, but purists should note that Krakatoa is actually *west* of Java.

	LOCATION	DATE	ESTIMATED NO. KILLED
5	**Nevado del Ruiz,** Colombia	Nov 13, 1985	22,940

The Andean volcano gave signs of erupting, but the decision to evacuate came too late. The steam, rocks, and ash ejected from Nevado del Ruiz melted its ice cap, resulting in a mudslide that completely engulfed the town of Armero.

6	**Mt. Etna,** Sicily	Mar 11 , 1669	over 20,000

Europe's largest volcano at 3,280 m (10,760 ft) has erupted frequently, but killed most people in 1669 when lava engulfed Catania, killing at least 20,000.

7	**Laki,** Iceland	Jan–June 1783	20,000

Events on the Laki volcanic ridge in 1783 culminated on June 11 with the largest ever recorded lava flow, up to 80 km (50 miles) long and 30 m (100 ft) deep. Many villages were engulfed and those who managed to escape were killed by poisonous gases released from the lava.

8	**Vesuvius,** Italy	Aug 24, AD 79	16–20,000

When the previously dormant Vesuvius erupted, Herculaneum was engulfed by a mud flow while Pompeii was buried under a vast layer of pumice and volcanic ash—which preserved it in a near-perfect state that was revealed by archaeological excavations that began in 1738 and continue to this day.

9	**Vesuvius,** Italy	Dec 16–17, 1631	up to 18,000

The next major cataclysm after that of AD 79 was almost as disastrous when lava and mud flows poured into surrounding towns, including Naples.

10	**Mt. Etna,** Sicily	1169	over 15,000

Large numbers died sheltering in Catania Cathedral, and more were killed when a tsunami caused by the eruption hit the port of Messina.

THE 10 WORST AVALANCHES AND LANDSLIDES*

	LOCATION	INCIDENT	DATE	ESTIMATED NO. KILLED
1	**Alps,** Italy	Avalanche	Oct 218 BC	18,000
2	**Yungay,** Peru	Landslide	May 31, 1970	17,500
3	**Italian Alps**	Avalanche	Dec 13, 1916	10,000
4	**Huarás,** Peru	Avalanche	Dec 13, 1941	5,000
5	**Nevada Huascaran,** Peru	Avalanche	Jan 10, 1962	3,500
6	**Chiavenna,** Italy	Landslide	Sept 4, 1618	2,427
7	**Plurs,** Switzerland	Avalanche	Sept 4, 1618	1,496
8	**Goldau Valley,** Switzerland	Landslide	Sept 2, 1806	800
9	**Medellin,** Colombia	Landslide	Sept 27, 1987	683
10	**Chungar,** Peru	Avalanche	Mar 19, 1971	600

* *Excluding those where most deaths resulted from flooding, earthquakes, volcanoes, etc, associated with landslides*

THE 10 WORST FLOODS

	LOCATION	DATE	ESTIMATED NO. KILLED
1	**Huang He River,** China	Aug 1931	3,700,000
2	**Huang He River,** China	Spring 1887	1,500,000
3	**Netherlands**	Nov 1, 1530	400,000
4	**Kaifong,** China	1642	300,000
5	**Henan,** China	Sept–Nov 1939	over 200,000
6	**Bengal,** India	1876	200,000
7	**Yangtze River,** China	Aug–Sept 1931	140,000
8	**Netherlands**	1646	110,000
9	**North Vietnam**	Aug 30, 1971	over 100,000
10 =	**Friesland,** Netherlands	1228	100,000
=	**Dort,** Netherlands	Apr 16, 1421	100,000
=	**Canton,** China	June 12, 1915	100,000
=	**Yangtze River,** China	Sept 1911	100,000

Records of floods caused by China's Huang He, or Yellow River, date back to 2297 BC. Since then, it has flooded at least 1,500 times, resulting in millions of deaths and giving it the nickname "China's Sorrow." According to some accounts, the flood of 1887 may have resulted in as many as six million deaths.

▼ Landslide Tragedy
The Villa Tina area of Medellin, Colombia, was engulfed in a mudslide in 1987. Although 183 bodies were recovered, a further 500 inhabitants disappeared completely and 200 were injured, leaving just 117 survivors.

LIFE ON EARTH

TOP 10 HEAVIEST PRIMATES

	PRIMATE	LENGTH* (IN)	(CM)	WEIGHT (LB)	(KG)
1	**Gorilla**	79	200	485	220
2	**Human**	70	177	170	77
3	**Orangutan**	54	137	165	75
4	**Chimpanzee**	36	92	110	50
5	= **Baboon**	39	100	99	45
	= **Mandrill**	37	95	99	45
7	**Gelada baboon**	30	75	55	25
8	**Proboscis monkey**	30	75	53	24
9	**Hanuman langur**	42	107	44	20
10	**Siamung gibbon**	35	90	29	13

* *Excluding tail*

The largest primates (including humans) and all the apes derive from the Old World (Africa, Asia, and Europe). Only one member of a New World species of monkeys (the Guatemalan howler at 91 cm/36 in; 9 kg/20 lb) is a close contender for the Top 10. The difference between the prosimians (primitive primates), great apes, lesser apes, and monkeys is more to do with shape than size, though the great apes mostly fill out the table.

TEST TUBE GORILLA!

FIRST FACT

Rosie, a lowland gorilla living at the Cincinnati Zoo in Ohio, produced her seventh baby, a female named Timu ("team" in Swahili), on October 9, 1995. Timu was the first gorilla ever born by in vitro fertilization, using the same technique that produced the first human test tube baby, Louise Brown, in 1978. An egg from Rosie had been fertilized by sperm from Mosuba, a male gorilla at Henry Doorly Zoo in Omaha, Nebraska, as part of a program to ensure the survival of this threatened species.

Great Ape
Gorillas are the heaviest primates. The largest on record was N'gagi, a male living at the San Diego Zoo in California from 1931 to 1944, whose peak weight was 310 kg (683 lb).

SNAKES WITH THE DEADLIEST BITES

	SNAKE (LATIN NAME)	ESTIMATED LETHAL DOSE FOR HUMANS (MG)	AVERAGE VENOM PER BITE (MG)	HUMANS POTENTIALLY KILLED PER BITE
1	**Coastal taipan** *(Oxyuranus scutellatus)*	1	120	120
2	**Common krait** *(Bungarus caeruleus)*	0.5	42	84
3	**Philippine cobra** *(Naja naja philippinensis)*	2	120	60
4	= **King cobra** *(Ophiophagus hannah)*	20	1,000	50
	= **Russell's viper** *(Daboia russelli)*	3	150	50
6	**Black mamba** *(Dendroaspis polyepis)*	3	135	45
7	**Yellow-jawed tommygoff** *(Bothrops asper)*	25	1,000	40
8	= **Multibanded krait** *(Bungarus multicinctus)*	0.8	28	35
	= **Tiger snake** *(Notechis scutatus)*	1	35	35
10	**Jararacussu** *(Bothrops jararacussu)*	25	800	32

This list represents the results of a comprehensive survey of the various factors that determine the relative danger posed by poisonous snakes. These include the strength of the venom (and hence the estimated lethal dose for an adult), and the amount injected per bite; most snakes inject about 15 per cent of their venom per bite. Some snakes are rare and seldom come into contact with humans, while the likelihood of death as a result of snake bite varies according to the availability of antivenom and medical treatment. The Common krait has the highest fatality rate of any snake on record: in one study, of 32 victims admitted to hospital in India after bites, only two survived. Bites by Russell's vipers have been known to cause death within 15 minutes.

FASTEST MAMMALS

	MAMMAL	MAXIMUM RECORDED SPEED (MPH)	(KM/H)
1	**Cheetah**	65	105
2	**Pronghorn antelope**	55	89
3	= **Mongolian gazelle**	50	80
	= **Springbok**	50	80
5	= **Grant's gazelle**	47	76
	= **Thomson's gazelle**	47	76
7	**Brown hare**	45	72
8	**Horse**	43	69
9	= **Greyhound**	42	68
	= **Red deer**	42	68

Although several animals on the list are capable of higher speeds, these figures are based on controlled measurements of average speeds over 0.4 km (0.25 miles). Charging lions can achieve 80 km/h (50 mph) over very short distances, while various members of the antelope family, wildebeests, elks, dogs, coyotes, foxes, hyenas, zebras, and Mongolian wild asses have all been credited with unsustained spurts of 64 km/h (40 mph) or more. Compare these figures with the top speed of the three-toed sloth, which is 0.2 km/h (0.12 mph).

HEAVIEST CARNIVORES

	CARNIVORE	LENGTH (FT)	(IN)	(M)	WEIGHT (LB)	(KG)
1	**Southern elephant seal**	21	4	6.5	7,716	3,500
2	**Walrus**	12	6	3.8	2,646	1,200
3	**Steller sea lion**	9	8	3.0	2,425	1,100
4	**Grizzly bear**	9	8	3.0	1,720	780
5	**Polar bear**	8	6	2.6	1,323	600
6	**Tiger**	9	2	2.8	661	300
7	**Lion**	6	3	1.9	551	250
8	**American black bear**	6	0	1.8	500	227
9	**Giant panda**	5	0	1.5	353	160
10	**Spectacled bear**	6	0	1.8	309	140

Only three marine carnivores have been included to make room for the terrestrial heavyweights. The polar bear is probably the largest land carnivore if shoulder height (when the animal is on all fours) is taken into account; it tops an awesome 1.6 m (5.3 ft) compared with the 1.2 m (4 ft) of its nearest rival, the grizzly.

TOP 10 HEAVIEST TERRESTRIAL MAMMALS

	MAMMAL	LENGTH (FT)	(M)	WEIGHT (LB)	(KG)
1	**African elephant**	24	7.3	14,432	7,000
2	**White rhinoceros**	14	4.3	7,937	3,600
3	**Hippopotamus**	13	4.0	5,512	2,500
4	**Giraffe**	19	5.8	3,527	1,600
5	**American bison**	13	4.0	2,205	1,000
6	**Arabian camel** (dromedary)	12	3.7	1,521	690
7	**Polar bear**	8	2.4	1,323	600
8	**Moose**	10	3.0	1,213	550
9	**Siberian tiger**	11	3.4	661	300
10	**Gorilla**	7	2.1	485	220

The list excludes domesticated cattle and horses. It also avoids comparing close kin such as the African and Indian elephants, highlighting instead the sumo stars within distinctive large mammal groups such as the bears, deer, big cats, primates, and bovines (oxlike mammals).

Flying Animals

TOP 10 HEAVIEST FLIGHTED BIRDS

	BIRD*	WINGSPAN (IN)	(CM)	WEIGHT (LB)	(OZ)	(KG)
1	**Mute swan**	94	238	49	6	22.50
2	**Kori bustard**	107	270	41	8	19.00
3 =	**Andean condor**	126	320	33	1	15.00
=	**Great white pelican**	142	360	33	1	15.00
5	**Black vulture** (Old World)	116	295	27	5	12.50
6	**Sarus crane**	110	280	26	9	12.24
7	**Himalayan griffon** (vulture)	122	310	26	5	12.00
8	**Wandering albatross**	138	350	24	9	11.30
9	**Steller's sea eagle**	104	265	19	8	9.00
10	**Marabou stork**	113	287	19	6	8.90

* *By species*

Source: *Chris Mead*

Wing size does not necessarily correspond to weight in flighted birds: the huge wingspan of the marabou stork, for example, is greater than that of species twice its weight. When laden with a meal of carrion, however, the voracious marabou can double its weight and needs all the lift it can get to take off. It often fails totally and has to put up with flightlessness until digestion takes its course.

TOP 10 BIRDS WITH THE LARGEST WINGSPANS

	BIRD*	MAXIMUM WINGSPAN (IN)	(CM)
1	**Great white pelican**	141	360
2	**Wandering albatross**#	138	351
3	**Andean condor**	126	320
4	**Himalayan griffon** (vulture)	122	310
5	**Black vulture** (Old World)	116	295
6	**Marabou stork**	113	287
7	**Lammergeier**	111	282
8	**Sarus crane**	110	280
9	**Kori bustard**	106	270
10	**Steller's sea eagle**	104	265

* *By species*

\# *Royal albatross, a close relative, is the same size*

Source: *Chris Mead*

Wingspans of up to 4.2 m (13.8 ft) have been claimed for the albatross, but the superstition that killing one would curse the crew of ship, the theme of Coleridge's poem *The Rime of the Ancient Mariner*, means that few have ever been captured.

TOP 10 SMALLEST BATS

	BAT (SCIENTIFIC NAME)/HABITAT	LENGTH (IN)	(CM)	WEIGHT (OZ)	(G)
1	**Kitti's hognosed bat** (*Craseonycteris thonglongyai*), Thailand	1.10	2.9	0.07	2.0
2	**Proboscis bat** (*Rhynchonycteris naso*), Central and South America	1.50	3.8	0.09	2.5
3	= **Banana bat** (*Pipistrellus nanus*), Africa	1.50	3.8	0.11	3.0
	= **Smoky bat** (*Furipterus horrens*), Central and South America	1.50	3.8	0.11	3.0
5	= **Little yellow bat** (*Rhogeessa mira*), Central America	1.57	4.0	0.12	3.5
	= **Lesser bamboo bat** (*Tylonycteris pachypus*), Southeast Asia	1.57	4.0	0.12	3.5
7	**Disc-winged bat** (*Thyroptera tricolor*), Central and South America	1.42	3.6	0.14	4.0
8	**Lesser horseshoe bat** (*Rhinolophus hipposideros*), Europe and Western Asia	1.46	3.7	0.18	5.0
9	**California myotis** (*Myotis californienses*), North America	1.69	4.3	0.18	5.0
10	**Northern blossom bat** (*Macroglossus minimus*), Southeast Asia to Australia	2.52	6.4	0.53	15.0

The minute Kitti's hognosed bat, the world's smallest mammal, is found only in a group of caves in Thailand. It is named after Kitti Thonglongya, who discovered it in 1973.

TOP 10 LONGEST BIRD MIGRATIONS

	BIRD	APPROXIMATE DISTANCE MILES	KM
1	**Pectoral sandpiper**	11,806	19,000*
2	**Wheatear**	11,184	18,000
3	**Slender-billed shearwater**	10,874	17,500*
4	**Ruff**	10,314	16,600
5	**Willow warbler**	10,128	16,300
6	**Arctic tern**	10,066	16,200
7	**Arctic skua**	9,693	15,600
8	**Swainson's hawk**	9,445	15,200
9	**Knot**	9,320	15,000
10	**Swallow**	9,258	14,900

* *Thought to be only half of the path taken during a whole year*

Source: *Chris Mead*

This list is of the likely extremes for a normal migrant, not one that has gotten lost and wandered into new territory. All migrant birds fly far longer than is indicated by the direct route. Many species fly all year, except when they come to land to breed, or in the case of seabirds, to rest on the sea. Such species include the albatross, petrel, tern, and some types of swift and house martin. The annual distance covered by these birds may range from 150,000 km (93,200 miles) to almost 300,000 km (186,415 miles).

TOP 10 FASTEST BIRDS

	BIRD	SPEED (MPH)	(KM/H)
1	**Common eider**	47	76
2	**Bewick's swan**	44	72
3	= **Barnacle goose**	42	68
	= **Common crane**	42	68
5	**Mallard**	40	65
6	= **Red-throated diver**	38	61
	= **Wood pigeon**	38	61
8	**Oyster catcher**	36	58
9	= **Pheasant**	33	54
	= **White-fronted goose**	33	54

Source: *Chris Mead*

◄ Big Wings

The Andean condor has one of the greatest total wing areas of any bird. The celebrated British mountaineer Edward Whymper encountered one in Ecuador in 1892 with wings 3.2 m (10.5 ft) from tip to tip.

Marine Animals

THE 10 COUNTRIES WITH THE MOST THREATENED FISH SPECIES

	COUNTRY/THREATENED SPECIES*	TOTAL NUMBER OF THREATENED FISH SPECIES
1	**US** Alabama sturgeon#, cuiui#, charalito chihuahua, White River spinedace#, Moapa dace#, Cahaba shiner#, Cape Fear shiner#, Leon Spring pupfish#, Pecos pupfish#, California black sea bass, Alabama cavefish#, shortnose cisco, Apache trout	131
2	**Mexico** Perrito de potosi# (extinct in the wild), cachorrito de charco palmal# (extinct in the wild), black-blotch pupfish# (extinct in the wild), butterfly splitfin# (extinct in the wild), golden skiffia# (extinct in the wild), charal de Alchichica#, *Cyprinella alvarezdelvillari*# (no common name), sardinita bocagrande#, sardinita quijarrona#, charalito saltillo#, charalito chihuahua, sardinita de tepelmene#, cachorrito de Mezquital#, cachorrito cabezon#, cachorrito de dorsal larga#, cachorrito de charco azul#, Cuatrocienegas killifish#, blackspot allotoca#, Mexclapique#, Turners hocklandkärpfling#, balsas hocklandkärpfling#, guayacon bocon#, broad-spotted molly#, molly del Teapa#, Monterrey platyfish#, black sea bass, totoaba#, Boccacio rockfish	88
3	**Indonesia** Sentani rainbowfish#, duck-bill poso minnow#, elongate poso minnow#, *Betta miniopinna*# (no common name), *Betta spilotogena*# (no common name), poso bungu#, *Encheloclarias kelioides*# (no common name)	67
4	**Australia** Red-finned blue-eye#, spotted handfish#, swan galaxias#, barred galaxias#, Clarence galaxias#, pedder galaxias#, Elizabeth Springs goby#, Edgbaston goby#, Mary River cod#	44
5	**China** Dabry's sturgeon#, Chinese paddlefish#	33
6	**South Africa** Twee River redfin#, border barb#, Clanwilliam sandfish#, Berg redfin#, Barnard's rock-catfish#, Incomati suckermouth#, river pipefish#	30
7	**Philippines** *Cephalakoompsus pachycheilus*# (no common name), manumbok#, bagangan#, bitungu#, pait#, baolan#, disa#, katapa-tapa#, *Puntius herrei*# (no common name), katolo#, kandar#, manalak#, tras#, palata#, dwarf pygmy goby#	28
8 =	**Cameroon** Dikume#, konye#, myaka#, pungu#, fissi#, blackbelly tilapia#, keppi#, kululu#, nsess#, mongo#, pindu#, *Clarias maclareni*# (no common name)	27
=	**Uganda** *Allochromis welcommei*# (no common name), *Astatotilapia latifasciata*# (no common name), *Haplochromis annectidens*# (no common name), *Harpagochromis worthingtoni*# (no common name), *Lipochromis "backflash cryptodon"*# (no common name), *Paralabidochromis beadlei*# (no common name), *Xystichromis "Kyoga flameback"*# (no common name)	27
10	**Turkey** Baltic/European sturgeon, *Aphanius splendens*# (no common name), *Aphanius sureyanus*# (no common name), *Aphanius transgrediens*# (no common name), flathead trout#	22
	Canada Shortnose cisco, boccacio rockfish	2

* *Listed as Critically Endangered on the IUCN Red List 2000, except where otherwise indicated*

\# *Found in no other countries*

Source: *2000 IUCN Red List of Threatened Species/UNEP-WCMC Animals of the World Database*

TOP 10 HEAVIEST MARINE MAMMALS

	MAMMAL	LENGTH (FT)	LENGTH (M)	WEIGHT (TONNES)
1	**Blue whale**	110.0	33.5	137.0
2	**Bowhead whale** (Greenland right)	65.0	20.0	86.0
3	**Northern right whale** (Black right)	60.0	18.6	77.7
4	**Fin whale** (common rorqual)	82.0	25.0	63.4
5	**Sperm whale**	59.0	18.0	43.7
6	**Gray whale**	46.0	14.0	34.9
7	**Humpback whale**	49.2	15.0	34.6
8	**Sei whale**	60.0	18.5	29.4
9	**Bryde's whale**	47.9	14.6	20.0
10	**Baird's whale**	5.5	18.0	12.1

Source: *Lucy T. Verma*

Probably the largest animal that ever lived, the blue whale dwarfs even the other whales listed here, all but one of which far outweigh the biggest land animal, the elephant. The elephant seal, with a weight of 3.5 tonnes, is the largest marine mammal that is not a whale.

TOP 10 HEAVIEST SHARKS

	SHARK	MAXIMUM WEIGHT (LB)	MAXIMUM WEIGHT (KG)
1	**Whale shark**	67,240	30,500
2	**Basking shark**	20,410	9,258
3	**Great white shark**	7,731	3,507
4	**Greenland shark**	2,224	1,009
5	**Tiger shark**	2,043	927
6	**Great hammerhead shark**	1,889	857
7	**Six-gill shark**	1,327	602
8	**Gray nurse shark**	1,243	564
9	**Mako shark**	1,221	554
10	**Thresher shark**	1,097	498

Source: *Lucy T. Verma*

Such is the notoriety of sharks that many accounts of their size are exaggerated, and this list should be taken as an approximate ranking based on best available evidence. The rare whale shark is also the largest fish, measuring up to 12.65 m (41.5 ft). First discovered in 1828, it is a plankton eater and consequently not a threat to swimmers.

TOP 10 HEAVIEST TURTLES

	TURTLE	MAXIMUM WEIGHT (LB)	MAXIMUM WEIGHT (KG)
1	**Pacific leatherback turtle***	1,552	704.4
2	**Atlantic leatherback turtle***	1,018	463.0
3	**Green sea turtle**	783	355.3
4	**Loggerhead turtle**	568	257.8
5	**Alligator snapping turtle#**	220	100.0
6	**Flatback (sea) turtle**	171	78.2
7	**Hawksbill (sea) turtle**	138	62.7
8	**Kemps Ridley turtle**	133	60.5
9	**Olive Ridley turtle**	110	49.9
10	**Common snapping turtle#**	85	38.5

* *One species, differing in size according to where they live*

\# *Freshwater species*

Source: *Lucy T. Verma*

The largest leatherback turtle ever recorded is a male found beached at Harlech, Wales, in 1988, measuring 2.9 m (9.5 ft) and weighing 961 kg (2,120 lb). It is now displayed in the National Museum of Wales, Cardiff.

Turtle
Having been hunted as food and for their shells, many of the world's largest turtles are endangered and under threat of extinction.

Invertebrates

TOP 10 MOST COMMON INSECTS*

	SPECIES (SCIENTIFIC NAME)	APPROXIMATE NO. OF KNOWN SPECIES
1	**Beetles** (*Coleoptera*)	400,000
2	**Butterflies and moths** (*Lepidoptera*)	165,000
3	**Ants, bees, and wasps** (*Hymenoptera*)	140,000
4	**True flies** (*Diptera*)	120,000
5	**Bugs** (*Hemiptera*)	90,000
6	**Crickets, grasshoppers, and locusts** (*Orthoptera*)	20,000
7	**Caddisflies** (*Trichoptera*)	10,000
8	**Lice** (*Phthiraptera/Psocoptera*)	7,000
9	**Dragonflies and damselflies** (*Odonata*)	5,500
10	**Lacewings** (*Neuroptera*)	4,700

* *By number of known species*

This list includes only species that have been discovered and named; it is surmised that many thousands of species still await discovery. It takes no account of the absolute numbers of each species, which are truly colossal. There are at least one million insects for each of the Earth's 6.3 billion humans; all together, the insects would weigh at least 12 times as much as the human race and at least three times as much as the combined weight of all other living animals. The most common insects in Canada are true flies, with 7,056 approximate known species, and beetles, with 6,758. Ants, bees, and wasps follow closely with 6,028 known species.

TOP 10 LARGEST MOLLUSKS*

	SPECIES (SCIENTIFIC NAME)	CLASS	LENGTH (IN)	(MM)
1	**Giant squid** (*Architeuthis sp.*)	Cephalopod	660	16,764#
2	**Giant clam** (*Tridacna gigas*)	Marine bivalve	51	1,300
3	**Australian trumpet** (*Syrus aruanus*)	Marine snail	30	770
4	***Hexabranchus sanguineus***	Sea slug	20	520
5	***Carinaria cristata***	Heteropod	19	500
6	**Steller's Coat of Mail shell** (*Cryptochiton stelleri*)	Chiton	18	470
7	**Freshwater mussel** (*Cristaria plicata*)	Freshwater bivalve	11	300
8	**Giant African snail** (*Achatina achatina*)	Land snail	7	200
9	**Tusk shell** (*Dentalium vernedi*)	Scaphopod	5	138
10	**Apple snail** (*Pila werneri*)	Freshwater snail	4	125

* *Largest species within each class*

\# *Estimated; actual length unknown*

There are over 60,000 species of mollusks, including octopuses, snails, slugs, and shellfish, of which these are the largest—although tales of the largest, the giant squid, attacking and sinking ships are in the realm of sailors' tall tales. The giant clam is noted for its longevity, lifespans of up to 150 years being claimed by some experts.

TOP 10 LARGEST BUTTERFLIES

	BUTTERFLY (SCIENTIFIC NAME)	WINGSPAN (IN)	(MM)
1	**Queen Alexandra's birdwing** (*Ornithoptera alexandrae*)	11.0	280
2	**African giant swallowtail** (*Papilio antimachus*)	9.1	230
3	**Goliath birdwing** (*Ornithoptera goliath*)	8.3	210
4	= **Buru opalescent birdwing** (*Troides prattorum*)	7.9	200
	= ***Trogonoptera trojana***	7.9	200
	= ***Troides hypolitus***	7.9	200
7	= **Chimaera birdwing** (*Ornithoptera chimaera*)	7.5	190
	= ***Ornithoptera lydius***	7.5	190
	= ***Troides magellanus***	7.5	190
	= ***Troides miranda***	7.5	190

The rare Queen Alexandra's birdwing is found only in Papua New Guinea. Females, which are usually larger than males, weigh up to 25 g (9/10 oz).

▶ **Leaf Beetle**
Almost one-third of all known animal species are beetles, with more than 25,000 species of leaf beetles among the 400,000 recorded.

TOP 10 FASTEST INSECT FLIERS

	SPECIES (SCIENTIFIC NAME)	SPEED (MPH)	(KM/H)
1	**Hawkmoth** (*Sphingidaei*)	33.3	53.6
2 =	**West Indian butterfly** (*Nymphalidae prepona*)	30.0	48.0
=	**Deer botfly** (*Cephenemyia pratti*)	30.0	48.0
4	**Deer botfly** (*Chrysops*)	25.0	40.0
5	**West Indian butterfly** (*Hesperiidae sp.*)	18.6	30.0
6	**Dragonfly** (*Anax parthenope*)	17.8	28.6
7	**Hornet** (*Vespa crabro*)	13.3	21.4
8	**Bumblebee** (*Bombus lapidarius*)	11.1	17.9
9	**Horsefly** (*Tabanus bovinus*)	8.9	14.3
10	**Honey bee** (*Apis mellifera*)	7.2	11.6

Hive of Activity
With its wings beating at a rate of 11,000 times a minute, the honey bee can fly surprisingly fast.

DEADLIEST SPIDERS

	SPIDER (SCIENTIFIC NAME)	RANGE
1	**Banana spider** (*Phonenutria nigriventer*)	Central and South America
2	**Sydney funnel web** (*Atrax robustus*)	Australia
3	**Wolf spider** (*Lycosa raptoria/erythrognatha*)	Central and South America
4	**Black widow** (*Latrodectus* species)	Widespread
5	**Violin spider/Recluse spider**	Widespread
6	**Sac spider**	Southern Europe
7	**Tarantula** (*Eurypelma rubropilosum*)	Neotropics
8	**Tarantula** (*Acanthoscurria atrox*)	Neotropics
9	**Tarantula** (*Lasiodora klugi*)	Neotropics
10	**Tarantula** (*Pamphobeteus* species)	Neotropics

This list ranks spiders according to their "lethal potential"—their venom yield divided by their venom potency. The banana spider, for example, yields 6 mg of venom, with 1 mg the estimated lethal dose in humans. However, few spiders are capable of killing humans. The tarantula produces 1.5 mg of venom, but its lethal dose for an adult human is 12 mg. Anecdotal evidence suggests that the Thailand and Sumatran black birdeaters may be equally dangerous, but insufficient data are available. Canada has about 1,400 species of spiders but none are considered deadly. Our two species of black widows—the western and the northern—are the only ones that are known to be potentially dangerous. Contrary to popular belief, no brown recluse spiders have ever been found in Canada.

THE 10 MOST COMMON ANIMAL PHOBIAS

	ANIMAL	MEDICAL TERM
1	**Spiders**	Arachnophobia or arachnephobia
2	**Bees and wasps**	Bees: Apiphobia, apiophobia, or melissophobia; wasps: spheksophobia
3	**Reptiles**	Batrachophobia
4	**Snakes**	Ophidiophobia, ophiophobia, ophiciophobia, herpetophobia, or snakephobia
5	**Mice**	Musophobia or muriphobia
6	**Dogs**	Cynophobia or kynophobia
7	**Birds**	Ornithophobia
8	**Frogs**	Batrachophobia
9	**= Ants**	Myrmecophobia
	= Horses	Hippophobia or equinophobia
	= Rats	No medical term

Not all phobias are completely irrational. Creatures that may bite or sting, or carry disease, such as rabid cats and dogs, are very wisely avoided.

THE 10 COUNTRIES THAT CATCH THE MOST WHALES

		CATCH IN 2000 (NUMBERS)		
	COUNTRY	SPERM AND PILOT WHALES	BLUE AND FIN WHALES	TOTAL
1	**Japan**	16,937	552	17,489
2	**Brazil**	861	-	861
3	**Norway**	-	487	487
4	**Argentina**	445	-	445
5	**France**	213	-	213
6	**US**	172	35	207
7	**Russia**	22	180	202
8	**South Korea**	95	79	174
9	**Greenland**	-	162	162
10	**UK**	46	3	49
	Canada	-	*1*	*1*

Source: *Food and Agriculture Organization of the United Nations*

Many of these countries have banned whaling; most of these whales were caught accidentally in fishing nets.

THE 10 COUNTRIES FOR IVORY SEIZURES

	COUNTRY	SEIZURES 1989–99
1	**US**	1,435
2	**Namibia**	409
3	**France**	375
4	**UK**	367
5	**Germany**	261
6	**Belgium**	237
7	**Tanzania**	210
8	**South Africa**	155
9	**Malawi**	132
10	**Zambia**	104
	World	*4,361*

Source: *The Elephant Trade Information System (ETIS)*

The records indicate that nearly 120 tonnes of ivory have been seized worldwide in the period 1989–99, representing some 28,319 tusks and pieces of raw ivory, 204,215 semi-worked ivory blocks, and 187,950 ivory products.

▼ **Death Rattle**
The fear of snakes is among the most common of all phobias—although with species such as this rattlesnake, there are good reasons.

THE 10 LATEST GENESIS AWARDS FOR BEST ANIMAL FEATURE FILM

YEAR	FILM
2003	**Spirit: Stallion of the Cimarron**
2002	**Dr. Dolittle 2**
2001	**Chicken Run**
2000	**Instinct**
1999	**Mighty Joe Young**
1998	**Shiloh**
1997	**Fly Away Home**
1996	**Babe**
1995	**Black Beauty**
1994	**Free Willy**

Source: *The Ark Trust*

Since 1986 the Ark Trust, Inc., a US animal rights and welfare charity, has been presenting the Genesis Awards, including one for the best animal feature film that raises such issues.

TOP 10 FILMS STARRING ANIMALS

	FILM	YEAR	ANIMAL
1	**Jaws**	1975	Shark
2	**101 Dalmatians**	1996	Dogs
3	**Doctor Dolittle**	1998	Various
4	**Babe**	1995	Pig
5	**Jaws 2**	1978	Shark
6	**Cats & Dogs**	2001	Cats, dogs
7	**The Horse Whisperer**	1998	Horses
8	**102 Dalmatians**	2000	Dogs
9	**Dr. Dolittle 2**	2001	Various
10	**Deep Blue Sea**	1999	Sharks

This list is of movies where real animals are central, rather than secondary characters. It excludes dinosaurs, fantasy creatures such as dragons, and humans costumed as animals (hence eliminating *Planet of the Apes*) as well as animated films and the eponymous stars of animated/live-action combinations such as *Who Framed Roger Rabbit?*, *Stuart Little*, and *Scooby-Doo*. With new technology, the line between real, animatronic, and computer-generated animals is becoming increasingly blurred.

Jaws of Death
Star of the 1975 film *Jaws*, the great white shark is responsible for more attacks on humans (254) and fatalities (67) than any other species, in attacks recorded between 1580 and 2001.

COUNTRIES WHERE MOST PEOPLE ARE ATTACKED BY SHARKS

	COUNTRY/STATE	FATAL ATTACKS	LAST FATAL ATTACK	TOTAL ATTACKS*
1	**US** (continental)	69	2001	855
2	**Australia**	152	2000	323
3	**South Africa**	43	1999	225
4	**US** (Hawaii)	19	1992	99
5	**Brazil**	20	1998	78
6	**Papua New Guinea**	31	2000	65
7	**New Zealand**	9	1968	53
8	**Bahamas**	1	1968	42
9	**Mexico**	21	1997	39
10	**Fiji**	10	2000	25

* *Including non-fatal*

Source: *International Shark Attack File/American Elasmobranch Society/Florida Museum of Natural History*

The International Shark Attack File monitors worldwide incidents, a total of more than 2,000 of which have been recorded since the 16th century. The 1990s had the highest attack total (536) of any decade, while 76 unprovoked attacks were recorded in 2001 alone. This upward trend is believed to reflect the increase in the numbers of people engaging in scuba diving and other aquatic activities.

MOST-COMMONLY USED ANIMALS IN SCIENTIFIC EXPERIMENTS IN CANADA*

	ANIMAL	NUMBER USED IN 2000
1	**Mice**	697,869
2	**Fish**	411,988
3	**Rats**	304,656
4	**Canadian wild species (birds, canines, rodents, ruminants, others)**	198,335
5	**Domestic birds (chickens, ducks, pigeons, turkeys, others)**	141,624
6	**Farm animals (cattle, goats, horses, sheep, swine, others)**	70,335
7	**Amphibia (frogs, salamanders, others)**	43,853
8	**Guinea pigs**	37,391
9	**Rabbits**	16,071
10	**Dogs**	8,789
	Total	*1,954,059*

* *Includes animals used in research, experiments, testing, and teaching*

Source: *Canadian Council on Animal Care,* CCAC Animal Use Survey, *2000*

Pet Power

TOP 10 DOG BREEDS IN CANADA

	BREED	NO. REGISTERED (2002)
1	**Labrador retriever**	10,286
2	**Golden retriever**	6,085
3	**German shepherd**	4,596
4	**Poodle**	2,992
5	**Shetland sheepdog**	2,636
6	**Yorkshire terrier**	2,133
7	**Miniature schnauzer**	2,073
8	**Shih tzu**	1,587
9	**Bichon frise**	1,469
10	**Boxer**	1,417
	Total registered	*70,449*

Source: *Canadian Kennel Club*

TOP 10 PET DOG POPULATIONS

	COUNTRY	ESTIMATED PET DOG POPULATION (2002)
1	**US**	61,080,000
2	**Brazil**	30,051,000
3	**China**	22,908,000
4	**Japan**	9,650,000
5	**Russia**	9,600,000
6	**South Africa**	9,100,000
7	**France**	8,150,000
8	**Italy**	7,600,000
9	**Poland**	7,520,000
10	**Thailand**	6,900,000
	Canada	*3,857,000*

Source: *Euromonitor*

The estimate for the US pet dog population represents a ratio of more than one dog for every two of the 104.7 million households in the country, but since multiple ownership is common, there are more dog-free homes than there are homes with a canine inhabitant.

TOP 10 PET BIRD POPULATIONS

	COUNTRY	ESTIMATED PET BIRD POPULATION (2002)
1	**China**	71,474,000
2	**Japan**	21,300,000
3	**US**	18,740,000
4	**Brazil**	17,254,000
5	**Indonesia**	14,842,000
6	**Italy**	13,000,000
7	**Turkey**	9,200,000
8	**Spain**	7,734,000
9	**Australia**	7,100,000
10	**France**	6,500,000
	Canada	*2,260,000*

Source: *Euromonitor*

TOP 10 PET FISH POPULATIONS

	COUNTRY	ESTIMATED PET FISH POPULATION (2000)
1	**US**	168,990,000
2	**China**	121,852,000
3	**Germany**	50,000,000
4	**Japan**	34,100,000
5	**Italy**	30,000,000
6	**France**	28,000,000
7	**UK**	23,900,000
8	**Russia**	20,600,000
9	**Australia**	12,900,000
10	**Sweden**	9,480,000
	Canada	*7,810,000*

Source: *Euromonitor*

◀ **Tanks a Lot**
Fish are kept as domestic pets, rather than for food, all over the world. The Chinese are particularly fond of them.

THE 10 PET CAT BREEDS IN CANADA

	BREED	NO. REGISTERED (2002)
1	**Himalayan**	437
2	**Persian**	359
3	**Ragdoll**	202
4	**Himalayan (non-pointed)**	112
5	**Exotic longhair**	91
6	**Abyssinian**	82
7	**Siamese**	72
8	**Maine coon**	71
9	**Birman**	68
10	**Scottish fold**	49
	Total registered	*2,046*

Source: *Canadian Cat Association*

▲ **Cool for Cats**
Ownership of pedigree cats, such as this Siamese, contributes to the substantial feline population of many Western countries. In developing parts of the world, cats continue their traditional role as domestic mousecatchers.

TOP 10 PET CAT POPULATIONS

	COUNTRY	ESTIMATED PET CAT POPULATION (2002)
1	**US**	76,430,000
2	**China**	53,100,000
3	**Russia**	12,700,000
4	**Brazil**	12,466,000
5	**France**	9,600,000
6	**Italy**	9,400,000
7	**UK**	7,700,000
8	**Ukraine**	7,350,000
9	**Japan**	7,300,000
10	**Germany**	7,000,000
	Canada	*6,811,000*

Source: *Euromonitor*

TOP 10 PET SMALL MAMMAL POPULATIONS

	COUNTRY	ESTIMATED PET SMALL MAMMAL POPULATION (2002)
1	**US**	20,930,000
2	**Germany**	6,400,000
3	**Russia**	4,700,000
4	**UK**	4,200,000
5	**Japan**	3,000,000
6	**France**	2,400,000
7	**Italy**	2,100,000
8	**China**	1,748,000
9	**Canada**	1,153,000
10	**Spain**	1,112,000

Source: *Euromonitor*

TOP 10 PET REPTILE POPULATIONS

	COUNTRY	ESTIMATED PET REPTILE POPULATION (1999)
1	**US**	7,680,000
2	**Russia**	4,500,000
3	**UK**	1,730,000
4	= **France**	1,100,000
	= **Italy**	1,100,000
6	**China**	612,000
7	**Spain**	200,000
8	**Canada**	190,000
9	**Thailand**	187,000
10	**Australia**	170,000

Source: *Euromonitor*

Trees & Forests

TOP 10 COUNTRIES WITH THE LARGEST AREAS OF FOREST

	COUNTRY	AREA (2000) (SQ MILES)	(SQ KM)
1	Russia	3,287,243	8,513,920
2	Brazil	2,100,359	5,439,905
3	Canada	944,294	2,445,710
4	US	872,564	2,259,930
5	China	631,200	1,634,800
6	Australia	596,678	1,545,390
7	Dem. Rep. of Congo	522,037	1,352,070
8	Indonesia	405,353	1,049,860
9	Angola	269,329	697,560
10	Peru	251,796	652,150
	World total	*14,888,715*	*38,561,590*

Source: *Food and Agriculture Organization of the United Nations, State of the World's Forests, 2001*

The world's forests occupy some 29 percent of the total land area of the planet. Just under half of Russia is forested, a total area that is almost the size of the whole of Brazil.

TOP 10 COUNTRIES WITH THE LARGEST AREAS OF TROPICAL FOREST

	COUNTRY	AREA (SQ MILES)	(SQ KM)
1	Brazil	1,163,222	3,012,730
2	Dem. Rep. of Congo	521,512	1,350,710
3	Indonesia	343,029	887,440
4	Peru	292,032	756,360
5	Bolivia	265,012	686,380
6	Venezuela	214,730	556,150
7	Columbia	205,352	531,860
8	Mexico	176,700	457,650
9	India	171,622	444,500
10	Angola	145,035	375,640
	World total	*5,434,964*	*14,076,490*

▼ **Tropical Forest**
The world's tropical forests are among Earth's most important resources, home to more than half the planet's plant and animal species. The vast forests of Brazil occupy an area greater than the whole of India.

TOP 10 TALLEST TREES IN NORTH AMERICA

	TREE	LOCATION	HEIGHT (M)
1	**Coast redwood**	Jedidiah Smith State Park, California	97.8
2	**Sitka spruce**	Carmanah Creek, British Columbia	96.0
3	**Coast redwood**	Prairie Creek Redwoods State Park, California	95.4
4	**Coast Douglas fir**	Coquitlam, British Columbia	94.5
5	**Coast redwood**	Jedidiah Smith State Park, California	93.6
6	**Coast Douglas fir**	Olympic National Forest, Washington	85.6
7	= **Coast Douglas fir**	Puntledge River, British Columbia	82.9
	= **Noble fir**	Mount St. Helens National Monument, Washington	82.9
9	**Sitka spruce**	West Walbran Creek, British Columbia	80.8
10	**General Sherman giant sequoia**	Sequoia National Park, California	79.6

Source: *National Register of Big Trees, American Forestry Association* and *British Columbia Register of Big Trees, BC Conservationa Data Centre*

The General Sherman giant sequoia is not only the biggest living tree but also the largest living object on the planet. It has been calculated that it is 266 trillion times heavier than the seed from which it sprouted some 2,500 years ago, and that if it were made into pencils, end to end they would reach around the equator, a distance of 40,075.02 km (24,901.46 miles).

▲ **Deforesting Countries**
In the 1990s the net loss of the world's forest (the difference between deforestation and increase by new planting) declined from 39,634,290 sq km (15,302,887 sq miles) to 38,694,550 sq km (14,940,051 sq miles), an average of 939,740 sq km (362,836 sq miles) a year.

THE 10 DEFORESTING COUNTRIES

	COUNTRY	ANNUAL FOREST COVER LOSS 1990–2000 (SQ MILES)	(SQ KM)
1	**Brazil**	8,915	23,090
2	**Indonesia**	5,065	13,120
3	**Sudan**	3,702	9,590
4	**Zambia**	3,286	8,510
5	**Mexico**	2,436	6,310
6	**Dem. Rep. of Congo**	2,054	5,320
7	**Myanmar**	1,996	5,170
8	**Nigeria**	1,537	3,980
9	**Zimbabwe**	1,235	3,200
10	**Argentina**	1,100	2,850

Source: *Food and Agriculture Organization of the United Nations*, State of the World's Forests, 2001

During the 1990s, deforestation—the permanent loss of forest when trees are felled to enable the land to be used for other purposes—resulted in the decline of Brazil's rain forests from 5,669,980 sq km (2,189,192 sq miles) to 5,439,050 sq km (2,100,029 sq miles).

TOP 10 MOST FORESTED COUNTRIES

	COUNTRY	PERCENTAGE FOREST COVER 2000
1	**French Guiana**	90.0
2	**Solomon Islands**	87.8
3	**Suriname**	86.4
4	**Gabon**	81.5
5	**Guyana**	78.5
6	**Brunei**	76.6
7	**Palau**	76.1
8	**Finland**	72.0
9	**North Korea**	68.1
10	**Sweden**	66.8
	Canada	26.5

Source: *Food and Agriculture Organization of the United Nations*

These countries have the greatest area of forest as a percentage of their total land area. Deforestation has caused the world average to fall from about 32 percent in 1972 to its present 29 percent.

TOP 10 TIMBER-PRODUCING COUNTRIES

	COUNTRY	ROUNDWOOD* PRODUCTION 2001 (CU FT)	(CU M)
1	**US**	16,989,640,251	481,092,992
2	**India**	10,461,406,517	296,234,016
3	**China**	10,061,503,477	284,910,024
4	**Brazil**	8,349,172,609	236,422,218
5	**Canada**	6,239,819,672	176,692,000
6	**Russia**	5,731,570,941	162,300,000
7	**Indonesia**	4,210,053,374	119,208,572
8	**Ethiopia**	3,223,648,197	91,283,543
9	**Dem. Rep. of Congo**	2,462,622,179	69,733,688
10	**Nigeria**	2,440,792,910	69,115,552
	World total	*117,513,661,774*	*3,327,616,024*

* *Logs, bolts, or other round sections cut from trees*

Source: *Food and Agriculture Organization of the United Nations*

Enough roundwood is produced annually to build more than 3,000 buildings with the volume of the Empire State Building, all constructed of solid wood.

Crops & Livestock

TOP 10 CEREAL CROPS

	CROP	PRODUCTION 2001 (TONNES)
1	**Corn**	614,219,025
2	**Rice** (paddy)	595,267,724
3	**Wheat**	589,871,831
4	**Barley**	143,067,330
5	**Sorghum**	58,732,210
6	**Millet**	28,900,100
7	**Oats**	26,950,177
8	**Rye**	23,283,404
9	**Triticale** (wheat/rye hybrid)	10,414,390
10	**Buckwheat**	2,577,044

Source: *Food and Agriculture Organization of the United Nations*

◀ Top of the Crops
Terraced rice cultivation in Indonesia, a leading producer of one of the world's most important crops. Worldwide, more than 1.5 million sq km (579,000 sq miles) are devoted to rice growing.

TOP 10 RICE-PRODUCING COUNTRIES

	COUNTRY	PRODUCTION* 2001 (TONNES)
1	**China**	179,303,895
2	**India**	136,580,992
3	**Indonesia**	50,096,000
4	**Bangladesh**	38,500,000
5	**Vietnam**	31,970,100
6	**Thailand**	26,954,068
7	**Myanmar**	20,600,000
8	**Philippines**	12,954,900
9	**Japan**	11,320,000
10	**Brazil**	10,195,400
	World total	*595,267,724*

* Paddy

Source: *Food and Agriculture Organization of the United Nations*

Rice has been cultivated since at least 4000 BC in Southeast Asia, from where it spread to India.

TOP 10 VEGETABLE CROPS*

	CROP	PRODUCTION 2001 (TONNES)
1	**Sugar cane**	1,273,370,750
2	**Potatoes**	309,306,566
3	**Sugar beet**	229,417,606
4	**Soybeans**	176,506,154
5	**Sweet potatoes**	135,447,539
6	**Tomatoes**	105,069,537
7	**Cabbages**	59,267,364
8	**Onions** (dry)	49,415,090
9	**Yams**	38,569,348
10	**Cucumbers**	35,017,554

* *Excluding cereals*

Source: *Food and Agriculture Organization of the United Nations*

The two leading crops exemplify the two-way traffic history of vegetable cultivation: sugar cane originated in India, but was taken to the Caribbean, while the potato, indigenous to the Americas, was transported to Europe, where it became a staple crop.

TOP 10 TOTAL STOCKS OF CANADIAN GRAINS

	CROP*	STOCKS OF GRAINS# (TONNES)
1	**All wheat**	13,405,000
2	**Corn for grain**	7,390,000
3	**Barley**	5,176,000
4	**Canola**	2,978,000
5	**Soybeans**	1,612,000
6	**Oats**	1,538,000
7	**Dry peas**	939,000
8	**Flaxseed**	399,000
9	**Lentils**	240,000
10	**Mustard seed**	130,000

* *Based on available data*

\# *As at December 31, 2002, estimates of crops stocks on farms and commercial grains stocks*

Source: *Statistics Canada, Agricultural Division,* Field Crop Reporting Series, *vol. 82, no. 1, 2003*

TOP 10 CATTLE COUNTRIES

	COUNTRY	CATTLE (2001)
1	**India**	219,642,000
2	**Brazil**	176,000,000
3	**China**	106,175,000
4	**US**	96,700,000
5	**Argentina**	50,369,000
6	**Sudan**	38,325,000
7	**Ethiopia**	34,500,000
8	**Mexico**	30,600,000
9	**Australia**	28,768,000
10	**Colombia**	27,000,000
	World	*1,360,475,620*
	Canada	*13,699,500*

Source: *Food and Agriculture Organization of the United Nations*

In addition to its symbolic and religious significance, the dairy cow has long been a crucial component of India's economy. The country's cattle population has more than quadrupled in the past century.

TOP 10 TYPES OF LIVESTOCK

	ANIMAL	WORLD STOCKS (2001)
1	**Chickens**	15,420,137,000
2	**Cattle**	1,360,475,620
3	**Sheep**	1,044,045,120
4	**Ducks**	947,525,000
5	**Pigs**	939,318,631
6	**Rabbits**	497,082,000
7	**Geese**	245,731,000
8	**Turkeys**	242,802,000
9	**Buffalo**	166,418,998
10	**Goats**	146,514,641

Source: *Food and Agriculture Organization of the United Nations*

In sheer numbers, chickens clearly rule the roost, with more than two chickens for every human on the planet. As well as providing meat, they produce some 880 billion eggs per annum, 337 billion of them in China alone—enough to make an omelet larger than Denmark!

▶ Getting the Goat
There are more than 60 countries in the world with one million or more goats. Worldwide, goats produce over 12 million tonnes of milk a year, while more than 300 million are slaughtered annually to provide meat and goatskin.

Fruit & Nuts

TOP 10 FRUIT-PRODUCING COUNTRIES

	COUNTRY	PRODUCTION* 2001 (TONNES)
1	**China**	75,770,921
2	**India**	53,540,274
3	**Brazil**	35,048,281
4	**US**	33,179,620
5	**Italy**	20,144,265
6	**Spain**	16,447,424
7	**Mexico**	15,671,564
8	**Iran**	12,972,692
9	**Philippines**	12,259,937
10	**France**	12,167,034
	World total	*516,170,055*
	Canada	*731,095*

* *Excluding melons*

Source: *Food and Agriculture Organization of the United Nations*

TOP 10 ALMOND-PRODUCING COUNTRIES

	COUNTRY	PRODUCTION 2001 (TONNES)
1	**US**	414,998
2	**Spain**	283,294
3	**Italy**	124,353
4	**Iran**	107,082
5	**Morocco**	90,191
6	**Greece**	60,921
7	**Syria**	54,550
8	**Turkey**	46,297
9	**Pakistan**	36,636
10	**Lebanon**	36,376
	World total	*1,466,427*

Source: *Food and Agriculture Organization of the United Nations*

TOP 10 FRUIT CROPS

	CROP	PRODUCTION 2001 (TONNES)
1	**Watermelons**	86,356,444
2	**Bananas**	75,494,803
3	**Oranges**	68,967,284
4	**Grapes**	67,514,025
5	**Apples**	64,676,038
6	**Coconuts**	55,729,507
7	**Plantains**	31,779,512
8	**Mangoes**	28,270,189
9	**Cantaloupes** and other melons	21,136,774
10	**Tangerines,** etc.	20,032,248

Source: *Food and Agriculture Organization of the United Nations*

About 70 percent of watermelons, the world's top fruit crop, are grown in China, where they have been cultivated since the 10th century.

TOP 10 WALNUT-PRODUCING COUNTRIES

	COUNTRY	PRODUCTION 2001 (TONNES)
1	**US**	304,998
2	**China**	278,164
3	**Iran**	185,222
4	**Turkey**	127,868
5	**Ukraine**	60,770
6	**Romania**	37,414
7	**India**	34,171
8	**France**	32,161
9	**Yugoslavia**	26,014
10	**Greece**	24,170
	World total	*1,246,259*

Source: *Food and Agriculture Organization of the United Nations*

◀ In a Nutshell

Walnuts were exported to the US from England and introduced into California in 1867, starting a state industry that today produces 99 percent of the US total and a major proportion of the world's supply.

TOP 10 NUT CROPS

	CROP	PRODUCTION 2001 (TONNES)
1	**Groundnuts** (in shell)	39,819,789
2	**Cashew nuts**	1,768,734
3	**Almonds**	1,466,427
4	**Walnuts**	1,373,765
5	**Chestnuts**	1,058,168
6	**Hazelnuts**	870,475
7	**Karite nuts** (sheanuts)	713,746
6	**Areca nuts** (betel)	711,173
9	**Tung nuts**	615,519
10	**Pistachios**	324,563

Source: *Food and Agriculture Organization of the United Nations*

Groundnuts, or peanuts, are native to Peru and Brazil, from where they spread to Asia and Africa. The modern peanut industry owes its origins to African-American agriculturalist George Washington Carver (1864–1943), who pioneered improved methods of cultivation and devised no fewer than 325 products based on peanuts, ranging from shampoo to shoe polish.

TOP 10 GRAPE-PRODUCING COUNTRIES

	COUNTRY	PRODUCTION 2001 (TONNES)
1	**Italy**	9,908,001
2	**France**	8,026,534
3	**US**	6,552,524
4	**Spain**	5,634,243
5	**China**	4,150,220
6	**Turkey**	3,582,511
7	**Iran**	2,774,181
8	**Argentina**	2,709,039
9	**Chile**	1,730,628
10	**Australia**	1,709,684
	World total	*67,514,025*
	Canada	*66,937*

Source: *Food and Agriculture Organization of the United Nations*

TOP 10 DATE-PRODUCING COUNTRIES

	COUNTRY	PRODUCTION 2001 (TONNES)
1	**Egypt**	1,227,170
2	**Iran**	964,505
3	**United Arab Emirates**	835,111
4	**Saudi Arabia**	810,198
5	**Iraq**	716,502
6	**Pakistan**	696,324
7	**Algeria**	407,855
8	**Oman**	273,878
9	**Sudan**	195,109
10	**Libya**	146,056
	World total	*6,760,388*

Source: *Food and Agriculture Organization of the United Nations*

▶ It's a Date

There are some 90 million date palms in the world, 64 million of them in Arab countries. Only female trees produce fruit—as much as 68 kg (150 lb) a year.

THE HUMAN WORLD

Human Body & Health

TOP 10 HEALTHIEST COUNTRIES

	COUNTRY	HEALTHY LIFE EXPECTANCY AT BIRTH*
1	Japan	73.6
2	Switzerland	72.8
3	San Marino	72.2
4	Sweden	71.8
5	Australia	71.6
6	= France	71.3
	= Monaco	71.3
8	Iceland	71.2
9	= Austria	71.0
	= Italy	71.0
	Canada	*69.9*

* *Average number of years expected to be spent in good health*

Source: *World Health Organization*, World Health Report 2002

Long Life
Diet and other factors have enabled Japanese healthy life expectancy to top the world league table.

THE 10 LEAST HEALTHY COUNTRIES

	COUNTRY	HEALTHY LIFE EXPECTANCY AT BIRTH*
1	Sierra Leone	26.5
2	Malawi	29.8
3	Zambia	30.9
4	Botswana	32.9
5	Niger	33.2
6	= Afghanistan	33.4
	= Lesotho	33.4
8	Burundi	33.7
9	Rwanda	33.8
10	Swaziland	33.9

* *Average number of years expected to be spent in good health*

Source: *World Health Organization*, World Health Report 2002

THE 10 MOST COMMON CAUSES OF HEALTH DISORDERS

DISORDERS AFFECTING MALES	% TOTAL*		DISORDERS AFFECTING FEMALES	% TOTAL*
Depression	9.7	1	**Depression**	14.0
Alcohol use	5.5	2	**Iron deficiency**	4.9
Hearing loss, adult onset	5.1	3	**Hearing loss,** adult onset	4.2
Iron deficiency	4.1	4	**Osteoarthritis**	3.5
Chronic obstructive pulmonary disease	3.8	5	**Chronic obstructive pulmonary disease**	2.9
Falls	3.3	6	**Schizophrenia**	2.7
Schizophrenia	3.0	7	**Manic depression**	2.4
Traffic accidents	2.7	8	**Falls**	2.3
Manic depression	2.6	9	**Alzheimer's and other dementias**	2.2
Osteoarthritis	2.5	10	**Obstructed labor**	2.1

* *Total includes other disorders not listed above*

Source: *World Health Organization*, World Health Report 2001

TOP 10 LONGEST BONES IN THE HUMAN BODY

	BONE	AVERAGE LENGTH (CM)	(IN)
1	**Femur** (thighbone—upper leg)	50.50	19.88
2	**Tibia** (shinbone—inner lower leg)	43.03	16.94
3	**Fibula** (outer lower leg)	40.50	15.94
4	**Humerus** (upper arm)	36.46	14.35
5	**Ulna** (inner lower arm)	28.20	11.10
6	**Radius** (outer lower arm)	26.42	10.40
7	**7th rib**	24.00	9.45
8	**8th rib**	23.00	9.06
9	**Innominate bone** (hipbone—half pelvis)	18.50	7.28
10	**Sternum** (breastbone)	17.00	6.69

These are average dimensions of the bones of an adult male measured from their extremities (ribs are curved, and the pelvis measurement is taken diagonally). The same bones in the female skeleton are usually 6 to 13 percent smaller, with the exception of the sternum, which is virtually identical.

TOP 10 MOST COMMON ALLERGENS

FOOD		ENVIRONMENTAL
Nuts	1	**House dust mites** (*Dermatophagoldes pteronyssinus*)
Shellfish/seafood	2	**Grass pollens**
Milk	3	**Tree pollens**
Wheat	4	**Cats**
Eggs	5	**Dogs**
Fresh fruit	6	**Horses**
Fresh vegetables	7	**Molds** (*Aspergillus fumigatus, Alternaria Cladosporium*, etc)
Cheese	8	**Birch pollens**
Yeast	9	**Weed pollens**
Soya protein	10	**Wasp/bee venoms**

An allergy has been defined as "an unpleasant reaction to foreign matter, specific to that substance, which is altered from the normal response and peculiar to the individual concerned."

TOP 10 BEST COUNTRIES TO LIVE IN

	COUNTRY	HDI VALUE (2000)*
1	**Norway**	0.942
2	**Sweden**	0.941
3	**Canada**	0.940
4	= **Australia**	0.939
	= **Belgium**	0.939
	= **US**	0.939
7	**Iceland**	0.936
8	**Netherlands**	0.935
9	**Japan**	0.933
10	**Finland**	0.930

* *The UN Human Development Index (HDI) measures average achievement in three basic dimensions of human development: health combined with longevity, education, and standard of living*

Source: *United Nations*, Human Development Report, 2002

TOP 10 MOST COMMON PHOBIAS

	OBJECT OF PHOBIA	MEDICAL TERM
1	**Spiders**	Arachnephobia or arachnophobia
2	**People and social situations**	Anthropophobia or sociophobia
3	**Flying**	Aerophobia or aviatophobia
4	**Open spaces**	Agoraphobia, cenophobia, or kenophobia
5	**Confined spaces**	Claustrophobia, cleisiophobia, cleithrophobia, or clithrophobia
6	= **Heights**	Acrophobia, altophobia, hypsophobia, or hypsiphobia
	= **Vomiting**	Emetophobia or emitophobia
8	**Cancer**	Carcinomaphobia, carcinophobia, carcinomatophobia, cancerphobia, or cancerophobia
9	**Thunderstorms**	Brontophobia or keraunophobia; related phobias are those associated with lightning (astraphobia), cyclones (anemophobia), and hurricanes and tornadoes (lilapsophobia)
10	= **Death**	Necrophobia or thanatophobia
	= **Heart disease**	Cardiophobia

A phobia is a morbid fear out of all proportion to the object of the fear. Many people would admit to being uncomfortable about these principal phobias, as well as others, but most do not become obsessive or allow such fears to rule their lives. True phobias often arise from an incident in childhood when a person has been afraid of some object and develops an irrational fear that persists into adulthood. Perhaps surprisingly, the Top 10 does not remain static, as "new" phobias become more common; although outside the Top 10, "technophobia," fear of modern technology such as computers, is increasingly reported. Nowadays, as well as the valuable work done by the Phobics Society in Britain and similar organizations elsewhere, phobias can be cured by taking special desensitization courses: for example, to conquer one's fear of flying.

Medicine & Healthcare

TOP 10 COUNTRIES WITH THE MOST HOSPITALS

	COUNTRY	BEDS PER 10,000 (1990–99)	HOSPITALS (1998)
1	**China**	17	69,105
2	**India**	8	15,067
3	**Vietnam**	17	12,500
4	**Nigeria**	2	11,588*
5	**Russia**	121	11,200
6	**Japan**	164	9,413#
7	**Egypt**	21	7,411
8	**South Korea**	55	6,446#
9	**Brazil**	31	6,410#
10	**US**	36	6,097

* *1993 data*

\# *1997 data*

TOP 10 COUNTRIES THAT SPEND THE MOST ON HEALTH CARE

	COUNTRY	HEALTH SPENDING PER CAPITA, 1995–99 (US$)
1	**US**	4,271
2	**Switzerland**	3,857
3	**Norway**	3,182
4	**Denmark**	2,785
5	**Germany**	2,697
6	**France**	2,288
7	**Japan**	2,243
8	**Netherlands**	2,173
9	**Sweden**	2,145
10	**Belgium**	2,137

Source: *World Bank,* World Development Indicators 2002

An average of US$12 per capita per annum is estimated to provide minimal health services, but many poor countries fall short of this figure. Ethiopia, for example, spends just US$4 per capita on health care.

TOP 10 DRUGS MOST PRESCRIBED IN CANADA

	DRUG/ (CONDITION/ILLNESS)	ESTIMATED NO. OF PRESCRIPTIONS DISPENSED (2002)*
1	**Synthroid** (Hypothyroidism)	7,050,000
2	**Lipitor** (High cholesterol)	7,046,000
3	**Altace** (Essential hypertension)	5,284,000
4	**Losec** (Excess stomach acid)	4,464,000
5	**Tylenol with codeine #3** (Pain)	4,462,000
6	**Premarin** (Estrogen deficiency)	4,385,000
7	**Novasen** (Inflammation, pain)	4,197,000
8	**Norvasc** (Hypertension)	3,838,000
9	**Paxil** (Depressive disorders)	3,476,000
10	**Vioxx** (Osteoarthritis, primary dysmenorrhea)	3,345,000

* *By Canadian retail pharmacies*

Source: *IMS Health, Canada,* Compuscript

▼ Babes in Arms
Despite its single-child policy, China's hospitals still have to deal with a proportion of the country's 20 million births a year.

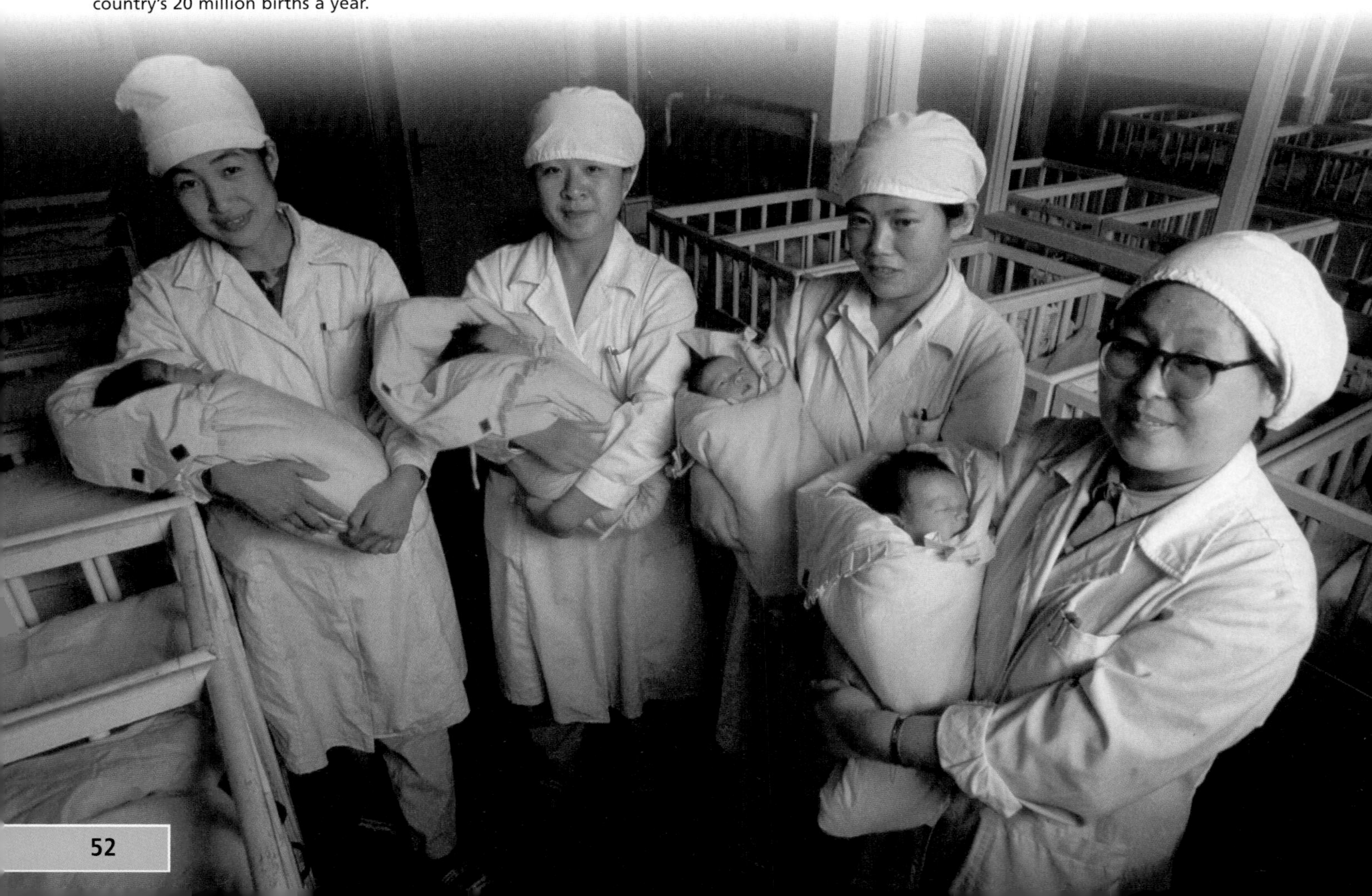

THE 10 COUNTRIES THAT SPEND THE MOST ON PRIVATE HEALTH CARE

	COUNTRY	PRIVATE HEALTH SPENDING PERCENTAGE OF GDP* (1995–99)
1	Lebanon	9.7
2	United Arab Emirates	7.6
3	Uruguay	7.3
4	US	7.1
5	Cambodia	6.3
6	Argentina	6.1
7	Kenya	5.5
8	Honduras	4.7
9	El Salvador	4.6
10	Sierra Leone	4.4

* *Gross domestic product*

Source: *World Bank,* World Development Indicators 2002

Expenditure on private health care is high both in countries where inhabitants are sufficiently wealthy to choose this option, and in some where the lack of state medicine makes it a necessity.

TOP 10 COUNTRIES THAT SPEND THE MOST ON PUBLIC HEALTH CARE

	COUNTRY	PUBLIC HEALTH SPENDING PERCENTAGE OF GDP* (1995–99)
1	Croatia	9.5
2	Nicaragua	8.5
3	Bosnia and Herzegovina	8.0
4	Germany	7.9
5	Switzerland	7.6
6	France	7.3
7	Norway	7.0
8	Denmark	6.9
9	Slovenia	6.7
10	= Canada	6.6
	= Czech Republic	6.6
	= Sweden	6.6

* *Gross domestic product*

Source: *World Bank,* World Development Indicators 2002

TOP 10 REASONS CANADIANS VISIT THEIR DOCTORS

	REASON FOR VISIT	ESTIMATED NO. OF VISITS (2002)*
1	Essential hypertension	18,937,000
2	Depressive disorder	8,513,000
3	Diabetes mellitus (without complications)	8,191,000
4	Routine general medical exam	7,790,000
5	Acute upper respiratory infection	6,070,000
6	Anxiety states	4,946,000
7	Normal pregnancy supervision	4,875,000
8	Unspecified otitis media (ear infection)	4,161,000
9	Hyperlipidemia (high cholesterol)	3,377,000
10	Acute bronchitis	3,258,000

* *Visits to Canadian office-based doctors*

Source: *IMS Health, Canada,* Canadian Disease and Therapeutic Index

THE 10 COUNTRIES WITH THE MOST PATIENTS PER DOCTOR

	COUNTRY	PATIENTS PER DOCTOR*
1	Malawi	49,118
2	Liberia	43,434
3	Mozambique	36,320
4	Eritrea	33,240
5	Chad	30,260
6	Ethiopia	30,195
7	Gambia	28,791
8	Central African Republic	28,600
9	Niger	28,560
10	Burkina Faso	27,158

* *In those countries, and latest year for which data are available*

TOP 10 COUNTRIES WITH THE FEWEST PATIENTS PER DOCTOR

	COUNTRY	PATIENTS PER DOCTOR*
1	Italy	169
2	Monaco	170
3	Cuba	188
4	Belarus	227
	= Georgia	227
6	Russia	238
7	Greece	243
8	Lithuania	250
9	Israel	256
10	Belgium	263
	Canada	476

* *In latest year for which data are available*

THE 10 MOST COMMON HOSPITAL ER CASES

	REASON FOR VISIT	VISITS (2000)
1	Stomach and abdominal pain, cramps, and spasms	6,759,000
2	Chest pain and related symptoms	5,798,000
3	Fever	4,383,000
4	Headache, pain in head	2,962,000
5	Shortness of breath	2,701,000
6	Back symptoms	2,595,000
7	Cough	2,592,000
8	Pain, unspecific	2,335,000
9	Laceration and cuts, upper body	2,322,000
10	Throat symptoms	2,043,000
	Total visits (including those not in Top 10)	*108,017,000*

Source: *National Ambulatory Medical Care Survey/ Center for Disease Control/National Center for Health Statistics*

Birth & Lifespan

TOP 10 COUNTRIES WITH THE HIGHEST BIRTH RATE

	COUNTRY	ESTIMATED BIRTH RATE (LIVE BIRTHS PER 1,000 POPULATION IN 2004)
1	**Niger**	48.8
2	**Mali**	47.5
3	**Chad**	46.7
4	**Uganda**	46.6
5	**Somalia**	46.0
6	**Angola**	45.4
7	**Liberia**	45.0
8	= **Dem. Rep. of Congo**	44.7
	= **Marshall Islands**	44.7
10	**Ethiopia**	43.7

Source: *US Census Bureau, International Data Base*

The countries with the highest birth rates are often among the poorest in the world. In these places, people often have large families so that their children can contribute to the family income.

TOP 10 COUNTRIES WITH THE LOWEST BIRTH RATE

	COUNTRY	ESTIMATED BIRTH RATE (LIVE BIRTHS PER 1,000 POPULATION IN 2004)
1	**Bulgaria**	8.0
2	**Italy**	8.6
3	**Germany**	8.7
4	= **Czech Republic**	8.9
	= **Latvia**	8.9
6	= **Hungary**	9.2
	= **Slovenia**	9.2
8	= **Andorra**	9.3
	= **Austria**	9.3
	= **Spain**	9.3
	Canada	*10.9*

Source: *US Census Bureau, International Data Base*

◄ **Baby Boom**
Mali and most of the other countries with high birth rates have rural economies that depend on large families to provide the required labor force.

TOP 10 COUNTRIES WITH THE HIGHEST LIFE EXPECTANCY

	COUNTRY	LIFE EXPECTANCY AT BIRTH (2004)
1	Andorra	83.5
2	San Marino	81.5
3	Japan	81.1
4	Singapore	80.5
5	Australia	80.2
6	= Sweden	80.1
	= Switzerland	80.1
8	= Canada	79.9
	= Iceland	79.9
10	= Italy	79.4
	= Liechtenstein	79.4
	= Monaco	79.4

Source: *US Census Bureau, International Data Base*

Life expectancy represents the average life span of a newborn child. A century ago the world average life expectancy was about 30 years; today it is more than double, but to achieve this average, there are countries with much higher expectancy, as well as those that fall below it.

THE 10 COUNTRIES WITH THE HIGHEST INFANT MORTALITY

	COUNTRY	ESTIMATED DEATH RATE PER 1,000 LIVE BIRTHS (2004)
1	Angola	187.5
2	Afghanistan	140.2
3	Sierra Leone	140.0
4	Mozambique	137.2
5	Liberia	125.7
6	Guinea	123.1
7	Niger	119.5
8	Somalia	118.5
9	Malawi	117.6
10	Mali	115.9

Source: *US Census Bureau, International Data Base*

With the exception of Afghanistan, which has experienced its own unique range of social and medical problems, all the countries in the Top 10 are in sub-Saharan Africa.

◄ Lease on Life
Japan was the first country to attain an average lifespan of over 80 years—more than double that of many less-developed countries.

THE 10 COUNTRIES WITH THE LOWEST LIFE EXPECTANCY

	COUNTRY	LIFE EXPECTANCY AT BIRTH (2004)
1	Botswana	32.3
2	Mozambique	33.7
3	Swaziland	34.2
4	Zimbabwe	35.3
5	Malawi	35.6
6	Namibia	36.1
7	Zambia	37.4
8	Rwanda	38.0
9	Central African Republic	43.1
10	Ethiopia	43.3

Source: *US Census Bureau, International Data Base*

TOP 10 COUNTRIES WITH THE MOST BIRTHS

	COUNTRY	ESTIMATED BIRTHS (2004)
1	India	24,579,788
2	China	19,506,042
3	Nigeria	5,220,326
4	Indonesia	5,057,950
5	Pakistan	4,423,638
6	US	4,025,868
7	Bangladesh	3,379,322
8	Ethiopia	3,111,374
9	Brazil	3,094,876
10	Dem. Rep. of Congo	2,614,438
	World	*131,471,559*
	Canada	*354,661*

Source: *US Census Bureau, International Data Base*

TOP 10 COUNTRIES WITH THE LOWEST INFANT MORTALITY

	COUNTRY	ESTIMATED DEATH RATE PER 1,000 LIVE BIRTHS (2004)
1	Sweden	3.40
2	Iceland	3.48
3	Singapore	3.55
4	Finland	3.70
5	Japan	3.77
6	Norway	3.83
7	Andorra	4.05
8	Netherlands	4.21
9	Austria	4.28
10	Switzerland	4.30
	Canada	*4.80*

Source: *US Census Bureau, International Data Base*

Marriage & Divorce

THE 10 COUNTRIES WITH THE HIGHEST DIVORCE RATES

	COUNTRY	DIVORCE RATE PER 1,000*
1	Maldives	10.97
2	Belarus	4.65
3	US	4.19
4	Panama	3.82
5	Russia	3.66
6	Estonia	3.65
7	Puerto Rico	3.61
8	Ukraine	3.59
9	Costa Rica	3.58
10	Cuba	3.54
	Canada	*2.25*

* *In those countries/latest year for which data available*

Source: *United Nations*

THE 10 COUNTRIES WITH THE LOWEST DIVORCE RATES

	COUNTRY	DIVORCE RATE PER 1,000*
1	Libya	0.24
2	Georgia	0.36
3	Mongolia	0.38
4	= Armenia	0.42
	= Chile	0.42
6	Italy	0.47
7	Mexico	0.48
8	El Salvador	0.49
9	= Macedonia	0.51
	= Turkey	0.51

* *In those countries/latest year for which data available*

Source: *United Nations*

TOP 10 WEDDING SONGS IN CANADA

	TITLE	ARTIST
1	Because You Loved Me	Celine Dion
2	Unforgettable	Nat King Cole & Natalie Cole
3	Amazed	Lonestar
4	At Last	Etta James
5	Unchained Melody	Righteous Brothers
6	The Look of Love	Diana Krall
7	Could I Have This Dance	Anne Murray
8	Have I Told You Lately	Van Morrison/ Rod Stewart
9	Can't Help Falling in Love	Elvis Presley
10	The Power of Love	Jennifer Rush/ Celine Dion

Source: *Weddings Canada at www.weddings.ca*

TOP 10 COUNTRIES WITH THE HIGHEST PROPORTION OF TEENAGE BRIDES

	COUNTRY	PERCENTAGE OF 15–19-YEAR-OLD GIRLS WHO HAVE BEEN MARRIED*
1	Dem. Rep. of Congo	74.2
2	Congo	55.0
3	Afghanistan	53.7
4	Bangladesh	51.3
5	Uganda	49.8
6	Mali	49.7
7	Guinea	49.0
8	Chad	48.6
9	Mozambique	47.1
10	Senegal	43.8
	Canada	*1.3*

* *In latest year for which data available*

Source: *United Nations*

TOP 10 COUNTRIES WITH THE HIGHEST PROPORTION OF TEENAGE GROOMS

	COUNTRY	PERCENTAGE OF 15–19-YEAR-OLD BOYS WHO HAVE BEEN MARRIED*
1	Iraq	14.9
2	Nepal	13.5
3	Congo	11.8
4	Uganda	11.4
5	Central African Republic	8.1
6	India	9.5
7	Afghanistan	9.2
8	Guinea	8.2
9	Guatemala	7.8
10	Columbia	7.7
	Canada	*0.3*

* *In latest year for which data available*

Source: *United Nations*

IN-FLIGHT WEDDINGS!

FIRST FACT

HOLDING WEDDINGS IN unusual locations is not a strictly modern phenomenon: the first marriage to take place in the air was in a balloon a mile above Cincinnati, Ohio, on October 19, 1874. A publicity stunt for showman Phineas T. Barnum's Great Roman Hippodrome circus, the balloonist was daredevil Washington Harrison Donaldson, the first person to ride a bicycle on a tightrope. Before 50,000 spectators, Donaldson piloted a huge gas balloon named P. T. Barnum, which also carried the bride, Mary Elizabeth Walsh (a horseback rider in Barnum's circus); the groom, Charles M. Colton; and, to conduct the airborne ceremony, Reverend Howard B. Jeffries.

TOP 10 COUNTRIES WITH THE HIGHEST MARRIAGE RATES

	COUNTRY	MARRIAGES PER 1,000 PER ANNUM*
1	**Antigua and Barbuda**	21.0
2	**Maldives**	20.1
3	**Barbados**	13.5
4	**Liechtenstein**	12.8
5	**Cyprus**	12.1
6	= **Seychelles**	11.5
	= **South Africa**	11.5
8	**Jamaica**	10.3
9	= **Ethiopia**	10.2
	= **Iran**	10.2
	Canada	*5.1*

* *In those countries/latest year for which data available*

Source: *United Nations*

TOP 10 COUNTRIES WITH THE MOST MARRIAGES

	COUNTRY	MARRIAGES PER ANNUM*
1	**US**	2,244,000
2	**Bangladesh**	1,181,000
3	**Russia**	911,162
4	**Japan**	784,595
5	**Brazil**	734,045
6	**Mexico**	704,456
7	**Ethiopia**	630,290
8	**Iran**	511,277
9	**Egypt**	493,787
10	**Turkey**	485,112
	Canada	*153,306*

* *In those countries/latest year for which data available*

Source: *United Nations*

This list, based on United Nations statistics, excludes certain large countries such as India, Indonesia, and Pakistan, which failed to provide accurate data.

▼ Viva Las Vegas
More than 110,000 people tie the knot in Las Vegas each year, including celebrities such as Frank Sinatra and Mia Farrow (1966), Elvis Presley and Priscilla Beaulieu (1967), and Bruce Willis and Demi Moore (1987).

MOST COMMON CAUSES OF DEATH BY NONCOMMUNICABLE DISORDERS

	CAUSE	APPROXIMATE DEATHS (2001)
1	**Ischemic heart disease**	7,181,000
2	**Cancers**	7,115,000
3	**Cerebrovascular disease**	5,454,000
4	**Chronic obstructive pulmonary disease**	2,672,000
5	**Perinatal conditions**	2,504,000
6	**Road traffic accidents**	1,194,000
7	**Neuropsychiatric disorders**	1,023,000
8	**Diabetes mellitus**	895,000
9	**Hypertensive heart disease**	874,000
10	**Self-inflicted injury**	849,000

Source: *World Health Organization,* World Health Report 2002

WHO estimates identify 33,077,000 deaths in 2001 resulting from noncommunicable conditions. These exclude a further 5,103,000 caused by injuries such as road traffic accidents, fires, and drowning.

GLOBAL DISEASES*

	DISEASE	PERCENTAGE OF TOTAL BURDEN OF DISEASE#†
1	**Neuropsychiatric disorders**	13.0
2	**Cardiovascular diseases**	9.8
3	**Lower respiratory infections**	6.2
4	**HIV/AIDS**	6.0
5	**Cancers**	5.2
6	= **Diarrheal diseases**	4.3
	= **Respiratory diseases** (noncommunicable)	4.3
8	**Digestive diseases**	3.4
9	**Childhood diseases**	3.3
10	**Malaria**	2.9

* *Those diseases that cause the highest total levels of disability worldwide*

\# *Measured in Disability-Adjusted Life Years (DALYs): a measure of the difference between a population's health and a normative goal of living in full health*

† *Total percentage includes injuries at 12.2%, maternal conditions at 2.1%, nutritional deficiencies at 2.2%, perinatal conditions at 6.7%*

Source: *World Health Organization,* World Health Report 2002

MOST COMMON CAUSES OF DEATH BY INFECTIOUS AND PARASITIC DISEASES

	CAUSE	APPROXIMATE DEATHS (2001)
1	**Lower respiratory infection**	3,871,000
2	**HIV/AIDS**	2,866,000
3	**Diarrhea** (including dysentery)	2,001,000
4	**Tuberculosis**	1,644,000
5	**Malaria**	1,124,000
6	**Measles**	745,000
7	**Whooping cough** (pertussis)	285,000
8	**Neonatal tetanus**	282,000
9	**Meningitis**	173,000
10	**Syphilis**	167,000

Source: *World Health Organization,* World Health Report 2002

Infectious and parasitic diseases—those listed here and many outside the 10 principal causes—were responsible for 10,937,000 deaths worldwide in 2001. Extending the parameters to encompass all communicable diseases, maternal and perinatal conditions and nutritional deficiencies extends the total to 18,374,000.

COUNTRIES WITH THE HIGHEST DEATH RATE

	COUNTRY	ESTIMATED DEATH RATE (DEATHS PER 1,000, 2003)
1	**Botswana**	33.6
2	**Mozambique**	30.9
3	**Angola**	25.9
4	**Lesotho**	24.8
5	**Zambia**	24.4
6	**Zimbabwe**	23.3
7	**Swaziland**	23.1
8	**Malawi**	23.0
9	**Rwanda**	21.9
10	**Niger**	21.5

Source: *US Census Bureau, International Data Base*

All 10 of the countries with the highest death rates are in Africa, with all but Niger and Rwanda located between 10° and 30° south latitude.

WORST EPIDEMICS

	EPIDEMIC	LOCATION	DATE	ESTIMATED NO. KILLED
1	**Black Death**	Europe/Asia	1347–51	75,000,000
2	**AIDS**	Worldwide	1981–	21,800,000
3	**Influenza**	Worldwide	1918–20	21,640,000
4	**Bubonic plague**	India	1896–1948	12,000,000
5	**Typhus**	Eastern Europe	1914–15	3,000,000
6	= **"Plague of Justinian"**	Europe/Asia	541–90	millions*
	= **Cholera**	Worldwide	1846–60	millions*
	= **Cholera**	Europe	1826–37	millions*
	= **Cholera**	Worldwide	1893–94	millions*
10	**Smallpox**	Mexico	1530–45	>1,000,000

* *No precise figures available*

Pandemics—epidemics spread over widespread geographical areas—have affected human populations since ancient times. The Black Death (bubonic plague) was the worst of all time, annihilating entire communities and decimating countries. After spreading throughout Asia, it reached Constantinople in 1347 and then spread to Europe, where it killed half the population of many cities, recurring at intervals in later centuries.

THE 10 MOST SUICIDAL COUNTRIES

	COUNTRY	SUICIDES PER 100,000 POPULATION*
1	**Lithuania**	42.0
2	**Russia**	35.3
3	**Belarus**	33.5
4	**Estonia**	33.2
5	**Hungary**	33.1
6	**Latvia**	31.4
7	**Slovenia**	29.7
8	**Ukraine**	28.8
9	**Kazakhstan**	26.8
10	**Finland**	23.8
	Canada	*12.3*

* *In those countries/latest year for which data available*

Source: *United Nations*

It is perhaps surprising that the highest suicide rates are not generally recorded in the poorest countries in the world. Suicide rates in many African countries are very low, maybe because of the strong extended family networks, as well as the cultural and religious taboos attached to suicide, but it is also difficult to obtain reliable figures for such countries.

THE 10 PROVINCES AND TERRITORIES WITH THE HIGHEST SUICIDE RATES

	PROVINCE/ TERRITORY	SUICIDE RATE PER 100,000* FEMALE	MALE
1	**Northwest Territories**	19.3	88.7
2	**Quebec**	9.5	33.4
3	**New Brunswick**	5.6	27.7
4	**Alberta**	6.4	25.9
5	**Yukon**	19.7	24.8
6	**Saskachewan**	3.2	24.6
7	**Nova Scotia**	4.6	22.5
8	**Manitoba**	5.6	21.3
9	**British Columbia**	4.6	18.3
10	**Ontario**	3.9	15.6

* *Age-standardized, population aged 10 or older, 1998; rates for Nunavut, created in 1999, are included in those of the NWT. Ranked by incidence in male population.*

Source: *Statistics Canada,* Health Reports, *vol. 13, no. 2*

Approximately 3,700 Canadians committed suicide in 1998. Males account for three to four times more suicides than females, largely due to their more lethal methods, though females were hospitalized for attempted suicide one and a half times more often than males.

THE 10 COUNTRIES WITH THE MOST DEATHS FROM HEART DISEASE

	COUNTRY	DEATH RATE PER 1,000
1	**Ukraine**	896.0
2	**Bulgaria**	891.2
3	**Russia**	746.6
4	**Latvia**	745.7
5	**Belarus**	741.3
6	**Romania**	736.8
7	**Hungary**	728.4
8	**Estonia**	715.6
9	**Georgia**	603.7
10	**Croatia**	594.5
	Canada	*150.1*

Source: *United Nations*

Cardiovascular (heart and blood vessel) diseases account for some 15 million deaths annually.

Buried Alive!
The specter of premature burial heightened the terror as the Black Death swept across Europe and Asia.

What's in a Name?

TOP 10 FIRST NAMES IN BRITISH COLUMBIA, 2002

GIRLS		BOYS
Emily	1	Ethan
Emma	2	Joshua
Hannah	3	Matthew
Sarah	4	Jacob
Jessica	5	Nicholas
Madison	6	Justin
Olivia	7	Ryan
Grace	8	Benjamin
Megan	9	Liam
Isabella	10	Alexander

Source: *British Columbia Vital Statistics Agency*

TOP 10 FIRST NAMES IN QUEBEC, 2001

GIRLS		BOYS
Gabrielle	1	Samuel
Camille	2	William
Maude	3	Gabriel
Laurie	4	Alexandre
Noemie	5	Jeremy
Audrey	6	Olivier
Sarah	7	Nicolas
Ariane	8	Vincent
Sabrina	9	Anthony
Catherine	10	Maxime

TOP 10 FIRST NAMES IN ENGLAND AND WALES, 2002

GIRLS				BOYS
Chloe		1		Jack
Emily		2	+1	Joshua
Jessica	+1	3	-1	Thomas
Ellie	+7	4		James
Sophie		5		Daniel
Megan	-3	6	+8	Benjamin
Charlotte		7	+6	William
Lucy	+2	8	-1	Samuel
Hannah	-1	9	-1	Joseph
Olivia	-1	10	+2	Oliver

+ Indicates rise in ranking since previous year

– Indicates decline in ranking since previous year

TOP 10 GIRLS' & BOYS' NAMES IN ENGLAND AND WALES 50 YEARS AGO*

GIRLS		BOYS
Susan	1	David
Linda	2	John
Christine	3	Stephen
Margaret	4	Michael
Janet	5	Peter
Patricia	6	Robert
Carol	7	Paul
Elizabeth	8	Alan
Mary	9	Christopher
Anne	10	Richard

* *Based on birth registrations in 1954*

TOP 10 LAST NAMES IN THE US

	NAME	% OF ALL US NAMES
1	Smith	1.006
2	Johnson	0.810
3	Williams	0.699
4 =	Brown	0.621
=	Jones	0.621
6	Davis	0.480
7	Miller	0.424
8	Wilson	0.339
9	Moore	0.312
10 =	Anderson	0.311
=	Taylor	0.311
=	Thomas	0.311

The Top 10 (or, in view of those in equal 10th place, 12) US surnames together make up over 6 percent of the entire US population—in other words, one American in every 16 bears one of these names.

TOP 10 FIRST NAMES IN THE US, 2001

GIRLS		BOYS
Emily	1	Jacob
Hannah	2	Michael
Madison	3	Joshua
Samantha	4	Matthew
Ashley	5	Andrew
Sarah	6	Joseph
Elizabeth	7	Nicholas
Kayla	8	Anthony
Alexis	9	Tyler
Abigail	10	Daniel

The Top 10 is based on a 1 percent sample of Social Security applications for the period January to August 2001. In 1999, Michael, which had been the most popular boy's name in the US since 1962 (when it ousted David), was replaced by Jacob; in 2000, David returned to its preeminent position before exchanging places with Jacob yet again in 2001.

▼ Jacob and Emily?
The fraught business of choosing names for their children results in many parents opting for those in the list of the most popular.

Pomp & Power

THE 10 FIRST FEMALE PRIME MINISTERS AND PRESIDENTS

	PRIME MINISTER/PRESIDENT	COUNTRY	FIRST PERIOD IN OFFICE
1	**Sirimavo Bandaranaike** (PM)	Sri Lanka	July 1960–Mar 1965
2	**Indira Gandhi** (PM)	India	Jan 1966–Mar 1977
3	**Golda Meir** (PM)	Israel	Mar 1969–June 1974
4	**Maria Estela Perón** (President)	Argentina	July 1974–Mar 1976
5	**Elisabeth Domitien** (PM)	Central African Republic	Jan 1975–Apr 1976
6	**Margaret Thatcher** (PM)	UK	May 1979–Nov 1990
7	**Maria Lurdes** Pintasilgo (PM)	Portugal	Aug 1979–Jan 1980
8	**Mary Eugenia Charles** (PM)	Dominica	July 1980–June 1995
9	**Vigdís Finnbogadóttir** (President)	Iceland	Aug 1980–Aug 1996
10	**Gro Harlem Brundtland** (PM)	Norway	Feb–Oct 1981

Sirimavo Bandaranaike (1916–2000) became the world's first female prime minister on July 21, 1960, when the Sri Lanka Freedom Party, founded by her assassinated husband Solomon Bandaranaike, won the general election. She held the position on three occasions, and her daughter Chandrika Kumaratunga also became prime minister and later president.

TOP 10 LONGEST-SERVING PRESIDENTS TODAY

	PRESIDENT	COUNTRY	TOOK OFFICE
1	**General Gnassingbé Eyadéma**	Togo	Apr 14, 1967
2	**El Hadj Omar Bongo**	Gabon	Dec 2, 1967
3	**Colonel Mu'ammar Gadhafi**	Libya	Sept 1, 1969*
4	**Zayid ibn Sultan al-Nuhayyan**	United Arab Emirates	Dec 2, 1971
5	**Fidel Castro**	Cuba	Nov 2, 1976
6	**France-Albert René**	Seychelles	June 5, 1977
7	**Ali Abdullah Saleh**	Yemen	July 17, 1978
8	**Maumoon Abdul Gayoom**	Maldives	Nov 11, 1978
9	**Teodoro Obiang Nguema Mbasogo**	Equatorial Guinea	Aug 3, 1979
10	**José Eduardo Dos Santos**	Angola	Sept 21, 1979

* *Since a reorganization in 1979, Colonel Gadhafi has held no formal position, but continues to rule under the ceremonial title of "Leader of the Revolution"*

All the presidents in this list have been in power for over 20 years, and some in excess of 30 years. Fidel Castro was prime minister of Cuba from February 1959. Since he was also chief of the army, and there was no opposition party, he effectively ruled as dictator from then. He was not technically president until the Cuban constitution was revised in 1976. Among those no longer in office, Abu Sulayman Hafiz al-Assad, president of Syria, died on June 10, 2000, after serving as leader of his country since February 22, 1971.

TOP 10 LONGEST-REIGNING MONARCHS

	MONARCH	COUNTRY	REIGN	AGE AT ACCESSION	REIGN YEARS
1	**King Louis XIV**	France	1643–1715	5	72
2	**King John II**	Liechtenstein	1858–1929	18	71
3	**Emperor Franz-Josef**	Austria-Hungary	1848–1916	18	67
4	**Queen Victoria**	Great Britain	1837–1901	18	63
5	**Emperor Hirohito**	Japan	1926–89	25	62
6	**Emperor K'ang Hsi**	China	1661–1722	8	61
7	**King Sobhuza II***	Swaziland	Dec 1921–Aug 1982	22	60
8	**Emperor Ch'ien Lung**	China	Oct 1735–Feb 1796	25	60
9	**King Christian IV**	Denmark	Apr 1588–Feb 1648	11	59
10	**King George III**	Great Britain	Oct 1760–Jan 1820	22	59

* *Paramount chief until 1967, when Great Britain recognized him as king with the granting of internal self-government*

TOP 10 LONGEST-REIGNING LIVING MONARCHS*

	MONARCH	COUNTRY	DATE OF BIRTH	ACCESSION
1	**Bhumibol Adulyadej**	Thailand	Dec 5, 1927	June 9, 1946
2	**Prince Rainier III**	Monaco	May 31, 1923	May 9, 1949
3	**Elizabeth II**	UK	Apr 21, 1926	Feb 6, 1952
4	**Malietoa Tanumafili II**	Samoa	Jan 4, 1913	Jan 1, 1962#
5	**Taufa'ahau Tupou IV**	Tonga	July 4, 1918	Dec 16, 1965†
6	**Haji Hassanal Bolkiah**	Brunei	July 15, 1946	Oct 5, 1967
7	**Sayyid Qaboos ibn Saidal-Said**	Oman	Nov 18, 1942	July 23, 1970
8	**Margrethe II**	Denmark	Apr 16, 1940	Jan 14, 1972
9	**Jigme Singye Wangchuk**	Bhutan	Nov 11, 1955	July 24, 1972
10	**Carl XVI Gustaf**	Sweden	Apr 30, 1946	Sept 19, 1973

* *Including hereditary rulers of principalities, dukedoms, etc*

Sole ruler since April 15, 1963

† *Full sovereignty from June 5, 1970, when British protectorate ended*

There are 28 countries that have emperors, kings, queens, princes, dukes, sultans, or other hereditary rulers as their heads of state. This list formerly included Birendra Bir Bikram Shah Dev, King of Nepal, since January 31, 1972. On June 1, 2001, he was shot dead by his own son, Crown Prince Dipendra, who then committed suicide.

TOP 10 LONGEST-SERVING PRIME MINISTERS IN CANADA

	PRIME MINISTER	MONTHS IN OFFICE
1	**William Lyon Mackenzie King**	258
2	**Sir John Alexander Macdonald**	229
3	**Pierre Elliott Trudeau**	185
4	**Sir Wilfrid Laurier**	183
5	**Joseph Jacques Jean Chrétien**	115*
6	= **Sir Robert Laird Borden**	105
	= **Martin Brian Mulroney**	105
8	**Louis Stephen Saint Laurent**	103
9	**John George Diefenbaker**	70
10	**Lester Bowles Pearson**	60

* *As at May 2003, still in office. In August 2002, Jean Chrétien announced that he would not be seeking a fourth term in office, and would be stepping down as prime minister in February 2004. At that time, he will have been in office for 124 months.*

THE 10 FIRST COUNTRIES TO GIVE WOMEN THE VOTE

	COUNTR	EAR
1	**New Zealand**	1893
2	**Australia** (South Australia 1894; Western Australia 1898; Australia united in 1901)	1902
3	**Finland** (then a Grand Duchy under the Russian Crown)	1906
4	**Norway** (restricted franchise; all women over 25 in 1913)	1907
5	**Denmark and Iceland** (a Danish dependency until 1918)	1915
6	= **Netherlands**	1917
	= **USSR**	1917
8	= **Austria**	1918
	= **Canada**	1918
	= **Germany**	1918
	= **Great Britain and Ireland** (Ireland part of the United Kingdom until 1921; women over 30 only—lowered to 21 in 1928)	1918
	= **Poland**	1918

Although not a country, the Isle of Man was the first place in Europe to give women the vote, in 1880. Until 1920, the only other European countries to enfranchise women were Sweden in 1919 and Czechoslovakia in 1920. Certain US states gave women the vote at earlier dates (Wyoming in 1869, Colorado in 1894, Utah in 1895, and Idaho in 1896), but it was not granted nationally until 1920. A number of countries, such as France and Italy, did not give women the vote until 1945. In certain countries, such as Saudi Arabia, women are not allowed to vote at all—but neither are men.

◄ **Head of State**
Leader of the Revolution and Supreme Commander of the Armed Forces, Colonel Muammar Gadhafi has been the controversial leader of Libya since the overthrow of the monarchy in 1969.

Crime & Punishment

THE 10 COUNTRIES WITH THE MOST EXECUTIONS

	COUNTRY	EXECUTIONS (1998)
1	**China**	1,067
2	**Dem. Rep. of Congo**	100
3	**US**	68
4	**Iran**	66
5	**Egypt**	48
6	**Belarus**	33
7	**Taiwan**	32
8	**Saudi Arabia**	29
9	**Singapore**	28
10 =	**Rwanda**	24
=	**Sierra Leone**	24

Source: *Amnesty International*

At least 80 countries in the world enforce the death penalty, with China consistently the leading practitioner of this ultimate sanction.

▶ Hot Seat

The electric chair has been introduced in very few countries outside the US, where it has been used since 1890. It remains the official execution method in only 10 of the 38 states that enforce the death penalty.

COUNTRIES WITH THE HIGHEST PRISON POPULATION RATES

	COUNTRY	TOTAL PRISON POPULATION*	PRISONERS PER 100,000
1	**US**	1,962,220	686
2	**Russia**	919,330	638
3	**Belarus**	56,000	554
4	**Kazakhstan**	84,000	522
5	**Turkmenistan**	22,000	489
6	**Belize**	1,097	459
7	**Suriname**	1,933	437
8	**Dominica**	298	420
9	**Bahamas**	1,280	416
10	**Maldives**	1,098	414

* *Includes pretrial detainees*

Source: *UK Home Office*, World Prison Population List *(4th ed.)*

THE 10 CANADIAN CITIES WITH THE HIGHEST CRIME RATES*

	CITY (CMA)#	CRIME RATE PER 100,000 (2001)
1	**Regina,** Saskatchewan	16,387
2	**Saskatoon,** Saskatchewan	13,360
3	**Vancouver,** British Columbia	11,314
4	**Winnipeg,** Manitoba	10,947
5	**Victoria,** British Columbia	9,996
6	**Halifax,** Nova Scotia	9,354
7	**Edmonton,** Alberta	9,032
8	**Thunder Bay,** Ontario	8,602
9	**London,** Ontario	7,894
10	**Sudbury,** Ontario	7,535

* *Includes violent, property, and other crimes*

\# *Census metropolitan area with population over 100,000*

Source: *Statistics Canada*

The CMAs with the lowest crime rates are located in the province of Quebec: Chicoutimi-Jonquière, Quebec City, and Trois-Rivières. The lowest crime rate among the provinces and territories, however, is shown in Newfoundland and Labrador, at 5,635.

THE 10 COUNTRIES WITH THE HIGHEST REPORTED BURGLARY RATES

	COUNTRY	RATE PER 100,000 (2000*)
1	**Netherlands**	3,100.40
2	**Australia**	2,280.82
3	**New Zealand**	2,153.66
4	**Scotland**	2,118.73
5	**Antigua and Barbuda**	2,071.99
6	**Denmark**	1,868.06
7	**England and Wales**	1,832.69
8	**St. Kitts and Nevis**	1,790.00
9	**Estonia**	1,699.95
10	**Finland**	1,690.52

* *Or latest year for which data available*

Source: *Interpol*

THE 10 MOST COMMON CRIMES IN CANADA*

	TYPE OF OFFENSE	NUMBER OF INCIDENTS (2001)
1	**Theft** ($5,000 and under)	665,961
2	**Mischief**	338,425
3	**Break and enter**	282,512
4	**Assault#**	239,163
5	**Motor vehicle theft**	170,213
6	**Drugs**	91,920
7	**Bail violation**	91,249
8	**Impaired driving**	90,454
9	**Disturbing the peace**	88,729
10	**Fraud**	88,332

* *Criminal Code and other federal statute incidents reported to police*

\# *Levels 1, 2, 3 only; does not include sexual and other assault (as defined by Statistics Canada)*

Source: *Statistics Canada, Canadian Centre for Justice Statistics,* Canadian Crime Statistics, 2001

THE 10 COUNTRIES WITH THE HIGHEST REPORTED CRIME RATES

	COUNTRY	RATE PER 100,000 (2000*)
1	**Iceland**	14,726.95
2	**Sweden**	13,455.08
3	**New Zealand**	12,586.64
4	**Grenada**	10,177.89
5	**Norway**	10,086.72
6	**England and Wales**	9,823.28
7	**Denmark**	9,460.38
8	**Finland**	8,697.37
9	**Scotland**	8,428.73
10	**Canada**	4,123.97

* *Or latest year for which data available*

Source: *Interpol*

THE 10 COUNTRIES WITH THE HIGHEST REPORTED CAR THEFT RATES

	COUNTRY	RATE PER 100,000 (2000*)
1	**Switzerland**	962.80
2	**New Zealand**	818.01
3	**England and Wales**	752.95
4	**Sweden**	738.47
5	**Australia**	726.19
6	**Denmark**	604.18
7	**Scotland**	555.33
8	**Italy**	537.00
9	**Canada**	521.20
10	**Norway**	518.25

* *Or latest year for which data available*

Source: *Interpol*

FIRST SPEEDING TICKET

FIRST FACT

THE WORLD'S FIRST automobile speeding ticket was issued in the UK on January 28, 1896, to Walter Arnold. He was charged with driving at 13 km/h (8 mph) in an area of Paddock Wood, Kent, that had a limit of 3 km/h (2 mph), hurtling past the house of a policeman, who gave chase on his bicycle. Arnold was fined one shilling (25 cents). On May 20, 1899, Jacob German became the first driver in the US arrested for speeding when he was caught driving an electric taxicab at a "breakneck speed" of 20 km/h (12 mph) on New York's Lexington Avenue—for which he was jailed.

Murder by Numbers

COUNTRIES WITH THE LOWEST MURDER RATES

	COUNTRY	REPORTED MURDERS PER 100,000 POPULATION (2000*)
1	**Iceland**	0.00
2	**Senegal**	0.33
3	= **Burkina Faso**	0.38
	= **Cameroon**	0.38
5	= **Finland**	0.71
	= **Gambia**	0.71
	= **Mali**	0.71
	= **Saudi Arabia**	0.71
9	**Mauritania**	0.76
10	**Oman**	0.91

* *Or latest year for which data are available*

Source: *Interpol*

The murder rate in Iceland has been so exceptionally low for many years that it is often excluded altogether from comparative international statistics.

COUNTRIES WITH THE HIGHEST MURDER RATES

	COUNTRY	REPORTED MURDERS PER 100,000 POPULATION (2000*)
1	**Honduras**	154.02
2	**South Africa**	121.91
3	**Swaziland**	93.32
4	**Colombia**	69.98
5	**Lesotho**	50.41
6	**Rwanda**	45.08
7	**Jamaica**	37.21
8	**El Salvador**	36.88
9	**Venezuela**	33.20
10	**Bolivia**	31.98

* *Or latest year for which data are available*

Source: *Interpol*

These figures should be viewed with caution: not all countries record or define crimes identically or use the same statistical methods in reporting rates.

MOST COMMON MURDER METHODS IN CANADA

	METHOD	PERCENTAGE (2001)
1	= **Shooting**	30.9
	= **Stabbing**	30.9
3	**Beating**	22.2
4	**Strangling/suffocating**	8.5
5	= **Fire** (burns, smoke inhalation)	1.4
	= **Poisoning**	1.4
	= **Shaken baby syndrome**	1.4
	= **Unknown**	1.4
9	= **Vehicle**	0.9
	= **Other***	0.9

* *Includes exposure, hypothermia, and heart attack*

Source: *Statistics Canada, Canadian Centre for Justice Statistics,* Homicide Survey, *September 2002*

In 2001, there were 171 homicide shootings involving handguns, rifles, shotguns, and fully-automatic as well as other unknown types of firearms.

WORST GUN MASSACRES*

	PERPETRATOR/LOCATION/DATE/CIRCUMSTANCES	KILLED
1	**Woo Bum Kong** Sang-Namdo, South Korea, April 28, 1982. Off-duty policeman Woo Bum Kong, 27, killed 57 and injured 38 during a drunken rampage with rifles and hand grenades, before blowing himself up with a grenade.	57
2	**Martin Bryant** Port Arthur, Tasmania, Australia, April 28, 1996. Bryant, a 28-year-old Hobart resident, began killing with a high-powered rifle and was eventually captured when he fled in flames from a guesthouse in which he had held three hostages.	35
3	**Baruch Goldstein** Hebron, occupied West Bank, Israel, February 25, 1994. Goldstein, a 42-year-old US immigrant doctor, massacred Palestinians at prayer at the Tomb of the Patriarchs before being beaten to death by the crowd.	29
4	**Campo Elias Delgado** Bogota, Colombia, December 4, 1986. Delgado, a Vietnamese war veteran, stabbed 2 and shot a further 26 people before being killed by police.	28
5	= **George Jo Hennard** Killeen, Texas, US, October 16, 1991. Hennard drove his truck through a café window and killed 22 with semiautomatic guns before shooting himself.	22
	= **James Oliver Huberty** San Ysidro, California, US, July 18, 1984. Huberty, aged 41, opened fire in a McDonald's restaurant before being shot dead by a SWAT marksman.	22
7	= **Thomas Hamilton** Dunblane, Stirling, UK, March 13, 1996. Hamilton, 43, shot 16 children and a teacher in Dunblane Primary School before killing himself.	17
	= **Robert Steinhäuser** Erfurt, Germany, April 26, 2002. Former student Steinhäuser returned to Johann Gutenberg secondary school and killed 14 teachers, two students, and a police officer with a handgun before shooting himself.	17
9	= **Michael Ryan** Hungerford, Berkshire, UK, August 19, 1987. Ryan, 26, shot 14 dead and wounded 16 others (2 of whom later died) before shooting himself.	16
	= **Ronald Gene Simmons** Russellville, Arkansas, US, December 28, 1987. Simmons killed 16, including 14 members of his own family, by shooting or strangling. After being caught, he was sentenced to death on February 10, 1989.	16
	= **Charles Joseph Whitman** Austin, Texas, US, July 31–August 1, 1966. Twenty-five-year-old ex-Marine marksman Whitman killed his mother and wife. The following day, he shot 14 and wounded 34 from the University of Texas at Austin campus tower observation deck, before being shot dead by police officers.	16

* *By individuals, excluding terrorist and military actions; totals exclude perpetrator*

Canada's worst gun massacre was that committed by Marc Lépine, an engineering student at the Université de Montréal, Quebec, who on December 6, 1989, went on an armed rampage, shooting 14 women before killing himself.

THE 10 MOST PROLIFIC SERIAL KILLERS*

	MURDERER (COUNTRY)	KILLED
1	**Behram** (India)	931
2	**Countess Erszébet Báthory** (Hungary)	up to 650
3	**Pedro Alonso López** (Colombia)	300
4	**Dr. Harold Shipman** (UK)	215
5	**Henry Lee Lucas** (US)	200
6	**Gilles de Rais** (France)	up to 200
7	**Hu Wanlin** (China)	196
8	**Luis Alfredo Garavito** (Colombia)	189
9	**Hermann Webster Mudgett** (US)	up to 150
10	**Dr. Jack Kevorkian** (US)	130

1 **Behram** (India) 931
Behram (or Buhram) was the leader of the Thugee cult in India, which it is believed was responsible for the deaths of up to two million people. At his trial, Behram was found guilty of 931 murders between 1790 and 1830, mostly by ritual strangulation with the cult's traditional cloth, known as a "ruhmal."

2 **Countess Erszébet Báthory** (Hungary) up to 650
In Hungary, in the period up to 1610, Báthory (1560–1614), known as "Countess Dracula," was alleged to have murdered between 300 and 650 girls (her personal list of 610 victims was described at her trial) in the belief that drinking their blood would prevent her from aging. She was eventually arrested in 1611. Tried and found guilty, she died on August 21, 1614, walled up in her own castle in Csejthe.

3 **Pedro Alonso López** (Colombia) 300
Captured in 1980, López, nicknamed the "Monster of the Andes," led police to 53 graves, but probably murdered at least 300 in Colombia, Ecuador, and Peru. He was sentenced to life imprisonment.

4 **Dr. Harold Shipman** (UK) 215
In January 2000, Manchester doctor Shipman was found guilty of the murder of 15 women patients. The official inquiry into his crimes put the figure at 215, with 45 possible further cases, but some authorities believe that the total could be as high as 400.

5 **Henry Lee Lucas** (US) 200
Lucas (1936–2001) admitted in 1983 to 360 murders, many with his partner-in-crime Ottis Toole. He died while on death row in Huntsville Prison, Texas.

6 **Gilles de Rais** (France) up to 200
A wealthy aristocrat, Gilles de Laval, Baron de Rais (1404–40), was accused of having kidnapped between 60 and 200 children, and killed them as sacrifices during black magic rituals. After being tried, tortured, and found guilty, he was strangled and his body burned in Nantes on October 25, 1440.

7 **Hu Wanlin** (China) 196
Posing as a doctor specializing in Chinese medicine, Hu Wanlin was given a 15-year sentence on October 1, 2000, for 3 deaths, but he is thought to have been responsible for 20 in Taiyuan, 146 in Shanxi, and 30 in Shangqui.

8 **Luis Alfredo Garavito** (Colombia) 189
Garavito confessed in 1999 to a spate of murders. On May 28, 2000, he was sentenced to a total of 835 years' imprisonment.

9 **Hermann Webster Mudgett** (US) up to 150
Mudgett (1860–96) was believed to have lured over 150 women to his Chicago "castle" of soundproofed cells equipped for torture, murder, and the disposal of bodies. Arrested and found guilty of the murder of an ex-partner, he confessed to 27 killings, but 200 victims' remains were thought to have been found. Mudgett was hanged in Moyamensing Prison on May 7, 1896.

10 **Dr. Jack Kevorkian** (US) 130
In 1999, Kevorkian, who admitted to assisting in 130 suicides since 1990, was convicted of second-degree murder. His appeal against his 10- to 25-year prison sentence was rejected on November 21, 2001.

* *Includes only individual murderers; excludes murders by bandits, terrorist groups, political and military atrocities, and gangland slayings*

► **Hand Gun**
In 2001, firearms were used in 8,719 murders in the US, with handguns accounting for some 6,790 of them.

War & Peace

THE 10 BATTLES WITH MOST CASUALTIES

	BATTLE/WAR	DATE	CASUALTIES*
1	**Stalingrad,** World War II	1942–43	2,000,000
2	**Somme River I,** World War I	1916	1,073,900
3	**Po Valley,** World War II	1945	740,000
4	**Moscow,** World War II	1941–42	700,000
5	**Verdun,** World War I	1916	595,000
6	**Gallipoli,** World War I	1915	500,000
7	**Artois-Loos,** World War I	1915	428,000
8	**Berezina,** War of 1812		400,000
9	**38th Parallel,** Korean War	1951	320,000
10	**Somme River II,** World War I	1918	300,000

* *Estimated total of military and civilian dead, wounded, and missing*

Source: *Alexis Tregenza*

Total numbers of casualties in the Battle of Stalingrad are at best estimates, but it was undoubtedly one of the longest battles—and almost certainly the bloodiest—of all time. Fought between German (with Hungarian, Romanian, and Italian troops also under German command) and Soviet forces, it continued from August 19, 1942 to February 2, 1943, with huge losses on both sides.

20TH CENTURY WARS WITH THE MOST MILITARY FATALITIES

	WAR	YEARS	ESTIMATED MILITARY FATALITIES
1	**World War II**	1939–45	15,843,000
2	**World War I**	1914–18	8,545,800
3	**Korean War**	1950–53	1,893,100
4	**Sino-Japanese War**	1937–41	1,200,000
5	**Biafra–Nigeria Civil War**	1967–70	1,000,000
6	**Spanish Civil War**	1936–39	611,000
7	**Vietnam War**	1961–75	546,000
8	**French Vietnam War**	1945–54	300,000
9	= **India–Pakistan War**	1947	200,000
	= **USSR invasion of Afghanistan**	1979–89	200,000
	= **Iran–Iraq War**	1980–88	200,000

The statistics of warfare has always been an imperfect science. Not only are battle deaths seldom recorded accurately, but figures are often deliberately inflated by both sides in a conflict. These figures therefore represent military historians' "best guesses"—and fail to take into account the enormous toll of deaths among civilian populations during the many wars that beset the twentieth century.

COUNTRIES SUFFERING THE GREATEST CIVILIAN LOSSES IN WORLD WAR II

	COUNTRY	KILLED
1	**China**	8,000,000
2	**USSR**	6,500,000
3	**Poland**	5,300,000
4	**Germany**	2,350,000
5	**Yugoslavia**	1,500,000
6	**France**	470,000
7	**Greece**	415,000
8	**Japan**	393,400
9	**Romania**	340,000
10	**Hungary**	300,000

As noted in the list of the 10 countries suffering the greatest military losses in World War II, deaths among civilians—many resulting from famine and internal purges, such as those in China and the USSR—were colossal, but they were less well documented than those among fighting forces. An estimate of 60,600 civilian deaths resulting from bomb and rocket attacks on the UK represents less than one-quarter of the total military deaths.

SHORTEST WAR EVER!

FIRST FACT

THE SHORTEST WAR ON RECORD was that between Britain and Zanzibar. On Thursday, August 27, 1896, the British fleet under Admiral Sir Henry Rawson arrived in Zanzibar harbor. Sultan Said Khaled, who had seized power two days earlier, regarded this as a provocative act and declared war, firing on the British from his sole warship, the *Glasgow*. The British fleet retaliated, sinking the ship, destroying the sultan's palace, and killing some 500 of his men. The sultan escaped to exile in Mombasa. The entire action had lasted 38 minutes, from 9:02 to 9:40 a.m.

THE 10 LATEST YEARS OF THE NOBEL PEACE PRIZE

PRIZE YEAR	WINNER(S)	COUNTRY
2002	Jimmy Carter	US
2001	Kofi Annan/United Nations	Ghana/international body
2000	Kim Dae Jung	South Korea
1999	Médecins Sans Frontières	Belgium
1998	John Hume/David Trimble	UK
1997	International Campaign to Ban Landmines/Jody Williams	International body/US
1996	Carlos Filipe Ximenes Belo/José Ramos-Horta	East Timor
1995	Joseph Rotblat	UK
1994	Yasser Arafat/Shimon Peres/Itzhak Rabin	Palestine/Israel
1993	Nelson Rolihlahla Mandela/Frederik Willem de Klerk	South Africa

Former US president Jimmy Carter was awarded the Nobel Peace Prize in 2002 "for his decades of untiring effort to find peaceful solutions to international conflicts, to advance democracy and human rights, and to promote economic and social development."

THE 10 COUNTRIES SUFFERING THE GREATEST MILITARY LOSSES IN WORLD WAR II

	COUNTRY	KILLED
1	**USSR**	13,600,000*
2	**Germany**	3,300,000
3	**China**	1,324,516
4	**Japan**	1,140,429
5	**British Empire**† (UK 264,000)	357,116
6	**Romania**	350,000
7	**Poland**	320,000
8	**Yugoslavia**	305,000
9	**US**	292,131
10	**Italy**	279,800
	Total	*21,268,992*

* *Total, of which 7,800,000 are battlefield deaths*

† *Including Australia, Canada, India, New Zealand, etc.*

The immense level of the military casualty rate of the USSR in particular is hard to comprehend. The combined armed forces of the USSR in World War II numbered 30,000,000.

THE 10 LONGEST WARS

	WAR	COMBATANTS	DATES	YRS
1	**Hundred Years' War**	France and England	1337–1453	116
2	**Greco-Persian Wars**	Greece and Persia	499–448 BC	51
3	= **Wars of the Roses**	Lancaster and York	1455–1485	30
	= **Thirty Years' War**	Catholics and Protestants	1618–1648	30
5	**Second Peloponnesian War**	Peloponnesian League (Sparta, Corinth, etc.) and Delian League (Athens, etc.)	432–404 BC	28
6	= **First Punic War**	Rome and Carthage	264–241 BC	23
	= **Napoleonic Wars**	France and other European countries	1792–1815	23
8	**Second Great Northern War**	Russia and Sweden and Baltic states	1700–21	21
9	**Vietnam War**	South Vietnam (with US support) and North Vietnam	1957–1975	18
10	**Second Punic War**	Rome and Carthage	219–202 BC	17

Source: *Alexis Tregenza*

It may be argued that the total period of the Crusades (fought by Christians and Muslims) constitutes one long single conflict spanning a total of 195 years from 1096 to 1291, rather than a series of nine short ones, in which case it ranks as the longest war ever. Similarly, if all the Punic Wars between 264 and 146 BC are taken as one, they would rank second at 118 years. The War of the Spanish Succession (1701–14) is the only other major conflict to have lasted more than 10 years, with the War of the Austrian Succession (1740–48), the American Revolution (1775–83), and the Chinese–Japanese War (1937–45) each lasting eight years.

▼ Siege of Stalingrad
The German army besieged Stalingrad, USSR, in 1942. The ensuing battle lasted almost six months and was the bloodiest in history.

Modern Military

NUCLEAR SUBMARINE

FIRST FACT

ALTHOUGH SUBMARINES had been used militarily for almost 100 years, it was not until January 21, 1954, that the first nuclear-powered vessel was launched, at Groton, Connecticut. It was named *Nautilus* after the submarine in Jules Verne's novel *20,000 Leagues Under the Sea*, and on August 3, 1958, it became the first submarine ever to cross beneath the North Pole, with 116 men on board. By 1979, after 25 years in service and having traveled a record of almost 804,672 km (500,000 miles), *Nautilus* was decommissioned and towed to Groton, where it joined the Submarine Force Museum. Designated a National Historic Landmark, it is also Connecticut's official state ship.

▲ **Sub Power**
The US submarine fleet is principally composed of nuclear-powered hunter-killers. Canada has no nuclear-powered subs; the current fleet consists of three diesel-electric–powered Victoria-class submarines, with one more to come.

TOP 10 COUNTRIES WITH THE MOST SUBMARINES

	COUNTRY	SUBMARINES
1	**US**	73
2	**China**	69
3	**Russia** (and associated states)	56
4	**North Korea**	26
5	**South Korea**	19
6	= **India**	16
	= **Japan**	16
	= **UK**	16
9	**Germany**	14
10	**Turkey**	13

TOP 10 COUNTRIES WITH THE MOST COMBAT AIRCRAFT*

	COUNTRY	COMBAT AIRCRAFT
1	**US**	3,939
2	**China**	2,900
3	**Russia**	2,636
4	**India**	738
5	**North Korea**	621
6	**Egypt**	580
7	**South Korea**	555
8	**Ukraine**	543
9	**Taiwan**	482
10	**France**	473
	Canada	*140*

* *Air force only, exluding long-range strike/attack aircraft*

TOP 10 COUNTRIES WITH THE LARGEST ARMIES

	COUNTRY	ARMY PERSONNEL
1	**China**	1,600,000
2	**India**	1,100,000
3	**North Korea**	950,000
4	**South Korea**	560,000
5	**Pakistan**	550,000
6	**US**	477,800
7	**Vietnam**	412,000
8	**Turkey**	402,000
9	**Iraq**	375,000
10	**Russia**	321,000
	Canada	*18,600*

Slight reductions in numbers have been made over the past few years, but recent heightenings in international tension since the September 11, 2001, terrorist attacks and ongoing disputes have put further imminent reductions "on hold."

TOP 10 COUNTRIES WITH THE LARGEST NAVIES

	COUNTRY	MANPOWER (2002)*
1	US	366,100
2	China	250,000
3	Russia	171,500
4	Taiwan	62,000
5	South Korea	60,000
6	= India	53,000
	= Turkey	53,000
8	North Korea	46,000
9	France	45,600
10	UK	43,530
	Canada	*9,000*

* *Including naval air forces and marines*

Along with other factors, the increasing reliance on technology rather than manpower in modern naval warfare led to reductions in numbers during the 1990s, but all the major powers remain capable of putting substantial forces to sea.

TOP 10 COUNTRIES WITH THE LARGEST DEFENSE BUDGETS

	COUNTRY	BUDGET (US$)
1	US	291,100,000,000
2	Russia	44,000,000,000
3	Japan	40,400,000,000
4	UK	34,000,000,000
5	Saudi Arabia	27,200,000,000
6	France	25,300,000,000
7	Germany	21,000,000,000
8	China	17,000,000,000
9	India	15,600,000,000
10	Italy	15,500,000,000
	Canada	*7,700,000,000*

The so-called "peace dividend"—the savings made as a consequence of the end of the Cold War between the West and the former Soviet Union—means that both the numbers of personnel and the defense budgets of many countries have been cut. That of the US has been reduced from its 1989 peak of US$303.6 billion.

TOP 10 COUNTRIES WITH THE HIGHEST MILITARY/CIVILIAN RATIO

	COUNTRY	RATIO (2002)*
1	North Korea	441
2	Israel	258
3	United Arab Emirates	253
4	Qatar	202
5	Syria	195
6	Iraq	190
7	Bahrain	176
8	Taiwan	167
9	Oman	162
10	Jordan	146
	Canada	*18*

* *Military personnel per 10,000 population*

People's Army
China's armed forces make up the world's largest military machine. At 18, male citizens are officially drafted into service for two years, but in practice conscription is selective.

World Religions

TOP 10 CHRISTIAN DENOMINATIONS

	DENOMINATION	MEMBERS
1	Roman Catholic	981,703,000
2	Orthodox	140,300,000
3	Pentecostal	128,405,000
4	Lutheran	82,271,000
5	Anglican	79,177,000
6	Baptist	73,383,000
7	Presbyterian	49,630,000
8	Methodist	26,576,000
9	Seventh Day Adventist	12,511,000
10	Churches of Christ	6,827,000

Source: *Christian Research*

Projections of the numbers of adherents to the world's Christian denominations estimate an overall growth to a total of 1,803 million by 2005, some 27 percent of the then world population, with Roman Catholics topping one billion members.

TOP 10 RELIGIOUS BELIEFS

	RELIGION	FOLLOWERS (2002)
1	Christianity	2,050,616,000
2	Islam	1,239,029,000
3	Hinduism	836,543,000
4	Nonreligion	780,557,000
5	Buddhism	367,538,000
6	Ethnic religion	234,341,000
7	Atheism	150,804,000
8	New religion	104,280,000
9	Sikhism	24,124,000
10	Judaism	14,670,000

Source: *David B. Barrett & Todd M. Johnson*, International Bulletin of Missionary Research, January 2002

◀ Buddhist Statue in China
Despite its suppression during the Cultural Revolution, Buddhism has survived in China, where it now has more than 100 million followers.

TOP 10 LARGEST BUDDHIST POPULATIONS

	COUNTRY	BUDDHIST POPULATION (2000)
1	**China**	105,829,000
2	**Japan**	69,931,000
3	**Thailand**	52,383,000
4	**Vietnam**	39,534,000
5	**Myanmar**	33,145,000
6	**Sri Lanka**	12,879,000
7	**Cambodia**	9,462,000
8	**India**	7,249,000
9	**South Korea**	7,174,000
10	**Taiwan**	4,686,000
	World	*359,981,757*

Source: *David B. Barrett & Todd M. Johnson,* World Christian Trends, *William Carey Library, 2001*

Buddhism originated in India in the 6th century BC. Its espousal of peace and tolerant coexistence ensured its appeal and encouraged its spread throughout Asia and beyond.

TOP 10 LARGEST HINDU POPULATIONS

	COUNTRY	HINDU POPULATION (2000)
1	**India**	755,135,000
2	**Nepal**	18,354,000
3	**Bangladesh**	15,995,000
4	**Indonesia**	7,259,000
5	**Sri Lanka**	2,124,000
6	**Pakistan**	1,868,000
7	**Malaysia**	1,630,000
8	**US**	1,032,000
9	**South Africa**	959,000
10	**Myanmar**	893,000

Source: *David B. Barrett & Todd M. Johnson,* World Christian Trends, *William Carey Library, 2001*

Claimed as the world's oldest organized religion, Hinduism is also the third-largest after Christianity and Islam, with an estimated total world population of at least 800 million.

TOP 10 LARGEST JEWISH POPULATIONS

	COUNTRY	JEWISH POPULATION (2001)
1	**US**	5,700,000
2	**Israel**	5,025,000
3	**France**	519,000
4	**Canada**	364,000
5	**UK**	273,500
6	**Russia**	265,000
7	**Argentina**	195,000
8	**Germany**	103,000
9	**Ukraine**	100,000
10	**Australia**	97,000
	World total	*13,330,000*

Source: American Jewish Year Book 2001, *vol. 101*

Results from the 2001 Census, showing Canada's religious group statistics, are available at the Statistics Canada website at www.statcan.ca.

TOP 10 LARGEST MUSLIM POPULATIONS

	COUNTRY	MUSLIM POPULATION (2000)
1	**Pakistan**	150,365,000
2	**India**	122,570,000
3	**Indonesia**	116,105,000*
4	**Bangladesh**	110,849,000
5	**Turkey**	64,714,000
6	**Iran**	64,707,000
7	**Egypt**	57,780,000
8	**Nigeria**	49,000,000
9	**Algeria**	30,442,000
10	**Morocco**	27,736,000

* *An additional 46 million people are considered Muslims by the Indonesian government but are more properly categorized as New Religionists (islamisized syncretistic religions)*

Source: *David B. Barrett & Todd M. Johnson,* World Christian Trends, *William Carey Library, 2001*

TOP 10 RELIGIOUS BRANCHES

	BRANCH/RELIGION	FOLLOWERS (2000)
1	**Roman Catholic,** Christianity	1,057,328,093
2	**Sunni,** Islam	1,002,542,801
3	**Vaishnavite,** Hinduism	549,583,323
4	**Protestant,** Christianity	342,001,605
5	**Sufi,** Islam	237,400,000
6	**Shaivite,** Hinduism	216,260,000
7	**Animist,** ethno-religion	216,160,890
8	**Orthodox,** Christianity	215,128,717
9	**Mahayana,** Buddhism	202,232,757
10	**Shia,** Islam	170,100,000

Source: *David B. Barrett & Todd M. Johnson,* World Christian Trends, *William Carey Library, 2001*

The world's religions are far from being homogenous: within each major religion there are often numerous branches often conflicting—sometimes fiercely—with others. This lists represents the 10 largest branches that share a common historical heritage and a proportion of doctrines or practices.

TOP 10 RELIGIOUS TRADITIONS WITH THE MOST MARTYRS

	RELIGIOUS TRADITION	MARTYRS
1	**Russian Orthodox**	21,626,000
2	**Assyrian or Nestoran** (East Syrian, Messihaye)	12,379,000
3	**Latin-rite Catholic**	11,024,000
4	**Ukrainian Orthodox**	3,500,000
5	**Armenian Orthodox** (Gregorian)	1,215,000
6	**Coptic Orthodox**	1,068,000
7	**Pentecostal** (Protestant, Classical Pentecostal)	1,021,000
8	=**Messianic Jewish**	1,000,000
	=**Quasi-Christians**	1,000,000
10	**Lutheran**	987,000

Source: *David B. Barrett & Todd M. Johnson,* World Christian Trends, *William Carey Library, 2001*

According to some authorities, some 70 million Christians have been martyred for their faith during the past 2,000 years, while other major religions also claim figures running into the millions.

TOWN & COUNTRY

Countries of the World

TOP 10 COUNTRIES WITH MOST NEIGHBORS

	COUNTRY/NEIGHBORS	NO. OF NEIGHBORS
1	**China** Afghanistan, Bhutan, India, Kazakhstan, Kyrgyzstan, Laos, Macau, Mongolia, Myanmar, Nepal, North Korea, Pakistan, Russia, Tajikistan, Vietnam	15
2	**Russia** Azerbaijan, Belarus, China, Estonia, Finland, Georgia, Kazakhstan, Latvia, Lithuania, Mongolia, North Korea, Norway, Poland, Ukraine	14
3	**Brazil** Argentina, Bolivia, Colombia, French Guiana, Guyana, Paraguay, Peru, Suriname, Uruguay, Venezuela	10
4 =	**Democratic Republic of Congo** Angola, Burundi, Central African Republic, Congo, Rwanda, Sudan, Tanzania, Uganda, Zambia	9
=	**Germany** Austria, Belgium, Czech Republic, Denmark, France, Luxembourg, Netherlands, Poland, Switzerland	9
=	**Sudan** Central African Republic, Chad, Democratic Republic of Congo, Egypt, Eritrea, Ethiopia, Kenya, Libya, Uganda	9
7 =	**Austria** Czech Republic, Germany, Hungary, Italy, Liechtenstein, Slovakia, Slovenia, Switzerland	8
=	**France** Andorra, Belgium, Germany, Italy, Luxembourg, Monaco, Spain, Switzerland	8
=	**Turkey** Armenia, Azerbaijan, Bulgaria, Georgia, Greece, Iran, Iraq, Syria	8
10 =	**Mali** Algeria, Burkina Faso, Côte d'Ivoire, Guinea, Mauritania, Niger, Senegal	7
=	**Niger** Algeria, Benin, Burkina Faso, Chad, Libya, Mali, Nigeria	7
=	**Saudi Arabia** Iraq, Jordan, Kuwait, Oman, Qatar, United Arab Emirates, Yemen	7
=	**Tanzania** Burundi, Kenya, Malawi, Mozambique, Rwanda, Uganda, Zambia	7
=	**Ukraine** Belarus, Hungary, Moldova, Poland, Romania, Russia, Slovakia	7
=	**Zambia** Angola, Democratic Republic of Congo, Malawi, Mozambique, Namibia, Tanzania, Zimbabwe	7

It should be noted that some countries have more than one discontinuous border with the same country; this has been counted only once.

Canadian Coastline
The coast of mainland Canada comprises 57,759 km (35,889 miles) of its total, the balance being the total coastline lengths of its 52,455 offshore islands.

TOP 10 COUNTRIES WITH THE LONGEST COASTLINES

	COUNTRY	TOTAL COASTLINE LENGTH (MILES)	(KM)
1	**Canada**	151,485	243,791
2	**Indonesia**	33,999	54,716
3	**Russia**	23,396	37,653
4	**Philippines**	22,559	36,289
5	**Japan**	18,486	29,751
6	**Australia**	16,007	25,760
7	**Norway**	13,624	21,925
8	**US**	12,380	19,924
9	**New Zealand**	9,404	15,134
10	**China**	9,010	14,500
	World	*221,208*	*356,000*

Including all its islands, the coastline of Canada is more than six times as long as the distance around the Earth at the equator, which is 40,076 km (24,902 miles).

LARGEST LANDLOCKED COUNTRIES

	COUNTRY/NEIGHBORS	AREA (SQ MILES)	(SQ KM)
1	**Kazakhstan,** China, Kyrgyzstan, Russia, Turkmenistan, Uzbekistan	1,049,156	2,717,300
2	**Mongolia,** China, Russia	604,250	1,565,000
3	**Niger,** Algeria, Benin, Burkina Faso, Chad, Libya, Mali, Nigeria	489,075	1,266,699
4	**Chad,** Cameroon, Central African Republic, Libya, Niger, Nigeria, Sudan	486,180	1,259,201
5	**Mali,** Algeria, Burkina Faso, Côte d'Ivoire, Guinea, Mauritania, Niger, Senegal	471,044	1,219,999
6	**Ethiopia,** Djibouti, Eritrea, Kenya, Somalia, Sudan	432,312	1,119,683
7	**Bolivia,** Argentina, Brazil, Chile, Paraguay, Peru	418,685	1,084,389
8	**Zambia,** Angola, Dem. Rep. of Congo, Malawi, Mozambique, Namibia, Tanzania, Zimbabwe	285,993	740,719
9	**Afghanistan,** China, Iran, Pakistan, Tajikistan, Turkmenistan, Uzbekistan	250,001	647,500
10	**Central African Republic**, Cameroon, Chad, Congo, Dem. Rep. of Congo, Sudan	240,534	622,980

SMALLEST LANDLOCKED COUNTRIES

	COUNTRY/NEIGHBORS	AREA (SQ MILES)	(SQ KM)
1	**Vatican City,** Italy	0.2	0.44
2	**San Marino,** Italy	23	60
3	**Liechtenstein,** Austria, Switzerland	62	161
4	**Andorra,** Spain, France	174	451
5	**Luxembourg,** Germany, Belgium, France	998	2,585
6	**Swaziland,** South Africa, Mozambique	6,641	17,200
7	**Rwanda,** Burundi, Dem. Rep. of Congo, Uganda, Tanzania	9,633	24,949
8	**Burundi,** Rwanda, Tanzania, Dem. Rep. of Congo	9,903	25,649
9	**Macedonia,** Yugoslavia, Bulgaria, Greece, Albania	9,928	25,713
10	**Armenia,** Azerbaijan, Georgia, Iran, Turkey	11,506	29,800

Source: *US Census Bureau, International Data Base*

Although the Vatican had become part of unified Italy in the 19th century, its identity as an independent state was recognized by treaty on February 11, 1929.

LARGEST COUNTRIES

	COUNTRY	AREA (SQ MILES)	(SQ KM)	PERCENTAGE OF WORLD TOTAL
1	**Russia**	6,592,850	17,075,400	13.0
2	**Canada**	3,855,383	9,984,670	7.6
3	**China**	3,600,948	9,326,411	7.1
4	**US**	3,539,245	9,166,601	6.9
5	**Brazil**	3,265,077	8,456,511	6.4
6	**Australia**	2,941,300	7,617,931	5.8
7	**India**	1,148,148	2,973,190	2.2
8	**Argentina**	1,056,642	2,736,690	2.1
9	**Kazakhstan**	1,049,155	2,717,300	2.1
10	**Algeria**	919,595	2,381,741	1.8
	World	*50,580,568*	*131,003,055*	*100.0*

Source: *US Census Bureau, International Data Base*

SMALLEST COUNTRIES

	COUNTRY	AREA (SQ MILES)	(SQ KM)
1	**Vatican City**	0.2	0.44
2	**Monaco**	0.7	2
3	**Nauru**	8	21
4	**Tuvalu**	10	26
5	**San Marino**	23	60
6	**Liechtenstein**	62	161
7	**Marshall Islands**	70	181
8	**Maldives**	116	300
9	**Malta**	124	321
10	**Grenada**	131	339

Source: *US Census Bureau, International Database*

The "country" status of Vatican City is questionable, since its government and other features are intricately linked with those of Italy.

Country Populations

TOP 10 COUNTRIES WITH THE OLDEST POPULATIONS

	COUNTRY	PERCENTAGE OVER 65 (2004 EST.)
1	**Monaco**	22.4
2	**Italy**	19.3
3	**Japan**	18.8
4	**Greece**	18.6
5	**Germany**	17.9
6	= **Spain**	17.5
	= **Sweden**	17.5
8	**Belgium**	17.4
9	**Bulgaria**	17.1
10	**San Marino**	16.7
	World	*7.2*
	Canada	*13.0*

Source: *US Census Bureau International Data Base*

Nine of the 10 countries with the oldest populations are in Europe, implying that this region has lower death rates and a higher life expectancy than the rest of the world. On average, one in every 6.6 people in Europe is over the age of 65 (15.7 percent).

TOP 10 MOST POPULATED COUNTRIES

	COUNTRY	POPULATION (2004 EST.)
1	**China**	1,305,625,273
2	**India**	1,077,116,060
3	**US**	285,522,555
4	**Indonesia**	239,259,710
5	**Brazil**	178,998,012
6	**Pakistan**	153,705,278
7	**Russia**	144,112,353
8	**Bangladesh**	137,650,588
9	**Nigeria**	136,514,807
10	**Japan**	127,295,333

Source: *US Census Bureau, International Data Base*

► Dense Tokyo
Japan is one of the world's most highly populated island countries, and only just fails to rank among the most densely populated.

TOP 10 COUNTRIES WITH THE YOUNGEST POPULATIONS

	COUNTRY	PERCENTAGE UNDER 15 (2004 EST.)
1	Uganda	50.5
2	Marshall Islands	48.7
3	Dem. Rep. of Congo	48.1
4	Chad	47.8
5	São Tomé and Príncipe	47.7
6	Niger	47.6
7	Ethiopia	47.3
8	Burkina Faso	47.0
	= Mali	47.0
10	Benin	46.8
	World	*28.4*
	Canada	*18.2*

Source: *US Census Bureau, International Data Base*

Countries with high proportions of their population under the age of 15 are usually characterized by high birth rates and high death rates.

TOP 10 LEAST POPULATED COUNTRIES

	COUNTRY	POPULATION (2004 EST.)
1	Tuvalu	11,468
2	Nauru	12,809
3	Palau	20,016
4	San Marino	28,503
5	Monaco	32,270
6	Liechtenstein	33,436
7	St. Kitts and Nevis	38,836
8	Antigua and Barbuda	68,320
9	Dominica	69,278
10	Andorra	69,865

Source: *US Census Bureau, International Data Base*

These are all independent countries, but there are numerous dependencies with even smaller populations, including the Falkland Islands (2,121) and the Pitcairn Islands, which were settled in 1790 by mutineers from the ship *Bounty*, and which have a population of 54. Another well-known small "country" is the Vatican City, with a population of 738. While it is an independent country, for some purposes and some statistics it is counted as part of Italy.

TOP 10 MOST HIGHLY POPULATED ISLAND COUNTRIES

	COUNTRY	POPULATION (2003 EST.)
1	Indonesia	239,259,710
2	Japan	127,295,333
3	Philippines	87,891,082
4	Malaysia	23,522,482
5	Taiwan	22,898,115
6	Sri Lanka	19,905,165
7	Madagascar	17,501,871
8	Cuba	11,301,850
9	Dominican Republic	9,005,285
10	Haiti	7,269,957

Source: *US Census Bureau, International Data Base*

There are 17 island countries in the world with populations of more than one million, of which these are the Top 10. Australia is regarded as a continental landmass, rather than an island, but if it were included, its 19,546,792 population would put it in sixth place. The UK (59,778,002) is also excluded, as it is not a self-contained island state.

TOP 10 MOST DENSELY POPULATED COUNTRIES

	COUNTRY	AREA (SQ KM)	POPULATION (2004 EST.)	POPULATION PER SQ KM
1	Monaco	1.95	37,270	19,112.8
2	Singapore	624	4,767,974	7,641.0
3	Malta	321	403,342	1,256.5
4	Maldives	300	339,330	1,131.1
5	Bahrain	619	677,886	1,095.1
6	Bangladesh	133,911	137,650,588	1,027.9
7	Taiwan	32,261	22,898,115	709.8
8	Mauritius	1,849	1,220,481	660.1
9	Barbados	430	279,157	649.2
10	Nauru	21	12,809	610.0
	World	*131,003,055*	*6,386,027,015*	*48.7*

Source: *US Census Bureau, International Data Base*

TOP 10 LEAST DENSELY POPULATED COUNTRIES

	COUNTRY	AREA (SQ KM)	POPULATION (2004 EST.)	POPULATION PER SQ KM
1	Mongolia	1,565,000	2,775,768	1.8
2	Namibia	823,291	1,857,619	2.3
3	Australia	7,617,931	19,913,144	2.6
4	= Botswana	585,371	1,587,782	2.7
	= Suriname	161,471	440,862	2.7
6	Iceland	100,251	282,151	2.8
7	Mauritania	1,030,400	2,998,563	2.9
8	Libya	1,759,540	5,631,585	3.2
9	Canada	9,220,970	32,507,874	3.5
10	Guyana	196,850	703,680	3.6

Source: *US Census Bureau, International Data Base*

In addition to these sparsely populated countries, there are several territories where one could be really alone: the Western Sahara with 0.30 people per 2.6 sq km (1 sq mile); and Greenland (Kalaallit Nunaat) with 0.01 people per 2.6 sq km (1 sq mile), or almost 39 sq km (15 sq miles) per person.

World Cities

TOP 10 MOST URBANIZED COUNTRIES

	COUNTRY	POPULATION LIVING IN URBAN AREAS (2001) TOTAL	PERCENTAGE
1	= **Hong Kong**	6,961,000	100.0
	= **Monaco**	34,000	100.0
	= **Nauru**	13,000	100.0
	= **Singapore**	4,108,000	100.0
	= **Vatican City**	1,000	100.0
6	**Belgium**	5,444,000	97.4
7	**Kuwait**	1,894,000	96.1
8	**Qatar**	534,000	92.9
9	**Iceland**	261,000	92.7
10	**Bahrain**	603,000	92.5
	World	*2,923,182,000*	*47.7*
	Canada	*24,472,000*	*78.9*

Source: *United Nations Population Division,* World Urbanization Prospects: The 2001 Revision

TOP 10 LARGEST CITIES IN CANADA*

	CITY/PROVINCE	POPULATION#
1	**Toronto,** Ontario	5,029,900
2	**Montreal,** Quebec	3,548,800
3	**Vancouver,** British Columbia	2,122,700
4	**Ottawa-Hull,** Ontario-Quebec	1,128,900
5	**Calgary,** Alberta	993,200
6	**Edmonton,** Alberta	967,200
7	**Quebec,** Quebec	697,800
8	**Hamilton,** Ontario	686,900
9	**Winnipeg,** Manitoba	685,500
10	**London,** Ontario	427,300

* *Based on census metropolitan area (CMA)*

\# *As at July 1, 2002*

Source: *Statistics Canada*

TOP 10 COUNTRIES WITH THE MOST PEOPLE LIVING IN LARGE CITIES

	COUNTRY	% POPULATION IN CITIES OF OVER 1 MILLION* (2002)
1	**Hong Kong**	100
2	**Singapore**	89
3	**Dominican Republic**	61
4	**Kuwait**	60
5	**Portugal**	57
6	**Australia**	56
7	= **Lebanon**	47
	= **South Korea**	47
9	= **Argentina**	41
	= **Congo**	41
	= **Germany**	41
	Canada	37

* *In those countries for which data available*

Source: *World Bank,* World Development Indicators, 2002

TOP 10 COUNTRIES WITH THE LARGEST URBAN POPULATIONS

	COUNTRY	ESTIMATED TOTAL URBAN POPULATION* (2005)
1	**China**	535,958,000
2	**India**	312,887,000
3	**US**	232,080,000
4	**Brazil**	151,925,000
5	**Indonesia**	104,048,000
6	**Russia**	102,731,000
7	**Japan**	101,831,000
8	**Mexico**	80,073,000
9	**Germany**	72,405,000
10	**Nigeria**	62,623,000
	World	*3,176,892,000*

* *In those countries for which data available*

Source: *United Nations Population Division,* World Urbanization Prospects: The 2001 Revision

City and State
Singapore City and the nation of Singapore are synonymous, as a result of which Singapore is considered a totally urbanized country.

TOP 10 LARGEST CITIES IN THE WORLD 100 YEARS AGO

	CITY	POPULATION*
1	**London,** UK	6,581,000
2	**New York,** New York, US	3,437,000
3	**Paris,** France	2,714,000
4	**Berlin,** Germany	1,889,000
5	**Chicago,** Illinois, US	1,699,000
6	**Vienna,** Austria	1,675,000
7	**Wuhan,** China	1,500,000
8	**Tokyo,** Japan	1,440,000
9	**Philadelphia,** Pennsylvania, US	1,294,000
10	**St. Petersburg,** Russia	1,265,000

* *Including adjacent suburban areas*

TOP 10 LARGEST CITIES

	CITY/COUNTRY	EST. POPULATION (2002)
1	**Tokyo,** Japan	35,100,000
2	**New York,** New York, US	21,650,000
3	**Seoul,** South Korea	21,350,000
4	**Mexico City,** Mexico	20,950,000
5	**São Paulo,** Brazil	19,900,000
6	**Mumbai** (Bombay), India	18,400,000
7	**Osaka,** Japan	18,050,000
8	**Delhi,** India	17,500,000
9	**Los Angeles,** California, US	16,900,000
10	**Jakarta,** Indonesia	16,050,000

Source: *Th. Brinkhoff:* The Principal Agglomerations of the World, *http://www.citypopulation.de, 1.05.2002*

TOP 10 FASTEST-GROWING CITIES*

	CITY/COUNTRY	AVERAGE ANNUAL POPULATION GROWTH RATE* (PERCENT) (2000–2005)
1	**Ansan,** South Korea	9.15
2	**Toluca,** Mexico	6.15
3	**Sana'a,** Yemen	5.83
4	**Niamey,** Niger	5.70
5	**Songnam,** South Korea	5.47
6	**P'ohang,** South Korea	5.43
7	**Rajshahi,** Bangladesh	5.29
8	**Kabul,** Afghanistan	5.10
9	= **Antananarivo,** Madagascar	5.05
	= **Campo Grande,** Brazil	5.05

* *Of urban agglomerations with 750,000 inhabitants or more*

Source: *United Nations Population Division,* World Urbanization Report: The 2001 Revision

Place Names

TOP 10 COUNTRIES WITH THE LONGEST OFFICIAL NAMES

	OFFICIAL NAME*	COMMON ENGLISH NAME	LETTERS
1	al-Jamāhīrīyah al-'Arabīyah al-Lībīyah ash-Sha'biyah al-Ishtirākiyah	Libya	59
2	al-Jūmhurīyah al-Jaza'irīyah ad-Dīmuqrātīyah ash-Sha'bīyah	Algeria	51
3	United Kingdom of Great Britain and Northern Ireland	United Kingdom	45
4	= Srī Lankā Prajātāntrika Samājavādī Janarajaya	Sri Lanka	41
	= Jumhurīyat al-Qumur al-Ittihādīyah al-Islāmīyah	The Comoros	41
6	República Democrática de São Tomé e Príncipe	Príncipe	38
7	al-Jūmhurīyah al-Islāmīyah al-Mūrītānīyah	Mauritania	36
8	= al-Mamlakah al-Urdunnīyah al-Hāshimīyah	Jordan	34
	= Sathalanalat Paxathipatai Paxaxôn Lao	Laos	34
10	Federation of St. Christopher and Nevis	St. Kitts and Nevis	33

* *Some official names have been transliterated from languages that do not use the Roman alphabet; their length may vary according to the method used*

There is clearly no connection between the length of names and the longevity of the nation-states that bear them, for since this list was first published in 1991, three countries have ceased to exist: Socijalisticka Federativna Republika Jugoslavija (Yugoslavia, 45 letters), Soyuz Sovetskikh Sotsialisticheskikh Respublik (USSR, 43) and Ceskoslovenská Socialistická Republika (Czechoslovakia, 36). Uruguay's official name of La República Oriental del Uruguay is sometimes given in full as the 38-letter La República de la Banda Oriental del Uruguay, which would place it in sixth position.

▶ The Long and Short of It
A bustling market in Libya. The country's short and commonly used name appeared in Egyptian hieroglyphics 4,000 years ago and is a fraction of the length of its modern official name, adopted on March 8, 1977, which means "The Great Socialist People's Libyan Arab Jamahiriya."

LONGEST PLACE NAMES*

	NAME	LETTERS
1	**Krung thep mahanakhon bovorn ratanakosin mahintharayutthaya mahadilok pop noparatratchathani burirom udomratchanivetmahasathan amornpiman avatarnsathit sakkathattiyavisnukarmprasit** When the poetic name of Bangkok, capital of Thailand, is used, it is usually abbreviated to "Krung Thep" (city of angels).	167
2	**Taumatawhakatangihangakoauauotamateaturipukakapiki-maungahoronukupokaiwhenuakitanatahu** This is the longer version (the other has a mere 83 letters) of the Maori name of a hill in New Zealand. It translates as "The place where Tamatea, the man with the big knees, who slid, climbed and swallowed mountains, known as land-eater, played on the flute to his loved one."	85
3	**Gorsafawddachaidraigddanheddogleddollônpenrhyn-areurdraethceredigion** A name contrived by the Fairbourne Steam Railway, Gwynedd, North Wales, for publicity purposes and in order to outdo its rival, No. 4. It means "The Mawddach station and its dragon teeth at the Northern Penrhyn Road on the golden beach of Cardigan Bay."	67
4	**Cape St. George-Petit Jardin-Grand Jardin-De Grau-Marches Point-Loretto** Canada's longest place name is of a community in Newfoundland.	64
5	**Llanfairpwllgwyngyllgogerychwyrndrobwllllantysiliogogogoch** This is the place in Gwynedd famed especially for the length of its railway tickets. It means "St. Mary's Church in the hollow of the white hazel near the rapid whirlpool of the church of St. Tysilo near the Red Cave." Its official name, however, comprises only the first 20 letters, and the full name appears to have been invented as a hoax in the 19th century by a local tailor.	57
6	**El Pueblo de Nuestra Señora la Reina de los Ángeles de la Porciúncula** The site of a Franciscan mission and the full Spanish name for the city of Los Angeles; it means "The town of Our Lady the Queen of the Angels of the Little Portion."	57
7	**Chargoggagoggmanchaugagoggchaubunagungamaug** The longest US place name, a lake near Webster, Massachusetts. Its Indian name, loosely translated, means "You fish on your side, I'll fish on mine, and no one fishes in the middle." However, it is an invented extension of its real name (Chabunagungamaug, or "boundary fishing place"), devised in the 1920s by Larry Daly, the editor of the *Webster Times*.	45
8	**Villa Real de la Santa Fé de San Francisco de Asis** The full Spanish name of Santa Fe, New Mexico, translates as "Royal city of the holy faith of St. Francis of Assisi."	40
9	**Te Whakatakanga-o-te-ngarehu-o-te-ahi-a-Tamatea** The Maori name of Hammer Springs, New Zealand; like the second name in this list, it refers to a legend of Tamatea, explaining how the springs were warmed by "the falling of the cinders of the fire of Tamatea."	38
10	**Meallan Liath Coire Mhic Dhubhghaill** The longest multiple name in Scotland, a place near Aultanrynie, Highland, alternatively spelled Meallan Liath Coire Mhic Chughaill (30 letters).	32

* *Including single-word, hyphenated, and multiple names*

LARGEST COUNTRIES NAMED AFTER REAL PEOPLE

	COUNTRY	NAMED AFTER	AREA (SQ MILES)	AREA (SQ KM)
1	**United States of America**	Amerigo Vespucci (Italy; 1451–1512)	3,539,245	9,166,601
2	**Saudi Arabia**	Abdul Aziz ibn-Saud (Nejd; 1882–1953)	830,000	2,149,690
3	**Bolivia**	Simón Bolívar (Venezuela; 1783–1830)	418,685	1,084,389
4	**Colombia**	Christopher Columbus (Italy; 1451–1506)	401,044	1,038,699
5	**Philippines**	Philip II (Spain; 1527–98)	115,124	298,171
6	**Falkland Islands**	Lucius Cary, 2nd Viscount Falkland (UK; *c.* 1610–43)	4,700	12,173
7	**Northern Mariana**	Maria Theresa (Austria; 1717–80)	184	477
8	**Wallis & Futuna**	Samuel Wallis (UK; 1728–95)	105	274
9	**Cook Islands**	Capt. James Cook (UK; 1728–79)	93	241
10	**Marshall Islands**	Capt. John Marshall (UK; 1748–after 1818)	70	181

Many countries were named after mythical characters, or saints of dubious historical authenticity—often because they were discovered on the saint's day—but these are all named after real people. It is questionable whether China is named after the Emperor Chin, but if so, it would rank first.

LONGEST STREAM NAMES IN CANADA

	NAME	LETTERS*
1	**Cours d'eau du Cordon des Terres des Sixième et Septième Rangs,** Quebec	52
2	**Cours d'eau de la Concession Sud-Est du Rang Saint-David,** Quebec	48
3	**Ruisseau Katakuschuwepaishit Kachikuschikepaisham,** Quebec	47
4	**Décharge des Neuvième Dixième et Onzième Concessions,** Quebec	46
5 =	**Lower North Branch Little Southwest Miramichi River,** New Brunswick	45
=	**Embranchement des Rangs Saint-Georges et Séraphine,** Quebec	45
7 =	**Rivière Eistustikwepaich Kaschewekahikanistikw,** Quebec	44
=	**Cours d'eau des Cinquième et Sixième Rangs de Milton,** Quebec	44
9 =	**Cours d'eau Première Route du Bas-de-la-Paroisse,** Quebec	43
=	**Embranchement de la Deuxième Concession Foucault,** Quebec	43

* *Including each letter, hyphen, and apostrophe; excluding spaces*

Source: *Geomatics Canada, Natural Resources Canada*

Great Buildings

TOP 10 TALLEST TELECOMMUNICATIONS TOWERS

	TOWER/LOCATION	YEAR COMPLETED	HEIGHT (FT)	(M)
1	**CN Tower,** Toronto, Canada	1975	1,821	555
2	**Ostankino Tower*,** Moscow, Russia	1967	1,762	537
3	**Oriental Pearl Broadcasting Tower,** Shanghai, China	1995	1,535	468
4	**Borj-e Milad Telecommunications Tower,** Tehran, Iran	U/C 2003	1,426	435
5	**Menara Telecom Tower,** Kuala Lumpur, Malaysia	1996	1,381	421
6	**Tianjin TV and Radio Tower,** Tianjin, China	1991	1,362	415
7	**Central Radio and TV Tower,** Beijing, China	1994	1,328	405
8	**TV Tower,** Tashkent, Uzbekistan	1983	1,230	375
9	**Liberation Tower,** Kuwait City, Kuwait	1998	1,220	372
10	**Alma-Ata Tower,** Kazakhstan	1983	1,215	370

** Severely damaged by fire, August 2000*

U/C = Under construction; scheduled completion date

◀ High Life
The striking, sail-like Burj Al Arab hotel, Dubai, is the world's tallest all-hotel building. The structure stands on a man-made island and contains a record-breaking 180-m (590.5-ft) atrium.

CANADA'S FIRST WORLD RECORD TOWER

FIRST FACT

WHILE EVER-TALLER HABITABLE BUILDINGS have seized the record in recent years, the CN Tower, Toronto, Canada, has retained its place as the world's tallest freestanding structure for almost 30 years. Built by some 1,537 construction workers between February 5, 1973, and April 2, 1975, the finished tower weighs 117,910 metric tons (130,000 tons). It features a glass floor at a height of 342 m (1,122 ft), across which brave visitors can walk while looking straight down at the world below.

TALLEST HOTELS

	HOTEL#/LOCATION/YEAR COMPLETED	STORIES	HEIGHT* (FT)	(M)
1	**Jin Mao Tower,** Shanghai, China, 1998 Grand Hyatt Hotel occupies floors 53 to 87	88	1,214	370
2	**Shimao International Plaza,** Shanghai, China, 2004† 48 floors of hotel occupancy proposed	60	1,093	333
3	**Baiyoke Tower 2,** Bangkok, Thailand, 1997 Baiyoke Sky Hotel occupies floors 22 to 74	89	1,013	309
4	**Burj Al Arab,** Dubai, United Arab Emirates, 1999	60	885	270
5	**Emirates Tower 2,** Dubai, United Arab Emirates, 1999	50	858	262
6	**Thai Wah Tower II,** Bangkok, Thailand, 1996 Westin Banyan Tree Hotel occupies floors 33 to 60	60	853	260
7	**Grand Duta Hyatt,** Kuala Lumpur, Malaysia, 2004†	60	798	243
8	**Four Seasons Hotel and Tower,** Miami, Florida, 2002 Hotel occupies lower floors	54	788	241
9	**JR Central Towers,** Nagoya, Japan, 1999	53	787	240
10	**Grand Gateway,** Shanghai, China (twin towers), 2002	52	765	233

** Excluding spire # Including mixed occupancy (hotel + residential/office) buildings*

† Under construction; scheduled completion date

TOP 10 TALLEST HABITABLE BUILDINGS

	BUILDING/LOCATION	YEAR COMPLETED	STORIES	HEIGHT* (FT)	(M)
1	**Union Square,** Hong Kong, China	U/C 2008	101	1,575	480
2	**Petronas Towers,** Kuala Lumpur, Malaysia	1996	96	1,482	452
3	**Taipei Financial Centre,** Taipei, China	U/C 2003*	101	1,470	448
4	**Sears Tower,** Chicago, IL	1974*	110	1,454	443
5	**Two International Financial Center,** Hong Kong, China	U/C 2003	88	1,350	412
6	**Jin Mao Building,** Shanghai, China	1997*	93	1,255	382
7	**Empire State Building,** New York, NY	1931*	102	1,250	381
8	**Tuntex and Chien-Tai Tower,** Kao-hsiung,Taiwan	1997*	85	1,142	348
9	**AON Building,** Chicago, IL	1973	80	1,136	346
10	**John Hancock Center,** Chicago, IL	1969*	100	1,127	343

** Excluding spires*

U/C = Under construction; scheduled completion date

TOP 10 TALLEST CATHEDRALS AND CHURCHES

	CHURCH/LOCATION	YEAR COMPLETED	HEIGHT (FT)	(M)
1	**Chicago Methodist Temple*,** Chicago, IL	1924	568	173
2	**Sagrada Familia,** Barcelona, Spain	U/C 2020	558	170
3	**Santuario de los Santos Mártires de Cristo Rey y Santa María de Guadalupe,** Tlaquepaque, Mexico	U/C 2004	551	168
4	**Ulm Cathedral,** Ulm, Germany	1890	528	161
5	**Notre Dame de la Paix,** Yamoussoukro, Côte d'Ivoire	1989	519	158
6	**Cologne Cathedral,** Cologne, Germany	1880	513	156
7	**Rouen Cathedral,** Rouen, France	1876	485	148
8	**St. Nicholas,** Hamburg, Germany	1847	475	145
9	**Notre Dame,** Strasbourg, France	1439	465	142
10	**Queen of Peace Shrine and Basilica,** Lichen, Poland	U/C	459	140

** Sited on top of a 25-story, 100-m (328-ft) building*

U/C = Under construction; scheduled completion date (where announced)

▶ Tall Temple

The Chicago Methodist Temple was completed in 1924 at a cost of US$3 million. It was the tallest building in the city until the Chicago Board of Trade was completed in 1930, but it remains the world's tallest church.

Under & Over

TOP 10 LONGEST CANTILEVER BRIDGES

	BRIDGE/LOCATION	YEAR COMPLETED	LENGTH OF MAIN SPAN (FT)	(M)
1	**Quebec,** Canada	1917	1,800	549
2	**Firth of Forth,** Scotland	1890	1,710	521
3	**Minato,** Osaka, Japan	1974	1,673	510
4	**Commodore John Barry,** New Jersey/Pennsylvania, US	1974	1,622	494
5	= **Greater New Orleans 1,** Louisiana, US	1958	1,575	480
	= **Greater New Orleans 2,** Louisiana, US	1958	1,575	480
7	**Howrah,** Calcutta, India	1943	1,500	457
8	**Gramercy,** Louisiana, US	1995	1,460	445
9	**Transbay,** San Francisco, US	1936	1,400	427
10	**Baton Rouge,** Louisiana, US	1969	1,235	376

The Quebec Bridge in Ste-Foy, Quebec, spans the St. Lawrence River. It has a history of two collapses, one in 1907 and one in 1916, killing a total of 86 people. After almost 20 years of planning and construction, the Quebec Bridge opened for traffic on December 3, 1917. It is recognized as an International Historic Civil Engineering Landmark by the Canadian Society for Civil Engineering and the American Society for Civil Engineers .

TOP 10 LONGEST SUSPENSION BRIDGES

	BRIDGE/LOCATION	YEAR COMPLETED	LENGTH OF MAIN SPAN (FT)	(M)
1	**Akashi-Kaikyo,** Kobe-Naruto, Japan	1998	6,532	1,991
2	**Izmit Bay,** Turkey	U/C	5,472	1,668
3	**Great Belt,** Denmark	1997	5,328	1,624
4	**Humber Estuary,** UK	1980	4,626	1,410
5	**Jiangyin,** China	1998	4,544	1,385
6	**Tsing Ma,** Hong Kong, China	1997	4,518	1,377
7	**Verrazano Narrows,** New York, US	1964	4,260	1,298
8	**Golden Gate,** San Francisco, US	1937	4,200	1,280
9	**Höga Kusten** (High Coast), Veda, Sweden	1997	3,970	1,210
10	**Mackinac Straits,** Michigan, US	1957	3,800	1,158

U/C = Under construction

The Messina Strait Bridge between Sicily and Calabria, Italy, received the go-ahead in June 2002, with work to begin in 2004–5; it will take five to six years to complete, and cost US$4.9 billion. It will have by far the longest center span of any bridge at 3,300 m (10,827 ft), although at 3,910 m (12,828 ft), Japan's Akashi-Kaikyo bridge, is the world's longest overall.

TOP 10 LONGEST STEEL ARCH BRIDGES

	BRIDGE/LOCATION	YEAR COMPLETED	LONGEST SPAN (FT)	(M)
1	**New River Gorge,** Fayetteville, West Virginia	1977	1,700	518
2	**Kill van Kull,** Bayonne, New Jersey/Staten Island, New York	1931	1,652	504
3	**Sydney Harbour,** Sydney, Australia	1932	1,650	503
4	**Wanxian,** Yangtze River, China	1997	1,378	420
5	**Fremont,** Portland, Oregon	1973	1,257	383
6	**Port Mann,** Vancouver, Canada	1964	1,200	366
7	**Thatcher Ferry,** Panama Canal, Panama	1962	1,128	344
8	**Laviolette,** Trois-Rivières, Canada	1967	1,100	335
9	**Zdákov,** Lake Orlik, Czech Republic	1967	1,083	330
10	**Runcorn-Widnes,** Mersey River, UK	1961	1,082	330

Longest Bridge So Far
The longest, tallest, and most expensive bridge in the world, Japan's Akashi-Kaikyo, measures 3,910 m (12,828 ft) overall. It was built to withstand winds of up to 290 km/h (180 mph) and earthquakes up to 8.5 on the Richter scale.

TOP 10 LONGEST UNDERWATER TUNNELS

	TUNNEL/LOCATION	YEAR COMPLETED	LENGTH (M)	(FT)
1	**Seikan,** Japan	1988	53,850	176,673
2	**Channel Tunnel,** France/England	1994	50,450	165,518
3	**Dai-Shimizu,** Japan	1982	22,221	72,904
4	**Shin-Kanmon,** Japan	1975	18,680	61,286
5	**Tokyo Bay Aqualine Expressway*,** Japan	1997	9,583	31,440
6	**Great Belt Fixed Link** (Eastern Tunnel), Denmark	1997	8,024	26,325
7	**Bømlafjord*,** Norway	2000	7,921	25,988
8	**Oslofjord*,** Norway	2000	7,260	23,819
9	**Severn,** UK	1886	7,008	22,992
10	**Magerøysund*,** Norway	1999	6,875	22,556

* *Road; others rail*

The need to connect the Japanese islands of Honshu, Kyushu, and Hokkaido has resulted in a recent wave of undersea tunnel building, with the Seikan the most ambitious project of all. Connecting Honshu and Hokkaido, 23.3 km (14.4 miles) of the tunnel is 100 m (328 ft) below the seabed, bored through strata that presented such enormous engineering problems that it took 24 years to complete.

TOP 10 LONGEST RAIL TUNNELS

	TUNNEL/LOCATION	YEAR COMPLETED	LENGTH (MILES)	(KM)
1	**Seikan,** Japan	1988	33.46	53.85
2	**Channel Tunnel,** France/England	1994	31.35	50.45
3	**Moscow Metro** (Medvedkovo/Belyaevo section), Russia	1979	19.07	30.70
4	**London Underground** (East Finchley/ Morden, Northern Line), UK	1939	17.30	27.84
5	**Hakkoda,** Japan	U/C	16.44	26.46
6	**Iwate,** Japan	U/C	16.04	25.81
7	**Iiyama,** Japan	U/C	13.98	22.50
8	**Dai-Shimizu,** Japan	1982	13.81	22.22
9	**Simplon II,** Italy/Switzerland	1922	12.31	19.82
10	**Simplon I,** Italy/Switzerland	1906	12.30	19.80

U/C = Under construction

The world's longest rail tunnel, the Gotthard AlpTransit, Switzerland, is scheduled for completion in 2010, and will measure 57.07 km (35.46 miles). Further rail tunnels over 20 km (12.43 miles) in length are in the planning stages in Austria, France, Italy, Spain, and Switzerland.

TOP 10 LONGEST ROAD TUNNELS

	TUNNEL/LOCATION	YEAR COMPLETED	LENGTH (FT)	(M)
1	**Laerdal,** Norway	2000	80,413	24,510
2	**Zhongnanshan,** China	U/C 2007	59,186	18,040
3	**St. Gotthard,** Switzerland	1980	55,505	16,918
4	**Arlberg,** Austria	1978	45,850	13,972
5	**Pinglin Highway,** Taiwan	U/C 2003	42,323	12,900
6	**Fréjus,** France/Italy	1980	42,306	12,895
7	**Mont-Blanc,** France/Italy	1965	38,094	11,611
8	**Gudvangen,** Norway	1991	37,493	11,428
9	**Folgefonn,** Norway	2001	36,417	11,100
10	**Kan-Etsu II** (southbound), Japan	1990	36,122	11,010

U/C = Under construction; scheduled completion date

Nos. 1, 3, 4, and 7 have all held the record as "world's longest road tunnel." Previous record-holders include the 5,854-m (19,206-ft) Grand San Bernardo (Italy-Switzerland; 1964), the 5,133-m (16,841-ft) Alfonso XIII or Viella (Spain; 1948), 3,237-m (10,620-ft) Queensway (Mersey) Tunnel (connecting Liverpool and Birkenhead, UK; 1934), and the 3,186-m (10,453-ft) Col de Tende (France-Italy; 1882), originally built as a rail tunnel and converted in 1928.

CULTURE & LEARNING

Mind Your Language

TOP 10 MOST WIDELY SPOKEN LANGUAGES

	LANGUAGE	APPROXIMATE NO. OF SPEAKERS
1	**Chinese (Mandarin)**	874,000,000
2	**Hindustani***	426,000,000
3	**Spanish**	358,000,000
4	**English**	341,000,000
5	**Bengali**	207,000,000
6	**Arabic#**	206,000,000
7	**Portuguese**	176,000,000
8	**Russian**	167,000,000
9	**Japanese**	125,000,000
10	**German** (standard)	100,000,000

* *Hindi and Urdu are essentially the same language—Hindustani. As the official language of Pakistan it is written in modified Arabic script and called Urdu; as the official language of India it is written in the Devanagari script and called Hindi.*

\# *Includes 16 variants of the Arabic language*

TOP 10 LANGUAGES OFFICIALLY SPOKEN IN THE MOST COUNTRIES

	LANGUAGE	COUNTRIES
1	**English**	57
2	**French**	33
3	**Arabic**	23
4	**Spanish**	21
5	**Portuguese**	7
6	= **Dutch**	5
	= **German**	5
8	= **Chinese (Mandarin)**	3
	= **Danish**	3
	= **Italian**	3
	= **Malay**	3

There are many countries in the world with more than one official language—both English and French are recognized officially in Canada, for example. English is used in numerous countries as the lingua franca, the common language that enables people who speak mutually unintelligible languages to communicate with each other.

TOP 10 COUNTRIES WITH THE MOST ENGLISH-LANGUAGE SPEAKERS

	LANGUAGE	APPROXIMATE NO. OF SPEAKERS*
1	**US**	237,320,000
2	**UK**	58,090,000
3	**Canada**	18,218,000
4	**Australia**	15,561,000
5	**Ireland**	3,720,000
6	**South Africa**	3,700,000
7	**New Zealand**	3,338,000
8	**Jamaica#**	2,460,000
9	**Trinidad and Tobago#†**	1,245,000
10	**Guyana#**	764,000

* *People for whom English is their mother tongue, rather than those who understand or speak it as a second language*

\# *Includes English Creole*

† *Trinidad English*

TOP 10 COUNTRIES WITH THE MOST FRENCH-LANGUAGE SPEAKERS

	COUNTRY	APPROXIMATE NO. OF SPEAKERS*
1	France	55,100,000
2	Canada	7,158,000
3	Haiti#	6,868,000
4	Belgium†	3,350,000
5	US★	2,250,000
6	Switzerland	1,380,000
7	Mauritius★	878,000
8	Réunion#	660,000
9	Guadeloupe★	407,000
10	Martinique★	372,000

* *People for whom French is their mother tongue*

French Creole

† *Walloon French*

★ *French/French Creole*

TOP 10 COUNTRIES WITH THE MOST SPANISH-LANGUAGE SPEAKERS

	COUNTRY	APPROXIMATE NO. OF SPEAKERS*
1	Mexico	91,080,000
2	Colombia	41,880,000
3	Argentina	35,860,000
4	Spain#	29,860,000
5	Venezuela	23,310,000
6	US	20,720,000
7	Peru	20,470,000
8	Chile	13,640,000
9	Ecuador	11,760,000
10	Dominican Republic	8,270,000

* *People for whom Spanish is their mother tongue*

Castilian Spanish

TOP 10 LANGUAGES USED ONLINE

	LANGUAGE	INTERNET ACCESS*
1	English	280,000,000
2	Chinese	170,000,000
3	Japanese	90,000,000
4	Spanish	68,000,000
5	German	62,000,000
6	Korean	43,000,000
7	French	41,000,000
8	Italian	35,000,000
9	Portuguese	32,000,000
10	Russian	23,000,000
	World total	*940,000,000*

* *Online population estimate for 2004*

Source: *Global Reach*

THE FIRST ENGLISH-LANGUAGE DICTIONARY

FIRST FACT

PUBLISHED IN LONDON in 1604, Robert Cawdrey's *A Table Alphabeticall, containing the true writing and understanding of hard usuall English wordes* is considered the first ever English-language dictionary. Cawdrey assembled a collection that originally contained 2,543 words, expanded to over 3,200 in later editions. Definitions are simple one-line entries, using 17th-century spelling, so "medicine" is defined as "remedie, or cure" and "corps" as "deade bodie." A single copy of Cawdrey's pioneering book survives.

◀ Chinese Whispers
Mandarin, the official Chinese dialect based on the pronunciation used in Beijing, is spoken by more than two-thirds of the Chinese population, making it the world's most-used language.

TOP 10 COUNTRIES WITH THE MOST GERMAN-LANGUAGE SPEAKERS

	COUNTRY	APPROX. NO. OF SPEAKERS*
1	Germany	75,060,000
2	Austria	7,444,000
3	Switzerland	4,570,000
4	US	1,850,000
5	Brazil	910,000
6	Poland	500,000
7	Canada	486,000
8	Kazakhstan	460,000
9	Russia	350,000
10	Italy	310,000

* *People for whom German is their mother tongue*

German is the national language of Germany and Austria, and is one of four official languages of Switzerland. However, as a result of the diaspora whereby more than seven million people emigrated from Germany to the US and many other parts of the world, German is spoken by expatriate groups in countries as far flung as Paraguay and Namibia.

TOP 10 COUNTRIES WITH THE MOST ARABIC-LANGUAGE SPEAKERS

	COUNTRY	APPROXIMATE NO. OF SPEAKERS*
1	Egypt	65,080,000
2	Algeria	26,280,000
3	Saudi Arabia	20,920,000
4	Morocco	18,730,000
5	Iraq	17,490,000
6	Yemen	17,400,000
7	Sudan	17,320,000
8	Syria	14,680,000
9	Tunisia#	6,710,000
10	Libya	4,910,000

* *People for whom Arabic is their mother tongue*

Another 2,520,000 people speak Arabic-French and 300,000 speak Arabic-English

Islamic invasions carried Arabic throughout the Middle East and North Africa, while certain Arabic words, including "alcohol," "giraffe," and "magazine," reached Europe and were adopted into the English language.

Libraries of the World

TOP 10 LARGEST LIBRARIES

	LIBRAR	OCATION	FOUNDED	BOOKS
1	**Library of Congress**	Washington, DC	1800	24,616,867
2	**National Library of China**	Beijing, China	1909	22,000,000
3	**Library of the Russian Academy of Science**	St. Petersburg, Russia	1714	20,000,000
4	**Deutsche Bibliothek***	Frankfurt, Germany	1990	16,593,000
5	**National Library of Canada**	Ottawa, Canada	1953	16,000,000
6	**British Library#**	London, UK	1753	15,000,000
7	**Harvard University Library**	Cambridge, MA	1638	14,437,361
8	**Institute for Scientific Information on the Social Sciences of Russian Academy of Science**	Moscow, Russia	1969	13,500,000
9	**Vernadsky Central Scientific Library of the National Academy of Sciences**	Kiev, Ukraine	1919	13,000,000
10	**Bibliothèque Nationale de France**	Paris, France	1400	11,000,000

* *Formed in 1990 through the unification of the Deutsche Bibliothek, Frankfurt (founded 1947), and the Deutsche Bucherei, Leipzig*

\# *Founded as part of the British Museum, 1753; became an independent body in 1973*

THE 10 LARGEST PUBLIC LIBRARIES IN CANADA

	LIBRARY/PROVINCE/ NO. OF BRANCHES	HOLDINGS
1	**Toronto Public Library,** ON, 103	10,606,221
2	**Bibliothèque de Montréal,** QC, 25	2,886,873
3	**Vancouver Public Library,** BC, 22	2,472,200
4	**Ottawa Public Library,** ON, 33	2,435,866
5	**Calgary Public Library,** AB, 17	2,054,454
6	**Edmonton Public Library,** AB, 16	1,650,858
7	**Winnipeg Public Library,** MB, 20	1,638,618
8	**Mississauga Library System,** ON, 15	1,568,204
9	**Hamilton Public Library,** ON, 27	1,484,681
10	**Halifax Regional Library,** NS, 15	1,239,145

Source: *Council of Administrators of Large Urban Public Libraries,* Canadian Public Library Statistics Report, 2001

Shelf Life
The founding of the National Library of Austria dates from 1368, when Archduke Albrecht III established it in the Imperial Castle, Vienna.

TOP 10 LARGEST UNIVERSITY LIBRARIES IN THE US

	LIBRARY	BOOKS
1	**Harvard University Library**	14,437,361
2	**Yale University Library**	10,492,812
3	**University of Illinois-Urbana Library**	9,469,620
4	**University of California-Berkeley Library**	9,107,757
5	**University of Texas-Austin Library**	7,935,540
6	**University of California-Los Angeles Library**	7,517,303
7	**University of Michigan-Ann Arbor Library**	7,348,360
8	**Stanford University Library**	7,286,437
9	**Columbia University-Main Division Library**	7,266,499
10	**Cornell University**	6,609,332

Source: *American Library Association*

TOP 10 LARGEST RESEARCH LIBRARIES IN CANADA

	LIBRARY	BOOKS*
1	**University of Toronto**	9,525,835
2	**National Library of Canada**	7,992,123
3	**University of Alberta**	5,768,464
4	**University of British Columbia**	4,819,117
5	**McGill University**	3,318,272
6	**University of Western Ontario**	2,838,293
7	**CISTI**#	2,612,082
8	**University of Montreal**	2,572,257
9	**Laval University**	2,529,751
10	**York University**	2,436,581

* *Based on volumes held 2001–2002* # *Canadian Institute for Scientific and Technical Information*

Source: *Canadian Association of Research Libraries*

Reading Room
The New York Public Library is one of the world's largest public libraries. In addition to its holdings of books, it houses over 30 million cataloged items.

TOP 10 OLDEST NATIONAL LIBRARIES

	LIBRARY/LOCATION	FOUNDED
1	**Národní Knihovne Ceské Republiky** National Library of the Czech Republic, Prague, Czech Republic	1366
2	**Österreichische Nationalbibliothek** National Library of Austria, Vienna, Austria	1368
3	**Biblioteca Nazionale Marciana,** Venice, Italy	1468
4	**Bibliothèque Nationale de France** National Library of France, Paris, France	1480
5	**National Library of Malta,** Valetta, Malta	1555
6	**Bayericsche Staatsbibliothek,** Munich, Germany	1558
7	**Bibliothèque Royale Albert 1er** National Library of Belgium, Brussels, Belgium	1559
8	**Nacionalna i Sveucilisna Knjiznica** Zagreb National and University Library, Zagreb, Croatia	1606
9	**Helsingin Yliopiston Kirjasto** National Library of Finland, Helsinki, Finland	1640
10	**Kongeligie Bibliotek** National Library of Denmark, Copenhagen, Denmark	1653

TOP 10 LARGEST PUBLIC LIBRARIES

	LIBRARY/NO. OF BRANCHES	LOCATION	FOUNDED	BOOKS
1	**Chicago Public Library** (79)	Chicago, IL	1872	10,994,943
2	**New York Public Library** (The Branch Libraries) (85)	New York, NY	1895*	10,608,570#
3	**Queens Borough Public Library** (62)	New York, NY	1896	10,357,159
4	**Public Library of Cincinnati and Hamilton County** (41)	Cincinnati, OH	1853	9,952,009
5	**County of Los Angeles Public Library** (85)	Los Angeles, CA	1872	8,255,100
6	**Shanghai Public Library**	Shanghai, China	1952	8,200,000
7	**Boston Public Library** (25)	Boston, MA	1852†	7,736,451
8	**Brooklyn Public Library** (58)	Brooklyn, New York, NY	1896	7,189,998
9	**Free Library of Philadelphia** (52)	Philadelphia, PA	1891	6,225,098
10	**Los Angeles Public Library** (67)	Los Angeles, CA	1872	6,023,257

* *Astor Library founded 1848; consolidated with Lenox Library and Tilden Trust to form New York Public Library, 1895*

Lending library and reference library holdings available for loan

† *Opened to the public 1996*

Schooling & Further Education

TOP 10 COUNTRIES SPENDING MOST ON EDUCATION

	COUNTR	PUBLIC EXPENDITURE AS PERCENTAGE OF GNP* 999/2000
1	Zimbabwe	11.05
2	Papua New Guinea	10.00
3	Botswana	9.32
4	Saudi Arabia	9.27
5	Denmark	8.04
6	St. Lucia	8.01
7	Lesotho	7.93
8	= Namibia	7.89#
	= Seychelles	7.89
10	Sweden	7.86
	Canada	*5.69*

* *Gross national product; in those countries for which data are available*

\# *1998/1999 data*

Source: *UNESCO*

If the Marshall Islands were a country, it would top this list, with the 1998/1999 public expenditure on education at 15.39 percent of this US territory's gross national income.

TOP 10 COUNTRIES WITH FEWEST PRIMARY SCHOOL PUPILS PER TEACHER

	COUNTR	PUPIL/TEACHER RATIO IN PRIMARY SCHOOLS 999/2000
1	San Marino	5.36
2	Libya	8.44*
3	Denmark	10.12
4	Hungary	10.71
5	Iceland	10.93
6	Italy	10.96
7	Cuba	11.50
8	Sweden	11.84
9	Saudi Arabia	11.99
10	Brunei	13.10

* *1998/1999*

Source: *UNESCO*

A Class of Their Own
Relatively small primary class sizes in such countries as Hungary contrast with those in some African countries, which may be up to five times as large.

TOP 10 COUNTRIES WITH THE LOWEST PERCENTAGE OF CHILDREN IN PRIMARY SCHOOL

	COUNTRY	% CHILDREN ENROLLED IN PRIMARY SCHOOL 1999/2000* GIRLS	BOYS	TOTAL
1	Niger	20.58	21.82	21.19
2	Angola	29.22	25.42	27.32
3	Djibouti	34.85	26.29	30.59
4	Ethiopia	34.46	27.74	31.11
5	Dem. Rep. of Congo	33.44	31.82	32.63#
6	Burkina Faso	34.63	28.31	34.63
7	Eritrea	43.28	37.39	40.34
8	Mali	50.71	35.89	43.32
9	Burundi	49.35	39.57	44.46
10	Sudan	48.60	40.75	44.74
	Canada	98.49	98.75	98.62

* *In those countries for which data are available*

\# *1998/1999*

Source: *UNESCO*

TOP 10 COUNTRIES WITH THE HIGHEST PERCENTAGE OF HIGH SCHOOL GRADUATES IN FURTHER EDUCATION

	COUNTRY	% HIGH SCHOOL GRADS IN FURTHER EDUCATION 1999/2000* FEMALE	MALE	TOTAL
1	Finland	83.79	91.89	76.01
2	South Korea	51.97	90.28	71.69
3	US	81.45	62.17	71.62
4	Norway	81.59	55.74	68.40
5	Sweden	79.05	54.17	66.32
6	New Zealand	80.25	53.04	66.31
7	Russia	72.99	57.38	65.10
8	Australia	69.80	56.51	63.00
9	Canada	68.82	51.57	59.99
10	Spain	62.32	53.01	57.56

* *Total enrollment in further education taken as a percentage of the five-year age group following on from high school graduation age; in those countries for which data is available*

\# *1998/1999*

Source: *UNESCO*

TOP 10 COUNTRIES OF ORIGIN OF UNIVERSITY STUDENTS STUDYING IN CANADA, 1999–2000

	COUNTRY	UNDERGRADUATE	GRADUATE	TOTAL
1	US	2,973	1,194	4,167
2	France	2,912	1,102	4,014
3	China	1,472	1,494	2,966
4	Hong Kong	1,720	125	1,845
5	Japan	1,090	329	1,419
6	UK	807	280	1,087
7	South Korea	801	261	1,062
8	Taiwan	772	62	834
9	India	387	430	817
10	Mexico	432	318	750

Source: *Canadian Bureau for International Education,* The National Report on International Students in Canada 2000/01

During the 1999–2000 school year, a total of 106,068 students from 207 countries came to Canada to study at all education levels, with university undergraduate programs showing the greatest increase in enrollment (30 percent) over the past decade.

TOP 10 FIELDS OF STUDY FOR UNIVERSITY GRADUATES IN CANADA

	FIELD	PERCENTAGE OF GRADUATES (2001)
1	Education (elementary, secondary, pre-primary)	14.26
2	Engineering	8.75
3	Business and commerce	7.98
4	Financial management	6.16
5	Psychology	3.52
6	Nursing	3.51
7	Computer science and applied mathematics	3.09
8	Law and jurisprudence	2.73
9	Economics	2.59
10	Medicine	2.45

Source: *Statistics Canada,* Education in Canada: Raising the Standard, 2001 Census

The top three fields among men were engineering, business and commerce, and education, with the largest growth in enrollment occurring in subjects relating to technology. Women gravitated toward education, nursing, and business and commerce, with the largest growth occurring in business- and finance-related fields.

By the Book

TOP 10 BESTSELLING PENGUIN CLASSICS

	AUTHOR	TITLE	FIRST PUBLISHED*
1	**Jane Austen**	Emma	1816
2	**Jane Austen**	Pride and Prejudice	1813
3	**Emily Brontë**	Wuthering Heights	1847
4	**Charlotte Brontë**	Jane Eyre	1847
5	**Geoffrey Chaucer**	The Canterbury Tales	1387–
6	**Charles Dickens**	Great Expectations	1862
7	**Homer**	The Odyssey	*c.*8th C. BC
8	**Niccolò Machiavelli**	The Prince	1513
9	**Plato**	The Republic	*c.*368 BC
10	**Mary Shelley**	Frankenstein	1818

* *In book form (some 19th-century novels were originally issued in weekly parts before appearing as books)*

The Penguin Classics series was started in 1946 by classicist E.V. Rieu (1887–1972), whose own translation of Homer's *Odyssey*, undertaken during World War II, became the first title published; it remains in the Top 10, having sold almost three million copies. The series now comprises some 850 titles, with about 60 additions annually.

◀ Pride of Place
Almost 200 years after they were written, Jane Austen's *Emma*, followed by her *Pride and Prejudice*, top the Penguin Classics bestseller list.

TOP 10 FICTION BESTSELLERS IN CANADA, 2002

	TITLE	AUTHOR
1	**Unless**	Carol Shields*
2	**Family Matters**	Rohinton Mistry*
3	**Quentins**	Maeve Binchy
4	**Crow Lake**	Mary Lawson*
5	**The Shelters of Stone**	Jean M. Auel
6	**The Navigator of New York**	Wayne Johnston*
7	**The Lovely Bones**	Alice Sebold
8	**Clara Callan**	Richard B. Wright*
9	**Atonement**	Ian McEwan
10	**The Last Crossing**	Guy Vanderhaeghe*

* *Author is Canadian*

Reprinted with permission from the Globe and Mail.

American-born Carol Shields, author of *Unless*, has been living in Canada since 1957. She won a Pulitzer Prize and the Governor General's Literary Award for her novel *The Stone Diaries*, and the Orange Prize for her novel *Larry's Party*. She is also co-editor of the non-fiction bestseller *Dropped Threads*, which has recently been joined by a sequel, *Dropped Threads 2*, a compilation of short stories by women.

TOP 10 NON-FICTION BESTSELLERS IN CANADA, 2002

	TITLE	AUTHOR/EDITOR
1	**Stupid White Men**	Michael Moore
2	**9-11**	Noam Chomsky
3	**How to Be a Canadian**	Will Ferguson* and Ian Ferguson*
4	**Dropped Threads**	edited by Carol Shields* and Marjorie Anderson*
5	**Souvenir of Canada**	Douglas Coupland*
6	**Lucky Man**	Michael J. Fox*
7	**On Equilibrium**	John Ralston Saul*
8	**Shakey**	Jimmy McDonough
9	**Jack: Straight from the Gut**	Jack Welch with Jack A. Byrne
10	**Negotiating with the Dead**	Margaret Atwood*

* *Author or editor is Canadian*

Reprinted with permission from the Globe and Mail.

Will Ferguson's novel *Happiness™* won the 2002 Leacock Medal for Humour and the 2002 Canadian Authors Association Award for Fiction. He recruited his brother Ian, a comedy writer, to help him write the bestseller *How to Be a Canadian*, a humorous guidebook to popular Canadian culture.

TOP 10 MASS MARKET PAPERBACK BESTSELLERS, 2002

	TITLE/AUTHOR	SALES
1	**The Summons,** John Grisham	3,965,000
2	**The Lord of the Rings: The Two Towers,** J.R.R. Tolkien	2,828,087
3	**Face the Fire,** Nora Roberts	2,700,269
4	**The Villa,** Nora Roberts	2,204,755
5	**Midnight Bayou,** Nora Roberts	2,034,602
6	**On the Street Where You Live,** Mary Higgins Clark	1,796,342
7	**The Lord of the Ring: The Fellowship of the Ring,** J.R.R. Tolkien	1,718,720
8	**The Hobbit,** J.R.R. Tolkien	1,710,430
9	**The Kiss,** Danielle Steel	1,610,000
10	**Isle of Dogs,** Patricia Cornwell	1,601,026

Source: *Publishers Weekly*

As the link between books and films has been increasingly exemplified in recent years, 2002 saw a surge in interest in the works of J.R.R. Tolkien resulting from the release and worldwide success of the movies *The Lord of the Rings: The Fellowship of the Ring* and *The Lord of the Rings: The Two Towers*. These novels, and J.K. Rowling's *Harry Potter* phenomenon, have also created a new enthusiasm for books featuring magic and wizardry, which Nora Roberts has skillfully woven into her Three Sisters Island trilogy, of which *Face the Fire* is the conclusion. Danielle Steel, a permanent resident of the fiction bestseller list since 1981—with every book going to No. 1, and with 390 consecutive weeks on the *New York Times* bestseller list—is in a class apart, with a total of more than 350 million copies of her books in print. Patricia Cornwell's *Isle of Dogs* was a surprising, albeit successful, departure from her usual writing in that it was a comic novel that did not feature her popular chief medical examiner character, Kay Scarpetta.

▲ Summons at the Summit
John Grisham's *The Summons* topped both the hardback and paperback bestseller lists in 2002, with cumulative sales of over 6.5 million.

TOP 10 BESTSELLING BOOKS OF ALL TIME

	BOOK/AUTHOR/FIRST PUBLISHED	APPROX. SALES
1	**The Bible,** *c.*1451–55	more than 6,000,000,000
2	**Quotations from the Works of Mao Tse-tung,** 1966	900,000,000
3	**The Lord of the Rings** (trilogy), J.R.R. Tolkien, 1954–55	more than 100,000,000
4	**American Spelling Book,** Noah Webster, 1783	up to 100,000,000
5	**The Guinness Book of Records** (now Guinness World Records), 1955	more than 92,000,000*
6	**World Almanac,** 1868	73,500,000*
7	**The McGuffey Readers,** William Holmes McGuffey, 1836	60,000,000
8	**The Common Sense Book of Baby and Child Care,** Benjamin Spock, 1946	more than 50,000,000
9	**A Message to Garcia,** Elbert Hubbard, 1899	up to 40,000,000
10 =	**In His Steps: What Would Jesus Do?** Rev. Charles Monroe Sheldon, 1896	more than 30,000,000
=	**Valley of the Dolls,** Jacqueline Susann, 1966	more than 30,000,000

* *Aggregate sales of annual publication*

TOP 10 CHILDREN'S HARDBACK TITLES IN THE US, 2002

	TITLE/AUTHOR	SALES
1	**The Carnivorous Carnival (A Series of Unfortunate Events #9),** Lemony Snicket, Brett Helquist (illustrator)	726,543
2	**The Bad Beginning (A Series of Unfortunate Events #1),** Lemony Snicket, Brett Helquist (illustrator)	681,019
3	**Harry Potter and the Goblet of Fire,** J.K. Rowling	654,000
4	**Goodnight Moon** (board book), Margaret Wise Brown, Clement Hurd (illustrator)	639,694
5	**If You Take a Mouse to School,** Laura Numeroff, Felicia Bond (illustrator)	526,008
6	**The Reptile Room (A Series of Unfortunate Events #2),** Lemony Snicket, Brett Helquist (illustrator)	504,964
7	**Green Eggs and Ham,** Dr. Seuss	497,772
8	**Oh, The Places You'll Go!,** Dr. Seuss	426,424
9	**Five Little Monkeys Jumping on the Bed** (board book), Eileen Christelow	412,000
10	**The Wide Window (A Series of Unfortunate Events #3),** Lemony Snicket, Brett Helquist (illustrator)	409,909

Source: *Publishers Weekly*

Literary Classics

THE 10 LATEST WINNERS OF THE MAN BOOKER PRIZE

YEAR	AUTHOR	BOOK
2002	Yann Martel	Life of Pi
2001	Peter Carey	True History of the Kelly Gang
2000	Margaret Atwood	The Blind Assassin
1999	J.M. Coetzee	Disgrace
1998	Ian McEwan	Amsterdam
1997	Arundhati Roy	The God of Small Things
1996	Graham Swift	Last Orders
1995	Pat Barker	The Ghost Road
1994	James Kelman	How Late It Was, How Late
1993	Roddy Doyle	Paddy Clarke Ha Ha Ha

As well as the two listed above (Martel and Atwood), other Canadian authors who have been shortlisted for the Man Booker Prize are: Rohinton Mistry (three times); Mordecai Richler and Carol Shields (twice); and Robertson Davies and Michael Ondaatje (once).

THE 10 LATEST WINNERS OF THE GOVERNOR GENERAL'S AWARD FOR ENGLISH FICTION

YEAR	AUTHOR	BOOK
2002	Gloria Sawai	A Song for Nettie Johnson
2001	Richard B. Wright	Clara Callan
2000	Michael Ondaatje	Anil's Ghost
1999	Matt Cohen	Elizabeth and After
1998	Diane Schoemperlen	Forms of Devotion
1997	Jane Urquhart	The Underpainter
1996	Guy Vanderhaeghe	The Englishman's Boy
1995	Greg Hollingshead	The Roaring Girl
1994	Rudy Wiebe	A Discovery of Strangers
1993	Carol Shields	The Stone Diaries

Source: *Canada Council for the Arts*

THE 10 LATEST WINNERS OF THE GOVERNOR GENERAL'S AWARD FOR FRENCH FICTION

YEAR	AUTHOR	BOOK
2002	Monique LaRue	La gloire de Cassiodore
2001	Andrée A. Michaud	Le ravissement
2000	Jean Marc Dalpé	Un vent se lève qui éparpille
1999	Lise Tremblay	La danse juive
1998	Christiane Frenette	La terre ferme
1997	Aude	Cette imperceptible mouvement
1996	Marie-Claire Blais	Soifs
1995	Nicole Houde	Les oiseaux de Saint-John Perse
1994	Robert Lalonde	Le petite aigle à tête blanche
1993	Nancy Huston	Cantique des plaines

Life Story
Canadian writer Yann Martel celebrates winning the prestigious Booker Prize for his surrealistic novel *Life of Pi*.

THE 10 LATEST WINNERS OF THE PULITZER PRIZE FOR FICTION

YEAR	AUTHOR/BOOK
2003	**Jeffrey Eugenides,** Middlesex
2002	**Richard Russo,** Empire Falls
2001	**Michael Chabon,** The Amazing Adventures of Kavalier & Clay
2000	**Jhumpa Lhiri,** Interpreter of Maladies
1999	**Michael Cunningham,** The Hours
1998	**Philip Roth,** American Pastoral
1997	**Steven Millhauser,** Martin Dressler: The Tale of an American Dreamer
1996	**Richard Ford,** Independence Day
1995	**Carol Shields,** The Stone Diaries
1994	**E. Annie Proulx,** The Shipping News

The Pulitzer Prize for Fiction has been awarded since 1915, with past recipients including Margaret Mitchell for *Gone with the Wind* (1937), and John Steinbeck for *The Grapes of Wrath* (1940).

TOP 10 MOST ANTHOLOGIZED ENGLISH POEMS

	POET/POEM	APPEARANCES
1	**William Blake (British; 1757–1827),** The Tyger	170
2	**Elizabeth Barrett Browning (British; 1806–61),** How Do I Love Thee? (Sonnet 42)	136
3	**William Blake (British; 1757–1827),** London	122
4	**Philip Sidney (British; 1554–86),** With how sad steps, O Moon, thou climb'st the skies (Sonnet 31)	98
5	**William Wordsworth (British; 1770–1850),** She dwelt among the untrodden ways ("Lucy")	97
6	**Samuel Taylor Coleridge (British; 1772–1834),** Kubla Khan	95
7	**John Keats (British; 1795–1821),** La Belle Dame sans Merci	92
8	**Andrew Marvell (British; 1621–78),** To His Coy Mistress	87
9	**Robert Frost (American; 1874–1963),** Stopping by Woods on a Snowy Evening	85
10	**George Herbert (British; 1593–1633),** Love ("Love bade me welcome but my soul drew back")	84

"Appearances" refers to the number of anthologies in which the poem is found, out of a total of more than 400 listed in *The Columbia Granger's Index to Poetry in Anthologies* (12th edition, Columbia University Press, 2002), which has been published since 1904.

THE 10 LATEST WINNERS OF THE GOVERNOR GENERAL'S AWARD FOR POETRY

YEAR	POET	TITLE
2002	**Roy Miki**	Surrender
2001	**George Elliott Clarke**	Execution Poems
2000	**Don McKay**	Another Gravity
1999	**Jan Zwicky**	Songs for Relinquishing the Earth
1998	**Stephanie Bolster**	White Stone: The Alice Poems
1997	**Dionne Brand**	Land to Light On
1996	**E.D. Blodgett**	Apostrophes: Woman at a Piano
1995	**Anne Szumigalski**	Voice
1994	**Robert Hilles**	Cantos from a Small Room
1993	**Don Coles**	Forest of the Medieval World

Source: *Canada Council for the Arts*

Roy Miki's collection of poems, *Surrender*, describes the history and language relating to the internment of Japanese-Canadians in the 1940s. He is a professor at Simon Fraser University in British Columbia. The Governor General's Literary Awards have been honoring Canadian authors and poets since 1937.

TOP 10 MOST POPULAR POEMS IN THE WORLD

	TITLE	POET
1	**Do Not Go Gentle into that Good Night**	Dylan Thomas
2	**The Tyger**	William Blake
3	**The Raven**	Edgar Allan Poe
4	**Stopping by Woods on a Snowy Evening**	Robert Frost
5	**Jabberwocky**	Lewis Carroll
6	**How Do I Love Thee? Let Me Count the Ways**	Elizabeth Barrett Browning
7	**There's a Certain Slant of Light**	Emily Dickinson
8	**Shall I Compare Thee to a Summer's Day**	William Shakespeare
9	**Because I Could Not Stop for Death**	Emily Dickinson
10	**Mending Wall**	Robert Frost

Source: *The Poetry Poll*

These are the Top 10 poems receiving the most votes in an international poll to discover the most popular poetry in the world. The poll, in which some 50,000 people participated, was conducted on the Internet over the six-year period 1992–98. Dylan Thomas's winning poem was written in 1951 in a verse style known as a villanelle, which has only two rhymes throughout.

TOP 10 BESTSELLING POETRY BOOKS IN THE US*

	AUTHOR (EDITOR)/BOOK/DATE	ESTIMATED SALES
1	**Kahlil Gibran,** The Prophet (1923)	6,000,000
2	**R.J. Cook (ed.),** 101 Famous Poems (1916)	up to 6,000,000
3	**M.E. Speare (ed.),** The Pocket Book of Verse (1940)	2,719,600
4	**Rod McKuen,** Listen to the Warm (1967)	2,025,000
5	**Rod McKuen,** Stanyan Street and Other Sorrows (1967)	1,500,000
6	**Ogden Nash,** Pocket Book of Ogden Nash (1955)	1,121,000
7	**Robert Frost (ed. Louis Untermeyer),** Anthology of Robert Frost's Poems (1949)	1,054,910
8	**Oscar Williams (ed.),** Immortal Poems of the English Language (1952)	1,054,500
9	**Edgar Guest,** A Heap O' Livin' (1916)	1,000,000
10	**Stephen Vincent Bénet,** John Brown's Body (1928)	755,630

* *Based on a survey of bestsellers in the US during the period 1895–1975*

Poetry books rarely sell in large numbers, so these multimillion sellers, as revealed by an extensive survey of sales in the US over an 80-year period, are exceptional.

Newspapers & Magazines

TOP 10 ENGLISH-LANGUAGE DAILY NEWSPAPERS

	NEWSPAPER	COUNTRY	AVERAGE DAILY CIRCULATION
1	**Sun**	UK	3,473,000
2	**Daily Mail**	UK	2,477,000
3	**Mirror**	UK	2,188,000
4	**USA Today**	US	2,150,000
5	**Times of India**	India	1,879,000
6	**Wall Street Journal**	US	1,781,000
7	**New York Times**	US	1,109,000
8	**The Daily Telegraph**	UK	1,021,000
9	**Daily Express**	UK	958,000
10	**Los Angeles Times**	US	944,000

Source: *World Association of Newspapers/ Audit Bureau of Circulations*

The *Sun* was founded on September 15, 1964, as the successor to the *Daily Herald*. By 1978, it had achieved the highest circulation of any English-language newspaper.

TOP 10 COUNTRIES WITH THE HIGHEST NEWSPAPER CIRCULATIONS

	COUNTRY	AVERAGE DAILY CIRCULATION
1	**China**	117,815,000
2	**Japan**	71,694,000
3	**US**	55,578,000
4	**India**	29,482,000
5	**Germany**	23,838,000
6	**UK**	17,899,000
7	**France**	8,597,000
8	**Russia**	7,850,000
9	**Brazil**	7,670,000
10	**Italy**	6,100,000
	Canada	*5,167,000*

Source: *World Association of Newspapers*

TOP 10 MAGAZINES IN CANADA BY REVENUE

	MAGAZINE (ISSUES PER YEAR)	TOTAL REVENUE ($), 2002*
1	**Chatelaine** (12)	42,653,596
2	**Reader's Digest** (12)	40,130,467
3	**Canadian Living** (12)	38,123,089
4	**Maclean's** (52)	37,764,702
5	**Time** (52)	26,110,602
6	**TV Guide** (52)	24,751,406
7	**7 Jours** (52)	15,991,814
8	**Canadian House & Home** (10)	14,369,662
9	**Starweek** (52)	13,582,701
10	**Flare** (12)	13,479,879

* *Estimated revenue from advertising and circulation for 2002, to the nearest dollar value*

Source: *MastheadOnline.com*

THE FIRST NEWSPAPER

FIRST FACT

CANADA'S FIRST NEWSPAPER is also North America's longest-running. The *Halifax Gazette* was first published on March 23, 1752, and continues today as the *Royal Gazette*, one of the Nova Scotia government's official publications. The first daily newspaper in the English language was the *London Gazette*. It was originally published on November 15, 1665, in Oxford as the *Oxford Gazette*. When it relocated to London, it changed its name, and is still published today.

TOP 10 NEWSSTAND MAGAZINES IN THE US

	MAGAZINE (ISSUES PER YEAR)	AVG SINGLE COPY CIRCULATION, 2001
1	**Cosmopolitan** (12)	1,875,735
2	**Family Circle** (17)	1,630,000
3	**National Enquirer** (52)	1,589,916
4	**Woman's World** (52)	1,573,764
5	**Woman's Day** (17)	1,555,059
6	**People** (52)	1,468,413
7	**Star** (52)	1,253,778
8	**TV Guide** (54)	1,163,379
9	**First for Women** (17)	1,145,056
10	**Good Housekeeping** (12)	1,037,995

Source: *Audit Bureau of Circulations/Magazine Publishers of America*

TOP 10 MAGAZINES IN CANADA BY CIRCULATION

	MAGAZINE	PAID CIRCULATION (2002)
1	**Westworld**	1,119,000
2	**Reader's Digest**	1,037,000
3	**Chatelaine**	705,000
4	**Leisureways**	685,000
5	**Starweek**	672,000
6	**Canadian Living**	540,000
7	**Homemaker's**	483,000
8	**Feature**	456,000
9	**TV Guide**	455,000
10	**Maclean's**	451,000

Source: *CARD, 2002*

Westworld is a travel and motoring magazine published by affiliates of the Canadian Automobile Association in British Columbia, Alberta, and Saskatchewan.

Newspapers
Despite the proliferation of new media, from TV to the Internet, traditional papers retain their international appeal as an accessible source of information and entertainment.

TOP 10 NEWSPAPERS IN THE US

	NEWSPAPER (EDITION)	AVERAGE CIRCULATION*
1	**USA Today** (daily)	2,610,225
2	**Wall Street Journal** (daily)	1,800,607
3	**New York Times** (Sunday)	1,671,865
4	**Los Angeles Times** (Sunday)	1,376,932
5	**Washington Post** (Sunday)	1,048,122
6	**Chicago Tribune** (Sunday)	1,012,240
7	**New York Daily News** (Sunday)	801,292
8	**Denver Post/Rocky Mountain News** (Sunday)	789,137
9	**Dallas Morning News** (Sunday)	784,905
10	**Philadelphia Inquirer** (Sunday)	747,969

* *Through September 30, 2002*

Source: *Audit Bureau of Circulations*

TOP 10 DAILY NEWSPAPERS IN CANADA

	NEWSPAPER	AVERAGE WEEKLY CIRCULATION*
1	**Toronto Star**	2,891,789
2	**Globe and Mail**	1,748,639
3	**Journal de Montréal**	1,637,790
4	**Toronto Sun**	1,413,958
5	**National Post**	1,257,264
6	**La Presse,** Montreal	1,254,736
7	**Vancouver Sun**	1,024,775
8	**Ottawa Citizen**	872,644
9	**Gazette,** Montreal	861,947
10	**Province,** Vancouver	843,037

* *Based on six months ended March 31, 2002*

Source: *Canadian Newspaper Association*

Art on Show

TOP 10 BEST-ATTENDED EXHIBITIONS AT THE METROPOLITAN MUSEUM OF ART, NEW YORK

	EXHIBITION	YEARS	ATTENDANCE
1	The Treasures of Tutankhamun	1978–79	1,226,467
2	Mona Lisa	1963	1,007,521
3	The Vatican Collection: The Papacy and Art	1983	896,743
4	Glory of Russian Costume	1976–77	835,862
5	Origins of Impressionism	1994–95	794,108
6	Romantic and Glamorous Hollywood	1974–75	788,665
7	The Horses of San Marco	1980	742,221
8	Man and the Horse	1984–85	726,523
9	Masterpiece of Fifty Centuries	1979–81	690,471
10	Seurat	1991–92	642,408

Source: *Metropolitan Museum of Art*

TOP 10 BEST-ATTENDED EXHIBITIONS AT THE NATIONAL GALLERY, WASHINGTON, DC

	EXHIBITION	YEARS	ATTENDANCE
1	Rodin Rediscovered	1981–82	1,053,223
2	Treasure Houses of Britain	1985–86	990,474
3	The Treasures of Tutankhamun	1976–77	835,924
4	Archaeological Finds of the People's Republic of China	1974–75	684,238
5	Ansel Adams: Classic Images	1985–86	651,652
6	The Splendor of Dresden	1978	620,089
7	The Art of Paul Gauguin	1988	596,058
8	Circa 1492: Art in the Age of Exploration	1991–92	568,192
9	Andrew Wyeth: The Helga Pictures	1987	558,433
10	Post Impressionism: Cross Currents in European & American Painting	1980	557,533

Source: *National Gallery*

Although the Rodin Rediscovered show holds the National Gallery's record, the exhibition was open for 307 days, while the Treasure Houses of Britain came a close second despite being open for just 153 days.

Behind the Mask
Held in the 1970s, the Treasures of Tutankhamun exhibition retains its record as the biggest crowd-pulling art show of all time in both New York and London.

TOP 10 ART EXHIBITIONS WITH THE BEST DAILY ATTENDANCE, 2002

	EXHIBITION/VENUE/CITY	DATES	ATTENDANCE TOTAL	DAILY
1	**Van Gogh and Gauguin,** Van Gogh Museum, Amsterdam	Feb 9–June 2	739,117	6,719
2	**Van Gogh and Gauguin,** Art Institute of Chicago, Chicago	Sept 22, 2001–Jan 13, 2002	690,951	6,281
3	**Masterpieces from the Prado Museum,** National Museum of Western Art, Tokyo	Mar 5–June 16	516,711	5,616
4	**Matisse/Picasso,** Tate Modern, London	May 11–Aug 18	467,166	4,671
5	**Surrealist Revolution,** Centre Georges Pompidou, Paris	Mar 6–June 24	450,000*	4,500
6	**The Artists of the Pharaohs,** Musée du Louvre, Paris	Apr 19–Aug 5	450,000*	4,285
7	**The Secret Gallery and the Nude,** Museo del Prado, Madrid	June 28–Sept 29	289,239	4,074
8	**Andy Warhol,** Tate Modern, London	Feb 7–Apr 1	218,801	4,052
9	**Treasures of Ancient Egypt,** National Gallery of Art, Washingon, D.C.	June 30–Oct 14	430,772	4,026
10	**Gerhard Richter,** Museum of Modern Art, New York	Feb 14–May 21	333,695	4,020

* *Approximate totals provided by museums*

Source: The Art Newspaper

TOP 10 BEST-ATTENDED EXHIBITIONS AT THE MONTREAL MUSEUM OF FINE ARTS

	EXHIBITION	YEAR	ATTENDANCE
1	**Pablo Picasso: Meeting in Montreal**	1985	517,000
2	**Leonardo da Vinci: Engineer and Architect**	1987	436,419
3	**From Renoir to Picasso**	2000	327,644
4	**Monet at Giverny**	1999	256,738
5	**Marc Chagall**	1989	245,883
6	**The 1920s: Age of the Metropolis**	1991	245,286
7	**The Passionate Eye: Impressionist and Other Master Paintings from the Emil G. Bührle Collection**	1990	201,205
8	**Picasso érotique**	2001	194,740
9	**Salvador Dali**	1990	192,963
10	**Moving Beauty**	1995	184,473

Source: *Montreal Museum of Fine Arts*

Art at Auction

TOP 10 MOST EXPENSIVE PAINTINGS

	PAINTING/ARTIST/SALE	PRICE (US$)
1	**Portrait of Dr. Gachet,** Vincent van Gogh (Dutch; 1853–90), Christie's, New York, May 15, 1990. Both this painting and the one in No. 2 position were bought by Ryoei Saito, chairman of the Japanese company Daishowa Paper Manufacturing.	75,000,000
2	**Au Moulin de la Galette,** Pierre-Auguste Renoir (French; 1841–1919), Sotheby's, New York, May 17, 1990	71,000,000
3	**Massacre of the Innocents,** Sir Peter Paul Rubens (Flemish; 1577–1640), Sotheby's, London, July 10, 2002	68,400,000 (£45,000,000)
4	**Portrait de l'Artiste Sans Barbe,** Vincent van Gogh, Christie's, New York, November 19, 1998	65,000,000
5	**Rideau, Cruchon et Compôtier,** Paul Cézanne (French; 1839–1906), Sotheby's, New York, May 10, 1999	55,000,000
6	**Les Noces de Pierrette 1905,** Pablo Picasso (Spanish, 1881–1973), Binoche et Godeau, Paris, November 30, 1989. This painting was sold by Swedish financier Fredrik Roos and bought by Tomonori Tsurumaki, a Japanese property developer, bidding from Tokyo by telephone.	51,671,920 (F.Fr 315,000,000)
7	**Femme aux Bras Croises,** Pablo Picasso, Christie's Rockefeller, New York, November 8, 2000	50,000,000
8	**Irises,** Vincent van Gogh, Sotheby's, New York, November 11, 1987. After much speculation, the painting's mystery purchaser was eventually confirmed as Australian businessman Alan Bond. However, because he was unable to pay for it in full, its former status as the world's most expensive work of art has been disputed. Painted in 1938, the work was part of the collection of cellist and conductor Daniel Saidenberg and his wife, Eleanore.	49,000,000
9	**Femme Assise Dans un Jardin,** Pablo Picasso, Sotheby's, New York, November 10, 1999	45,000,000
10	**Le Rêve,** Pablo Picasso, Christie's, New York, November 10, 1997. Victor and Sally Ganz had paid $7,000 for this painting in 1941.	44,000,000

TOP 10 MOST EXPENSIVE PIECES OF SCULPTURE

	SCULPTURE/ARTIST/SALE	PRICE (US$)
1	**Danaïde,** Constantin Brancusi (Romanian; 1876–1956), Christie's Rockefeller, New York, May 7, 2002	16,500,000
2	**Grande Femme Debout I,** Alberto Giacometti (Swiss; 1901–66), Christie's Rockefeller, New York, November 8, 2000	13,000,000
3	**La Serpentine Femme à la Stele—l'Araignée,** Henri Matisse (French; 1869–1954), Sotheby's, New York, May 10, 2000	12,750,000
4	**Grande Tête de Diego,** Alberto Giacometti, Sotheby's, New York, May 8, 2002	12,500,000
5	**La Forêt,** Alberto Giacometti, Christie's Rockefeller, New York, May 7, 2002	12,000,000
6	**Figure Decorative,** Henri Matisse, Sotheby's, New York, May 10, 2001	11,500,000
7	**Petite Danseuse de Quatorze Ans,** Edgar Degas (French; 1834–1917), Sotheby's, New York, November 11, 1999	11,250,000
8	**Petite Danseuse de Quatorze Ans,** Edgar Degas, Sotheby's, New York, November 12, 1996	10,800,000
9	**Petite Danseuse de Quatorze Ans,** Edgar Degas , Sotheby's, London, June 27, 2000	10,570,000 (£7,000,000)
10	**The Dancing Faun,** Adriaen de Vries (Dutch; c.1550–1626), Sotheby's, London, December 7, 1989	9,796,000 (£6,200,000)

TOP 10 MOST EXPENSIVE WORKS OF ART BY LIVING ARTISTS

	WORK/ARTIST/SALE	PRICE (US$)
1	**False Start,** Jasper Johns (American; 1930–), Sotheby's, New York, November 10, 1988	15,500,000
2	**Two Flags,** Jasper Johns, Sotheby's, New York, November 8, 1989	11,000,000
3 =	**Henry Moore Bound to Fail, Back View,** Bruce Nauman (American; 1941–), Christie's Rockefeller, New York, May 17, 2001	9,000,000
=	**0 Through 9,** Jasper Johns, Christie's Rockefeller, New York, November 13, 2002	9,000,000
5	**Corpse and Mirror,** Jasper Johns, Christie's, New York, November 10, 1997	7,600,000
6	**White Numbers,** Jasper Johns, Christie's, New York, November 10, 1997	7,200,000
7	**Two Flags,** Jasper Johns, Christie's Rockefeller, New York, May 13, 1999	6,500,000
8	**White Flag,** Jasper Johns, Christie's, New York, November 9, 1988	6,400,000
9	**Large Interior, WII,** Lucian Freud (British/German; 1922–), Sotheby's, New York, May 14, 1998	5,300,000
10 =	**Michael Jackson and Bubbles,** Jeff Koons (American; 1955–), Sotheby's, New York, May 15, 2001	5,100,000
=	**Untitled,** Cy Twombly (American; 1929–), Sotheby's, New York, November 12, 2002	5,100,000

In 2002, a painting by Paul Kane, *Scene in the Northwest—Portrait*, sold for $4,600,000, the largest amount for any Canadian work of art.

TOP 10 MOST EXPENSIVE GOUACHE/PASTEL WORKS

	WORK/ARTIST/SALE	PRICE (US$)
1	**Acrobate et Jeune Arlequin,** Pablo Picasso (Spanish; 1881–1973), Christie's, London, November 28, 1988	35,530,000 (£19,000,000)
2	**Danseuses au Repos,** Edgar Degas (French; 1834–1917), Sotheby's, London, June 28, 1999	25,280,000 (£16,000,000)
3	**Au Musée du Louvre (Miss Cassatt) ,** Edgar Degas, Sotheby's, New York, May 8, 2002	15,000,000
4	**Famille de l'Arlequin,** Pablo Picasso, Christie's, New York, November 14, 1989	14,000,000
5	**La Moisson en Provence,** Vincent van Gogh (Dutch; 1853–90), Sotheby's, London, June 24, 1997	13,280,001 (£8,000,000)

	WORK/ARTIST/SALE	PRICE ($)
6	**Danseuse Assise aux Bas Roses,** Henri de Toulouse-Lautrec (French; 1864–1901), Christie's, New York, May 12, 1997	13,200,000
7	**La Vis,** Henri Matisse (French; 1869–1954), Sotheby's, New York, November 3, 1993	12,500,000
8	**Portrait de Mme. K,** Joan Miró (Spanish; 1893–1983), Christie's Rockefeller, New York, November 6, 2001	11,500,000
9	**Garçon à la Collerette,** Pablo Picasso, Christie's, New York, November 7, 1995	11,000,000
10	**Danseuses,** Edgar Degas, Sotheby's, New York, May 13, 1997	10,000,000

While the world's most costly paintings are oils, a number of drawings, sketches, and studies in gouache (a type of watercolor) and pastel (a kind of crayon) have also attained substantial sums at auction. Both media were widely employed by the Impressionists and ideally suited to their fleeting style.

▲ Prima Ballerina
At a 1999 auction, the price paid for Degas's pastel and gouache study of dancers at rest, owned by the same family for over 100 years, broke the world record for a drawing.

TOP 10 MOST EXPENSIVE MUSICAL INSTRUMENTS

	INSTRUMENT**/SALE	PRICE (US$)
1	**John Lennon's Steinway Model Z upright piano,** teak veneered, complete with cigarette burns, on which Lennon played at Woodstock in 1969. Fleetwood-Owen online auction, Hard Rock Café, London and New York, October 17, 2000.	2,150,000 (£1,450,000)
2	**"Kreutzer" violin by Antonio Stradivari,** Christies, London, April 1, 1998	1,582,847 (£946,000)
3	**"Cholmondeley" violincello by Antonio Stradivari,** Sotheby's, London, June 22, 1998	1,141,122 (£682,000)
4	**"Brownie," one of Eric Clapton's favorite electric guitars,** Clapton used the 1956 sunburst Fender Stratocaster to record the whole *Layla* album. It sold to an anonymous telephone bidder for double the expected price, making it the most expensive guitar ever auctioned. Christie's, New York, June 24, 1999.	497,500
5	**Steinway grand piano, decorated by Lawrence Alma-Tadema and Edward Poynter for Henry Marquand, 1884–87,** Sotheby Parke Bernet, New York, March 26, 1980	390,000
6	**Single-manual harpsichord by Joseph Joannes Couchet, Antwerp, 1679,** Sotheby's, London, November 21, 2001	378,004 (£267,500)
7	**Acoustic guitar owned by David Bowie, Paul McCartney, and George Michael,** Christie's, London, May 18, 1994	339,856 (£220,000)
8	**Double bass by Domenico Montagnana,** Sotheby's, London, March 16, 1999	250,339 (£155,500)
9	**Verne Powell's platinum flute,** Christie's, New York, October 18, 1986	187,000
10	**Viola by Giovanni Paolo Maggini,** Christie's, London, November 20, 1984	161,121 (£129,000)

◀Classic Clapton
Eric Clapton and his record-breaking "Brownie" Fender Stratocaster guitar, sold in aid of a drug rehabilitation charity.

TOP 10 MOST EXPENSIVE ITEMS OF POP MEMORABILIA*

	ITEM/SALE	PRICE (US$)#
1	**John Lennon's 1965 Rolls-Royce Phantom V touring limousine,** Sotheby's, New York, June 29, 1985. Finished in psychedelic paintwork.	2,299,000
2	**Bernie Taupin's handwritten lyrics for the rewritten *Candle in the Wind*,** Christie's, Los Angeles, February 11, 1998. Played by Elton John at the funeral of Diana, Princess of Wales; sold to Diana's brother, Earl Spencer. The sale, part of a charity auction, established a world record for pop lyrics.	400,000
3	**Paul McCartney's handwritten lyrics for *Getting Better*,** 1967, Sotheby's, London, September 14, 1995	249,380 (£161,000)
4	**John Lennon's 1970 Mercedes-Benz 600 Pullman four-door limousine,** Christie's, London, April 27, 1989	232,169 (£137,500)
5	**John Lennon's 1965 Ferrari 330 GT 2+2 two-door coupe, right-hand drive,** Fleetwood-Owen online auction, Hard Rock Café, London and New York, October 17, 2000	188,304
6	**Mal Evan's notebook, compiled 1967–68,** which includes a draft by Paul McCartney of the lyrics for *Hey Jude*, Sotheby's, London, September 15, 1998	187,110 (£111,500)
7	**Elvis Presley's 1963 Rolls–Royce Phantom V touring limousine,** Sotheby's, London, August 28, 1986	163,240 (£110,000)
8	**Page of lyrics in John Lennon's hand for *I Am The Walrus*, 1967, in black ink,** Christie's, London, September 30, 1999	129,500 (£78,500)
9	**Reel-to-reel tape recording of 16-year-old John Lennon singing with the Quarrymen at a church fair in Liverpool on July 6, 1957,** Sotheby's, London, September 15, 1994	122,774 (£78,500)
10	**Recording of John Lennon with his stepdaughter Kyoko Cox,** Christie's, London, April 30, 2002	109,747 (£75,200)

*** Most expensive example only given for each category of instrument*

** Excluding musical instruments*

 # Including 10 percent buyer's premium, where appropriate

Pioneered particularly by Sotheby's in London, pop memorabilia has become big business – especially if it involves personal association with mega-stars such as the Beatles. Even such items as the Liverpool birthplace of Ringo Starr, the barber's shop mentioned in the Beatles song *Penny Lane*, and a door from John Lennon's house have been offered for sale as artefacts from the archaeology of the Beatles.

MOST EXPENSIVE ITEMS OF FILM MEMORABILIA

	ITEM/SALE	PRICE (US$)
1	**David O. Selznick's Oscar for *Gone With the Wind* (1939),** Sotheby's, New York, June 12, 1999 (bought by Michael Jackson)	1,542,500
2	**Judy Garland's ruby slippers from *The Wizard of Oz* (1939),** Christie's, New York, May 26, 2000	666,000
3	**Clark Gable's Oscar for *It Happened One Night*,** Christie's, Los Angeles, December 15, 1996	607,500
4	**Bette Davis's Oscar for *Jezebel*,** Christie's, New York, July 19, 2001	578,000
5	**Vivien Leigh's Oscar for *Gone with the Wind*,** Sotheby's, New York, December 15, 1993	562,500
6	**Statue of the Maltese Falcon from *The Maltese Falcon* (1941),** Christie's Rockefeller, New York, December 5, 1994	398,500
7	**James Bond's Aston Martin DB5 from *Goldfinger*,** Sotheby's, New York, June 28, 1986	275,000
8	= **Clark Gable's personal script for *Gone with the Wind*,** Christie's, Los Angeles, December 15, 1996	244,500
	= **Herman J. Mankiewicz's Oscar for co-writing *Citizen Kane* (1941),** Christie's, New York, November 18, 1999	244,500
10	**"Rosebud" sled from *Citizen Kane*,** Christie's, Los Angeles, December 15, 1996	233,500

MOST VALUABLE AMERICAN COMICS

	COMIC	VALUE (US$)*
1	***Action Comics* No. 1** Published in June 1938, the first issue of *Action Comics* marked the original appearance of Superman.	350,000
2	***Detective Comics* No. 27** Issued in May 1939, it is prized as the first comic book to feature Batman.	300,000
3	***Marvel Comics* No. 1** The Human Torch and other heroes were first introduced in the issue dated October 1939.	250,000
4	***Superman* No. 1** The first comic book devoted to Superman, reprinting the original *Action Comics* story, was published in Summer 1939.	210,000
5	***All American Comics* No. 16** The Green Lantern made his debut in the issue dated July 1940.	115,000
6	= ***Batman* No. 1** Published in Spring 1940, this was the first comic book devoted to Batman.	100,000
	= ***Captain America Comics* No. 1** Published in March 1941, this was the original comic book in which Captain America appeared.	100,000
8	= ***Flash Comics* No. 1** Dated January 1940, and featuring The Flash, it is rare because it was produced in small numbers for promotional purposes, and was unique as issue No. 2 was retitled *Whiz Comics*.	85,000
	= ***Whiz Comics* No. 1** Published in February 1940—and confusingly numbered "2"— it was the first comic book to feature Captain Marvel.	77,000
10	***More Fun Comics* No. 52** The Spectre made his debut in the issue dated February 1940.	72,000

Source: The Overstreet Comic Book Price Guide, *No. 32, 2002. ©2002 Gemstone Publishing, Inc. All rights reserved.*

Glittering Prize

First presented in 1929, the gold-plated Oscar statuette is coveted not only by its recipients but also by collectors of film memorabilia.
©A.M.P.A.S.®

MUSIC & MUSICIANS

Songs & Songwriters

TOP 10 LATEST JUNO SONGWRITERS OF THE YEAR

YEAR	SONGWRITER(S)
2003	Chad Kroeger and Nickelback
2002	Jann Arden
2001	Nelly Furtado
2000	Shania Twain and Robert John "Mutt" Lange
1999	Bryan Adams, Phil Thornally, and Eliot Kennedy
1998	Sarah McLachlan and Pierre Marchand
1997	Alanis Morissette
1996	Alanis Morissette
1995	Jann Arden
1994	Leonard Cohen

Source: *Canadian Academy of Recording Arts and Sciences*

THE 10 LATEST GRAMMY SONGS OF THE YEAR

YEAR	SONG	SONGWRITER(S)
2002	Don't Know Why	Jesse Harris
2001	Fallin'	Alicia Keys
2000	Beautiful Day	U2
1999	Smooth	Itaal Shur and Rob Thomas
1998	My Heart Will Go On	James Horner and Will Jennings
1997	Sunny Came Home	Shawn Colvin
1996	Change the World	Gordon Kennedy, Wayne Kirkpatrick, and Tommy Sims
1995	Kiss From a Rose	Seal
1994	Streets of Philadelphia	Bruce Springsteen
1993	A Whole New World	Alan Menken and Tim Rice

The National Academy of Recording Arts & Sciences was founded in 1957. Awards have been presented annually since 1959, for recordings of the preceding year. In the category "Song of the Year," the award is made to the songwriter rather than the performer. The first winner was *Nel Blu Dipinto di Blu (Volare)*, written by Domenico Modugno. Subsequent winners represent many songs that are now regarded as classics, as well as some of the biggest-selling singles of all time, among them *Moon River* by Henry Mancini and Johnny Mercer, from the film *Breakfast at Tiffany's* (1961), and *We Are the World*, by Michael Jackson and Lionel Richie (1985).

▼ Wonder Land
Stevie Wonder is the most recent recipient of the Songwriters Hall of Fame Sammy Cahn Lifetime Achievement Award, created to honor the legendary songwriter (1913–93).

THE 10 LATEST RECIPIENTS OF THE SONGWRITERS HALL OF FAME SAMMY CAHN LIFETIME ACHIEVEMENT AWARD

YEAR	RECIPIENT(S)
2002	Stevie Wonder
2001	Gloria and Emilio Estefan
2000	Neil Diamond
1999	Kenny Rogers
1998	Berry Gordy
1997	Vic Damone
1996	Frankie Laine
1995	Steve Lawrence and Eydie Gorme
1994	Lena Horne
1993	Ray Charles

Source: *National Academy of Popular Music*

The National Academy of Popular Music's most prestigious award is named for Sammy Cahn, who served for 20 years as the Academy's president.

TOP 10 ROCK SONGS OF ALL TIME*

	SONG	ARTIST OR GROUP
1	**(I Can't Get No) Satisfaction**	Rolling Stones
2	**Respect**	Aretha Franklin
3	**Stairway to Heaven**	Led Zeppelin
4	**Like a Rolling Stone**	Bob Dylan
5	**Born to Run**	Bruce Springsteen
6	**Hotel California**	Eagles
7	**Light My Fire**	Doors
8	**Good Vibrations**	Beach Boys
9	**Hey Jude**	Beatles
10	**Imagine**	John Lennon

* *Determined by a panel of 700 voters assembled by the music network VH1*

This Top 10 is extracted from an all-time top 100 list dominated by songs dating from the 1960s. Within it are no fewer than nine Beatles songs (in addition to John Lennon's *Imagine*), as well as five by the Rolling Stones, four by Elvis Presley, and three each by the Beach Boys, Bob Dylan, Marvin Gaye, and Led Zeppelin. Surprisingly, a number of notable artists are represented by a single song only, including Chuck Berry's *Johnny B Goode*, David Bowie's *Space Oddity*, The Doors' *Light My Fire*, The Eagles' *Hotel California*, Jimi Hendrix's *Purple Haze*, Little Richard's *Good Golly, Miss Molly*, Roy Orbison's *Oh, Pretty Woman*, and Stevie Wonder's *Superstition*.

TOP 10 HITS IN CANADA COMPOSED BY DIANE WARREN

	TITLE/YEAR	CHARTING ARTIST OR GROUP
1	**Nothing's Gonna Stop Us Now** (1987)	Starship
2	**Blame It on the Rain** (1990)	Milli Vanilli
3	**Because You Loved Me** (1996)	Celine Dion
4	**Unbreak My Heart** (1997)	Toni Braxton
5	**How Do I Live** (1997)	Leann Rimes
6	**Love Will Lead You Back** (1990)	Taylor Dayne
7	**Rhythm of the Night** (1985)	DeBarge
8	**I'll Be Your Shelter** (1990)	Taylor Dayne
9	**If You Asked Me To** (1992)	Celine Dion
10	**How Can We Be Lovers** (1990)	Michael Bolton

Source: *Music Data Research*

One of America's most prolific songwriters, Diane Warren has been writing hit records for more than 20 years. Most recently she wrote Leann Rimes' top 30 hit *Can't Fight the Moonlight* (from the film *Coyote Ugly*) and Faith Hill's *There You'll Be* (from the film *Pearl Harbor*).

TOP 10 HITS IN CANADA COMPOSED BY SARAH MCLACHLAN

	TITLE/YEAR	CHARTING ARTIST OR GROUP
1	**Building a Mystery** (1997)	Sarah McLachlan
2	**Adia** (1998)	Sarah McLachlan
3	**Sweet Surrender** (1998)	Sarah McLachlan
4	**Angel** (1999)	Sarah McLachlan
5	**I Will Remember You** (Live) (1999)	Sarah McLachlan
6	**Good Enough** (1994)	Sarah McLachlan
7	**I Will Remember You** (1995)	Sarah McLachlan
8	**Silence** (1999)	Delirium
9	**Possession** (1993)	Sarah McLachlan
10	**Into the Fire** (1991)	Sarah McLachlan

Source: *Music Data Research*

Even though Sarah McLachlan has been recording since 1988, the Nova Scotia–born singer/songwriter emerged as a driving force in popular music only in the late 1990s. Each of her top five hits charted in the latter part of the decade; the top three are from her 1997 No. 1 album, *Surfacing*.

Record Firsts

THE 10 FIRST MILLION-SELLING ALBUMS IN CANADA

	TITLE/ARTIST	DATE
1	**Rumours,** Fleetwood Mac	May 1978
2	**Saturday Night Fever,** Soundtrack	June 1978
3	**Grease,** Soundtrack	Nov 1978
4	**Bat Out of Hell,** Meat Loaf	Mar 1979
5	**Breakfast in America,** Supertramp	Oct 1979
6	**Crime of the Century,** Supertramp	Nov 1979
7	**Dark Side of the Moon,** Pink Floyd	Aug 1980
8	**Kenny Rogers' Greatest Hits,** Kenny Rogers	May 1981
9	**Led Zeppelin IV,** Led Zeppelin	Dec 1982
10	**Thriller,** Michael Jackson	Nov 1983

Source: *Canadian Recording Industry Association*

THE 10 FIRST GRAMMY RECORDS-OF-THE-YEAR

YEAR	RECORD/ARTIST
1958	**Nel Blu Dipinto di Blu (Volare),** Domenico Modugno
1959	**Mack the Knife,** Bobby Darin
1960	**Theme from "A Summer Place,"** Percy Faith
1961	**Moon River,** Henry Mancini
1962	**I Left My Heart In San Francisco,** Tony Bennett
1963	**The Days of Wine and Roses,** Henry Mancini
1964	**The Girl from Ipanema,** Stan Getz & Astrud Gilberto
1965	**A Taste of Honey,** Herb Alpert & the Tijuana Brass
1966	**Strangers In the Night,** Frank Sinatra
1967	**Up Up and Away,** 5th Dimension

◀ **The King Rules**
Elvis Presley's *Heartbreak Hotel*, his first single to sell a million copies, was the biggest-selling single of 1956. In that year, he sold a record total of 10 million discs.

THE 10 FIRST PLATINUM SINGLES IN CANADA

	SINGLE/ARTIST	YEAR
1	**That's the Way I Like It,** K.C. & the Sunshine Band	Feb 1976
2	**Feelings,** Morris Albert	June 1976
3	= **I Love to Love,** Tina Charles	Aug 1976
	= **Love Hurts,** Nazareth	Aug 1976
5	**A Fifth of Beethoven,** Walter Murphy & the Big Apple Band	Oct 1976
6	= **Disco Duck,** Rick Dees & His Cast of Idiots	Dec 1976
	= **Don't Go Breaking My Heart,** Elton John & Kiki Dee	Dec 1976
8	**I Feel Love,** Donna Summer	Nov 1977
9	**You Light Up My Life,** Debby Boone	Dec 1977
10	**The Unicorn,** Irish Rovers	Feb 1978

Source: *Canadian Recording Industry Association*

Until 2003, singles achieving sales in excess of 100,000 in Canada were certified platinum. In 2003, due to dwindling singles sales, the minimum requirement was reduced to 10,000.

THE 10 FIRST FEMALE SINGERS TO HAVE A NO. 1 CANADIAN HIT

	ARTIST/TITLE	DATE AT NO. 1
1	**Maxine Nightingale,** Right Back Where We Started From	Apr 24, 1976
2	**Diana Ross,** Love Hangover	July 3, 1976
3	**Barbra Streisand,** Love Theme from "A Star is Born" (Evergreen)	Mar 19, 1977
4	**Debby Boone,** You Light Up My Life	Nov 16, 1977
5	**Bonnie Tyler,** It's a Heartache	June 14, 1978
6	**Donna Summer,** MacArthur Park	Nov 29, 1978
7	**Donna Summer,** Hot Stuff	June 27, 1979
8	**Anita Ward,** Ring My Bell	July 25, 1979
9	**Barbra Streisand,** Woman in Love	Nov 15, 1980
10	**Sheena Easton,** Morning Train (9 to 5)	Apr 25, 1981

Source: *Canadian Recording Industry Association*

THE 10 FIRST MILLION-SELLING ROCK 'N' ROLL SINGLES IN THE US

	TITLE/ARTIST	YEAR
1	**Rock Around the Clock,** Bill Haley & His Comets	1954
2	**Shake Rattle and Roll,** Bill Haley & His Comets	1954
3	**Maybellene,** Chuck Berry	1955
4	**Ain't That a Shame,** Fats Domino	1955
5	**Ain't That a Shame,** Pat Boone	1955
6	**Seventeen,** Boyd Bennett	1955
7	**I Hear You Knocking,** Gale Storm	1955
8	**See You Later Alligator,** Bill Haley & His Comets	1955
9	**Tutti Frutti,** Little Richard	1955
10	**Heartbreak Hotel,** Elvis Presley	1956

Widely regarded as the first rock 'n' roll hit, *Rock Around the Clock* saw the dawn of a new musical era, a hybrid of R & B and country, which would explode as its own genre in the mid-1950s.

THE 10 ALBUMS IN THE FIRST US ALBUMS TOP 10

	TITLE	ARTIST
1	**Al Jolson (Volume III)**	Al Jolson
2	**A Presentation of Progressive Jazz**	Stan Kenton
3	**Emperor's Waltz**	Bing Crosby
4	**Songs of Our Times**	Carmen Cavallaro
5	**Wizard at the Organ**	Ken Griffin
6	**Glenn Miller Masterpieces**	Glenn Miller
7	**Busy Fingers**	Three Suns
8	**Songs of Our Times**	B. Grant Orchestra
9	**Glenn Miller**	Glenn Miller
10	**Theme Songs**	Various artists

Source: Billboard

This first list of album best-sellers appeared in *Billboard* on March 24, 1945, but was restricted to a Top 5, with The King Cole Trio at No. 1. This, the first ever album Top 10, was published by *Billboard* on September 3, 1948.

FIRST MUSIC CHANNEL

FIRST FACT

AUGUST 31, 1984, marked a milestone in Canadian music history. MuchMusic, the Nation's Music Channel, debuted, and ushered Canadians into the music-video age. The first 10 videos aired reflected the music of the day. However, there was one exception: the very first clip shown, Eubi Blake and Noble Sissle's *Snappy Songs*, written in 1922, which was the first song ever to be produced as a video.The other nine music videos featured were Rush's *The Enemy Within*, Prince & the Revolution's *Let's Go Crazy*, Frankie Goes to Hollywood's *Relax*, Culture Club's *Love Is Love* and *Karma Chameleon* (Live), Billy Idol's *Flesh for Fantasy*, Bruce Springsteen's *Dancing in the Dark*, Peter Wolf's *Lights Out*, and the Fixx's *Are We Ourselves*.

Stars of the Decades

TOP 10 SOLO SINGERS OF THE 1970s IN CANADA

	SINGER	HITS
1	Paul McCartney	12
2 =	Elton John	11
=	Barry Manilow	11
4	Donna Summer	9
5	Rod Stewart	8
6 =	Burton Cummings	7
=	Linda Ronstadt	7
8 =	Billy Joel	6
=	Olivia Newton-John	6
10	Andy Gibb	5

Source: *Music Data Research*

As well as penning chart hits in the 1970s, Paul McCartney was further acknowledged for his song-writing talents in 1973, when he was nominated for an Academy Award for "Best Song" for the theme to the James Bond film *Live and Let Die.*

Material Girl
Since her first chart hit, *Holiday*, in 1984 Madonna has achieved more chart hits than any other female artist.

TOP 10 SOLO SINGERS OF THE 1980s IN CANADA

	SINGER	HITS
1	Elton John	20
2 =	Michael Jackson	18
=	Madonna	18
4 =	John Cougar Mellencamp*	16
=	Prince	16
6	Billy Joel	15
7	Bruce Springsteen	14
8	Lionel Richie	13
9	Phil Collins	12
10	Cyndi Lauper	11

* *This artist recorded under the name John Cougar until 1983, at which time he affixed his real surname, Mellencamp, onto his albums for the rest of the decade*

Source: *Music Data Research*

TOP 10 GROUPS OF THE 1970s IN CANADA

	GROUP	HITS
1	Bee Gees	13
2 =	ABBA	11
=	Electric Light Orchestra	11
4	Trooper	9
5	Bay City Rollers	8
6 =	Captain & Tennille	7
=	Commodores	7
=	Eagles	7
=	Earth, Wind & Fire	7
=	Fleetwood Mac	7

Source: *Music Data Research*

Not surprisingly, the Bee Gees assume the top spot among the most popular groups of the 1970s. In the late 1970s, the brothers Gibb scored No. 1 hits with *Night Fever* and *Stayin' Alive*, both from the "Saturday Night Fever" soundtrack.

TOP 10 GROUPS OF THE 1980s IN CANADA

	GROUP	HITS
1 =	Duran Duran	13
=	Eurythmics	13
=	Daryl Hall & John Oates	13
4	Huey Lewis & the News	12
5	Genesis	11
6 =	Culture Club	10
=	The Police	10
8 =	Chicago	9
=	Loverboy	9
=	Pointer Sisters	9

Source: *Music Data Research*

TOP 10 SOLO SINGERS OF THE 1990s IN CANADA

	SINGER	HITS
1	Madonna	25
2	Janet Jackson	23
3 =	Mariah Carey	22
=	Celine Dion	22
5	Bryan Adams	20
6	Alanis Morrissette	17
7 =	Whitney Houston	16
=	Prince	16
9	Elton John	15
10	Michael Bolton	14

Source: *Music Data Research*

Madonna has the distinction of being the top solo act of both the 1980s and 1990s. Since achieving her first Top 40 hit in 1984 with *Holiday*, she has consistently appeared in the charts, and has reached No. 1 with such hits as *Like a Virgin*, *Like a Prayer*, and *Deeper and Deeper*.

ROCK 'N' ROLL

FIRST FACT

THE ROCK 'N' ROLL ERA is generally dated from the release of Bill Haley & His Comets' single *(We're Gonna) Rock Around the Clock*. Recorded in New York's Pythian Temple Studios on April 12, 1954, it was first released later that year, but became a smash hit only after it appeared in the teen film "Blackboard Jungle," which opened in the US on March 25, 1955. On July 9, it became the first rock record to top the US chart, where it stayed for eight weeks, and on October 14, it became the first rock record ever to top the UK chart.

All the Right Moves
Led by (John) Michael Stipe, American band R.E.M., named after the rapid eye movement dream phase of the sleep cycle, was among the most successful of the 1990s.

TOP 10 GROUPS OF THE 1990s IN CANADA

	GROUP	HITS
1	Boyz II Men	14
2	Aerosmith	13
3	Backstreet Boys	11
4	= Bon Jovi	10
	= R.E.M.	10
	= Roxette	10
7	= Def Leppard	9
	= Metallica	9
	= New Kids on the Block	9
	= TLC	9

Source: *Music Data Research*

Despite emerging in the last few years of the 1990s, the Backstreet Boys were able to capture the No. 2 spot among the top groups of the decade. The Boys scored several No. 1 singles, including *I Want It That Way* in 1999.

TOP 10 SINGLES OF ALL TIME

	TITLE/ARTIST OR GROUP/YEAR	SALES EXCEED
1	**Candle in the Wind 1997/Something About the Way You Look Tonight,** Elton John, 1997	37,000,000
2	**White Christmas,** Bing Crosby, 1942	30,000,000
3	**Rock Around the Clock,** Bill Haley and His Comets, 1954	17,000,000
4	**I Want to Hold Your Hand,** The Beatles, 1963	12,000,000
5	=**Hey Jude,** The Beatles, 1968	10,000,000
	=**I Will Always Love You,** Whitney Houston, 1992	10,000,000
	=**It's Now or Never,** Elvis Presley, 1960	10,000,000
8	=**Diana**, Paul Anka, 1957	9,000,000
	=**Hound Dog/Don't Be Cruel,** Elvis Presley, 1956	9,000,000
10	=**(Everything I Do) I Do It for You,** Bryan Adams, 1991	8,000,000
	=**I'm a Believer,** Monkees, 1966	8,000,000

Global sales are notoriously difficult to calculate since, for many decades, little statistical research on record sales was done in a large part of the world. "Worldwide" is thus usually taken to mean the known minimum "Western world" sales. It took 55 years for a record to overtake Bing Crosby's 1942 *White Christmas*, although the song, as also recorded by others and sold as sheet music, has achieved such enormous total sales that it would still appear in first position on many lists of best-selling songs.

TOP 10 SINGLES OF ALL TIME IN CANADA

	TITLE/ARTIST OR GROUP/YEAR	ESTIMATED SALES
1	**Candle in the Wind 1997/Something About the Way You Look Tonight,** Elton John, 1997	1,900,000
2	=**Tears Are Not Enough,** Northern Lights, 1985	300,000
	=**We Are the World,** USA for Africa, 1985	300,000
	=**I Just Called to Say I Love You,** Stevie Wonder, 1984	300,000
5	=**Le Freak,** Chic, 1979	200,000
	=**YMCA,** Village People, 1979	200,000
7	=**(Everything I Do) I Do It For You,** Bryan Adams, 1991	100,000
	=**Heart of Glass,** Blondie, 1979	100,000
	=**Flashdance... What a Feelin',** Irene Cara, 1983	100,000
	=**Live Is Life,** Opus, 1986	100,000

Source: *Music Data Research*

Even though singles sales have gone down dramatically in the past 15 years, the bestselling single of all time charted in 1997. The overwhelming response to the death of Diana, Princess of Wales, catapulted Elton John's *Candle in the Wind 1997* to the top of the single sales charts for 46 weeks and made it the No. 1 single of all time.

TOP 10 "GREATEST HITS" ALBUMS IN CANADA

	TITLE/ARTIST OR GROUP	YEAR OF ENTRY
1	**Their Greatest Hits, 1971–1975,** Eagles	1976
2	**The Best of Bon Jovi: Crossroads,** Bon Jovi	1994
3	**Greatest Hits,** Kenny Rogers	1981
4	**ABBA Gold,** ABBA	1993
5	**Greatest Hits,** Elton John	1974
6	**So Far So Good,** Bryan Adams	1993
7	**Greatest Hits,** Anne Murray	1980
8	**Classic Queen,** Queen	1992
9	**Greatest Hits Volume II,** Olivia Newton-John	1983
10	**Greatest Hits,** ABBA	1977

Source: *Music Data Research*

Some of the biggest of these hits compilations have achieved truly immense sales in Canada—far more, in most cases, than the hit singles they anthologize. All the albums above have sold in excess of 500,000 copies, while the Eagles' album has topped 2 million units. Bon Jovi and Kenny Rogers are both over the 1 million mark.

TOP 10 NORTH AMERICAN CONCERT TOURS

	ARTIST OR GROUP	TOUR/YEAR	GROSS (US$)
1	**Rolling Stones**	Voodoo Lounge, 1994	121,200,000
2	**U2**	Elevation, 2001	109,700,000
3	**Pink Floyd**	The Division Bell, 1994	103,500,000
4	**Paul McCartney**	Driving USA, 2002	103,300,000
5	**Rolling Stones**	Steel Wheels, 1989	98,000,000
6	**Rolling Stones**	Bridges to Babylon, 1997	89,300,000
7	**Rolling Stones**	Licks, 2002	87,900,000
8	***NSYNC**	Popodyssey, 2001	86,800,000
9	**Backstreet Boys**	Black and Blue, 2001	82,100,000
10	**Tina Turner**	Twenty-Four Seven, 2000	80,200,000

Source: Fortune/*Pollstar*

This survey was conducted when the Rolling Stones were embarking on their 2002–2003 Licks world tour, which will no doubt top the next version of the list. The band already leads the field with all-time total tour earnings of US$864,300,000.

TOP 10 ARTISTS WITH MOST GRAMMY AWARDS

	ARTIST	YEARS	AWARDS*
1	Sir Georg Solti	1962–97	38
2	Pierre Boulez	1969–2001	29
3	= Vladimir Horowitz	1962–92	26
	= Quincy Jones	1963–93	26
5	Stevie Wonder	1973–98	22
6	= Leonard Bernstein	1961–2001	20
	= Henry Mancini	1958–70	20
8	John T. Williams	1975–2000	18
9	= Eric Clapton	1972–2001	16
	= Itzhak Perlman	1977–95	16

* *Excludes Lifetime Achievement awards*

The Grammy Awards are considered to be the most prestigious in the music industry. Winners are selected annually by the 7,000-member Recording Academy of NARAS (National Academy of Recording Arts & Sciences). The proliferation of classical artists in this Top 10 reflects the number of classical award categories at the Grammys, which have only lately been overshadowed by the rise of pop and rock.

TOP 10 ALBUMS OF ALL TIME IN CANADA

	ARTIST OR GROUP	ESTIMATED SALES
1	= **Their Greatest Hits, 1971–1975**, Eagles, 1976	2,000,000
	= **Rumours**, Fleetwood Mac, 1977	2,000,000
	= **Thriller**, Michael Jackson, 1983	2,000,000
	= **Led Zeppelin IV**, Led Zeppelin, 1971	2,000,000
	= **Bat Out of Hell**, Meat Loaf, 1978	2,000,000
	= **Jagged Little Pill**, Alanis Morissette, 1996	2,000,000
	= **The Wall**, Pink Floyd, 1980	2,000,000
	= **Come On Over**, Shania Twain, 1997	2,000,000
	= **The Woman in Me**, Shania Twain, 1995	2,000,000
10	**Brothers In Arms**, Dire Straits, 1985	1,000,000

Source: *Music Data Research*

Before precise accounting of record sales came into effect in Canada in 1996, exact sales were difficult to determine. Instead, certifications and approximate data from the Canadian Recording Industry Association (CRIA) were used.

TOP 10 ARTISTS WITH MOST WEEKS ON THE CANADIAN ALBUMS CHART

	ARTIST OR GROUP	TOTAL WEEKS
1	Celine Dion	666
2	Garth Brooks	512
3	Madonna	465
4	U2	435
5	Rod Stewart	431
6	Bryan Adams	389
7	Elton John	362
8	Tragically Hip	341
9	Sarah McLachlan	334
10	Backstreet Boys	317

Source: *Music Data Research*, Top Albums: The Essential Chart Guide

Bell Ringer

Along with those for the majority of the top-earning concert tours, the dramatic stage set for Pink Floyd's 1994 Division Bell tour was designed by British architect Mark Fisher.

Today's Stars

TOP 10 ALBUMS OF 2002 IN CANADA

	ALBUM	ARTIST OR GROUP
1	**The Eminem Show**	Eminem
2	**A New Day Has Come**	Celine Dion
3	**Elv1s 30 #1 Hits**	Elvis Presley
4	**Up!**	Shania Twain
5	**MuchDance 2002**	Various artists
6	**Under Rug Swept**	Alanis Morissette
7	**Let Go**	Avril Lavigne
8	**Now! 7**	Various artists
9	**Laundry Service**	Shakira
10	**Drive**	Alan Jackson

Source: *Music Data Research*

The Eminem Show sold over 800,000 copies in Canada and was No. 1 for nine weeks—longer than any other album in 2002.

TOP 10 SINGLES OF 2002 IN CANADA

	SINGLE	ARTIST OR GROUP
1	**I'm Gonna Getcha Good!**	Shania Twain
2	**A New Day Has Come**	Celine Dion
3	**Complicated**	Avril Lavigne
4	**Hero**	Chad Kroeger featuring Josey Scott
5	**Electrical Storm**	U2
6	**Wherever You Will Go**	The Calling
7	**Soak Up the Sun**	Sheryl Crow
8	**Get the Party Started**	Pink
9	**Brother Down**	Sam Roberts
10	**Just Like a Pill**	Pink

Source: *Music Data Research*

Canadians dominated the top singles of 2002 with the top four spots being held by domestic acts; in fact, Canadian artists were No 1 for a record-breaking 37 weeks.

THE 10 LATEST GRAMMY RECORDS OF THE YEAR

YEAR	RECORD/ARTIST OR GROUP
2002	**Don't Know Why,** Norah Jones
2001	**Walk On,** U2
2000	**Beautiful Day,** U2
1999	**Smooth,** Santana featuring Rob Thomas
1998	**My Heart Will Go On,** Celine Dion
1997	**Sunny Came Home,** Shawn Colvin
1996	**Change the World,** Eric Clapton
1995	**Kiss From a Rose,** Seal
1994	**All I Wanna Do,** Sheryl Crow
1993	**I Will Always Love You,** Whitney Houston

The Grammys are awarded retrospectively. Thus the 45th awards were presented in 2003 in recognition of musical accomplishments during 2002.

TOP 10 COUNTRY SONGS OF 2002 IN CANADA

	SONG	ARTIST OR GROUP
1	**Somebody Like You**	Keith Urban
2	**19 Somethin'**	Mark Wills
3	**Drive (For Daddy Gene)**	Alan Jackson
4	**Young**	Kenny Chesney
5	**She'll Leave You With a Smile**	George Strait
6	**The Cowboy in Me**	Tim McGraw
7	**Long Time Gone**	Dixie Chicks
8	**Blessed**	Martina McBride
9	**The Good Stuff**	Kenny Chesney
10	**My Heart Is Lost to You**	Brooks & Dunn

Source: *Music Data Research*

Australian singer Keith Urban tops the country charts of 2002 with *Somebody Like You*, a song that was later remixed and featured in the 2003 romantic-comedy movie *How to Lose a Guy in 10 Days*.

TOP 10 ADULT CONTEMPORARY SONGS OF 2002 IN CANADA

	SONG	ARTIST OR GROUP
1	**A New Day Has Come**	Celine Dion
2	**The Game of Love**	Santana featuring Michelle Branch
3	**A Thousand Miles**	Vanessa Carlton
4	**Soak Up the Sun**	Sheryl Crow
5	**I'm Alive**	Celine Dion
6	**Superman**	Five for Fighting
7	**Surrender**	Laura Pausini
8	**I'm Gonna Getcha Good!**	Shania Twain
9	**I Need You**	Marc Anthony
10	**Here I Am**	Bryan Adams

Source: *Music Data Research*

2002 marked the return of Celine Dion after a three-year hiatus. Her album *A New Day Has Come* went straight to No. 1 as did the title track, spending 16 weeks topping the Adult Contemporary chart.

THE 10 LATEST GRAMMY NEW ARTISTS OF THE YEAR

YEAR	ARTIST OR GROUP
2002	**Norah Jones**
2001	**Alicia Keys**
2000	**Shelby Lynne**
1999	**Christina Aguilera**
1998	**Lauryn Hill**
1997	**Paula Cole**
1996	**Leann Rimes**
1995	**Hootie & the Blowfish**
1994	**Sheryl Crow**
1993	**Toni Braxton**

Most recent winner Norah Jones swept the Grammys, winning an unprecedented five awards at the 45th annual ceremony (held on February 23, 2003, honoring 2002 releases). The week after the event, her album *Come Away With Me*,winner of the "Album of the Year Grammy," sold 621,000 units, rocketing to No. 1.

BEST-PAID ROCK AND POP STARS

	ARTIST OR GROUP	EST. EARNINGS 2001–02 (US$)*
1	**U2**	69,000,000
2	**Mariah Carey**	58,000,000
3	**Dave Matthews Band**	50,000,000
4	**Madonna**	43,000,000
5	***NSYNC**	42,300,000
6	**Britney Spears**	39,200,000
7	**Jennifer Lopez**	37,000,000
8	**Backstreet Boys**	36,800,000
9	**Elton John**	30,000,000
10	**Aerosmith**	25,000,000

* *For the period June 2001–June 2002*

Source: Forbes

THE 10 LATEST JUNO SINGLES OF THE YEAR

YEAR	SINGLE/ARTIST OR GROUP
2003	**Complicated,** Avril Lavigne
2002	**How You Remind Me,** Nickelback
2001	**I'm Like a Bird,** Nelly Furtado
2000	**Bobcaygeon,** Tragically Hip
1999	**One Week,** Barenaked Ladies
1998	**Building a Mystery,** Sarah McLachlan
1997	**Ironic,** Alanis Morissette
1996	**You Oughta Know,** Alanis Morissette
1995	**Could I Be Your Girl,** Jann Arden
1994	**Fare Thee Well Love,** The Rankin Family

Complicated was named "Single of the Year" in 2003, a crowning achievement in the young career of Avril Lavigne, a pop-punk singer from Napanee, Ontario.

▶ Pro Bono
The combined revenue from record sales and concert tours has propelled U2 to the head of the rock star earnings league.

Chart Toppers

TOP 10 ARTISTS WITH THE MOST WEEKS AT NO. 1 ON THE ALBUMS CHART IN CANADA

	ARTIST	WEEKS
1	U2	45
2	Supertramp	34
3	Madonna	32
4	Bruce Springsteen	31
5	The Police	29
6	Phil Collins	28
7	Bryan Adams	26
8	Alanis Morissette	25
9	Whitney Houston	23
10	= Eminem	22
	= Rolling Stones	22

Source: *Music Data Research,* Top Albums: The Essential Chart Guide

TOP 10 ARTISTS WITH THE MOST NO. 1 ALBUMS ON THE ALBUMS CHART IN CANADA

	ARTIST	NO. 1 HITS
1	= Celine Dion	7
	= Tragically Hip	7
3	= Bruce Springsteen	6
	= U2	6
5	= Backstreet Boys	5
	= Phil Collins	5
	= Madonna	5
	= Rolling Stones	5
9	= Bryan Adams	4
	= Rod Stewart	4

Source: *Music Data Research,* Top Albums: The Essential Chart Guide

TOP 10 ARTISTS WITH THE MOST NO. 1 SINGLES IN THE UK

	ARTIST	NO. 1 SINGLES
1	Elvis Presley	18
2	Beatles	17
3	Cliff Richard	14
4	Westlife*	11
5	Madonna	10
6	= ABBA	9
	= Spice Girls	9
8	= Rolling Stones	8
	= Take That	8
10	= Michael Jackson	7
	= George Michael	7

* *Including one with Mariah Carey*

Source: *Music Information Database*

TOP 10 SINGLES WITH THE MOST WEEKS AT NO. 1 IN CANADA

	TITLE/YEAR	ARTIST	WEEKS
1	**Candle in the Wind 1997/Something About the Way You Look Tonight,** 1997	Elton John	46
2	**Goodbye,** 1998	Spice Girls	15
3	**I'm Gonna Getcha Good,** 2002	Shania Twain	14
4	**I'll Be Missing You,** 1992	Puff Daddy & Faith Evans (feat. 112)	13
5	=**(Everything I Do) I Do It For You,** 1991	Bryan Adams	12
	=**Said I Loved You... But I Lied,** 1993	Michael Bolton	12
	=**You Light Up My Life,** 1977	Debby Boone	12
	=**Fantasy**, 1995	Mariah Carey	12
	=**A New Day Has Come,** 2002	Celine Dion	12
	=**The Power of Love,** 1994	Celine Dion	12
	=**Pop Muzik,** 1979	M	12
	=**Faith,** 1987	George Michael	12

Source: *Music Data Research*

TOP 10 ALBUMS WITH THE MOST WEEKS AT NO. 1 IN CANADA

	TITLE	ARTIST	YEAR RELEASED	WEEKS AT AT NO. 1
1	**Breakfast in America**	Supertramp	1979	26
2	=**Jagged Little Pill**	Alanis Morissette	1995	23
	=**Synchronicity**	The Police	1983	23
4	=**Grease**	Soundtrack	1978	22
	=**Saturday Night Fever**	Soundtrack	1978	22
6	**Rumours**	Fleetwood Mac	1977	20
7	**Brothers in Arms**	Dire Straits	1985	18
8	=**Unplugged**	Eric Clapton	1992	17
	=**Whitney Houston**	Whitney Houston	1986	17
	=**The Joshua Tree**	U2	1987	17

Source: *Music Data Research,* Top Albums: The Essential Chart Guide

Wings over North America

As well as enjoying more weeks at US No. 1 than any other artist, Paul McCartney has also reached No. 1 in Canada as a member of the Beatles, a member of Wings, and as a solo artist.

TOP 10 OLDEST ARTISTS TO HAVE A NO. 1 SINGLE IN CANADA

	ARTIST/YEAR	TITLE	AGE YRS	MTHS
1	**Eric Clapton,** 1996	Change the World	51	4
2	**Willie Nelson,** 1984	To All the Girls I've Loved Before*	51	1
3	**Elton John,** 1997	Candle in the Wind 1997/Something About the Way You Look Tonight	50	5
4	**Tina Turner,** 1985	We Don't Need Another Hero	45	9
5	**Kenny Rogers,** 1983	Islands in the Stream#	45	2
6	**John Mellencamp,** 1996	Key West Intermezzo (I Saw You First)	44	11
7	**Bruce Springsteen,** 1994	Streets of Philadelphia	44	7
8	**Madonna,** 2000	Music	42	1
9	**Paul McCartney,** 1984	Say, Say, Say†	41	6
10	**Michael Bolton,** 1993	Said I Love You... But I Lied	40	9

* *Duet with Julio Iglesias*

Duet with Dolly Parton

† *Duet with Michael Jackson*

Source: *Music Data Research*

TOP 10 YOUNGEST ARTISTS TO HAVE A NO. 1 SINGLE IN CANADA

	ARTIST/YEAR	TITLE	AGE YRS	MTHS
1	**Britney Spears,** 1998	...Baby One More Time	16	11
2	**Monica,** 1998	The Boy is Mine	17	7
3	**Shaun Cassidy,** 1977	Da Doo Ron Ron	17	10
4	**Debbie Gibson,** 1988	Foolish Beat	17	11
5	**Christina Aguilera,** 1999	Genie in a Bottle	18	8
6	**Brandy,** 1998	The Boy is Mine	19	3
7	**Andy Gibb,** 1977	I Just Want to Be Your Everything	19	6
8	**Mariah Carey,** 1990	Vision of Love	20	5
9	**Bobby Brown,** 1989	On Our Own	20	6
10	**Kylie Minogue,** 1988	The Locomotion	20	7

Source: *Music Data Research*

Gold, Platinum & Diamond

TOP 10 GROUPS WITH THE MOST PLATINUM ALBUMS IN CANADA

	GROUP	PLATINUM ALBUMS
1	U2	37
2	Pink Floyd	22
3	= Van Halen	20
	= Dire Straits	20
5	Bee Gees	18
6	= Def Leppard	17
	= Bon Jovi	17
8	Boston	15
9	= Simon & Garfunkel	14
	= Rush	14

Source: *Canadian Recording Industry Association*

They Just Keep Rolling Along
The Rolling Stones have achieved six Canadian platinum albums, though they have been releasing best-selling albums for over 40 years.

TOP 10 GROUPS WITH THE MOST GOLD ALBUMS IN THE US

	GROUP	GOLD ALBUMS
1	Beatles	41
2	Rolling Stones	38
3	= Kiss	23
	= Aerosmith	23
5	= Alabama	22
	= Chicago	22
	= Rush	22
8	= Beach Boys	20
	= Jefferson Airplane/Starship	20
10	AC/DC	19

Source: *Recording Industry Association of America*

The RIAA's Gold Awards have been presented since 1958 to artists who have sold 500,000 units of a single, album, or multidisc set. Multiple Gold Awards were presented up to 1976, when Platinum Awards, honoring million-selling discs, were introduced.

TOP 10 GROUPS WITH THE MOST PLATINUM ALBUMS IN THE US

	GROUP	PLATINUM ALBUMS*
1	Beatles	92
2	Eagles	81
3	Led Zeppelin	80
4	AC/DC	60
5	Aerosmith	59
6	Pink Floyd	54
7	Van Halen	50
8	U2	45
9	= Alabama	44
	= Fleetwood Mac	44

* *By number of album awards, rather than number of albums qualifying for awards; double/triple albums counted once*

THE 10 LATEST DIAMOND ALBUMS IN CANADA

	TITLE/ARTIST	DATE
1	**Up!,** Shania Twain	Dec 2002
2	= **Use Your Illusion II,** Guns 'N' Roses	Mar 2001
	= **Nevermind,** Nirvana	Mar 2001
4	**The Best of Bon Jovi,** Bon Jovi	Nov 2000
5	**Supernatural,** Santana	July 2000
6	**ABBA Gold,** ABBA	May 2000
7	**Amanda Marshall,** Amanda Marshall	Apr 2000
8	= **Ricky Martin,** Ricky Martin	Dec 1999
	= **...Baby One More Time,** Britney Spears	Dec 1999
10	**Come On Over,** Shania Twain	Apr 1999

Source: *Canadian Recording Industry Association*

Diamond albums in Canada are those that have achieved sales of one million units.

TOP 10 MALE ARTISTS WITH THE MOST PLATINUM ALBUMS IN CANADA

	ARTIST	PLATINUM ALBUMS
1	**Kenny Rogers**	32
2	**Billy Joel**	25
3	= **John Mellencamp**	20
	= **Bruce Springsteen**	20
5	= **Bob Seger**	17
	= **Bryan Adams**	17
7	**Elton John**	16
8	**Michael Jackson**	15
9	**Neil Diamond**	12
10	**Corey Hart**	11

Source: *Canadian Recording Industry Association*

Platinum albums in Canada are those that have achieved sales of 100,000 units.

TOP 10 FEMALE ARTISTS WITH THE MOST PLATINUM ALBUMS IN CANADA

	ARTIST	PLATINUM ALBUMS
1	**Celine Dion**	24
2	**Anne Murray**	18
3	**Mariah Carey**	17
4	= **Whitney Houston**	16
	= **Pat Benatar**	16
6	**Barbra Streisand**	14
7	**Olivia Newton-John**	13
8	**Madonna**	12
9	**Cyndi Lauper**	10
10	**Tina Turner**	9

Source: *Canadian Recording Industry Association*

Whitney Houston
Including her two soundtrack albums, Whitney Houston has had 16 platinum and multiplatinum albums in Canada.

TOP 10 R & B/HIP-HOP ALBUMS IN CANADA, 2002

	ALBUM/ARTIST OR GROUP	ESTIMATED SALES
1	**The Eminem Show,** Eminem	600,000
2	**Songs in a Minor,** Alicia Keys	500,000
3	= **Missundaztood,** Pink	400,000
	= **Nellyville,** Nelly	400,000
5	**Pain Is Love,** Ja Rule	300,000
6	**No More Drama,** Mary J. Blige	200,000
7	= **Ashanti,** Ashanti	100,000
	= **MTV Unplugged 2.0,** Lauryn Hill	100,000
	= **The Way I Feel,** Remy Shand	100,000
	= **Bad Dreams,** Swollen Members	100,000

Source: *Music Data Research*

TOP 10 RAP SINGLES IN CANADA

	SINGLE/ARTIST OR GROUP	YEAR
1	**Rapper's Delight,** Sugarhill Gang	1980
2	**I'll Be Missing You,** Puff Daddy & Faith Evans (featuring 112)	1997
3	**Push It,** Salt-N-Pepa	1988
4	**Let Your Backbone Slide,** Maestro Fresh-Wes	1990
5	**Wild Thing,** Tone Loc	1989
6	**U Can't Touch This,** M.C. Hammer	1990
7	**Bust a Move,** Young M.C.	1989
8	**Walk This Way,** Run D.M.C.	1986
9	**Insane in the Brain,** Cypress Hill	1993
10	**I'll Be There for You/ You're All I Need (To Get By),** Method Man (featuring Mary J. Blige)	1995

Source: *Music Data Research*

Ironically, *Rapper's Delight*, the biggest rap record ever in Canada, charted in the early 1980s, long before the heyday of rap in the 1990s. It spent eight weeks at No. 1 and sold in excess of 200,000 copies—more than any other rap single in history.

TOP 10 ROCK ALBUMS IN CANADA

	ALBUM/ARTIST OR GROUP	YEAR OF ENTRY
1	**Jagged Little Pill,** Alanis Morissette	1995
2	**Dark Side of the Moon,** Pink Floyd	1980
3	**Rumours,** Fleetwood Mac	1977
4	**The Wall,** Pink Floyd	1980
5	**Bat Out of Hell,** Meat Loaf	1978
6	**Their Greatest Hits 1971–1975,** The Eagles	1976
7	**Led Zeppelin IV,** Led Zeppelin	1975
8	**Waking Up the Neighbors,** Bryan Adams	1991
9	**Supernatural,** Santana	2000
10	**Dookie,** Green Day	1995

Source: *Music Data Research*

▼ Always First
Ja Rule and Ashanti individually had two of Canada's bestselling R & B albums in 2002, as well as a global chart-topping single with their duet

TOP 10 COUNTRY SINGLES IN CANADA

	TITLE/ARTIST OR GROUP	YEAR
1	**Islands in the Stream,** Kenny Rogers & Dolly Parton	1983
2	**To All the Girls I've Loved Before,** Julio Iglesias & Willie Nelson	1984
3	**My Way,** Elvis Presley	1977
4	**You Needed Me,** Anne Murray	1998
5	**Queen of Hearts,** Juice Newton	1981
6	**Coward of the County,** Kenny Rogers	1980
7	**Lady,** Kenny Rogers	1980
8	**Angel of the Morning,** Juice Newton	1981
9	**Southern Nights,** Glen Campbell	1977
10	**Don't It Make My Brown Eyes Blue,** Crystal Gayle	1977

Some of these artists have enjoyed a certain amount of crossover success; for example, reached No. 1 on the Canadian Top-40 pop singles chart, and Anne Murray was awarded a "Best Pop Vocal" Grammy for .

TOP 10 MUSIC GENRES IN THE US

	TYPE OF MUSIC	PERCENTAGE MARKET SHARE (2000)
1	Rock	24.8
2	Pop	11.0
3	Country	10.7
4	Rap	10.3
5	R & B/Urban	9.7
6	Religious	4.8
7	Jazz	2.9
8	Classical	2.7
9	Hip hop	2.6
10	Oldies	0.9

Source: *Recording Industry Association of America*

The music sales market breaks down into CD sales, representing 89.3 percent; cassettes (4.9 percent); singles (2.5 percent); music videos (0.8 percent); and vinyl LPs (0.5 percent).

► High-Profile J-Lo
Jennifer Lopez's *Jenny from the Block* was one of the biggest pop songs on radio in 2002.

TOP 10 POP RADIO TRACKS IN CANADA, 2002

	TITLE	ARTIST OR GROUP
1	Complicated	Avril Lavigne
2	Can't Get You Out of My Head	Kylie Minogue
3	Just Like a Pill	Pink
4	Don't Let Me Get Me	Pink
5	Sk8Er Boi	Avril Lavigne
6	Jenny from the Block	Jennifer Lopez
7	Die Another Day	Madonna
8	Escape	Enrique Iglesias
9	The Game of Love	Santana featuring Michelle Branch
10	Hands Clean	Alanis Morissette

Source: *Music Data Research*

TOP 10 MOST PROLIFIC CLASSICAL COMPOSERS

	COMPOSER/NATIONALITY/DATES	HOURS OF MUSIC
1	**Joseph Haydn** (Austrian; 1732–1809)	340
2	**George Handel** (German-English; 1685–1759)	303
3	**Wolfgang Amadeus Mozart** (Austrian; 1756–91)	202
4	**Johann Sebastian Bach** (German; 1685–1750)	175
5	**Franz Schubert** (German; 1797–1828)	134
6	**Ludwig van Beethoven** (German; 1770–1827)	120
7	**Henry Purcell** (English; 1659–95)	116
8	**Giuseppe Verdi** (Italian; 1813–1901)	87
9	**Anton Dvorák** (Czech; 1841–1904)	79
10	= **Franz Liszt** (Hungarian; 1811–86)	76
	= **Peter Tchaikovsky** (Russian; 1840–93)	76

Based on a survey by *Classical Music* magazine, which ranked classical composers by the total number of hours of music each composed. If the length of the composer's working life is taken into account, Schubert wins: his 134 hours were composed in a career of 18 years—an average of 7 hours 27 minutes per annum. This method puts Tchaikovsky ahead of Liszt. Although both composed 76 hours, Tchaikovsky worked for 30 years, Liszt for 51, giving them annual averages of 2 hours 32 minutes and 1 hour 29 minutes respectively.

THE FIRST ENGLISH OPERA

FIRST FACT

THE IDENTITY OF THE FIRST OPERA in English is the subject of debate. It may have been Richard Flecknoe's *Ariadne* (1654), or *The Siege of Rhodes* by English poet laureate Sir William D'Avenant (1606–68), performed at Rutland House, London in September 1656. The latter was described by John Evelyn in his Diary as "'...a new opera after the Italian way, in recitative music and scenes." It was the first theatrical production with painted perspective stage sets, and the first with a female performer, Mrs. Edward Coleman, as Ianthe.

TOP 10 CITIES STAGING THE MOST OPERAS

	CITY	PRODUCTIONS*
1	**Vienna,** Austria	32
2	**Berlin,** Germany	21
3	**Prague,** Czech Republic	20
4	**Paris,** France	16
5	**Hamburg,** Germany	13
6	= **London,** UK	12
	= **Zurich,** Switzerland	12
8	= **New York,** US	11
	= **Munich,** Germany	11
10	**Hanover,** Germany	10

* *International sample during a 12-month period*

TOP 10 LARGEST OPERA THEATERS

	THEATER/LOCATION	CAPACITY*
1	**Arena di Verona#,** Verona, Italy	16,663
2	**Municipal Opera Theater#,** St. Louis, MO	11,745
3	**Teatro alla Scala,** Milan, Italy	3,600
4	**Civic Opera House,** Chicago, IL	3,563
5	= **The Metropolitan,** Lincoln Center, New York, NY	3,500
	= **Teatro San Carlo,** Naples, Italy	3,500
7	**Music Hall,** Cincinnati, OH	3,417
8	= **The Hummingbird Centre,** Toronto, Canada	3,200
	= **Teatro Massimo,** Palermo, Italy	3,200
10	**Halle aux Grains,** Toulouse, France	3,000

* *Indoor venues—seating capacity only given, although capacity is often larger when standing capacity is included*

\# *Open-air venue*

Although there are more venues in the world where opera is regularly performed, the above list is limited to those where the principal performances are opera.

TOP 10 MOST PERFORMED OPERA COMPOSERS

	COMPOSER	PRODUCTIONS*
1	**Giuseppe Verdi** (Italian; 1813–1901)	58
2	**Giacomo Puccini** (Italian; 1858–1924)	44
3	**Wolfgang Amadeus Mozart** (Austrian; 1756–91)	40
4	**Gioacchino Rossini** (Italian; 1792–1868)	23
	= **Richard Strauss** (German; 1864–1949)	23
6	**Richard Wagner** (German; 1813–83)	22
7	**Gaetano Donizetti** (Italian; 1797–1848)	21
8	= **Leoš Janáček** (Czech; 1854–1928)	10
	= **Jacques Offenbach** (German; 1819–80)	10
10	**Georges Bizet** (French; 1838–75)	9

* *International sample during a 12-month period*

TOP 10 MOST PERFORMED OPERAS

	OPERA	PRODUCTIONS	PERFORMANCES*
1	**La Bohème**	11	52
2	**Tosca**	12	48
3	**Madama Butterfly**	9	42
4	**Die Zauberflöte**	11	37
5	**Un Ballo in Maschera**	8	35
6	**Don Giovanni**	9	31
7	**Otello**	9	30
8	**Les Contes d'Hoffmann**	7	29
9	**Il Barbiere di Siviglia**	9	27
10	= **La Traviata**	8	24
	= **Salome**	6	24

* *Based on a sample of 180 international productions*

TOP 10 CLASSICAL ALBUMS OF ALL TIME IN CANADA

	PERFORMER(S)	TITLE	YEAR
1	Andrea Bocelli	Romanza	1997
2	Andrea Bocelli	Sogno	1999
3	José Carreras, Placido Domingo, Luciano Pavarotti	The Three Tenors in Concert 1994	1994
4	Josh Groban	Josh Groban	2002
5	Sarah Brightman	Time to Say Goodbye	1998
6	Andrea Bocelli	Sacred Arias	1999
7	Andrea Bocelli	Cieli Di Toscana	2001
8	Charlotte Church	Voice of an Angel	1999
9	Luciano Pavarotti	Pavarotti and Friends 2	1995
10	Placido Domingo	Perhaps Love	1981

Source: *Music Data Research*

Sales of classical music boomed to unprecedented heights at the end of the 1980s and in the early 1990s, primarily because of the popularity of a select band of superstars—José Carreras, Placido Domingo, and Luciano Pavarotti, known collectively as the Three Tenors. Their 1994 album went to No. 3.

TOP 10 OPERAS MOST FREQUENTLY PERFORMED AT THE METROPOLITAN OPERA HOUSE, NEW YORK

	OPERA	COMPOSER	PERFORMANCES
1	La Bohème	Giacomo Puccini	1,126
2	Aïda	Giuseppi Verdi	1,066
3	Carmen	Georges Bizet	908
4	La Traviata	Giuseppi Verdi	881
5	Tosca	Giacomo Puccini	839
6	Madama Butterfly	Giacomo Puccini	768
7	Rigoletto	Giuseppi Verdi	753
8	Faust	Charles Gounod	713
9	Pagliacci	Ruggero Leoncavallo	688
10	Cavalleria Rusticana	Pietro Mascagni	648

* *As of end of 2002-2003 season*

Source: *Metropolitan Opera*

Nights at the Opera
Tosca, here sung by Luciano Pavarotti with Carole Vanes, is one of the most performed productions at the principal opera houses on both sides of the Atlantic.

Broadcast Music

THE 10 LATEST RECIPIENTS OF THE MTV VMA "BEST VIDEO" AWARD

	ARTIST/TITLE
2002	**Eminem,** Without Me
2001	**Christina Aguilera (featuring Mya, Pink, L'il Kim, Missy "Misdeameanor" Elliott),** Lady Marmalade
2000	**Eminem,** The Real Slim Shady
1999	**Lauryn Hill,** Doo Wop (That Thing)
1998	**Madonna,** Ray of Light
1997	**Jamiroquai,** Virtual Insanity
1996	**The Smashing Pumpkins,** Tonight, Tonight
1995	**TLC,** Waterfalls
1994	**Aerosmith,** Cryin'
1993	**Pearl Jam,** Jeremy

THE 10 LATEST RECIPIENTS OF THE MTV VMA "BEST GROUP VIDEO" AWARD

	ARTIST/TITLE
2002	**No Doubt (featuring Bounty Killer),** Hey Baby
2001	***NSYNC,** POP
2000	**Blink 182,** All the Small Things
1999	**TLC,** No Scrubs
1998	**Backstreet Boys,** Everybody (Backstreet's Back)
1997	**No Doubt,** Don't Speak
1996	**Foo Fighters,** Big Me
1995	**TLC,** Waterfalls
1994	**Aerosmith,** Cryin'
1993	**Pearl Jam,** Jeremy

No Doubt about It

The video of *Hey Baby*, co-written by Dave Stewart and performed by Gwen Stefani of No Doubt, received the accolade as MTV's "Best Group Video."

TOP 10 SINGLES OF TV THEME TUNES IN CANADA

	TITLE/ARTIST	PROGRAM
1	**I'll Be There for You,** The Rembrandts	Friends
2	**How Do You Talk to an Angel,** The Heights	The Heights
3	**Theme from "The Greatest American Hero" (Believe It or Not)** Joey Scarbury	The Greatest American Hero
4	**Nadia's Theme (The Young and the Restless),** Barry DeVorzon & Perry Botkin, Jr.	The Young and the Restless
5	**Welcome Back,** John Sebastian	Welcome Back Kotter
6	**Miami Vice Theme,** Jan Hammer	Miami Vice
7	**Closer to Free,** Bodeans	Party of Five
8	**Happy Days,** Pratt & McClain	Happy Days
9	**Searching My Soul,** Vonda Shepard	Ally McBeal
10	**Makin' It,** David Naughton	Makin' It

Source: *Music Data Research*

Former member of the Lovin' Spoonful John Sebastian wrote *Welcome Back* for the 1970s TV series *Welcome Back Kotter*. Sebastian's expanded version of the theme song topped the chart and became his first million seller.

THE 10 FIRST MUSIC VIDEOS ON MUCHMUSIC

	TITLE/ARTIST
1	**Snappy Songs,** Eubi Blake and Noble Sissle
2	**The Enemy Within,** Rush
3	**Let's Go Crazy,** Prince
4	**Relax,** Frankie Goes to Hollywood
5	**Love Is Love,** Culture Club
6	**Karma Chameleon (Live),** Culture Club
7	**Flesh for Fantasy,** Billy Idol
8	**Dancing in the Dark,** Bruce Springsteen
9	**Lights Out,** Peter Wolf
10	**Are We Ourselves,** The Fixx

Source: *MusicMusic*

MuchMusic debuted on August 31, 1984.

THE 10 LATEST RECIPIENTS OF THE MTV VMA "BEST FEMALE VIDEO" AWARD

	ARTIST/TITLE
2002	**Pink,** Get the Party Started
2001	**Eve (featuring Gwen Stefani),** Let Me Blow Ya Mind
2000	**Aaliyah,** Try Again
1999	**Lauryn Hill,** Doo Wop (That Thing)
1998	**Madonna,** Ray of Light
1997	**Jewel,** You Were Meant for Me
1996	**Alanis Morissette,** Ironic
1995	**Madonna,** Take a Bow
1994	**Janet Jackson,** If
1993	**k.d. lang,** Constant Craving

Launched in 1981 as a cable channel, MTV started presenting its Video Music Awards (VMA) in 1984.

THE 10 LATEST RECIPIENTS OF THE MTV VMA "BEST MALE VIDEO" AWARD

	ARTIST/TITLE
2002	**Eminem,** Without Me
2001	**Moby (featuring Gwen Stefani),** South Side
2000	**Eminem,** The Real Slim Shady
1999	**Will Smith,** Miami
1998	**Will Smith,** Just the Two of Us
1997	**Beck,** Devil's Haircut
1996	**Beck,** Where It's At
1995	**Tom Petty and the Heartbreakers,** You Don't Know How It Feels
1994	**Tom Petty and the Heartbreakers,** Mary Jane's Last Dance
1993	**Lenny Kravitz,** Are You Gonna Go My Way

THE 10 LATEST RECIPIENTS OF THE MUCHMUSIC "BEST MUSIC VIDEO" AWARD

YEAR*	TITLE	ARTIST
2002	**Too Bad**	Nickelback
2000	**Load Me Up**	Matthew Good Band
1999	**Steal My Sunshine**	Len
1998	**Sweet Surrender**	Sarah McLachlan
1997	**Tangerine**	Moist
1996	**Ahead by a Century**	Tragically Hip
1995	**Insensitive**	Jann Arden
1994	**Hasn't Hit Me Yet**	Blue Rodeo
1993	**Locked in the Trunk of a Car**	Tragically Hip
1992	**She-la**	54.40

* The 2001 MuchMusic Video Awards, scheduled for September 23, 2001, were canceled because of the September 11 terrorist attacks in the US.

Source: *MusicMusic*

The Real Slim Shady
Eminem's award-winning video of his single *Without Me* depicts the rap star both as himself and in a diverse range of provocative personae, from a fat Elvis to Osama bin Laden.

Movie Music

TOP 10 MUSICAL FILMS

	FILM	YEAR
1	Grease	1978
2	Saturday Night Fever	1977
3	The Sound of Music	1965
4	Evita	1996
5	The Rocky Horror Picture Show	1975
6	Staying Alive	1983
7	American Graffiti	1973
8	Mary Poppins	1964
9	Flashdance	1983
10	Fantasia 2000	2000

Traditional musicals (films in which the cast actually sing) and films in which a musical soundtrack is a major component of the film are included here. The era of the blockbuster musical film may be over, but in recent years animated films with an important musical content appear to have taken over from them—*Beauty and the Beast*, *Aladdin*, *The Lion King*, *Pocahontas*, *The Prince of Egypt*, and *Tarzan* all won "Best Original Song" Oscars—while the film soundtrack album of *Titanic* is the bestselling of all time.

TOP 10 ORIGINAL SOUNDTRACK ALBUMS IN CANADA

	SOUNDTRACK	YEAR OF RELEASE
1	Saturday Night Fever	1978
2	Grease	1978
3	Dirty Dancing	1987
4	Titanic	1998
5	The Bodyguard	1992
6	Armageddon	1998
7	Dangerous Minds	1995
8	Forrest Gump	1994
9	Cocktail	1988
10	The Lion King	1994

Source: *Music Data Research*

TOP 10 FILMS WITH TITLES DERIVED FROM SONG TITLES

	FILM/SONG	YEAR OF SONG RELEASE*
1	American Pie	1972
2	Bad Boys	1983
3	One Fine Day	1963
4	Sweet Home Alabama	1976
5	Something to Talk About	1991
6	The Crying Game	1964
7	Addicted to Love	1986
8	My Girl	1965
9	Stand By Me	1961
10	When a Man Loves a Woman	1966

* *Release of first hit version*

Remarkably, the first film with a title derived from a song title was *How Would You Like to Be the Ice Man?*, released on April 21, 1899.

Grease is the Word
Although it has celebrated its 25th anniversary, *Grease*, starring John Travolta (as Danny) and Olivia Newton-John (as Sandy), remains unbeaten as the highest-earning musical film.

TOP 10 "BEST SONG" ACADEMY AWARD–WINNING SINGLES IN CANADA

	TITLE/ARTIST OR GROUP	YEAR
1	**I Just Called to Say I Love You,** Stevie Wonder	1984
2	**Flashdance... What a Feeling,** Irene Cara	1983
3	**You Light Up My Life,** Debby Boone	1977
4	**Say You, Say Me,** Lionel Richie	1986
5	**Evergreen** (Love Theme from *A Star Is Born*), Barbra Streisand	1977
6	**Take My Breath Away,** Berlin	1986
7	**The Way We Were,** Barbra Streisand	1974
8	**Up Where We Belong,** Joe Cocker & Jennifer Warnes	1982
9	**(I've Had) The Time of My Life,** Bill Medley & Jennifer Warnes	1987
10	**Beauty and the Beast,** Celine Dion & Peabo Bryson	1992

Source: *Music Data Research*

The "Best Song" Oscar was instituted at the 1934 Academy Awards ceremony, when it was won by *The Continental* from the film *The Gay Divorcee*. Stevie Wonder's *I Just Called to Say I Love You* spent 11 weeks at No. 1 and sold more than 300,000 copies in Canada.

TOP 10 JAMES BOND FILM THEMES IN CANADA

	TITLE (FILM*)/ARTIST OR GROUP	YEAR
1	**A View to a Kill,** Duran Duran	1985
2	**Live and Let Die,** Paul McCartney & Wings	1973
3	**Nobody Does It Better** (from *The Spy Who Loved Me*), Carly Simon	1977
4	**Die Another Day,** Madonna	2002
5	**Goldfinger,** Shirley Bassey	1965
6	**Goldfinger,** John Barry	1965
7	**For Your Eyes Only,** Sheena Easton	1981
8	**Thunderball,** Tom Jones	1966
9	**All Time High** (from *Octopussy*), Rita Coolidge	1983
10	**You Only Live Twice,** Nancy Sinatra	1967

* *If different from song title*

Source: *Music Data Research*

Note two appearances for *Goldfinger*—a vocal version by Shirley Bassey and an instrumental version by John Barry.

TOP 10 FILM MUSICALS ADAPTED FROM STAGE VERSIONS

	STAR	THEATER OPENING	FILM RELEASE
1	**Grease**	1972	1978
2	**The Sound of Music**	1959	1965
3	**Evita**	1978	1996
4	**The Rocky Horror (Picture) Show**	1973	1975
5	**Chicago**	1975	2002
6	**Fiddler on the Roof**	1964	1971
7	**My Fair Lady**	1956	1964
8	**The Best Little Whorehouse in Texas**	1978	1982
9	**Annie**	1977	1982
10	**West Side Story**	1957	1961

The adapting of stage musicals as films has a long history, with these the most successful cinematic versions of, in most instances, long-running theatrical productions. Some followed an even longer progress from stage to screen, having been non-musical theatrical productions before being adapted as stage musicals, among them the recent success *Chicago*, which started life in 1926 as a play by Maurine Dallas Watkins and was made into two films, *Chicago* (1927) and *Roxie Hart* (1942), before Bob Fosse wrote the 1975 musical.

TOP 10 POP STAR FILM DEBUTS

	POP STAR	FILM	YEAR
1	**Whitney Houston**	The Bodyguard	1992
2	**Eminem**	8 Mile	2002
3	**Meat Loaf**	The Rocky Horror Picture Show	1975
4	**Dolly Parton**	9 to 5	1980
5	**Spice Girls**	Spice World	1998
6	**Aaliyah**	Romeo Must Die	2000
7	**Britney Spears**	Crossroads	2002
8	**Barbra Streisand**	Funny Girl	1968
9	**Ice-T**	New Jack City	1991
10	**Mandy Moore**	A Walk to Remember	2002

Since Al Jolson's debut role in the pioneering talkie *The Jazz Singer* (1927), many popular vocalists have made the transition to films, with those listed representing the most successful (although some had minor parts, often uncredited, in films before starring in these). Since the 1930s, this catalog has included artists of the caliber of Bing Crosby, Marlene Dietrich, Elvis Presley, The Beatles, David Bowie, Sting, Madonna, and Björk.

STAGE & SCREEN

BERTELSMANN
Time To Fly
Virgin
LOEWS
Cola
AALIYAH
SELLECK
D CLOWN

The Play's the Thing

THE 10 LATEST DORA AWARDS FOR "OUSTANDING MUSICAL PRODUCTION"

YEAR	MUSICAL PRODUCTION
2002	Anything That Moves
2001	Billy Budd
2000	Cabaret
1999	Norma
1998	Oedipus Rex
1997	Ragtime
1996	A Little Night Magic
1995	Tommy
1994	Crazy for You
1993	Kiss of the Spiderwoman

THE 10 LATEST DORA AWARDS FOR "OUTSTANDING PRODUCTION OF A PLAY"

YEAR	PLAY
2002	The Island
2001	Platanov
2000	Endgame
1999	The Drawer Boy
1998	Patience
1997	The Three Lives of Lucie Cabrol
1996	The Seven Streams of the River Ota
1995	Molly Wood
1994	Homeward Bound
1993	Whale

The Dora Mavor Moore Awards, established in 1981, honor outstanding achievements in Toronto theater and dance.

THE 10 LATEST DRAMA DESK AWARDS FOR AN ACTRESS

YEAR	ACTRESS/DRAMA
2002	**Lindsay Duncan,** Private Lives
2001	**Mary-Louise Parker,** Proof
2000	**Eileen Heckart,** The Waverly Gallery
1999	**Kathleen Chalfant,** Wit
1998	**Cherry Jones,** Pride's Crossing
1997	**Janet McTeer,** A Doll's House
1996	**Zoë Caldwell,** Master Class
1995	**Glenn Close,** Sunset Boulevard
1994	**Myra Carter,** Three Tall Women
1993	**Jane Alexander,** The Sisters Rosensweig

Source: *New York Drama Desk*

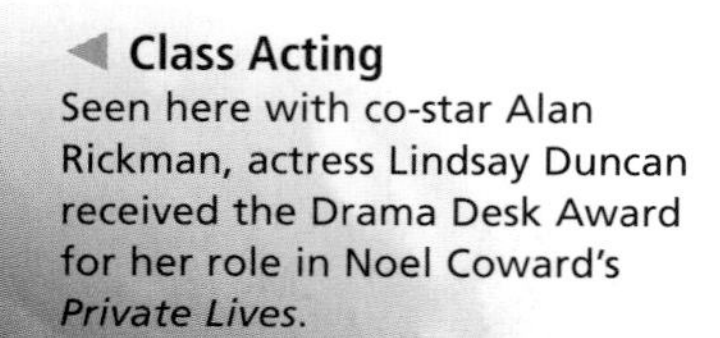

Class Acting
Seen here with co-star Alan Rickman, actress Lindsay Duncan received the Drama Desk Award for her role in Noel Coward's *Private Lives.*

TOP 10 PRODUCTIONS OF SHAKESPEARE ON BROADWAY

	PLAY	PRODUCTIONS
1	Hamlet	61
2	The Merchant of Venice	46
3	Macbeth	40
4	Romeo and Juliet	32
5	Twelfth Night	29
6	As You Like It	22
7	Othello	20
8	= Julius Caesar	19
	= Richard III	19
	= The Taming of the Shrew	19

Source: *The League of American Theaters and Producers*

The least popular productions have been *The Two Gentlemen of Verona* (never produced—except as a musical written by the composers of *Hair*), *All's Well That Ends Well, The Comedy of Errors, Timon of Athens, Coriolanus, Henry IV Part I,* and *Henry IV Part II,* which have been produced just once.

TOP 10 LONGEST-RUNNING NON-MUSICALS ON BROADWAY

	SHOW/YEARS RUNNING	PERFORMANCES
1	**Oh! Calcutta!**, 1976–89	5,959
2	**Life With Father**, 1939–47	3,224
3	**Tobacco Road**, 1933–41	3,182
4	**Abie's Irish Rose**, 1922–27	2,327
5	**Gemini**, 1977–81	1,819
6	**Deathtrap**, 1978–82	1,793
7	**Harvey**, 1944–49	1,775
8	**Born Yesterday**, 1946–49	1,642
9	**Mary, Mary**, 1961–64	1,572
10	**The Voice of the Turtle**, 1943–48	1,557

Source: *The League of American Theaters and Producers*

More than half of the longest-running non-musical shows on Broadway began their runs before World War II; the others all date from the period up to the 1970s, before the long-running musical completely dominated the Broadway stage.

TOP 10 LONGEST-RUNNING THRILLERS ON BROADWAY

	SHOW/YEARS RUNNING	PERFORMANCES
1	**Deathtrap**, 1978–82	1,793
2	**Arsenic and Old Lace**, 1941–44	1,444
3	**Angel Street**, 1941–1944	1,295
4	**Sleuth**, 1970–73	1,222
5	**Dracula**, 1977–80	925
6	**Witness for the Prosecution**, 1954–56	645
7	**Dial M for Murder**, 1952–54	556
8	**Sherlock Holmes**, 1974–76	471
9	**An Inspector Calls**, 1994–95	454
10	**Ten Little Indians**, 1944–45	426

Source: *The League of American Theaters and Producers*

Canada's longest-running thriller is Agatha Christie's *The Mousetrap*, which opened August 19, 1977, at the Toronto Truck Theatre. With more than 8,500 performances, it is currently in its 28th season.

THE 10 LATEST PULITZER DRAMA AWARDS

YEAR*	PLAYWRIGHT/DRAMA
2003	**Nilo Cruz**, Anna in the Tropics
2002	**Suzan-Lori Parks**, Topdog/Underdog
2001	**David Auburn**, Proof
2000	**Jhumpa Lahiri**, Dinner With Friends
1999	**Margaret Edson**, Wit
1998	**Paula Vogel**, How I Learned to Drive
1996	**Jonathan Larson**, Rent
1995	**Horton Foote**, The Young Man from Atlanta
1994	**Edward Albee**, Three Tall Women
1993	**Tony Kushner**, Angels in America: Millennium Approaches

* *No award in 1997*

The Pulitzer Drama Award is made for "an American play, preferably original and dealing with American life." Regarded as the most prestigious of all drama awards, it is presented to playwrights; the first winner, in 1918, was Jesse Lynch Williams for *Why Marry?*

TOP 10 LONGEST-RUNNING MUSICALS ON BROADWAY

	SHOW/YEARS RUNNING	PERFORMANCES
1	**Cats**, 1982–2000	7,485
2	**Les Misérables**, 1987–2003	6,684
3	**The Phantom of the Opera**, 1988–	6,231*
4	**A Chorus Line**, 1975–90	6,137
5	**Miss Saigon**, 1991–2001	4,095
6	**Beauty and the Beast**, 1994–	3,556*
7	**42nd Street**, 1980–89	3,486
8	**Grease**, 1972–80	3,388
9	**Fiddler on the Roof**, 1964–72	3,242
10	**Hello, Dolly!** 1964–71	2,844

* *Still running; total as of January 1, 2003*

Source: *The League of American Theaters and Producers*

▶ The Cats' Whiskers
Cats made theater history by topping the long-running musicals chart on both sides of the Atlantic.

Blockbusters

TOP 10 HIGHEST-GROSSING FILMS WORLDWIDE

	FILM	YEAR	GROSS INCOME (US$) CANADA & US	OVERSEAS	WORLD TOTAL
1	**Titanic***	1997	600,800,000	1,234,600,000	1,835,400,000
2	**Harry Potter and the Philosopher's Stone**	2001	317,600,000	649,400,000	967,000,000
3	**Star Wars: Episode I—The Phantom Menace**	1999	431,100,000	492,000,000	923,100,000
4	**Jurassic Park**	1993	334,800,000	547,000,000	881,800,000
5	**The Lord of the Rings: The Two Towers**	2002	333,600,000	533,000,000	866,600,000
6	**Harry Potter and the Chamber of Secrets**	2002	261,700,000	604,000,000	865,700,000
7	**The Lord of the Rings: The Fellowship of the Ring**	2001	313,400,000	547,200,000	860,600,000
8	**Independence Day**	1996	306,300,000	505,000,000	811,200,000
9	**Spider-Man**	2002	403,700,000	402,000,000	805,700,000
10	**Star Wars#**	1977	461,000,000	337,000,000	798,000,000

* *Winner of the Academy Award for "Best Picture"*

\# *Later retitled* Star Wars: Episode IV—A New Hope

In March 2003, *Harry Potter and the Chamber of Secrets* became only the third film ever (after *Titanic* and *Harry Potter and the Philosopher's Stone*) to make more than US$600 million at the international box office—a remarkable achievement, since only four films have ever made more than US$500 million and three over US$400 million outside the US prior to that.

TOP 10 FILM BUDGETS

	FILM	YEAR	BUDGET (US$)
1	**Titanic**	1997	200,000,000
2	= **Waterworld**	1995	175,000,000
	= **Wild, Wild West**	1999	175,000,000
4	**Terminator 3: Rise of the Machines**	2003	170,000,000
5	**Tarzan***	1999	145,000,000
6	**Die Another Day**	2002	142,000,000
7	= **Armageddon**	1998	140,000,000
	= **Lethal Weapon 4**	1998	140,000,000
	= **Men in Black II**	2002	140,000,000
	= **Pearl Harbor**	2001	140,000,000
	= **Treasure Planet**	2002	140,000,000

* *Animated*

The two most expensive films ever made are water-based, their use of large-scale special effects being a major contributing factor to their escalating budgets. The two blockbuster films of 2001, *Harry Potter and the Philosopher's Stone* and *Lord of the Rings: The Fellowship of the Ring*, had budgets of US$125 million and US$109 million respectively, and hence do not make the Top 10.

▼ **Star quality**
Queen Padmé Amidala, played by Natalie Portman, is the heroine of *Star Wars: Episode I—The Phantom Menace*, second only to *Titanic* as the highest-grossing film of the 20th century.

TOP 10 HIGHEST-GROSSING FILMS IN THE US

	FILM	YEAR	GROSS US INCOME (US$)
1	Titanic*	1997	600,800,000
2	Star Wars#	1977	461,000,000
3	E.T. the Extra-Terrestrial	1982	435,000,000
4	Star Wars: Episode I—The Phantom Menace	1999	431,100,000
5	Spider-Man	2002	403,700,000
6	Jurassic Park	1993	357,100,000
7	The Lord of the Rings: The Two Towers	2002	334,800,000
8	Forrest Gump*	1994	329,700,000
9	Harry Potter and the Philosopher's Stone†	2001	317,600,000
10	The Lord of the Rings: The Fellowship of the Ring	2001	313,400,000

* *Winner of the Academy Award for "Best Picture"*

Later retitled Star Wars: Episode IV—A New Hope

† *Titled* Harry Potter and the Philosopher's Stone *for the US market only*

Only 14 films have ever earned more than US$300 million in the US. The four movies not on this Top 10 list, *The Lion King* (1994), *Star Wars: Episode II— Attack of the Clones* (2002), *Star Wars: Episode VI—Return of the Jedi* (1983), and *Independence Day* (1996), have recently been bumped by the *Harry Potter* and *Lord of the Rings* films.

TOP 10 FILMS IN CANADA

	FILM	BOX OFFICE GROSS ($)*
1	The Lord of the Rings: The Fellowship of the Ring	53,100,000
2	Spider-Man	47,000,000
3	Harry Potter and the Philosopher's Stone	39,400,000
4	Star Wars: Episode II—Attack of the Clones	33,100,000
5	Austin Powers in Goldmember	25,000,000
6	My Big Fat Greek Wedding	23,800,000
7	Signs	21,500,000
8	A Beautiful Mind	21,200,000
9	Ice Age	19,000,000
10	Men in Black 2	18,100,000

* *Earnings from November 9, 2001 to November 7, 2002*

Source: *Motion Picture Theatre Associations of Canada*

Nia Vardalos, originally from Winnipeg, Manitoba, starred in and wrote the screenplay for the sleeper hit *My Big Fat Greek Wedding*. The film, based on her one-woman play, was mainly filmed in Toronto, where local venues filled in for what were portrayed as Chicago locations in the film. It is one of the most profitable films, and the highest-grossing independent film, of all time.

TOP 10 MOST PROFITABLE FILMS OF ALL TIME*

	FILM	YEAR	BUDGET (US$)	WORLD GROSS (US$)	PROFIT RATIO
1	The Blair Witch Project	1999	35,000	248,662,839	7,104.65
2	American Graffiti	1973	750,000	115,000,000	153.33
3	Snow White and the Seven Dwarfs#	1937	1,488,000	187,670,866	126.12
4	The Rocky Horror Picture Show	1975	1,200,000	139,876,417	116.56
5	Rocky†	1976	1,100,000	117,235,147	106.58
6	Gone With the Wind†	1939	3,900,000	390,555,278	100.14
7	The Full Monty	1997	3,500,000	256,950,122	73.41
8	Star Wars★	1977	11,000,000	797,998,007	72.55
9	E.T. the Extra-Terrestrial	1982	10,500,000	756,774,579	72.07
10	My Big Fat Greek Wedding	2002	5,000,000	353,906,779	70.78

* *Minimum entry US$100 million world gross*

Animated

† *Winner of the Academy Award for "Best Picture"*

★ *Later retitled* Star Wars: Episode IV—A New Hope

It should be noted that budget for *The Blair Witch Project* represents only the cost of making the film: further post-production costs, for example to enhance the sound quality, were incurred prior to theatrical release.

THE 10 LATEST GOLDEN REEL AWARD WINNERS*

YEAR	FILM	DOMESTIC BOX OFFICE ($)
2002	Les Boys III	5,334,504
2001	Nuit de Noces	2,054,074
2000	The Art of War	4,500,000
1999	Les Boys II	5,500,000
1998	Les Boys	6,800,000
1997	Air Bud	over 1,600,000
1996	Crash	over 1,230,000
1995	Johnny Mnemonic	over 3,000,000
1994	Louis 19, le roi des ondes	1,800,000
1993	La Florida	1,640,000

* *Given by the Academy of Canadian Cinema & Televisiton (ACC&T) to the Canadian film earning the most revenue at the box office*

Source: *ACC&T*

World Movies

TOP 10 FILMS IN INDIA

	FILM*	YEAR	TOTAL INDIA GROSS (IRs)
1	**Gadar**	2001	650,000,000
2	**Hum Aapke Hai Kaun**	1994	600,000,000
3	**Dilwale Dulhania Le Jayenge**	1995	500,000,000
4	**Raja Hindustani**	1996	450,000,000
5	**Kuch Kuch Hota Hai**	1998	425,000,000
6	**Kabhi Khushi Kabhie Gham**	2001	380,500,000
7	**Kaho Na Pyaar Hai**	2000	350,000,000
8	**Karan Arjun**	1995	320,000,000
9	= **Border**	1997	300,000,000
	= **Lagaan**	2001	300,000,000

** All from India*

▼ Bollywood blockbuster
Aditya Chopra's popular directorial debut *Dilwale Dulhania Le Jayenge* (The Brave-Hearted Will Take the Bride), starring Shahrukh Khan and Kajol, was a huge hit.

TOP 10 FILMS IN FRANCE

	FILM*	YEAR	TOTAL FRANCE GROSS (US$)
1	**Titanic**	1998	138,928,349
2	**Astérix & Obélix: Mission Cleopatra** (France)	2002	75,846,048
3	**Taxi 2** (France)	2000	63,703,757
4	**Astérix & Obélix contre César** (France)	1999	59,154,242
5	**Star Wars: Episode I—The Phantom Menace**	1999	55,825,511
6	**The Fifth Element**	1997	54,080,230
7	**Les Visiteurs II: Les couloirs du temps** (France)	1998	53,898,537
8	**Le Dîner de Cons** (France)	1998	53,155,025
9	**Harry Potter and the Chamber of Secrets**	2002	53,141,000
10	**Harry Potter and the Philosopher's Stone**	2001	48,745,200

** All US unless otherwise stated*

France's all-time Top 10 films mirror the country's cosmopolitan movie tastes, with half the films from among a selection of Hollywood blockbusters and half from the homegrown output.

TOP 10 FILMS IN AUSTRALIA

	FILM*	YEAR	TOTAL AUSTRALIA GROSS (AUS$)
1	**Titanic**	1997	57,642,943
2	**Crocodile Dundee** (Australia)	1986	47,707,045
3	**The Lord of the Rings: The Fellowship of the Ring**	2001	46,851,327
4	**The Lord of the Rings: The Two Towers**	2002	45,183,872
5	**Harry Potter and The Philosopher's Stone**	2001	42,310,037
6	**Star Wars: Episode I—The Phantom Menace**	1999	38,828,310
7	**Harry Potter and the Chamber of Secrets**	2002	37,009,842
8	**Babe** (Australia/US)	1995	36,776,544
9	**Star Wars: Episode II—Attack of the Clones**	2002	33,811,334
10	**Jurassic Park**	1993	33,002,776

** All US unless otherwise stated*

Australia's most popular films reflect the international box office, but with a distinct Antipodean bias: *Crocodile Dundee* is the most successful Australian film ever, earning over US$300 million worldwide, while *Babe* was an Australian/US co-production filmed in Australia with an Australian director (Chris Noonan). Australian films earned US$25 million, 4.9 percent of the total, at the Australian box office in 2002.

FILMS IN JAPAN

	FILM*	YEAR	TOTAL JAPAN GROSS (US$)
1	**Sen to Chihiro no Kamikakushi (Spirited Away)#** (Japan)	2001	228,612,367
2	**Harry Potter and the Chamber of Secrets**	2002	142,786,414
3	**Harry Potter and the Philosopher's Stone**	2001	127,687,138
4	**Titanic**	1997	101,800,644
5	**The Lord of the Rings: The Two Towers**	2002	59,156,943
6	**Star Wars: Episode I—The Phantom Menace**	1999	50,812,345
7	**Mononoke Hime (Princess Mononoke)#** (Japan)	1997	49,959,609
8	**Kindaichi Shonen no Jikenbo (The Case Book of Young Kindaichi)#** (Japan)	1997	47,637,131
9	**Armageddon**	1998	45,533,387
10	**Independence Day**	1996	44,239,833

** All US unless otherwise stated*

 # Animated

The Japanese Top 10 feature a number of global successes while representing the local enthusiasm for anime—animation, often with a fantasy element, aimed to appeal to adults

High spirits
The popular Japanese anime production *Spirited Away* was the first film ever to earn more than US$200 million before it opened in the US.

TOP 10 FOREIGN LANGUAGE FILMS IN THE US

	FILM	YEAR	ORIGINAL LANGUAGE*	TOTAL US GROSS (US$)
1	**Crouching Tiger, Hidden Dragon**	2001	Mandarin	128,078,872
2	**Life Is Beautiful (La vita è bella)**	1999	Italian	57,600,759
3	**Amélie**	2001	French	33,225,499
4	**The Gods Must Be Crazy**	1984	Afrikaans	30,031,783
5	**The Postman (Il Postino)**	1995	Italian	21,845,977
6	**Like Water for Chocolate**	1993	Spanish	21,665,468
7	**La Dolce Vita**	1966	Italian	19,500,000
8	**Brotherhood of the Wolf**	2002	French	18,828,863
9	**I Am Curious (Yellow)**	1969	Swedish	18,570,318
10	**La Cage aux Folles**	1979	French	17,921,489

** Some dubbed in English, others subtitled*

TOP 10 FILMS IN RUSSIA

	FILM*	YEAR	TOTAL RUSSIA GROSS ($US)
1	**The Lord of the Rings: The Fellowship of the Ring**	2002	7,123,940
2	**Harry Potter and the Philosopher's Stone**	2002	5,332,760
3	**Titanic**	1998	5,200,000
4	**Star Wars: Episode II—Attack of the Clones**	2002	4,986,420
5	**Spider-Man**	2002	3,452,610
6	**Ocean's Eleven**	2002	3,183,270
7	**The Mummy Returns**	2001	3,050,000
8	**Sibirskiy Cirulnik** (Russia)	1999	2,600,000
9	**Star Wars: Episode I—The Phantom Menace**	1999	2,300,000
10	**Planet of the Apes**	2001	2,180,000

** All US unless otherwise stated*

Movie Genres

TOP 10 WAR FILMS

	FILM	YEAR
1	Saving Private Ryan	1998
2	Pearl Harbor	2001
3	Schindler's List	1993
4	The English Patient	1996
5	Life Is Beautiful (La vita è bella)	1997
6	Braveheart	1995
7	Black Hawk Down	2001
8	U-571	2000
9	Three Kings	1999
10	Enemy at the Gates	2001

In recent years—until the hugely successful *Saving Private Ryan*—surprisingly few war films appeared in the high-earning bracket, which led some to consider that the days of big-budget films in this genre were over. However, excluding military-themed but non-war films, recent blockbusters, including "historical" war films such as *Pearl Harbor* and Mel Gibson's two notable successes, *Braveheart* and *The Patriot*, appear to have disproved this prediction.

TOP 10 SUPERHERO FILMS

	FILM	YEAR
1	Spider-Man	2002
2	Batman	1989
3	Batman Forever	1995
4	The Mask	1994
5	Superman	1978
6	X-Men	2000
7	Batman Returns	1992
8	Batman & Robin	1997
9	Teenage Mutant Ninja Turtles	1990
10	Blade II	2002

Spider-Man has earned over $47 million in Canada since its release in 2002. It surpassed *Harry Potter and the Philosopher's Stone* in its opening weekend in Canadian theaters, grossing $12 million.

TOP 10 SCIENCE-FICTION FILMS

	FILM	YEAR
1	Star Wars: Episode I—The Phantom Menace	1999
2	Jurassic Park	1993
3	Independence Day	1996
4	Star Wars	1977
5	Spider-Man	2002
6	E.T. the Extra-Terrestrial	1982
7	Star Wars: Episode II—Attack of the Clones	2002
8	The Lost World: Jurassic Park	1997
9	Men in Black	1997
10	Star Wars: Episode VI—Return of the Jedi	1983

The first six films in this list are also on the all-time Top 10, and all 10 are among the 16 most successful films ever, having earned in excess of US$570 million each—a total of more than US$7.4 billion at the worldwide box office.

▼ **Worldwide web**
With global earnings of over US$800 million, *Spider-Man* established itself as the most successful superhero film ever.

TOP 10 MAGIC, WITCHES, AND WIZARDS FILMS

	FILM	YEAR
1	**Harry Potter and the Philosopher's Stone**	2001
2	**The Lord of the Rings: The Two Towers**	2002
3	**The Lord of the Rings: The Fellowship of the Ring**	2001
4	**Harry Potter and the Chamber of Secrets**	2002
5	**Shrek***	2001
6	**Beauty and the Beast***	1991
7	**The Blair Witch Project**	1999
8	**Sleepy Hollow**	1999
9	**Snow White and the Seven Dwarfs***	1937
10	**Fantasia/2000***	1999

* *Animated*

► Golden ring
The second of the *Lord of the Rings* trilogy, *The Two Towers* has outearned its predecessor to become the fifth highest-earning film of all time.

DINOSAUR FILMS

	FILM	YEAR
1	**Jurassic Park**	1993
2	**The Lost World: Jurassic Park**	1997
3	**Godzilla**	1998
4	**Jurassic Park III**	2001
5	**Dinosaur***	2000
6	**Fantasia***	1940
7	**T-Rex: Back to the Cretaceous**	1998
8	**The Flintstones in Viva Rock Vegas**	2000
9	**The Land Before Time***	1988
10	**Super Mario Bros.**	1993

* *Animated; others live-action with mechanical or computer-generated animation sequences*

The animated *Gertie the Dinosaur* (1914) was the first notable example in a catalog of well over 100 films to feature prehistoric monsters.

TOP 10 JAMES BOND FILMS

	FILM	BOND ACTOR	YEAR
1	**The World Is Not Enough**	Pierce Brosnan	1999
2	**GoldenEye**	Pierce Brosnan	1995
3	**Tomorrow Never Dies**	Pierce Brosnan	1997
4	**Die Another Day**	Pierce Brosnan	2002
5	**Moonraker**	Roger Moore	1979
6	**The Living Daylights**	Timothy Dalton	1987
7	**For Your Eyes Only**	Roger Moore	1981
8	**The Spy Who Loved Me**	Roger Moore	1977
9	**Octopussy**	Roger Moore	1983
10	**License to Kill**	Timothy Dalton	1990

Ian Fleming wrote 12 James Bond novels, of which the film versions of only two, *Moonraker* (1955) and *The Spy Who Loved Me* (1962), figure in this Top 10. After his death in 1964, *For Your Eyes Only*, *Octopussy*, *The Living Daylights*, and *GoldenEye* were developed by other writers from his short stories, while subsequent releases were written without reference to Fleming's writings. *Casino Royale* (book 1953, film 1967), featuring 56-year-old David Niven as the retired spy Sir James Bond, is an oddity in that it was presented as a comedy. This film and *Never Say Never Again* (1983), effectively a remake of *Thunderball*, are not considered "official" Bond films, making the 2002 release of *Die Another Day* the 20th in the canonical series.

Leading Men

TOP 10 ACTORS AT THE US BOX OFFICE

	ACTOR*	FILMS	TOTAL US BOX OFFICE EARNINGS (US$)
1	**Harrison Ford**	30	3,187,215,057
2	**Samuel L. Jackson**	56	2,832,308,762
3	**Tom Hanks**	30	2,805,563,647
4	**Tom Cruise**	25	2,389,498,678
5	**James Earl Jones**	36	2,326,924,965
6	**Eddie Murphy**	27	2,300,000,784
7	**Mel Gibson**	31	2,285,154,698
8	**Robin Williams**	41	2,230,226,135
9	**Jim Cummings**	24	2,193,119,817
10	**Rance Howard**	38	2,190,866,163

** Appeared in or provided voice in animated film*

Although a volatile list, this presents a snapshot of the actors who, to date, have appeared in the films or provided the voice of a character in an animated film that cumulatively have earned the most in the US. Such is the box office appeal of Harrison Ford that US distributors voted him "Star of the Century."

TOP 10 RUSSELL CROWE FILMS

	FILM	YEAR
1	**Gladiator***	2000
2	**A Beautiful Mind**	2001
3	**L.A. Confidential**	1997
4	**The Insider**	1999
5	**The Quick and the Dead**	1995
6	**Proof of Life**	2000
7	**Virtuosity**	1995
8	**Mystery, Alaska**	1999
9	**The Sum of Us**	1994
10	**Proof**	1991

** Won Academy Award for "Best Actor"*

After appearing in Australian TV series, including *Neighbours* (1987), New Zealand–born Russell Crowe gained his first Hollywood role with *The Quick and the Dead* (1985).

TOP 10 PIERCE BROSNAN FILMS

	FILM	YEAR
1	**Mrs. Doubtfire**	1993
2	**Die Another Day**	2002
3	**The World Is Not Enough**	1999
4	**GoldenEye**	1995
5	**Tomorrow Never Dies**	1997
6	**Dante's Peak**	1997
7	**The Thomas Crown Affair**	1999
8	**Mars Attacks!**	1996
9	**The Mirror Has Two Faces**	1996
10	**The Lawnmower Man**	1992

Pierce Brosnan, now best known as James Bond, provided the voice of King Arthur in the animated *Quest for Camelot* (1998). If included, it would be ranked ninth. Each of the eight leading films in his Top 10 has earned in excess of US$100 million worldwide.

TOP 10 BRAD PITT FILMS

	FILM	YEAR
1	**Ocean's Eleven**	2001
2	**Se7en**	1995
3	**Interview with the Vampire: The Vampire Chronicles**	1994
4	**Sleepers**	1996
5	**Twelve Monkeys**	1995
6	**Legends of the Fall**	1994
7	**The Devil's Own**	1997
8	**Meet Joe Black**	1998
9	**Seven Years in Tibet**	1997
10	**Spy Game**	2001

Brad Pitt is a member of an elite group of actors, all of whose 10 highest-earning films have made more than US$100 million in total at the world box office. Pitt's runners-up to this Top 10 list, *The Mexican* (2001) and *Fight Club* (1999), also fall into this high-earning category.

FIRST FACT

THE FIRST MILLION-DOLLAR FILM STAR

IN 1921—after ironically appearing in a film called *The Dollar a Year Man*—silent-film star Roscoe ("Fatty") Arbuckle (1887–1933) signed a three-year contract with Paramount that would have made him the first film star ever to earn US$1 million a year. However, at a party to celebrate his success, a starlet named Virginia Rappe was injured and later died, and he was charged with her manslaughter. Although he was acquitted, the scandal meant Arbuckle became the first star to be banned from acting. He began working as a director under the pseudonym William Goodrich and, in 1933, agreed a deal with Warner Bros. Fatefully, he died, aged 46, on the day he signed the contract that would have enabled his return to the screen.

TOP 10 BRUCE WILLIS FILMS

	FILM	YEAR
1	**The Sixth Sense**	1999
2	**Armageddon**	1998
3	**Die Hard: With a Vengeance**	1995
4	**The Fifth Element**	1997
5	**Unbreakable**	2000
6	**Die Hard 2**	1990
7	**Pulp Fiction**	1994
8	**Twelve Monkeys**	1995
9	**The Jackal**	1997
10	**Death Becomes Her**	1992

Although discounted here, it is somewhat ironic to consider that the fourth most successful film role of an actor whose screen persona is of a tough guy would otherwise be that of a baby in *Look Who's Talking* (1989)—with that part consisting only of Willis's dubbed voice.

TOP 10 LEONARDO DiCAPRIO FILMS

	FILM	YEAR
1	**Titanic**	1997
2	**Catch Me If You Can**	2002
3	**The Man in the Iron Mask**	1998
4	**The Beach**	2000
5	**Gangs of New York**	2002
6	**Romeo + Juliet**	1996
7	**The Quick and the Dead**	1995
8	**Marvin's Room**	1996
9	**What's Eating Gilbert Grape?**	1993
10	**Celebrity**	1998

A film career of only 10 years has seen Leonardo DiCaprio star in six films earning in excess of US$100 million, including the biggest blockbuster of all time, *Titanic*. His role in *What's Eating Gilbert Grape?* also garnered him an Oscar nomination.

▼ Leonardo Masterpiece
Leonardo DiCaprio stars as conman Frank Abagnale Jr. in *Catch Me If You Can*, which has netted over US$300 million worldwide.

TOP 10 TOM CRUISE FILMS

	FILM	YEAR
1	**Mission: Impossible II**	2000
2	**Mission: Impossible**	1996
3	**Rain Man**	1988
4	**Top Gun**	1986
5	**Minority Report**	2002
6	**Jerry Maguire**	1996
7	**The Firm**	1993
8	**A Few Good Men**	1992
9	**Interview with the Vampire: The Vampire Chronicles**	1994
10	**Vanilla Sky**	2001

Few actors have matched Tom Cruise's commercial success: every one of his Top 10 films has earned more than US$200 million worldwide, a total of US$3.3 billion.

Leading Women

TOP 10 ACTRESSES AT THE US BOX OFFICE

	ACTRESS*	FILMS	TOTAL US BOX OFFICE EARNINGS (US$)
1	**Julia Roberts**	27	1,889,883,547
2	**Carrie Fisher**	25	1,760,869,785
3	**Whoopi Goldberg**	41	1,683,352,258
4	**Kathy Bates**	31	1,447,092,182
5	**Drew Barrymore**	27	1,303,932,619
6	**Cameron Diaz**	21	1,289,627,290
7	**Maggie Smith**	20	1,286,055,060
8	**Bonnie Hunt**	16	1,270,837,762
9	**Sally Field**	20	1,237,398,519
10	**Glenn Close**	28	1,236,979,789

* *Appeared in or provided voice in animated film*

As with their actor counterparts, these are the actresses whose films (and voice-only parts in animated films) have earned the most cumulatively in the US. Julia Roberts has appeared in nine films that have made over US$100 milion in the US, and 13 that have netted more than that amount worldwide.

TOP 10 JULIANNE MOORE FILMS

	FILM	YEAR
1	**The Lost World: Jurassic Park**	1997
2	**The Fugitive**	1993
3	**Hannibal**	2001
4	**Nine Months**	1995
5	**The Hand that Rocks the Cradle**	1992
6	**Evolution**	2001
7	**Assassins**	1995
8	**The Hours**	2002
9	**Magnolia**	1999
10	**Boogie Nights**	1997

Julianne Moore's early screen appearances were in TV series and TV films. Following her break into mainstream movies, her relatively minor role in *The Fugitive* so impressed Steven Spielberg that he cast her in *The Lost World: Jurassic Park*, films No. 1 and No. 2 of her personal Top 10.

TOP 10 MERYL STREEP FILMS

	FILM	YEAR
1	**Out of Africa**	1985
2	**The Bridges of Madison County**	1995
3	**Death Becomes Her**	1992
4	**Kramer vs. Kramer**	1979
5	**The River Wild**	1994
6	**The Hours**	2002
7	**The Deer Hunter**	1978
8	**Manhattan**	1979
9	**Postcards from the Edge**	1990
10	**Silkwood**	1983

Meryl Streep has been nominated for Academy Awards on a total of 13 occasions, winning "Best Supporting Actress" for her role in *Kramer vs. Kramer* and "Best Actress" for *Sophie's Choice* (1982). She provided the voice of the Blue Fairy in *A.I.: Artificial Intelligence* (2001), which, if it were taken into account for this list, would appear in second place.

TOP 10 NICOLE KIDMAN FILMS

	FILM	YEAR
1	**Batman Forever**	1995
2	**Moulin Rouge!***	2001
3	**The Others**	2001
4	**Days of Thunder**	1990
5	**Eyes Wide Shut**	1999
6	**The Peacemaker**	1997
7	**Practical Magic**	1998
8	**Far and Away**	1992
9	**The Hours#**	2002
10	**Malice**	1993

* *Nominated for Academy Award for "Best Actress"*

\# *Winner of Academy Award for "Best Actress"*

Honolulu-born Nicole Kidman was raised in Australia, where she acted on TV before her break into films. She has pursued a highly successful movie career: more than half her Top 10 films have earned in excess of US$100 million worldwide.

TOP 10 GWYNETH PALTROW FILMS

	FILM	YEAR
1	**Se7en**	1995
2	**Hook**	1991
3	**Shakespeare in Love***	1998
4	**Shallow Hal**	2001
5	**A Perfect Murder**	1998
6	**The Talented Mr. Ripley**	1999
7	**The Royal Tenenbaums**	2001
8	**Sliding Doors**	1998
9	**Great Expectations**	1998
10	**Malice**	1993

* *Winner of Academy Award for "Best Actress"*

Noted for her faultless English accent in her Academy Award–winning role in *Shakespeare in Love* and in other movies, Gwyneth Paltrow has achieved an enviable box office feat: her Top 10 films have cumulatively earned more than US$1.5 billion globally in just over a decade.

TOP 10 CAMERON DIAZ FILMS

	FILM	YEAR
1	**There's Something About Mary**	1998
2	**The Mask**	1994
3	**My Best Friend's Wedding**	1997
4	**Charlie's Angels**	2000
5	**Vanilla Sky**	2001
6	**Gangs of New York**	2002
7	**Any Given Sunday**	1999
8	**Being John Malkovich**	1999
9	**The Sweetest Thing**	2002
10	**A Life Less Ordinary**	1997

Cameron Diaz's Top 10 films include several that are among the highest earning of recent years. She also provided the voice of Princess Fiona in *Shrek* (2001), which has outearned all of them. Her uncredited cameo role as "woman on metro" in *Minority Report* (2002) has not been included in this list, but would appear in second place if it was.

CATHERINE ZETA-JONES FILMS

	FILM	YEAR
1	The Mask of Zorro	1998
2	Entrapment	1999
3	Traffic	2000
4	Chicago*	2002
5	The Haunting	1999
6	America's Sweethearts	2001
7	High Fidelity	2000
8	The Phantom	1996
9	Christopher Columbus: The Discovery	1992
10	Splitting Heirs	1993

* *Winner of Academy Award for "Best Supporting Actress"*

After a debut as Sheherezade in the French film *Les Mille et Une Nuits* (1990), Welsh-born Catherine Zeta-Jones rose to prominence as Mariette Larkin in the British TV series *The Darling Buds of May* before her first Hollywood screen role in *Christopher Columbus: The Discovery* (1992).

▶ From Chicago to Toronto
Catherine Zeta-Jones took the Oscar for "Best Supporting Actress" as Velma Kelly in *Chicago*, a movie filmed almost entirely in Toronto, which very often stands in for the Windy City.

RENEE ZELLWEGER FILMS

	FILM	YEAR
1	Bridget Jones's Diary	2001
2	Jerry Maguire	1996
3	Chicago	2002
4	Me, Myself & Irene	2000
5	Nurse Betty	2000
6	One True Thing	1998
7	The Bachelor	1999
8	Reality Bites	1994
9	8 Seconds	1994
10	White Oleander	2002

Apart from some unmemorable early parts in films such as *The Return of the Texas Chainsaw Massacre* (1994), Reneé Zellweger has followed an ever-upward trajectory in her film career. Her title role in *Bridget Jones's Diary* and *Nurse Betty* earned her two Golden Globe awards, and she was nominated for the "Best Actress" Oscar for her performance in *Chicago*.

Oscar-Winning Films

THE 10 LATEST "BEST PICTURE" OSCAR WINNERS

YEAR	FILM	DIRECTOR
2002	Chicago	Rob Marshall*
2001	A Beautiful Mind	Ron Howard
2000	Gladiator	Ridley Scott*
1999	American Beauty	Sam Mendes
1998	Shakespeare in Love	John Madden*
1997	Titanic	James Cameron
1996	The English Patient	Anthony Minghella
1995	Braveheart	Mel Gibson
1994	Forrest Gump	Robert Zemeckis
1993	Schindler's List	Steven Spielberg

** Did not win "Best Director" Oscar*

The 2002 film *Chicago* captured Oscars for Canadians Gordon Sim, a set decorator, for "Best Art Direction" and sound engineer David Lee, for "Best Sound."

TOP 10 HIGHEST-EARNING "BEST PICTURE" OSCAR WINNERS*

	FILM	YEAR#
1	Titanic	1997
2	Forrest Gump	1994
3	Gladiator	2000
4	Dances With Wolves	1990
5	Rain Man	1988
6	Gone With the Wind	1939
7	American Beauty	1999
8	Schindler's List	1993
9	A Beautiful Mind	2001
10	Shakespeare in Love	1998

** Ranked by world box office income*

 # Of release; Oscars are awarded the following year

THE 10 LATEST BLACK & WHITE FILMS TO WIN "BEST PICTURE" OSCARS

	FILM	YEAR
1	Schindler's List	1993
2	The Apartment	1960
3	Marty	1955
4	On the Waterfront	1954
5	From Here to Eternity	1953
6	All About Eve	1950
7	All the King's Men	1949
8	Hamlet	1948
9	Gentleman's Agreement	1947
10	The Best Years of Our Lives	1946

Gone With the Wind (1939) was the first color film to win the Oscar for "Best Picture." Since then, black-and-white winners have been the exception, but include such monochrome classics as Alfred Hitchcock's *Rebecca* (1940), and *Casablanca* (1943).

STUDIOS WITH THE MOST "BEST PICTURE" OSCARS

	STUDIO	AWARDS
1	= Columbia	12
	= United Artists	12
3	Paramount	11
4	MGM	9
5	20th Century Fox	7
6	= Universal	6
	= Warner Bros.	6
8	Orion	4
9	= DreamWorks	3
	= Miramax	3

In the 75 years of the Academy Awards prior to the 2003 ceremony, these studios—along with RKO Radio Pictures, with two wins (1931 and 1946)—are the only studios to have won a "Best Picture" Oscar.

◀ Top Gere
Richard Gere as astute lawyer Billy Flynn in *Chicago*. The film, an adaptation of a stage musical, won "Best Picture" and five other Academy Awards.

TOP 10 FILMS TO WIN THE MOST OSCARS*

	FILM	YEAR	NOMINATIONS	AWARDS
1	= Ben-Hur	1959	12	11
	= Titanic	1997	14	11
3	West Side Story	1961	11	10
4	= Gigi	1958	9	9
	= The Last Emperor	1987	9	9
	= The English Patient	1996	12	9
7	= Gone With the Wind	1939	13	8#
	= From Here to Eternity	1953	13	8
	= On the Waterfront	1954	12	8
	= My Fair Lady	1964	12	8
	= Cabaret	1972	10	8
	= Gandhi	1982	11	8
	= Amadeus	1984	11	8

* *Oscar® is a registered trademark*

\# *Plus two special awards*

Ten other films have won seven Oscars each: *Going My Way* (1944), *The Best Years of Our Lives* (1946), *The Bridge on the River Kwai* (1957), *Lawrence of Arabia* (1962), *Patton* (1970), *The Sting* (1973), *Out of Africa* (1985), *Dances With Wolves* (1991), *Schindler's List* (1993), and *Shakespeare in Love* (1998). *Titanic* (1997) matched the previous record of 14 nominations set by *All About Eve* (1950), but outshone it by winning 11, compared with the predecessor's 6.

TOP 10 FILMS NOMINATED FOR THE MOST OSCARS

	FILM	YEAR	AWARDS	NOMINATIONS
1	= All About Eve	1950	6	14
	= Titanic	1997	11	14
3	= Gone With the Wind	1939	8*	13
	= From Here to Eternity	1953	8	13
	= Mary Poppins	1964	5	13
	= Who's Afraid of Virginia Woolf?#	1966	5	13
	= Forrest Gump	1994	6	13
	= Shakespeare in Love	1998	7	13
	= The Lord of the Rings: The Fellowship of the Ring	2001	4	13
	= Chicago	2002	6	13

* *Plus two special awards*

\# *Did not win "Best Picture"*

Thirteen is clearly not unlucky where Oscar nominations are concerned; no fewer than eight films having received that number. These films, and the two with 14 nominations each, are those that received the greatest share of votes from Academy members using a system that creates a shortlist of five nominees in each of 24 categories other than special, honorary, and technical awards. However, eliminating such specialist categories as "Best Foreign Language," "Live Action Short," and "Animated Feature" reduces the potential number of awards for which a film may be nominated; those that are eligible may be nominated in one category but not another—screenplays, for example, are separately nominated according to whether they are based on material previously produced or published, or written directly for the screen.

TOP 10 FILMS WITH THE MOST NOMINATIONS WITHOUT A SINGLE WIN

	FILM	YEAR	NOMINATIONS
1	= The Turning Point	1977	11
	= The Color Purple	1985	11
3	Gangs of New York	2002	10
4	= The Little Foxes	1941	9
	= Peyton Place	1957	9
6	= Quo Vadis	1951	8
	= The Nun's Story	1959	8
	= The Sand Pebbles	1966	8
	= The Elephant Man	1980	8
	= Ragtime	1981	8
	= The Remains of the Day	1993	8

Gangs of New York is the latest of a number of films to have received an impressive tally of nominations, but no wins in any category. *Mutiny on the Bounty* (1935) was the last to win "Best Picture" but no other awards.

THE 10 LATEST "BEST FOREIGN LANGUAGE FILM" OSCAR WINNERS

YEAR	ENGLISH TITLE	ORIGINAL LANGUAGE TITLE	COUNTRY
2002	Nowhere in Africa	Nirgendwo in Afrika	Germany
2001	No Man's Land	Nicija zemlja	Bosnia, Herzegovina
2000	Crouching Tiger, Hidden Dragon	Wo hu cang long	Taiwan
1999	All About My Mother	Todo sobre mi madre	Spain
1998	Life Is Beautiful	La vita è bella	Italy
1997	Character	Karakter	Netherlands
1996	Kolya		Czech Republic
1995	Antonia's Line	Antonia	Netherlands
1994	Burnt by the Sun	Utomlyonnye solntsem	Russia
1993	The Age of Beauty	Belle époque	Spain

Prior to 1956, when *La Strada* won this award, foreign language films received awards in special or honorary categories.

Oscar-Winning Stars

THE 10 LATEST "BEST ACTRESS" OSCAR WINNERS

YEAR	ACTRESS	FILM
2002	**Nicole Kidman**	The Hours
2001	**Halle Berry**	Monster's Ball
2000	**Julia Roberts**	Erin Brockovich
1999	**Hilary Swank**	Boys Don't Cry
1998	**Gwyneth Paltrow**	Shakespeare in Love*
1997	**Helen Hunt**	As Good As It Gets
1996	**Frances McDormand**	Fargo
1995	**Susan Sarandon**	Dead Man Walking
1994	**Jessica Lange**	Blue Sky
1993	**Holly Hunter**	The Piano

** Won "Best Picture" Oscar*

Only one actress has ever won the "Best Actress in a Leading Role" Oscar in consecutive years—Katharine Hepburn in 1967 and 1968 (shared with Barbra Streisand), with further wins in 1933 and 1981. Just 10 other actresses have won twice: Ingrid Bergman, Bette Davis, Olivia de Havilland, Sally Field, Jane Fonda, Jodie Foster, Glenda Jackson, Vivien Leigh, Luise Rainer, and Elizabeth Taylor.

Unafraid of Virginia Woolf
Nicole Kidman gained her first "Best Actress" Oscar nomination for *Moulin Rouge!* (2001), but won for her role as Virginia Woolf in *The Hours* (2002).

THE 10 LATEST "BEST ACTOR" OSCAR WINNERS

YEAR	ACTO	ILM
2002	**Adrien Brody**	The Pianist
2001	**Denzel Washington**	Training Day
2000	**Russell Crowe**	Gladiator*
1999	**Kevin Spacey**	American Beauty*
1998	**Roberto Benigni**	Life Is Beautiful (La vita è bella)
1997	**Jack Nicholson**	As Good As It Gets
1996	**Geoffrey Rush**	Shine
1995	**Nicolas Cage**	Leaving Las Vegas
1994	**Tom Hanks**	Forrest Gump*
1993	**Tom Hanks**	Philadelphia

** Won "Best Picture" Oscar*

Tom Hanks shares the honor of two consecutive wins with Spencer Tracy (1937: *Captains Courageous*, and 1938: *Boys Town*). Only four other actors have ever won twice: Marlon Brando (1954; 1972), Gary Cooper (1941; 1952), Dustin Hoffman (1977; 1988), and Jack Nicholson (1975; 1997).

THE 10 LATEST WINNERS OF AN OSCAR FOR THEIR DEBUT FILM*

	ACTOR/ACTRESS	FILM	YEAR
1	**Anna Paquin#**	The Piano	1993
2	**Marlee Matlin†**	Children of a Lesser God	1986
3	**Haing S. Ngor†#**	The Killing Fields	1984
4	**Timothy Hutton#**	Ordinary People	1980
5	**Tatum O'Neal#**	Paper Moon	1973
6	**Barbra Streisand†**	Funny Girl	1968
7	**Julie Andrews†**	Mary Poppins	1964
8	**Lila Kedrova#**	Zorba the Greek	1964
9	**Miyoshi Umeki#**	Sayonara	1957
10	**Anna Magnani†**	The Rose Tattoo	1955

** In a film eligible for a "Best" or "Best Supporting Actor/Actress" Oscar win (hence excluding previous TV movies, etc.)*

 # "Best Actor/Actress in a Supporting Role"

† "Best Actor/Actress in a Leading Role"

TOP 10 ACTRESSES WITH THE MOST OSCAR NOMINATIONS*

	ACTRESS	WINS SUPPORTING	WINS BEST	NOMINATIONS
1	Meryl Streep	1	1	13
2	Katharine Hepburn	0	4	12
3	Bette Davis	0	2	10
4	Geraldine Page	0	1	8
5	= Ingrid Bergman	1	2	7
	= Jane Fonda	0	2	7
	= Greer Garson	0	1	7
8	= Ellen Burstyn	0	1	6
	= Deborah Kerr	0	0	6
	= Jessica Lange	1	1	6
	= Vanessa Redgrave	1	0	6
	= Thelma Ritter	0	0	6
	= Norma Shearer	0	0	6
	= Maggie Smith	1	1	6
	= Sissy Spacek	0	1	6

* *In all acting categories*

TOP 10 ACTORS WITH THE MOST OSCAR NOMINATIONS*

	ACTOR	WINS SUPPORTING	WINS BEST	NOMINATIONS
1	Jack Nicholson	1	3	12
2	Laurence Olivier	0	1	10
3	= Paul Newman	0	1	9
	= Spencer Tracy	0	2	9
5	= Marlon Brando	0	2	8
	= Jack Lemmon	1	1	8
	= Al Pacino	0	1	8
8	= Richard Burton	0	0	7
	= Dustin Hoffman	0	2	7
	= Peter O'Toole	0	0	7

* *In all acting categories*

Several of the actors listed here were also nominated for, and sometimes won, awards in non-acting categories. Laurence Olivier won not only the "Best Actor" Oscar for his leading role in *Hamlet* (1948), but also the "Best Picture" award as the film's producer; he was also nominated as "Best Director." Paul Newman, as the producer, was a nominee for *Rachel, Rachel* (1968) in the "Best Picture" category. In 2003, Peter O'Toole initially declined an honorary Academy Award on the grounds that, as his career was not yet over, he retained hopes of winning one for an acting role. O'Toole has had seven "Best Actor" nominations, but has never won.

THE 10 LATEST ACTORS AND ACTRESSES TO RECEIVE THREE OR MORE CONSECUTIVE OSCAR NOMINATIONS

	ACTOR/ACTRESS	NOMINATIONS	YEARS
1	Russell Crowe	3	1999–2001
2	William Hurt	3	1985–87
3	Glenn Close	3	1982–84
4	Meryl Streep	3	1981–83
5	Jane Fonda	3	1977–79
6	Jack Nicholson	3	1973–75
7	Al Pacino	4	1972–75
8	Richard Burton	3	1964–66
9	Elizabeth Taylor	4	1957–60
10	Deborah Kerr	3	1956–58

In the earlier years of the Academy Awards, two actresses were nominated for "Best Actress" Oscars on a record five consecutive occasions: Bette Davis, with wins in 1935 and 1939; and Greer Garson, who never won.

THE 10 LATEST OSCAR NOMINATIONS FOR ACTORS AND ACTRESSES FOR NON-ENGLISH-LANGUAGE PERFORMANCES

	ACTOR/ACTRESS	FILM	LANGUAGE	YEAR
1	Javier Bardem	Before Night Falls	Spanish	2000
2	Roberto Benigni*	Life Is Beautiful (La vita è bella)	Italian	1998
3	Fernanda Montenegro	Central Station	Portuguese	1998
4	Massimo Troisi	The Postman (Il Postino)	Italian	1995
5	Catherine Deneuve	Indochine	French	1992
6	Gerard Depardieu	Cyrano de Bergerac	French	1990
7	Isabelle Adjani	Camille Claudel	French	1989
8	Max von Sydow	Pelle the Conqueror	Swedish	1988
9	Marcello Mastroianni	Dark Eyes	Italian	1987
10	Marlee Matlin*	Children of a Lesser God	American sign language	1986

* *Won Oscar*

And the Winner Is...

▲Palme Winner
Adrien Brody, in the title role in *The Pianist*, the latest winner of the prestigious Cannes Film Festival Palme d'Or.

THE 10 LATEST WINNERS OF THE CANNES PALME D'OR FOR "BEST FILM"

YEAR	FILM	COUNTRY
2002	**The Pianist**	UK, France, Germany, Netherlands, Poland)
2001	**The Son's Room** (La stanza del figlio)	Italy/ France
2000	**Dancer in the Dark**	Denmark
1999	**Rosetta**	France
1998	**Eternity and a Day** (Mia aioniotita kai mia mera)	Greece/France Italy
1997 =	**The Eel** (Unagi)	Japan
=	**The Taste of Cherries** (Ta'm e guilass)	Iran
1996	**Secrets and Lies**	UK
1995	**Underground** (Bila jednom jedna zemlja)	Yugoslavia/Germany/ France/Hungary
1994	**Pulp Fiction**	US

In its early years, there was no single "Best Film" award at the Cannes Film Festival, several films being honored jointly, including such unlikely bedfellows as David Lean's *Brief Encounter* and Walt Disney's *Dumbo*.

THE 10 LATEST GOLDEN GLOBE AWARDS FOR "BEST FOREIGN LANGUAGE FILM"

YEAR	FILM	COUNTRY
2002	**Talk to Her** (Habla con ella)	Spain
2001	**Amélie**	France
2000	**Crouching Tiger, Hidden Dragon** (Wo hu conag long)	Hong Kong/ China/ Taiwan/US
1999	**All About My Mother** (Todo sobre mi madre)	Spain
1998	**Central Station** (Central do Brasil)	Brazil/ France
1997	**My Life in Pink** (Ma Vie en Rose)	France/ Belgium/UK
1996	**Kolya**	Czech Republic
1995	**Les Misérables**	France
1994	**Farinelli**	Belgium
1993	**Farewell My Concubine** (Ba wang bie ji)	China/ Hong Kong

THE 10 LATEST GOLDEN GLOBE AWARDS FOR "BEST MOTION PICTURE—DRAMA"

YEAR	FILM
2002	**The Hours**
2001	**A Beautiful Mind**
2000	**Billy Elliott**
1999	**American Beauty**
1998	**Saving Private Ryan**
1997	**Titanic**
1996	**The English Patient**
1995	**Sense and Sensibility**
1994	**Forrest Gump**
1993	**Schindler's List**

THE 10 LATEST WINNERS OF THE "BEST MOTION PICTURE" GENIE AWARD

YEAR*	FILM
2002	Ararat
2001	Atanarjuat (The Fast Runner)
2000	Maelstöm
1999	Sunshine
1998	The Red Violin
1997	The Sweet Hereafter
1996	Lilies – Les Feluettes
1996	Le Confessionnal
1994	Exotica
1993	Thirty-Two Short Films About Glenn Gould

* *Two awards were given in 1996 and none in 1995 due to broadcast changes*

Source: *Academy of Canadian Cinema & Television*

THE 10 LATEST GOLDEN GLOBE AWARDS FOR "BEST DIRECTOR"

YEAR	DIRECTOR/FILM
2002	**Martin Scorsese,** Gangs of New York
2001	**Robert Altman,** Gosford Park
2000	**Ang Lee,** Crouching Tiger, Hidden Dragon
1999	**Sam Mendes,** American Beauty
1998	**Steven Spielberg,** Saving Private Ryan
1997	**James Cameron,** Titanic
1996	**Milos Forman,** The People vs. Larry Flynt
1995	**Mel Gibson,** Braveheart
1994	**Robert Zemeckis,** Forrest Gump
1993	**Steven Spielberg,** Schindler's List

The Golden Globe awards, which take place a month before the Academy Awards, are often seen as predictions of Oscars to come. In this category, awards for *American Beauty, Saving Private Ryan, Titanic, Braveheart, Forrest Gump,* and *Schindler's List* were all mirrored by their subsequent "Best Director" Academy Award wins.

THE 10 LATEST RECIPIENTS OF THE AMERICAN FILM INSTITUTE "LIFE ACHIEVEMENT" AWARD

YEAR	ACTOR/ACTRESS
2002	Robert De Niro
2001	Tom Hanks
2000	Barbra Streisand
1999	Harrison Ford
1998	Dustin Hoffman
1997	Robert Wise
1996	Martin Scorsese
1995	Clint Eastwood
1994	Steven Spielberg
1993	Jack Nicholson

The first recipient of the American Film Institute's Life Achievement Award was veteran director and actor John Ford, who was honored in 1973, the year he died. Subsequent winners have included many of the most illustrious figures in the film world, including Orson Welles, Alfred Hitchcock, and, in 1977, Bette Davis, the first female winner.

THE 10 LATEST WINNERS OF THE "ACHIEVEMENT IN DIRECTION" GENIE AWARD

YEAR*	DIRECTOR/FILM
2002	**David Cronenberg,** Spider
2001	**Zacharias Kunuk,** Atanarjuat (The Fast Runner)
2000	**Denis Villeneuve,** Maelstöm
1999	**Jeremy Podeswa,** The Five Senses
1998	**François Girard,** The Red Violin
1997	**Atom Egoyan,** The Sweet Hereafter
1996	**David Cronenberg,** Crash
1996	**Robert Lepage,** Le Confessionnal
1994	**Atom Egoyan,** Erotica
1993	**François Girard,** Thirty-Two Short Films About Glenn Gould

* *Two awards were given in 1996 and none in 1995 due to broadcast changes*

Source: *ACC&T*

THE 10 LATEST WINNERS OF THE GOLDEN RASPBERRY AWARD FOR "WORST PICTURE"

YEAR	FILM
2002	Swept Away
2001	Freddy Got Fingered
2000	Battlefield Earth
1999	Wild Wild West
1998	An Alan Smithee Film: Burn, Hollywood, Burn!
1997	The Postman
1996	Striptease
1995	Showgirls
1994	Color of Night
1993	Indecent Proposal

FIRST FILM AWARDS

FIRST FACT

Pre-dating the Academy Awards by almost a decade and the Golden Globes by more than two, the *Photoplay* Medal of Honor was the first-ever annual film award. Presented by the US film magazine *Photoplay*, which had been founded in 1911, it was initially based on a poll of its readers, who in its debut year voted for *Humoresque*, a drama directed by Frank Borzage, later the winner of two Oscars. After 1930, when *All Quiet on the Western Front* won both the *Photoplay* Medal and the "Best Picture" Oscar, the winners often coincided. "Most Popular Star" and other categories were later added to the *Photoplay* awards, the last of which were presented in 1968. The magazine itself closed down in 1980.

Funny Business

TOP 10 GROSS-OUT COMEDY FILMS

	FILM	YEAR
1	There's Something About Mary	1998
2	Austin Powers: The Spy Who Shagged Me	1999
3	Austin Powers in Goldmember	2002
4	Scary Movie	2001
5	American Pie 2	2001
6	Dumb & Dumber	1994
7	Big Daddy	1999
8	American Pie	1999
9	The Waterboy	1998
10	Nutty Professor II: The Klumps	2000

TOP 10 COMEDY FILMS*

	FILM	YEAR
1	Forrest Gump	1994
2	Men in Black	1997
3	Home Alone	1990
4	Ghost	1990
5	Pretty Woman	1990
6	Men in Black II	2002
7	Mrs. Doubtfire	1993
8	Ocean's Eleven	2001
9	What Women Want	2001
10	Notting Hill	1999

* *Excluding animated*

Canada's top box office success is the 1981 teen sex comedy, *Porky's*, which has earned over US$105.5 million worldwide to date, and won the 1983 Golden Reel Award for highest-grossing film in Canada.

THE 10 LATEST WINNERS OF THE GEMINI AWARD FOR BEST COMEDY PROGRAM OR SERIES

YEAR*	PROGRAM
2002	An American in Canada
2001	Made in Canada
2000	This Hour Has 22 Minutes
1999	Made in Canada
1998	This Hour Has 22 Minutes
1997	This Hour Has 22 Minutes
1996	This Hour Has 22 Minutes
1995	This Hour Has 22 Minutes
1994	The Kids in the Hall
1993	The Kids in the Hall

* *Gemini Awards were not given in this category each year*

Source: *Academy of Canadian Cinema and Television*

▼ **Sky-High Pie**
American Pie 2 figures among the recent wave of popular gross-out comedies designed to appeal to the young and repel older audiences.

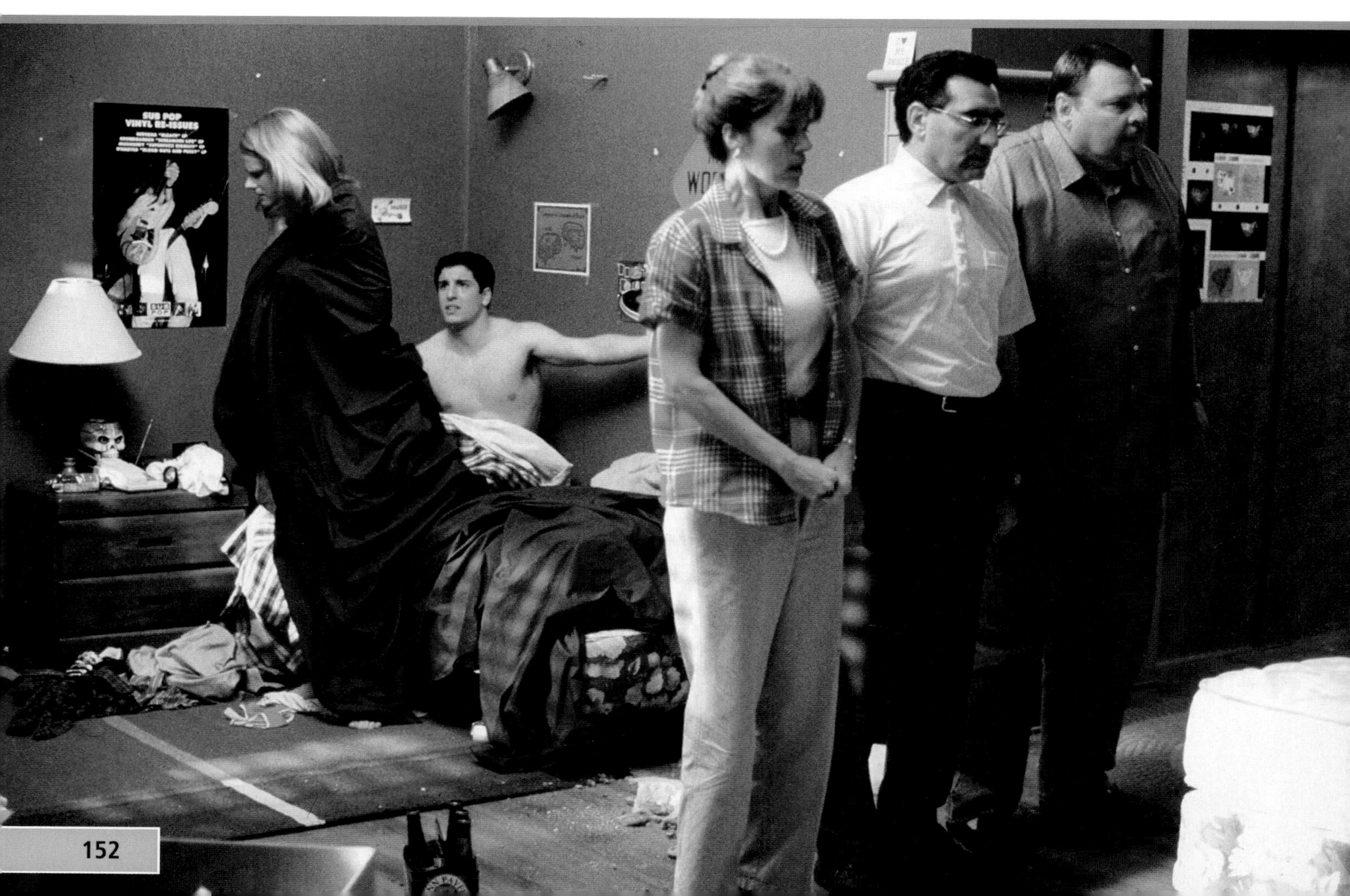

THE 10 LONGEST-RUNNING STAGE COMEDIES OF ALL TIME ON BROADWAY

	COMEDY/YEARS RUNNING	PERFORMANCES
1	**Life With Father,** 1939–47	3,224
2	**Abie's Irish Rose,** 1922–27	2,327
3	**Gemini,** 1977–81	1,819
4	**Harvey,** 1944–49	1,775
5	**Born Yesterday,** 1946–49	1,642
6	**Mary, Mary,** 1961–64	1,572
7	**The Voice of the Turtle,** 1943–48	1,557
8	**Barefoot in the Park,** 1963–67	1,530
9	**Same Time Next Year,** 1975–78	1,454
10	**Brighton Beach Memoirs,** 1983–86	1,299

Source: *The League of American Theaters and Producers*

Shown at the Empire Theatre in New York, Howard Lindsay and Russel Crouse's *Life With Father*, adapted from stories in *The New Yorker*, owed its success in part to the show's nostalgic view of a bygone America that appeared under threat as it opened on the eve of World War II.

THE 10 MOST-WATCHED TELEVISION COMEDY/ VARIETY SHOWS OF ALL TIME

	PROGRAM	AIR DATE	RATING
1	**M*A*S*H Special**	Feb 28, 1983	60.2
2	**Bob Hope Christmas Show**	Jan 15, 1970	46.6
3	**Cheers**	May 20, 1993	45.5
4	**Ed Sullivan**	Feb 9, 1964	45.3
5	**Bob Hope Christmas Show**	Jan 14, 1971	45.0
6	**The Beverly Hillbillies**	Jan 8, 1964	44.0
7	**Ed Sullivan**	Feb 16, 1964	43.8
8	**42nd Academy Awards Ceremony**	Apr 7, 1970	43.4
9	**The Beverly Hillbillies**	Jan 15, 1964	42.8
10	**The Beverly Hillbillies**	Feb 26, 1964	42.4

Source: *Nielsen Media Research*

The three-hour *M*A*S*H Special*, the farewell episode also known as "Goodbye, Farewell, and Amen," depicted the events surrounding the 4,077th M*A*S*H unit in the closing stages of the Korean War. It had been running since 1972 and attracted consistently high audiences, with this final program registering an estimated 50.15 million out of a then total of 83 million "TV households" in the US, thereby producing the highest-ever rating for a comedy show.

TOP 10 HORROR SPOOF FILMS

	FILM	YEAR
1	**Scary Movie**	2000
2	**Scream**	1996
3	**Scream 2**	1997
4	**Scream 3**	2000
5	**Scary Movie 2**	2001
6	**Young Frankenstein**	1974
7	**Love at First Bite**	1979
8	**An American Werewolf in London**	1981
9	**An American Werewolf in Paris**	1997
10	**Fright Night**	1985

While many films combine comedy and horror elements—among them *Ghoulies* (1985), the two *Gremlins* movies (1984 and 1990), *Little Shop of Horrors* (1986), and *Arachnophobia* (1990)—those in this Top 10 represent the most successful of a species of parodies of classic horror films that began more than half a century ago with such examples as *Abbott and Costello Meet Frankenstein* (1948). Such has been the success of the most recent crop that each movie in the *Scream* and *Scary Movie* franchise has earned more than US$100 million globally.

TOP 10 FUNNIEST MOVIES VOTED FOR BY THE AMERICAN FILM INSTITUTE

	FILM	YEAR
1	**Some Like It Hot**	1959
2	**Tootsie**	1982
3	**Dr. Strangelove, or: How I Learned to Stop Worrying and Love the Bomb**	1964
4	**Annie Hall**	1977
5	**Duck Soup**	1933
6	**Blazing Saddles**	1974
7	**M*A*S*H**	1970
8	**It Happened One Night**	1934
9	**The Graduate**	1967
10	**Airplane!**	1980

Source: *American Film Institute*

This list is the cream of the 500 titles nominated and 100 selected by a panel of 1,500 film experts for the AFI's "100 Years 100 Laughs" list, published on June 13, 2000. The Top 100 included comedy movies that ranged in time from Buster Keaton's 1924 silent classic *The Navigator* (in 84th place) to 1998 box office hit *There's Something About Mary* (27th).

Animation

TOP 10 ANIMATED FILMS

	FILM	US RELEASE	WORLDWIDE TOTAL GROSS (US$)
1	**The Lion King***	1994	771,900,000
2	**Monsters, Inc.***	2001	529,000,000
3	**Aladdin***	1992	502,400,000
4	**Toy Story 2***	1999	485,800,000
5	**Shrek**	2001	477,000,000
6	**Tarzan***	1999	449,400,000
7	**Ice Age**	2002	366,300,000
8	**A Bug's Life***	1998	363,400,000
9	**Toy Story***	1995	361,500,000
10	**Dinosaur***	2000	356,100,000

** Disney*

TOP 10 BUDGETS FOR ANIMATED FILMS

	FILM	DATE	BUDGET (US$)
1	= **Tarzan**	1999	150,000,000
	= **The Polar Express**	2004	150,000,000
3	**Treasure Planet**	2002	140,000,000
4	**Final Fantasy: The Spirits Within**	2001	137,000,000
5	**Dinosaur**	2000	128,000,000
6	**Monsters, Inc.**	2001	115,000,000
7	**The Emperor's New Groove**	2000	100,000,000
8	**The Road to El Dorado**	2000	95,000,000
9	**Finding Nemo**	2003	94,000,000
10	**The Incredibles**	2004	92,000,000

Animated film budgets have come a long way since *Snow White and the Seven Dwarfs* (1937) established a then record of US$1.49 million. The US$2.6 million budget for *Pinocchio* (1940), and US$2.28 million for the original *Fantasia* (1940) were the two biggest of the 1940s, while *Sleeping Beauty* (1959) at US$6 million was the highest of the 1950s. *Robin Hood* (1973) had a budget of US$15 million, a record that remained unbroken until 1985, when *The Black Cauldron* (1985) became the first to break the US$25-million barrier. Since the 1990s, budgets of US$50 million to US$100 million or more have become commonplace.

▼ Towering Success

One of the most successful movies derived from a TV series, *Rugrats in Paris*, the US$30 million–budget sequel to *The Rugrats Movie* (1988), has made over US$100 million worldwide.

TOP 10 PART ANIMATION/PART LIVE ACTION FILMS

	FILM	YEAR
1	**Who Framed Roger Rabbit?**	1988
2	**Casper**	1995
3	**Space Jam**	1996
4	**9 to 5**	1980
5	**Mary Poppins**	1964
6	**Fantasia/2000**	2000
7	**Small Soldiers**	1998
8	**Song of the South**	1946
9	**James and the Giant Peach**	1996
10	**Pete's Dragon**	1977

Many recent movies, from *Jurassic Park* to *Stuart Little*, contain computer-generated three-dimensional images with live action, but these stand out as the highest-earning that combine the traditional animation of imaginary characters alongside live action as a key element. *Fantasia* (1940) may arguably warrant a place in the list, but the only combination sequence is a brief encounter between Mickey Mouse and the conductor Leopold Stokowski in what is otherwise an animated film. *The Adventures of Rocky and Bullwinkle* (2000) does not make the grade, having failed to earn more than a fraction of its reputed US$76 million budget.

THE 10 LATEST OSCAR-WINNING ANIMATED FILMS*

YEAR	FILM	DIRECTOR/COUNTRY
2002	**The ChubbChubbs!**	Eric Armstrong, Canada
2001	**For the Birds**	Ralph Eggleston, US
2000	**Father and Daughter**	Michael Dudok de Wit, Netherlands
1999	**The Old Man and the Sea**	Aleksandr Petrov, US
1998	**Bunny**	Chris Wedge, US
1997	**Geri's Game**	Jan Pinkava, US
1996	**Quest**	Tyron Montgomery, UK
1995	**Wallace & Gromit: A Close Shave**	Nick Park, UK
1994	**Bob's Birthday**	David Fine and Alison Snowden, Canada/UK
1993	**Wallace & Gromit: The Wrong Trousers**	Nick Park, UK

* *In the category "Short Films (Animated)"*

An Oscar was first awarded in the category "Short Subjects (Cartoons)"—later "Short Subjects (Animated Films)" and "Short Films (Animated)"—in 1932, when it was won by Walt Disney for *Flowers and Trees*, the first-ever color animated short. During the award's first decade, and with few exceptions up to 1968, it was won annually by Walt Disney. The new category "Best Animated Feature" has existed only since 2001 (when *Shrek* won the award that year); prior to this, films such as *Snow White and the Seven Dwarfs* (1937) and *Fantasia* (1940) received honorary Oscars.

THE 10 LATEST GENIE-AWARD WINNING BEST ANIMATED SHORTS

YEAR*	FILM	CREATORS
2002	**The Hungry Squid**	Marcy Page, John Weldon
2001	**The Boy Who Saw the Iceberg**	Paul Driessen, Marcy Page
2000	**Village of Idiots**	David Verrall, Michael Scott, Rose Newlove, Eugene Fedorenko
1999	**When the Day Breaks**	David Verrall, Wendy Tilby, Amanda Forbis
1998	**Bingo**	Kevin Tureski, Chris Landreth, Andy Jones
1997	**The Old Lady and the Pigeons**	Sylvain Chomet, Bernard Lajoie, Didier Brunner
1993	**Pearl's Diner**	Lynn Smith
1992	**Strings**	Wendy Tilby
1990	**Juke Bar**	Martin Barry
1989	**The Cat Came Back**	Richard Condie, Cordell Barker

* *Genie Awards, presented by the Academy of Canadian Cinema and Television, were not given in this category each year*

TOP 10 ANIMATED FILM OPENING WEEKENDS IN THE US

	FILM	US RELEASE	OPENING WEEKEND GROSS (US$)
1	**Monsters, Inc.**	Nov 2, 2001	62,577,067
2	**Toy Story 2***	Nov 26, 1999	57,388,839
3	**Ice Age**	Mar 15, 2002	46,312,454
4	**Shrek**	May 18, 2001	42,347,760
5	**The Lion King**	June 24, 1994	40,888,194
6	**Dinosaur**	May 19, 2000	38,854,851
7	**Lilo & Stitch**	June 21, 2002	35,260,212
8	**Tarzan**	June 18, 1999	34,221,968
9	**A Bug's Life***	Nov 28, 1998	33,258,052
10	**Pokémon: The First Movie**	Nov 12, 1999	31,036,678

* *Second weekend; opening weekend release in limited number of theaters only*

The popularity of animated feature films in recent years has initiated the new phenomenon of the US$20 million-plus opening weekend, with these high earners closely trailed by slightly less impressive successes including *Pocahontas* (1995), *Toy Story* (1995), *The Rugrats Movie* (1998), and *Mulan* (1998).

Kids' Stuff

▲ The Price of Fame
Youngest-ever Oscar winner Shirley Temple said, "I stopped believing in Santa Claus when my mother took me to see him in a department store and he asked for my autograph."

THE 10 YOUNGEST OSCAR WINNERS

	ACTOR/ACTRESS	AWARD	AWARD YEAR	AGE YRS	MTHS	DAYS
1	**Shirley Temple**	Special Award (outstanding contribution during 1934)	1934	6	10	4
2	**Vincent Winter**	Special Award (*The Little Kidnappers*)	1954	7	3	1
3	**Margaret O'Brien**	Special Award (outstanding child actress of 1944)	1944	8	2	0
4	**Jon Whiteley**	Special Award (*The Little Kidnappers*)	1954	10	1	11
5	**Tatum O'Neal**	"Best Supporting Actress" (*Paper Moon*)	1973	10	4	27
6	**Anna Paquin**	"Best Supporting Actress" (*The Piano*)	1993	11	7	28
7	**Ivan Jandl**	Special Award (*The Search*)	1948	12	0	27
8	**Claude Jarman Jr.**	Special Award (*The Yearling*)	1946	12	5	16
9	**Bobby Driscoll**	Special Award (outstanding juvenile actor)	1949	13	0	20
10	**Hayley Mills**	Special Award (outstanding juvenile performance)	1960	13	11	29

The Academy Awards ceremony usually takes place in March of the year after the film was released, so winners are generally at least a year older when they receive their Oscars than when they acted in their films. Hayley Mills, the 12th and last winner of the Special Award miniature Oscar (presented to her by its first winner, Shirley Temple), won her award one day before her 14th birthday. Subsequent winners have had to compete on the same basis as adult actors and actresses for the major awards. Tatum O'Neal is the youngest winner of—as well as the youngest ever nominee for—an "adult" Oscar. The youngest winner of the "Best Actor" award is Richard Dreyfuss (for *The Goodbye Girl* at the 1977 Academy Awards). The youngest winner in the "Best Supporting Actor" category is Timothy Hutton, who was age 20 when he won in 1980 for his role in *Ordinary People*.

TOP 10 MOST-RENTED CHILDREN'S VIDEOS IN CANADA, 2002

	VIDEO
1	**Monsters, Inc.**
2	**Ice Age**
3	**Lilo & Stitch**
4	**101 Dalmations II: Patch's London Adventure**
5	**Cinderella II: Dreams Come True**
6	**Return to Never Land**
7	**The Land Before Time: Journey to Big Water**
8	**Scooby-Doo: Winter Wonderdog**
9	**Barney: Round and Round We Go**
10	**Bob the Builder: The Knights of Fix-a-Lot**

Source: *Rogers Video*

TOP 10 PROGRAMS MOST WATCHED BY CHILDREN ON CANADIAN TELEVISION, 2001–02*

	PROGRAM/DAYS	NETWORK	TIME	AUDIENCE
1	**Powerpuff Girls** (Mon–Fri)	YTV	4:30 pm	174,000
2	**Hey Arnold** (Mon–Fri)	YTV	4:30 pm	152,000
3	**Pokémon** (Mon–Fri)	YTV	5:00 pm	145,000
4	**Jackie Chan** (Mon–Fri)	YTV	5:30 pm	137,000
5	**Jackie Chan** (Mon–Fri)	YTV	5:00 pm	136,000
6	**Dexter's Laboratory** (Mon–Fri)	YTV	4:00 pm	135,000
7	**Salt Lake City Winter Olympics Games** (Mon–Sun)	CBC	6:00 pm	131,000
8	**Digimon** (Mon–Fri)	YTV	5:30 pm	130,000
9	**Movie** (Sat and Sun)	Teletoon	5:00 pm	127,000
10	**Powerpuff Girls** (Mon–Fri)	YTV	4:00 pm	125,000

* *On English-language networks; five or more telecasts from October 1, 2001, to September 1, 2002, watched by children*

TOP 10 FILMS WITH CHILD STARS

	FILM	YEAR
1	Harry Potter and the Philosopher's Stone	2001
2	Star Wars: Episode I—The Phantom Menace	1999
3	Jurassic Park	1993
4	Harry Potter and the Chamber of Secrets	2002
5	E.T. the Extra-Terrestrial	1982
6	The Sixth Sense	1999
7	Home Alone	1990
8	Mrs. Doubtfire	1993
9	Signs	2002
10	Jurassic Park III	2001

Family films, especially those with child stars, are among the highest-earning of all time: all those in the Top 10 have earned upward of US$365 million each worldwide. Several of those appearing here featured children early in their careers, with Drew Barrymore one of the most notable. Having appeared in *Altered States* (1980) at the age of four, she took the role of Gertie in *E.T. the Extra-Terrestrial* while still only six, going on to pursue a successful adult career in such films as *Batman Forever* (1995) and *Charlie's Angels* (2000).

▲ **Secret Success**
Child stars Rupert Grint (Ron) and Daniel Radcliffe (Harry) take to the air in a flying Ford Anglia in box office smash hit *Harry Potter and the Chamber of Secrets.*

THE 10 LATEST WINNERS OF THE GEMINI AWARD FOR "BEST CHILDREN'S PROGRAM OR SERIES"*

YEAR#	PROGRAM
1997	The Adventures of Dudley the Dragon
1996	Are You Afraid of the Dark?
1995	The Big Comfy Couch
1994	Lamb Chop's Play-Along
1993	Shining Time Station
1992	The Garden
1990	Raffi in Concert with the Rise and Shine Band
1989	Mr. Dressup
1988	They Look a Lot Like Us
1987	Down at Fraggle Rock: Behind the Scenes/ Degrassi Junior High

* *After 1997, award category renamed "Best Children's or Youth Program or Series"*

\# *Gemini Awards were not given in this category each year*

Source: *Academy of Canadian Cinema & Television*

THE 10 LATEST WINNERS OF THE "OUTSTANDING CHILDREN'S SERIES" DAYTIME EMMY AWARD

SEASON ENDING	PROGRAM
2002	Sesame Street
2001	Reading Rainbow
2000	Bill Nye the Science Guy
1999	Sesame Street (pre-school); Bill Nye the Science Guy (school age)
1998	Sesame Street
1997	Sesame Street (pre-school); Reading Rainbow (school age)
1996	Reading Rainbow
1995	Nick News
1994	Sesame Street
1993	Reading Rainbow

Several of the multiple award winners are not only among the most popular children's series but also some of the longest runners: *Sesame Street* was first screened in 1969, *Reading Rainbow* in 1983, and *Bill Nye the Science Guy* in 1993. *Reading Rainbow* host LeVar Burton gained additional recognition by appearing in the show while also starring in *StarTrek: The Next Generation.*

DVD & Video

TOP 10 VIDEO-BUYING COUNTRIES

	COUNTRY	PERCENTAGE DVD	TOTAL SPENDING, 2001 (US$)
1	US	34	20,549,000,000
2	Japan	35	4,768,000,000
3	UK	36	2,857,000,000
4	France	41	1,681,000,000
5	Canada	34	1,666,000,000
6	Germany	39	1,027,000,000
7	Australia	29	595,000,000
8	South Korea	3	556,000,000
9	Italy	23	540,000,000
10	Spain	31	405,000,000

Source: *Screen Digest*

The availability of comparative international statistics lags behind the rapidly moving video (VHS and DVD) business, but figures for the US for 2002 revealed that the home-video industry in the US—DVD and VHS rentals and sales—was worth US$20.3 billion, more than double the US$9.37 billion generated by domestic movie releases.

TOP 10 VIDEO PIRACY COUNTRIES

	COUNTRY	PIRACY RATE (PERCENTAGE)	EST. LOSSES, 2002 (US$)*
1	Russia	80	250,000,000
2	China	91	168,000,000
3	Italy	20	140,000,000
4	Brazil	35	120,000,000
5	India	60	75,000,000
6	Turkey	45	50,000,000
7	= Malaysia	75	42,000,000
	= Taiwan	44	42,000,000
9	= Colombia	90	40,000,000
	= Saudi Arabia	35	40,000,000
	= Ukraine	90	40,000,000

* *Preliminary figures*

Source: *International Intellectual Property Alliance (IIPA)*

Despite international attempts to curb video piracy by both legal and technological means, it has reached epidemic proportions in many countries.

TOP 10 MOST-RENTED VIDEOS OF ALL TIME IN THE US

	TITLE	YEAR*	REVENUE (US$)
1	Titanic	1997	324,430,000
2	Star Wars: Episode IV—A New Hope	1977	270,920,000
3	E.T. the Extra-Terrestrial	1982	228,170,000
4	Jurassic Park	1993	212,950,000
5	Star Wars: Episode VI—Return of the Jedi	1983	191,650,000
6	Independence Day	1996	177,190,000
7	Star Wars: Episode V—The Empire Strikes Back	1980	173,810,000
8	The Lion King	1994	173,060,000
9	Forrest Gump	1994	156,000,000
10	Batman	1989	150,500,000

* *Of cinema release*

Video rentals have declined since the arrival of DVDs in 1997. Total DVD and VHS rentals in 2002 were US$8.2 billion, compared with US$12.1 billion for sales.

TOP 10 BESTSELLING VIDEOS IN THE US

	TITLE	YEAR*	SALES(US$)#
1	Shrek	2001	228,000,000
2	Tarzan	2000	210,000,000
3	Dr. Seuss's How the Grinch Stole Christmas	2001	192,000,000
4	Dinosaur	2001	153,000,000
5	Toy Story 2	2000	145,300,000
6	Monsters, Inc.	2002	145,200,000
7	Star Wars: Episode I—The Phantom Menace	2000	133,400,000
8	Harry Potter and the Philosopher's Stone	2002	131,300,000
9	Pearl Harbor	2001	119,200,000
10	Lady and the Tramp II: Scamp's Adventure	2001	119,100,000

* *Of video release in the US; 21st century only*

\# *In release year*

Source: *VSDA VidTrac*

TOP 10 BESTSELLING VIDEOS IN THE US, 2002

	TITLE	SALES(US$)*
1	Monsters, Inc.	145,200,000
2	Harry Potter and the Philosopher's Stone	131,300,000
3	Spider-Man	84,000,000
4	Lilo & Stitch	81,700,000
5	Cinderella II: Dreams Come True	76,500,000
6	The Lord of the Rings: The Fellowship of the Ring	72,800,000
7	Atlantis: The Lost Empire	70,400,000
8	Miss Congeniality	63,000,000
9	Spirit: Stallion of the Cimarron	58,000,000
10	Snow Dogs	52,700,000

* *In release year*

Source: *VSDA VidTrac*

Monsters, Inc. also earned some US$202 million from DVD sales, compared to just US$23.5 million from VHS and US$14.36 million from DVD rentals. This reflects the shift in the ratio between renting and buying as increasing numbers prefer to own their favorite movies.

TOP 10 MOST-RENTED VIDEOS IN CANADA, 2002

	TITLE
1	Ocean's Eleven
2	Don't Say a Word
3	Training Day
4	Rat Race
5	Spy Game
6	Shallow Hal
7	I Am Sam
8	A Beautiful Mind
9	Vanilla Sky
10	The Others

Source: *Rogers Video*

TOP 10 MOST-RENTED DVDs IN CANADA, 2002

	TITLE
1	Ocean's Eleven
2	Training Day
3	Spy Game
4	Don't Say a Word
5	The Sum of All Fears
6	Black Hawk Down
7	Shallow Hal
8	Behind Enemy Lines
9	Rat Race
10	Panic Room

Source: *Rogers Video*

TOP 10 HORROR FILM RENTALS IN CANADA, 2002

	TITLE
1	The Others
2	The Mothman Prophecies
3	Blade 2
4	From Hell
5	Jeepers Creepers
6	Thirteen Ghosts
7	Resident Evil
8	Queen of the Damned
9	Scary Movie 2
10	Jason X

Source: *Rogers Video*

TOP 10 DVD GENRES IN THE US, 2002

	GENRE	NO. OF FILMS IN TOP-500 RENTALS
1	Comedy	155
2	Drama	96
3	Action	95
4	Suspense	59
5	Horror	27
6	Family	17
7	Children's	16
8	Science fiction	14
9	Romance	11
10	Western	2

Source: *VSDA VidTrac*

▼ Ocean Wave
Ocean's Eleven, the most rented DVD of 2002, made a total of US$192.2 million from DVD and VHS sales and rentals.

Top TV

THE 10 LATEST WINNERS OF THE GEMINI CANADA AWARD

YEAR		PROGRAM
2002		Film Club
2001		Made in China
2000		Unwanted Soldiers
1999		Loyalties
1998	=	The Rez, Season 2
	=	The Road Taken
1997		The Mind of a Child
1996		Nuhoniyeh: Our Story
1995		For Angela
1994		Speak It! From the Heart of Black Nova Scotia

Source: *Academy of Canadian Cinema and Television*

The Canada Award honors excellence in television programming that reflects Canada's diversity.

▼ TV Age

The proliferation of terrestrial and satellite television in recent years has transformed both the industry and the skylines of today's cities.

THE 10 LATEST WINNERS OF THE GEMINI AWARD FOR "BEST DRAMATIC SERIES"

YEAR	PROGRAM
2002	DaVinci's Inquest
2001	DaVinci's Inquest
2000	DaVinci's Inquest
1999	DaVinci's Inquest
1998	Traders
1997	Due South
1996	Due South
1995	Due South
1994	E.N.G.
1993	E.N.G.

PUBLIC TV BROADCASTS

FIRST FACT

ALTHOUGH THERE WERE earlier low-definition experimental transmissions, the world's first daily high-definition public broadcasting television service was launched by the BBC on November 2, 1936. Television's debut in the United States dates from April 30, 1939, when NBC showed an outside broadcast of the opening of the New York World's Fair by Franklin D. Roosevelt—who thereby became the first American president to appear on television. In Canada, the CBC aired its first public television programs from stations in Montreal and Toronto in September 1952.

TOP 10 SATELLITE TELEVISION COUNTRIES

	COUNTRY	HOME SATELLITE ANTENNAE (2000)
1	US	16,000,000
2	Germany	12,900,000
3	Japan	10,620,000
4	UK	5,200,000
5	France	4,300,000
6	Indonesia	3,900,000
7	Algeria	3,500,000
8	Poland	2,500,000
9	Saudi Arabia	1,914,000
10	Spain	1,840,000
	Canada	*967,800*

Source: *International Telecommunication Union,* World Telecommunication Development Report, 2002

TOP 10 TELEVISION-OWNING COUNTRIES

	COUNTRY	TVs PER 1,000 POPULATION (2000)
1	Qatar	869
2	US	854
3	Denmark	807
4	Latvia	789
5	Australia	738
6	Japan	725
7	Canada	715
8	Finland	692
9	Norway	669
10	UK	653
	World average	270

Source: *International Telecommunication Union,* World Telecommunication Development Report 2002

TOP 10 PRIMETIME PROGRAMS ON NETWORK TELEVISION, 2001–02*

	PROGRAM	AVERAGE VIEWERS PERCENT	TOTAL
1	**Academy Awards 2002**	25.4	26,832,000
2	**Friends** (Special)	17.2	18,154,000
3	**On the Red Carpet: The Oscars 2002**	17.1	17,999,000
4	**Friends**	16.6	17,462,000
5	**Golden Globe Awards 2002**	14.9	15,718,000
6	**Emmy Awards 2002**	13.5	14,397,000
7	**Survivor: Thailand Special**	13.2	14,124,000
8	**Survivor: Marquesas Finale**	13.4	14,122,000
9	**Law and Order: Criminal Intent**	12.9	13,628,000
10	**CSI: Crime Scene Investigation**	12.9	13,588,000

* *Excluding sports; highest-ranked screening only listed*

Source: *Nielsen Media Research*

TOP 10 DAYTIME DRAMAS ON US TELEVISION, 2001–02*

	DRAMA	NETWORK	AVERAGE VIEWERS PERCENT	TOTAL
1	**Young and the Restless**	CBS	5.0	5,293,000
2	**Bold and the Beautiful**	CBS	3.9	4,103,000
3	**Days of Our Lives**	NBC	3.6	3,804,000
4	**General Hospital**	ABC	3.4	3,611,000
5	**As the World Turns**	CBS	3.3	3,448,000
6	**All My Children**	ABC	3.3	3,443,000
7	**One Life to Live**	ABC	3.2	3,336,000
8	**Guiding Light**	CBS	2.9	3,076,000
9	**Passions**	NBC	2.1	2,185,000
10	**Port Charles**	ABC	1.8	1,854,000

* *Excludes specials*

Source: *Nielsen Media Research*

TOP 10 MOST-WATCHED PROGRAMS ON CANADIAN TELEVISION, 2001–02*

	PROGRAM	NETWORK	AUDIENCE
1	**CSI: Crime Scene Investigation** (Mon, Thu)	CTV	1,666,000
2	**ER**	CTV	1,647,000
3	**Law and Order**	CTV	1,451,000
4	**CTV Evening News**	CTV	1,320,000
5	**National Newsworld: Salt Lake City Winter Olympic Games**	CBC	1,302,000
6	**Weakest Link**	CTV	1,296,000
7	**Law and Order: Special Victims Unit**	CTV	1,221,000
8	**Ally McBeal**	CTV	1,209,000
9	**CSI: Crime Scene Investigation** (Fri, Sat)	CTV	1,194,000
10	**Law and Order: Criminal Intent**	CTV	1,190,000

* *On English-language networks; five or more telecasts from September 3, 2001, to September 1, 2002; excluding individual sports event telecasts*

TOP 10 MOST-WATCHED SPECIALS ON CANADIAN TELEVISION, 2001–02*

	SPECIAL	NETWORK	AUDIENCE
1	**Academy Awards 2002**	CTV	4,659,000
2	**Academy Awards 2002 Pre-Show**	CTV	3,332,000
3	**Golden Globe Awards 2002**	CTV	2,393,000
4	**Trudeau**	CBC	1,879,000
5	**Barbara Walters Academy Awards 2002 Special**	CTV	1,838,000
6	**Emmy Awards 2002**	CTV	1,629,000
7	**American Music Awards 2002**	CTV	1,469,000
8	**Royal Canadian Air Farce: Best of 2001**	CBC	1,388,000
9	**Golden Globe Awards 2002 Pre-Show**	CTV	1,385,000
10	**People's Choice Awards 2002**	CBC	1,376,000

* *On English-language networks; one or two telecasts from September 3, 2001, to September 1, 2002; excluding sports event telecasts*

Radio Days

TOP 10 RADIO-OWNING COUNTRIES

	COUNTRY	RADIOS PER 1,000 POPULATION (2000)
1	**US**	2,118
2	**Australia**	1,908
3	**Finland**	1,623
4	**UK**	1,432
5	**Denmark**	1,349
6	**Estonia**	1,096
7	**Canada**	1,047
8	**South Korea**	1,033
9	**Switzerland**	1,002
10	**New Zealand**	997
	World	*419*

Source: *World Bank*, World Development Indicators 2002/*UNESCO*

THE 10 FIRST PROGRAMS BROADCAST ON CBC*

	PROGRAM	TIME
1	**G.R. Markowsky and His Chateau Laurier Concert Trio**	5:30 pm
2	**Closing stock quotations** (TSE)	5:45 pm
3	**The Hitmakers,** variety presentation with Percy Faith's orchestra	6:00 pm
4	**Overseas program,** rebroadcast of BBC Empire transmission	6:30 pm
5	**At the Organ,** popular organ recital by Ernest Dainty	7:00 pm
6	**Les Cavaliers de LeSalle,** novelty orchestra direction by Arthur Vander Haegue	7:15 pm
7	**Adventure,** tales of adventure in far-off lands	7:30 pm
8	**Au Rhythme de la Rhumba**	7:45 pm
9	**Fanfare,** orchestra and soloists	8:00 pm
10	**Bob Chester and orchestra**	8:30 pm

* *Broadcast on the first official day of CBC's English-language station, November 2, 1936. Separate programming was broadcast to Quebec and eastern Canada simultaneously.*

Source: *CBC Radio Archives*

THE 10 LATEST INDUCTEES TO THE CANADIAN ASSOCIATION OF BROADCASTERS HALL OF FAME, 2002*

	HONOREE	CLAIM TO FAME
1	**Liette Champagne**	Executive vice-president, Telemedia Radio Quebec
2	**Bruce Cockburn**	Singer/songwriter
3	**Rita Deverell**	Multicultural broadcaster
4	**Denise Donlon**	President, Sony Music Canada
5	**Jerry Lawrence**	On-air host
6	**Johnny Lombardi**	Founder, CHIN radio
7	**Clarence Mack**	Morning radio host
8	**Trina McQueen**	Former president and COO, CTV
9	**Jim Robson**	Sports announcer/"The Voice of the Vancouver Canucks"
10	**Pamela Wallin**	On-air host

* *For outstanding achievements and contributions to private broadcasting and Canada*

Source: *Canadian Association of Broadcasters, prepared by Hennessy & Bray Communications*

Candidates are nominated annually by five regional broadcasting associations and the Canadian Association of Broadcasters Executive Committee. There are currently 187 members of the Hall of Fame.

TOP 10 MOST-LISTENED TO RADIO STATIONS IN CANADA

	STATION	CITY	FORMAT	WEEKLY CIRCULATION*
1	**CHFI-FM**	Toronto, ON	Adult contemporary	1,100,530
2	**CKOI-FM**	Montreal, QC	Contemporary hit radio	1,097,500
3	**CHUM-FM**	Toronto, ON	Adult hits	1,090,470
4	**CFTR**	Toronto, ON	All news	956,500
5	**CKFM-FM**	Toronto, ON	Hot adult comtemporary	909,200
6	**CILQ-FM**	Toronto, ON	Classic rock	883,100
7	**CISS-FM**	Toronto, ON	Contemporary hit radio	874,300
8	**CBLA-FM**	Toronto, ON	News/talk	842,300
9	**CITE-FM**	Montreal, QC	Light adult comtemporary	786,600
10	**CFRB**	Toronto, ON	News/talk	735,900

* *Total number of listeners aged 12 and older tuning to a staion during an average week*

Source: *Hennessy & Bray Communications; based on a BBM Bureau of Measurement fall 2002 survey*

TOP 10 MOST POPULAR CBC RADIO ONE PROGRAMS

	PROGRAM	NUMBER OF LISTENERS*
1	**World Report**	780,000
2	**Local Monday–Friday Morning Show** (6–9 am)	605,000
3	**The House**	422,000
4	= **GO**	356,000
	= **Workology**	356,000
6	**Vinyl Café**	352,000
7	= **Local Saturday Morning Show** (6–9 am)	350,000
	= **World at Six**	350,000
9	**This Morning**	344,000
10	**Canada at Five**	343,000

* *Based on BBM Bureau of Measurement fall 2002 figures*

Source: *CBC Research*

Radio Head
Radio listeners maintain loyalty to their favorite stations, ensuring large audiences for the leading broadcasters.

TOP 10 MOST POPULAR CBC RADIO TWO PROGRAMS

	PROGRAM	NUMBER OF LISTENERS*
1	**Vinyl Café**	156,000
2	**World Report**	139,000
3	**Canada at Five**	125,000
4	**I Hear Music**	117,000
5	**Disc Drive**	113,000
6	**Music & Company**	107,000
7	**Sound Advice**	105,000
8	**Take Five**	103,000
9	**Choral Concert**	100,000
10	**Saturday Afternoon at the Opera**	90,000

* *Based on BBM Bureau of Measurement fall 2002 figures*

Source: *CBC Research*

RADIO BROADCAST

FIRST FACT

ALTHOUGH WIRELESS messages had been broadcast earlier using Morse code, the first ever to transmit sound and music took place on Christmas Eve, December 24, 1906. Canadian physicist and inventor Reginald Fessenden (1866–1932) set up a radio station and a 128-m (420-ft) mast at Brant Rock Station in Massachusetts, from where he opened the broadcast with an explanation of what he proposed to do, followed by a phonograph recording of Handel's *Largo*, after which he sang and played violin. This first-ever radio show was repeated on New Year's Eve, and received as far afield as the West Indies, and by ships at sea. Over the years, radio continued as a means of communications between ships, but did not become established as a popular medium until the 1920s.

THE COMMERCIAL WORLD

World Finance

TOP 10 GLOBAL INDUSTRIAL COMPANIES

	COMPANY/LOCATION/SECTOR	REVENUE IN 2001 (US$)
1	**Wal-Mart Stores, Inc.,** US, retailing	219,812,000,000
2	**Exxon Mobil,** US, oil, gas, fuel	191,581,000,000
3	**General Motors Corp.,** US, motor vehicles	177,260,000,000
4	**BP plc,** UK, oil, gas	174,218,000,000
5	**Ford Motor Co.,** US, motor vehicles	162,412,000,000
6	**Enron Corp.*,** US, gas, electricity	138,718,000,000
7	**DaimlerChrysler AG,** Germany, motor vehicles	136,897,300,000
8	**Royal Dutch/Shell Group,** Netherlands/UK, oil, gas, chemicals	135,211,000,000
9	**General Electric,** US, electronics, electrical equipment	125,913,000,000
10	**Toyota Motor Corp.,** Japan, motor vehicles	120,814,400,000

* *Revenue for nine months Jan–Sept 2001; filed for bankruptcy December 2, 2001.*

Source: Fortune, *The 2002 Global 500, July 22, 2002*

Sam Walton opened his first Wal-Mart store in Rogers, Arkansas, in 1962. It has undergone phenomenal growth in the past 40 years, to become the world's No. 1 company. On the day after Thanksgiving, 2001, it achieved the largest single day's sales in retail history, taking in US$1.25 billion.

TOP 10 RICHEST COUNTRIES

	COUNTRY	GDP* PER CAPITA IN 2000 (US$)
1	**Luxembourg**	50,061
2	**US**	34,142
3	**Norway**	29,918
4	**Ireland**	29,866
5	**Iceland**	29,581
6	**Switzerland**	28,769
7	**Canada**	27,840
8	**Denmark**	27,627
9	**Belgium**	27,178
10	**Austria**	26,765
	World average	7,446

* *Gross Domestic Product*

Source: *United Nations,* Human Development Indicators 2002

Retail Giant
Wal-Mart was founded in 1962. By 1979, it was achieving sales of over US$1 billion a year; by 1993 it did so in a week, and can now sell that amount in a single day.

TOP 10 PRICE GAINS ON THE TORONTO STOCK EXCHANGE

	STOCK (CLOSE PRICE, $)	NET CHANGE 2002
1	**Winpak Ltd.** (121.00)	45.50
2	**Royal Gold, Inc.** (39.93)	31.96
3	**E-L Financial Corporation Ltd.** (230.00)	25.00
4	**Niko Resources Ltd.** (25.80)	18.05
5	**Algoma Central Corporation** (45.00)	16.00
6	**iUnits S&P/TSX Canadian Gold Index Fund Units** (50.15)	14.85
7	**Gildan Activewear Inc.** (37.04)	14.24
8	**McGraw-Hill Ryerson Ltd.** (33.25)	13.75
9	**Northstar Energy Corporation** (73.49)	13.09
10	**Glamis Gold Ltd.** (17.80)	12.07

Source: *Toronto Stock Exchange*

TOP 10 FASTEST-GROWING ECONOMIES

	COUNTRY	GDP* PER CAPITA 2000 (US$)	GDP PER CAPITA ANNUAL GROWTH RATE 1990–2000 (%)
1	**Equatorial Guinea**	15,073	18.9
2	**China**	3,976	9.2
3	**Ireland**	29,866	6.5
4	**Vietnam**	1,996	6.0
5	**Sudan**	1,797	5.6
6	**Maldives**	4,485	5.4
7	**Chile**	9,417	5.2
8	**Guyana**	3,963	5.0
9	**Myanmar**	1,500	4.8
10 =	**St. Kitts and Nevis**	12,510	4.7
=	**Singapore**	23,356	4.7
=	**South Korea**	17,380	4.7
	World	*7,446*	*1.2*
	Canada	*27,840*	*1.9*

* *Gross Domestic Product*

Source: *United Nations*, Human Development Indicators 2002

THE 10 POOREST COUNTRIES

	COUNTRY	GDP* PER CAPITA 2000 (US$)
1	**Sierra Leone**	490
2	**Tanzania**	523
3	**Burundi**	591
4	**Malawi**	615
5	**Ethiopia**	668
6	**Niger**	746
7	**Guinea-Bissau**	755
8	**Dem. Rep. of Congo**	765
9	**Mali**	797
10	**Congo**	825

* *Gross Domestic Product*

Source: United Nations, Human Development Indicators 2001

THE 10 COUNTRIES MOST IN DEBT

	COUNTRY	TOTAL EXTERNAL DEBT IN 2000 (US$)
1	**Brazil**	237,953,000,000
2	**Russia**	160,300,000,000
3	**Mexico**	150,288,000,000
4	**China**	149,800,000,000
5	**Argentina**	146,172,000,000
6	**Indonesia**	141,803,000,000
7	**South Korea**	134,417,000,000
8	**Turkey**	116,209,000,000
9	**India**	100,367,000,000
10	**Thailand**	79,675,000,000

Source: *World Bank*, World Development Indicators 2002

TOP 10 BIGGEST EXPORTERS

	COUNTRY	EXPORTS, 2000 (US$)
1	**US**	1,065,740,000,000
2	**Germany**	633,052,000,000
3	**Japan**	528,751,000,000
4	**UK**	401,385,000,000
5	**France**	377,274,000,000
6	**Canada**	321,693,000,000
7	**Italy**	294,852,000,000
8	**China**	279,562,000,000
9	**Netherlands**	258,951,000,000
10	**Hong Kong (China)**	244,004,000,000

Source: *World Bank*, World Development Indicators 2002

TOP 10 NOBEL ECONOMIC SCIENCES PRIZE-WINNING COUNTRIES

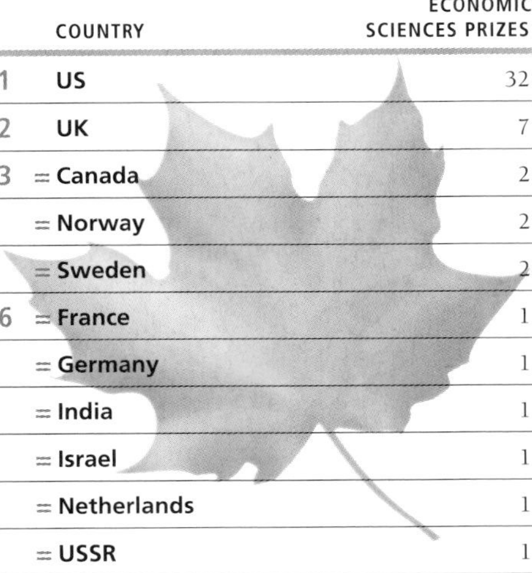

	COUNTRY	ECONOMIC SCIENCES PRIZES
1	**US**	32
2	**UK**	7
3	= **Canada**	2
	= **Norway**	2
	= **Sweden**	2
6	= **France**	1
	= **Germany**	1
	= **India**	1
	= **Israel**	1
	= **Netherlands**	1
	= **USSR**	1

Workers of the World

THE 10 COUNTRIES WITH THE HIGHEST PROPORTION OF CHILD WORKERS

	COUNTRY	TOTAL	10–14 YEAR OLDS AT WORK IN 2000 PERCENTAGE*
1	**Mali**	726,000	51.14
2	**Bhutan**	136,000	51.10
3	**Burundi**	445,000	48.50
4	**Uganda**	1,343,000	43.79
5	**Niger**	609,000	43.62
6	**Burkina Faso**	686,000	43.45
7	**Ethiopia**	3,277,000	42.45
8	**Nepal**	1,154,000	42.05
9	**Rwanda**	413,000	41.35
10	**Kenya**	1,699,000	39.15
	World	*67,444*	*11.24*

* *Excludes unpaid work*

Source: *International Labor Organization*

It is estimated that there are some 21 million children aged from five to 14 years working around the world, including as many as 111 million who are involved in tasks that are hazardous.

COUNTRIES WITH HIGHEST PROPORTION OF ELDERLY PEOPLE AT WORK*

	COUNTRY	EST. PERCENTAGE OF OVER-64 YEAR OLDS ECONOMICALLY ACTIVE IN 2000
1	**Mozambique**	77.24
2	**Malawi**	74.85
3	**Ghana**	71.30
4	**Central African Republic**	70.91
5	**Tanzania**	69.80
6	**Gambia**	61.60
7	**Uganda**	61.01
8	**Congo**	60.07
9	**Madagascar**	57.92
10	**Solomon Islands**	57.91

* *Excludes unpaid work*

Source: *International Labor Organization*

The concept of retirement is a Western phenomenon that is unavailable to many, especially subsistence farmers in Africa.

TOP 10 COUNTRIES WITH LOWEST PROPORTION OF ELDERLY PEOPLE AT WORK*

	COUNTRY	EST. PERCENTAGE OF OVER-64 YEAR OLDS ECONOMICALLY ACTIVE IN 2000
1	**Hungary**	0.46
2	**Belgium**	0.93
3	**Netherlands**	1.14
4	**Luxembourg**	1.16
5	**Austria**	1.26
6	**France**	1.52
7	**Spain**	2.04
8	**Germany**	2.30
9	**Finland**	2.35
10	**Martinique**	3.00
	World	*18.77*
	Canada	*6.06*

* *Excludes unpaid work*

Source: *International Labor Organization*

THE 10 COUNTRIES WITH THE MOST STRIKES AND LOCKOUTS

	COUNTRY	WORKERS INVOLVED	DAYS LOST	STRIKES AND LOCKOUTS IN 2000
1	**Denmark**	75,656	124,800	1,081
2	**Italy**	687,000	884,100	966
3	**Russia**	31,000	236,400	817
4	**Spain**	2,067,287	3,616,907	750
5	**Australia**	325,400	469,100	698
6	**India**	689,592	16,720,762	656
7	**Morocco**	43,619	395,703	484
8	**Tunisia**	35,886	47,549	411
9	**Canada**	143,570	1,661,620	377
10	**Guyana**	no data	56,175	268

Source: *International Labour Organization*

Strikes are temporary work stoppages precipitated by workers attempting, for example, to enforce their demands, while lockouts involve the closure of workplaces to employees by management until contract terms have been agreed.

TOP 10 COUNTRIES WITH THE HIGHEST PROPORTION OF FARMERS

	COUNTRY	WORKERS IN AGRICULTURE (2000) TOTAL	PERCENTAGE OF WORK FORCE
1	**Bhutan**	942,000	93
2	= **Burkina Faso**	5,062,000	92
	= **Nepal**	10,109,000	92
4	= **Burundi**	3,022,000	90
	= **Rwanda**	3,734,000	90
6	**Niger**	4,388,000	87
7	= **Ethiopia**	22,891,000	82
	= **Guinea Bissau**	454,000	82
9	= **Mali**	4,500,000	80
	= **Uganda**	9,130,000	80

Source: *Food and Agriculture Organization of the United Nations*

Despite a global trend toward urbanization, a very high proportion of the populations of many Asian and African countries depend on farming for their livelihoods.

TOP 10 COUNTRIES WITH HIGHEST PROPORTION OF WOMEN WORKING IN SERVICE INDUSTRIES

	COUNTRY	PERCENTAGE FEMALE LABOR FORCE IN SERVICES* (1998–2000)
1	Argentina	89
2	= Hong Kong (China)	88
	= Norway	88
	= Panama	88
5	= Canada	87
	= Sweden	87
	= UK	87
8	= Australia	86
	= Belgium	86
	= France	86
	= Israel	86
	= Peru	86
	= US	86

* *Service industries include wholesale and retail trade, restaurants and hotels; transportation, storage, and communications; financing, insurance, real estate, and business services; and community, social, and personal services*

Source: *World Bank*, World Development Indicators 2002

TOP 10 COUNTRIES WITH HIGHEST PROPORTION OF MEN WORKING IN SERVICE INDUSTRIES

	COUNTRY	PERCENTAGE MALE LABOR FORCE IN SERVICES* (1998–2000)
1	= Columbia	71
	= Hong Kong (China)	71
3	= Peru	67
	= Singapore	67
5	Argentina	65
6	= Australia	64
	= US	64
8	= Canada	63
	= Ecuador	63
	= France	63
	= Morocco	63
	= Netherlands	63

* *Service industries include wholesale and retail trade, restaurants and hotels; transportation, storage, and communications; financing, insurance, real estate, and business services; and community, social, and personal services*

Source: *World Bank*, World Development Indicators 2002

THE 10 COUNTRIES WITH HIGHEST UNEMPLOYMENT

	COUNTRY	EST. PERCENT OF LABOR FORCE UNEMPLOYED IN 2001*
1	Liberia	70
2	Zimbabwe	60
3	= Djibouti	50
	= East Timor	50
	= Zambia	50
6	Senegal	48
7	Nepal	47
8	Lesotho	45
9	= Bosnia and Herzegovina	40
	= Botswana	40
	= Kenya	40
	Canada	7.2

* *Or latest year; in those countries for which data available*

Source: *CIA*, The World Factbook 2002

Leading the Field

The Himalayan kingdom of Bhutan tops the list of countries with the highest percentage of its people involved in agriculture, mainly growing rice, vegetables, and fruit.

Hazards at Home & Work

TOP 10 MOST COMMON CAUSES OF FIRE IN CANADA

	SOURCE OF IGNITION	NO. OF FIRES, 1999
1	**Cooking equipment**	6,143
2	**Heating equipment**	4,857
3	**Electrical distribution equipment**	4,803
4	**Smoker's material or "open flame," unclassified**	4,177
5	**Smoker's material**	2,868
6	**Other electrical equipment**	2,819
7	**Match, lighter*, lamp, candle, taper**	2,693
8	**Exposure**	2,433
9	**Appliances and equipment**	2,346
10	**Cutting torch, welding equipment, varied torches**	839

* *Not used with smoking*

Source: Canadian Council of Fire Marshals and Fire Commissioners, Annual Report, Fire Losses in Canada, 1999

TOP 10 CAUSES OF UNNATURAL DEATH IN BRITISH COLUMBIA

	CAUSE	NO. OF PEOPLE, 2001
1	**Cancer**	7,767
2	**Cardiovascular disease**	6,887
3	**Cerebrovascular disease**	2,272
4	**Chronic lung disease**	1,210
5	**Pneumonia/influenza**	1,163
6	**Unintentional injury/accident**	1,060
7	**Diabetes**	784
8	**Digestive system** (excludes liver disease)	776
9	**Nervous system** (excludes Alzheimer's disease)	605
10	**Circulatory system** (excludes cardio/cerebrovascular disease)	575

Source: *BC Vital Statistics*

◀ Kitchen Conflagration

Kitchen fires are the most common among almost 400,000 annual incidents. Domestic fires cause over 3,000 deaths,15,000 injuries, and cost US$5.5 billion in property damage.

THE 10 COUNTRIES WITH THE MOST FATAL INJURIES AT WORK

	COUNTRY	FATAL INJURIES PER 100,000 WORKERS IN 2000
1	**Austria**	39.0
2	**Canada**	31.2
3	**India**	31.0
4	**Turkey**	24.6
5	**Argentina**	18.6
6	**Tunisia**	15.1
7	= **Chile**	14.0
	= **Mexico**	14.0*
9	**Togo**	11.7
10	**Brazil**	11.5

* *Partial data*

Source: *International Labour Organization*

THE 10 WORST INDUSTRIAL DISASTERS*

	LOCATION/DAT	NCIDENT	NO. KILLED
1	**Bhopal,** India, December 3, 1984	Methyl isocyanate gas escape at Union Carbide plant	up to 3,849
2	**Jesse,** Nigeria, October 17, 1998	Oil pipeline explosion	more than 700
3	**Oppau,** Germany, September 21, 1921	Chemical plant explosion	561
4	**San Juanico,** Mexico, November 19, 1984	Explosion at a PEMEX liquified petroleum gas plant	540
5	**Cubatão,** Brazil, February 25, 1984	Oil pipeline explosion	508
6	**Durunkah,** Egypt, November 2, 1994	Fuel storage depot fire	more than 500
7	**Novosibirsk,** USSR, precise date unknown, April 1979	Anthrax infection following an accident at a biological and chemical warfare plant	up to 300
8	**Adeje,** Nigeria, July 10, 2000	Oil pipeline explosion	250
9	**Guadalajara,** Mexico, April 22, 1992	Explosions caused by a gas leak into sewers	230
10	**Ludwigshafen,** Germany, July 28, 1948	Dimethyl ether explosion in a lacquer plant	184

* *Including industrial sites, factories, and fuel depots and pipelines; excluding military, munitions, bombs, mining, marine and other transport disasters, dam failures, and mass poisonings*

THE 10 COUNTRIES WITH THE MOST INJURIES AT WORK

	COUNTRY	NONFATAL INJURIES PER 100,000 WORKERS IN 2000
1	**Costa Rica**	15,994
2	**Chile**	7,964
3	**Argentina**	7,747
4	**Spain**	7,549
5	**Portugal**	5,471
6	**Slovenia**	5,091
7	**Nicaragua**	4,150
8	**Italy**	4,030
9	**Germany**	4,001
10	**Tunisia**	3,962
	Canada	3,145

Source: *International Labour Organization*

Work injuries are those sustained during the course of employment, including acts of violence, but excluding long-term occupational diseases or accidents while traveling to and from work.

THE 10 MOST DANGEROUS INDUSTRIES IN CANADA

	INDUSTRY	NUMBER OF FATALITIES, 2001
1	**Manufacturing**	192
2	**Construction**	185
3	**Transportation and storage**	124
4	**Mining, quarrying, and oil wells**	95
5	**Government services**	62
6	**Logging and forestry**	40
7	**Wholesale trade**	31
8	= **Business services**	30
	= **Retail trade**	30
10	**Communication and other utilities**	20

Source: *Association of Workers' Compensation Boards of Canada,* Work Injuries and Diseases, 1999–2001

A death occurring in the workplace is recorded statistically during the year when the claim was accepted by a Workers' Compensation Board, which is not necessarily the year in which the accident causing the death actually occurred.

THE 10 CAUSES OF INJURIES AT WORK IN CANADA

	EVENT	NO. OF TIME-LOSS INJURIES, 2001
1	**Overexertion**	87,440
2	**Bodily reaction**	49,492
3	**Struck by object**	48,747
4	**Fall on same level**	32,337
5	**Struck against object**	22,724
6	**Fall to lower level**	20,323
7	**Caught in or compressed by equipment or objects**	18,145
8	**Repetitive motion**	12,860
9	**Bodily reaction and exertion**	10,243
10	**Rubbed or abraded by friction or pressure**	9,735

Source: *Association of Workers' Compensation Boards of Canada,* Work Injuries and Diseases, 1999–2001

Advertising & Brands

TOP 10 ADVERTISING CATEGORIES

	CATEGORY	EST. GLOBAL ADVERTISING EXPENDITURE IN 2001 (US$)
1	**Automotives**	19,334,400,000
2	**Food**	11,220,700,000
3	**Personal care**	10,300,200,000
4	**Electronics,** computers	6,557,500,000
5	**Media and entertainment**	6,285,400,000
6	**Pharmaceuticals**	5,655,800,000
7	**Fast food**	2,989,400,000
8	**Household cleaners**	2,203,500,000
9	**Telecommunications**	1,733,000,000
10	**Financial services,** credit	1,156,300,000

Source: Advertising Age *Special Report, November 11, 2002*

TOP 10 CORPORATE ADVERTISERS IN CANADA

	CORPORATION	AD SPENDING IN 2001 ($)
1	**BCE**	79,160,000
2	**Procter & Gamble Company**	65,450,000
3	**General Motors Corporation**	60,520,000
4	**Hudson's Bay Company**	56,110,000
5	**Philip Morris Companies**	55,920,000
6	**Government of Canada**	53,430,000
7	**CanWest Global Communications Corporation**	45,870,000
8	**Sears, Roebuck & Company**	39,630,000
9	**Viacom**	38,210,000
10	**Wendy's International**	33,680,000

Source: *Nielsen Media Research. Reprinted with permission from the November 2002 issue of* Advertising Age Global. © *Crain Communications Inc.*

FIRST TV SOAP AD

FIRST FACT

THE FIRST TELEVISION BROADCAST of a live major league baseball game was also the occasion of the first screening of a soap advertisement. The two events took place on August 21, 1939, when the Brooklyn Dodgers met the Cincinnati Reds at Ebbets Field, Brooklyn, New York. TV station W2XBS broadcast the event, but since television was in its infancy, barely 400 people—all in New York—were able to tune in. Those who did saw an advertisement for Procter & Gamble's Ivory soap.

TOP 10 GLOBAL MARKETERS

	COMPANY/BASE	MEDIA SPENDING IN 2001 (US$)
1	**Procter & Gamble Company,** US	3,820,100,000
2	**General Motors Corporation,** US	3,028,900,000
3	**Unilever,** Netherlands/UK	3,005,500,000
4	**Ford Motor Company,** US	2,309,000,000
5	**Toyota Motor Corporation,** Japan	2,213,300,000
6	**AOL Time Warner,** US	2,099,800,000
7	**Philip Morris Companies,** US	1,934,600,000
8	**DaimlerChrysler,** Germany/US	1,835,300,000
9	**Nestlé,** Switzerland	1,798,500,000
10	**Volkswagen,** Germany	1,574,100,000

Source: Advertising Age Global

◄ Car Production
With cars being one of the costliest of all items of consumer expenditure, advertising budgets for automobiles figure prominently among the highest for any product.

TOP 10 CORPORATE ADVERTISERS IN THE US

	CORPORATION/HEADQUARTERS	TOTAL AD SPENDING 2001 (US$)
1	**General Motors Corporation,** Detroit, US	3,374,400,000
2	**Proctor & Gamble Company,** Cincinnati, US	2,540,600,000
3	**Ford Motor Company,** Dearborn, US	2,408,200,000
4	**PepsiCo,** Purchase, US	2,189,500,000
5	**Pfizer,** New York, US	2,189,500,000
6	**DaimlerChrysler,** Auburn Hills, US/Stuttgart, Germany	1,985,300,000
7	**AOL Time Warner,** New York, US	1,885,300,000
8	**Philip Morris Companies,** New York, US	1,815,700,000
9	**Walt Disney Company,** Burbank, US	1,757,300,000
10	**Johnson & Johnson,** New Brunswick, US	1,618,100,000

Source: *Taylor Nelson Sofres'* Competitive Media Reporting *and Yellow Pages Integrated Media Association*/Advertising Age

TOP 10 MOST VALUABLE GLOBAL BRANDS

	BRAND NAME*	INDUSTRY	BRAND VALUE IN 2002 (US$)
1	**Coca-Cola**	Beverages	69,637,000,000
2	**Microsoft**	Technology	64,091,000,000
3	**IBM**	Technology	51,188,000,000
4	**General Electric**	Diversified	41,311,000,000
5	**Intel**	Technology	30,861,000,000
6	**Nokia,** Finland	Technology	29,970,000,000
7	**Disney**	Leisure	29,256,000,000
8	**McDonald's**	Food retail	26,375,000,000
9	**Marlboro**	Tobacco	24,151,000,000
10	**Mercedes,** Germany	Automobiles	21,010,000,000

** All US-owned unless otherwise stated*

Source: *Interbrand*/BusinessWeek

Brand consultants Interbrand use a method of estimating value that takes into account the profitability of individual brands within a business (rather than the companies that own them), as well as such factors as their potential for growth. Well over half of the 75 most valuable global brands surveyed by Interbrand are US-owned, with European ownership accounting for another 30 percent.

▶ **Things Go Better…**
The Coca-Cola brand stands alone as a symbol of American culture, the most valued international beverage and one of the best-selling products in the world.

Shopping Lists

TOP 10 GLOBAL RETAILERS

	COMPANY/COUNTRY	RETAIL SALES IN 2001 (US$)*
1	**Wal-Mart,** US	217,799,000,000
2	**Carrefour,** France	61,565,000,000
3	**Ahold,** Netherlands	57,976,000,000
4	**Home Depot,** US	53,553,000,000
5	**Kroger Company,** US	50,098,000,000
6	**METRO AG,** Germany	43,357,000,000
7	**Target,** US	39,455,000,000
8	**Albertson's,** US	37,931,000,000
9	**Kmart,** US	36,151,000,000
10	**Sears, Roebuck,** US	35,843,000,000

* *Financial year*

Source: Stores, *Top 200 Global Retailers*

In 1887, watch retailer Richard Sears and watchmaker Alvah C. Roebuck formed Sears, Roebuck. It flourished to become the world's largest mail-order company before opening its first stores in the 1920s.

TOP 10 COUNTRIES WITH THE MOST STORES

	COUNTRY	STORES IN 2000
1	**China**	19,306,800
2	**India**	10,537,080
3	**Brazil**	1,595,062
4	**Japan**	1,240,237
5	**Mexico**	1,087,995
6	**Spain**	780,247
7	**Vietnam**	727,268
8	**South Korea**	704,032
9	**Italy**	697,853
10	**US**	685,367
	World	*44,443,840*
	Canada	*104,844*

Source: *Euromonitor*

Less developed countries tend to have a high ratio of small stores to population: China has 1 store per 67 people, whereas the ratio in the US is 1 to 400.

► Street Trader
India's tradition of entrepreneurship and trade has given rise to a culture in which small shops play a prominent part.

TOP 10 SUPERMARKET-SHOPPING COUNTRIES

	COUNTRY	SPENDING PER CAPITA IN 2000 (US$)
1	**US**	1,600.2
2	**UK**	1,366.5
3	**Sweden**	1,339.2
4	**Switzerland**	1,318.9
5	**Australia**	1,301.7
6	**Norway**	1,234.6
7	**Japan**	1,229.4
8	**Netherlands**	1,087.9
9	**Canada**	1,077.9
10	**Belgium**	1,051.0
	World	*244.6*

Source: *Euromonitor*

TOP 10 MERCHANDISERS IN CANADA

	MERCHANDISER	REVENUES, 2001 ($)
1	**Hudson's Bay Co.**	7,445,813,000
2	**Costco Wholesale Canada Ltd.**	7,044,960,000
3	**Sears Canada Inc.**	6,726,400,000
4	**Canadian Tire Corp., Ltd.**	5,374,759,000
5	**Liquor Control Board of Ontario**	2,734,937,000
6	**Future Shop Ltd.**	1,985,177,000
7	**RONA Inc.**	1,834,544,000
8	**British Columbia Liquor Distribution**	1,719,182,000
9	**Société des alcools du Québec**	1,547,911,000
10	**United Farmers of Alberta Co-operative Ltd.**	833,517,000

Source: National Post Business, FP500, *June 2002*

TOP 10 INTERNET RETAILERS

	COMPANY	WEBSITE	EST. US SALES (US$)*
1	**eBay**	eBay.com	3,500–3,700,000,000
2	**Amazon.com**	amazon.com	1,700–1,900,000,000
3	**Dell**	dell.com	1,100–1,300,000,000
4	**buy.com**	buy.com	700–800,000,000
5	= **Egghead.com** (formerly OnSale.com)	Egghead.com	500–600,000,000
	= **Gateway**	Gateway.com	500–600,000,000
7	**Quixtar**	Quixtar.com	400–450,000,000
8	= **Barnes & Noble**	bn.com	275–325,000,000
	= **uBid.com**	uBid.com	275–325,000,000
10	= **Cyberian Outpost**	Outpost.com	200–250,000,000
	= **MicroWarehouse**	MicroWarehouse.com	200–250,000,000
	= **Value America**#	va.com	200–250,000,000

* *In latest financial year* # *Ceased retail operations*

Source: Stores/*VeriFone and Russell Reynold Associates, Top 100 Internet Retailers, Sept 2001 © NRF Enterprises, Inc.*

TOP 10 SPECIALTY RETAILERS

	COMPANY/HEADQUARTERS	SPECIALTY	RETAIL SALES IN 2001 (US$)
1	**Home Depot, Inc.,** US	Home improvement supplies	53,553,000,000
2	**Lowe's Companies, Inc.,** US	Home improvement supplies	22,111,000,000
3	**AutoNation, Inc.,** US	Car dealers	19,989,000,000
4	**Best Buy Co. Inc.,** US	Consumer electronics	19,597,000,000
5	**The Gap, Inc.,** US	Clothing	13,848,000,000
6	**Circuit City Stores, Inc.,** US	Consumer electronics	12,791,000,000
7	**Toys "R" Us, Inc.,** US	Toys	11,019,000,000
8	**TJX Companies, Inc.,** US	Clothing and accessories	10,709,000,000
9	**IKEA,** Sweden	Home furnishing	10,359,000,000
10	**Staples, Inc.,** US	Office supplies	10,100,000,000

Source: Stores, *Top 200 Global Retailers*

TOP 10 MAIL-ORDER SHOPPING COUNTRIES

	COUNTRY	SPENDING PER CAPITA IN 2000 (US$)
1	**US**	520.6
2	**Germany**	228.6
3	**UK**	198.6
4	**Denmark**	171.7
5	**Switzerland**	149.1
6	**Austria**	137.4
7	**France**	111.7
8	**Norway**	109.2
9	**Sweden**	102.8
10	**Finland**	56.5
	Canada	*42.1*

Source: *Euromonitor*

Despite a general global market slowdown, driven by new technologies such as the Internet, the mail-order sector in many countries is growing: in the US, for example, it expanded by almost 9 percent between 1999 and 2000 (the latest year for which comparative country data are available) to reach a total value of US$142.7 billion.

Rich Lists

TOP 10 RICHEST AMERICAN MEN

	NAME	COMPANY	NET WORTH (US$)
1	**William H. Gates III**	Microsoft	40,700,000,000
2	**Warren Edward Buffett**	Berkshire Hathaway	30,500,000,000
3	**Paul Gardner Allen**	Microsoft	20,100,000,000
4	**Lawrence Joseph Ellison**	Oracle	16,600,000,000
5	= **Jim C. Walton**	Wal-Mart	16,500,000,000
	= **John T. Walton**	Wal-Mart	16,500,000,000
	= **S. Robson Walton**	Wal-Mart	16,500,000,000
8	**Steven Anthony Ballmer**	Microsoft	11,100,000,000
9	**John Werner Kluge**	Metromedia	10,500,000,000
10	= **Forrest E. Mars Jr.**	Mars Inc.	10,000,000,000
	= **John F. Mars**	Mars Inc.	10,000,000,000

Source: Forbes, *The World's Richest People, February 27, 2003*

TOP 10 RICHEST NON-AMERICAN MEN*

	NAME/COUNTRY	SOURCE	NET WORTH (US$)
1	**Karl and Theo Albrecht,** Germany	Retail	25,600,000,000
2	**Prince Alwaleed Bin Talal Alsaud,** Saudi Arabia	Investments	17,700,000,000
3	**Kenneth Thomson and family,** Canada	Publishing	14,000,000,000
4	**Ingvar Kamprad,** Sweden	Home furnishings	13,000,000,000
5	**Amancio Ortega,** Spain	Clothing	10,300,000,000
6	**Mikhail B. Khodorkovsky,** Russia	Banking and oil	8,000,000,000
7	**Li Ka-shing,** Hong Kong	Diversified	7,800,000,000
8	**Hans Rausing,** Sweden	Packaging	7,700,000,000
9	**Gerald Cavendish Grosvenor (Duke of Westminster),** UK	Land and property	7,500,000,000
10	**Carlos Slim Helu,** Mexico	Telecommunications	7,400,000,000

* *Excluding rulers*

Source: Forbes, *The World's Billionaires, February 27, 2003*

TOP 10 BEST PAID EXECUTIVES IN CANADA

	EXECUTIVE	COMPANY	TOTAL COMPENSATION ($)*
1	**Frank Stronach**	Magna International Inc.	58,137,280
2	**Richard Currie**	George Weston Ltd.	48,058,056
3	**Galen Weston**	George Weston Ltd.	31,996,185
4	**Pierre Lessard**	Metro Inc.	28,310,200
5	**Robert Burton**	Moore Corp.	20,932,279
6	**Richard George**	Suncor Energy Inc.	14,077,955
7	**Randall Oliphant**	Barrick Gold Corp.	13,837,890
8	**Frank Weise**	Cott Corp.	13,248,375
9	**Siegfried Wolf**	Magna International Inc.	12,776,839
10	**William McCallum**	Great-West Lifeco Inc.	12,191,715

* *Total of base salary and, if applicable, annual bonus, share units, option gains, and all other payments or cash value of benefits*

Source: Globe and Mail *Report on Business, May 2003. Reprinted with permission from the* Globe and Mail.

World's Richest
Microsoft co-founder William H. Gates III has led both the list of richest Americans and that of world's richest for the past 10 years.

TOP 10 RICHEST WOMEN*

	NAME/COUNTRY#	SOURCE	NET WORTH (US$)
1	= Alice L. Walton	Retail	16,500,000,000
	= Helen R. Walton	Retail	16,500,000,000
3	Liliane Bettencourt, France	Beauty products	14,500,000,000
4	Birgit Rausing and family, Sweden	Inheritance/packaging	12,900,000,000
5	= Barbara Cox Anthony	Media	10,300,000,000
	= Anne Cox Chambers	Media	10,300,000,000
7	Jacqueline Mars	Candy	10,000,000,000
8	Abigail Johnson	Mutual funds	8,200,000,000
9	Susanne Klatten, Germany	Inheritance	5,300,000,000
10	Maria-Elisabeth and Georg Schaeffler (mother and son), Germany	Roller bearings	3,800,000,000

* *Excluding rulers*

\# *From the US unless otherwise specified*

Source: Forbes, *The World's Richest People, February 27, 2003*

TOP 10 HIGHEST-EARNING CELEBRITIES

	CELEBRITY	PROFESSION	EARNINGS 2001–02 (US$)
1	George Lucas	Film producer/director	200,000,000
2	Oprah Winfrey	TV host/producer	150,000,000
3	Steven Spielberg	Film producer/director	100,000,000
4	= Tiger Woods	Golfer	69,000,000
	= U2	Rock band	69,000,000
6	Michael Schumacher	Race car driver	67,000,000
7	Mariah Carey	Pop singer	58,000,000
8	Stephen King	Writer/film director	52,400,000
9	Dave Matthews Band	Rock band	50,000,000
10	Tom Clancy	Writer	47,800,000

* *June 2001–June 2002*

Source: Forbes, *The Celebrity 100*

TOP 10 RICHEST CANADIANS

	NAME	SOURCE	NET WORTH (US$)
1	Kenneth Thomson and family	Publishing	14,000,000,000
2	Galen Weston and family	Retail	6,200,000,000
3	James, Arthur, and John Irving	Oil	3,500,000,000
4	Jeffrey S. Skoll	eBay	2,800,000,000
5	= Charles R. Bronfman	Media	2,200,000,000
	= Jim Pattison	Diversified	2,200,000,000
	= Bernard (Barry) Sherman	Pharmaceuticals	2,200,000,000
8	Wallace McCain	Food processing	1,800,000,000
9	Paul Desmarais and family	Diversified	1,700,000,000
10	Harrison McCain	Food processing	1,500,000,000

Source: Forbes, *The World's Richest People 2003*

Super Celebrity
Oprah Winfrey has consistently figured among—sometimes topping—the list of highest-earning entertainers since the 1980s.

Energy & Environment

TOP 10 PAPER-RECYCLING COUNTRIES

	COUNTRY	PRODUCTION PER 1,000 PEOPLE IN 2001 (TONNES)
1	Switzerland	167.36
2	Sweden	164.61
3	Austria	157.77
4	Netherlands	155.30
5	US	144.14
6	Germany	140.55
7	Finland	134.80
8	Japan	116.55
9	Norway	98.26
10	France	93.62
	Canada	*48.05*

Source: *Food and Agriculture Organization of the United Nations*

TOP 10 COUNTRIES WITH THE GREATEST CRUDE OIL RESERVES

	COUNTRY	2001 RESERVES (TONNES)
1	Saudi Arabia	36,000,000,000
2	Iraq	15,100,000,000
3	Kuwait	13,300,000,000
4	United Arab Emirates	13,000,000,000
5	Iran	12,300,000,000
6	Venezuela	11,200,000,000
7	Russia	6,700,000,000
8	= Libya	3,800,000,000
	= Mexico	3,800,000,000
10	US	3,700,000,000

Source: *BP Amoco Statistical Review of World Energy 2002*

THE 10 CARBON DIOXIDE-EMITTING COUNTRIES

	COUNTRY	CO_2 EMISSIONS PER CAPITA, 2001 (TONNES OF CARBON)
1	Qatar	13.66
2	United Arab Emirates	13.31
3	Bahrain	9.47
4	Kuwait	8.32
5	Singapore	7.57
6	Trinidad and Tobago	6.25
7	Luxembourg	5.61
8	US	5.51
9	Canada	5.22
10	Guam	5.18
	World	*1.07*

Source: *Energy Information Administration*

TOP 10 ENERGY-CONSUMING COUNTRIES

	COUNTRY	ENERGY CONSUMPTION IN 2001* OIL	GAS	COAL	NUCLEAR	HEP#	TOTAL
1	US	895.6	554.6	555.7	183.2	48.3	2,237.3
2	China	231.9	24.9	520.6	4.0	58.3	839.7
3	Russia	122.3	335.4	114.6	30.9	39.8	643.0
4	Japan	247.2	71.1	103.0	72.7	20.4	514.5
5	Germany	131.6	74.6	84.4	38.7	5.8	335.2
6	India	71.1	23.7	173.5	4.4	16.1	314.7
7	Canada	88.0	65.4	28.9	17.4	75.0	274.6
8	France	95.8	36.6	10.9	94.9	18.1	256.4
9	UK	76.1	85.9	40.3	20.4	1.5	224.0
10	South Korea	103.1	20.8	45.7	25.4	0.9	195.9
	World	*3,510.6*	*2,164.3*	*2,255.1*	*601.2*	*594.5*	*9,124.8*

* *Millions of tonnes of oil equivalent*

\# *Hydroelectric power*

Source: *BP Amoco Statistical Review of World Energy 2002*

◄ **Paper Chase**
Every tonne of recycled paper uses 64 percent less energy, 50 percent less water, causes 74 percent less air pollution, and saves 17 trees compared with the same quantity derived from new wood pulp.

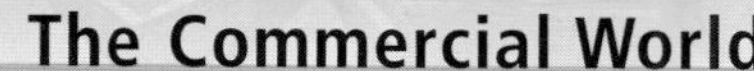

COUNTRIES WITH MOST RELIANCE ON NUCLEAR POWER

	COUNTRY	NUCLEAR ELECTRICITY AS PERCENTAGE OF TOTAL (2001)
1	Lithuania	78
2	France	77
3	Belgium	58
4	Slovakia	53
5	Ukraine	46
6	Sweden	44
7	Bulgaria	42
8	= Hungary	39
	= Slovenia	39
	= South Korea	39
	Canada	*13*

Source: *International Atomic Energy Agency*

ALTERNATIVE POWER*-CONSUMING COUNTRIES

	COUNTRY	CONSUMPTION KW/HR (2001)
1	US	84,800,000,000
2	Germany	22,600,000,000
3	Japan	19,100,000,000
4	Brazil	14,800,000,000
5	Philippines	12,200,000,000
6	Spain	9,200,000,000
7	Finland	8,400,000,000
8	= Italy	7,800,000,000
	= Luxembourg	7,800,000,000
10	Canada	7,200,000,000
	World	*251,100,000,000*

* *Includes geothermal, solar, wind, wood, and waste electric power*

Source: *Energy Information Administration*

◀ **Wind Power**
Some countries have taken the lead in the amount of electricity they generate by wind turbines: Germany's capacity is now double that of the US.

Science & Technology

TOP 10 INTERNATIONAL COMPANIES FOR RESEARCH AND DEVELOPMENT

	COMPANY/COUNTRY	INDUSTRY	R & D SPENDING (2001) (US$)
1	**Ford Motor,** US	Automobiles and parts	7,400,000,000
2	**General Motors,** US	Automobiles and parts	6,200,000,000
3	**Siemens,** Germany	Electronic and electrical	5,980,550,000
4	**DaimlerChrysler,** Germany	Automobiles and parts	5,231,880,000
5	**Pfizer,** US	Pharmaceuticals	4,847,000,000
6	**IBM,** US	Software and IT services	4,620,000,000
7	**Ericsson,** Sweden	IT hardware	4,410,410,000
8	**Microsoft,** US	Software and IT services	4,379,000,000
9	**Motorola,** US	IT hardware	4,318,000,000
10	**Matsushita Electric,** Japan	Electronic and electrical	4,310,440,000

Source: *The Financial Times Ltd., 2002*

The 300 international companies featured in the *Financial Times*' survey spent a total of US$267.6 trillion on research and development. Of them, some 70 firms spent in excess of US$1 billion a year, with automobile manufacturers the most prominent among the world's biggest R & D spenders.

TOP 10 INDUSTRIES FOR RESEARCH AND DEVELOPMENT

	INDUSTRY	R & D SPENDING (2001) (US$)
1	**IT hardware**	69,687,090,000
2	**Automobiles and parts**	47,877,160,000
3	**Pharmaceuticals**	46,553,340,000
4	**Electronic and electrical**	28,751,540,000
5	**Software and IT services**	15,925,250,000
6	**Chemicals**	11,725,580,000
7	**Aerospace and defense**	11,367,060,000
8	**Engineering and machinery**	5,941,040,000
9	**Telecommunications**	5,898,190,000
10	**Health**	4,727,640,000

Source: *The Financial Times Ltd., 2002*

THE 10 FIRST PATENTS IN THE US

	PATENT	PATENTEE	DATE
1	**Making potash and pearl ash**	Samuel Hopkins	July 31, 1790
2	**Making candles**	Joseph S. Sampson	Aug 6, 1790
3	**Making flour and meal**	Oliver Evans	Dec 18, 1790
4	= **Punches for type**	Francis Bailey	Jan 29, 1791
	= **Improvement in distilling**	Aaron Putnam	Jan 29, 1791
6	**Driving piles**	John Stone	Mar 10, 1791
7	= **Threshing machine**	Samuel Mullikin	Mar 11, 1791
	= **Breaking hemp**	Samuel Mullikin	Mar 11, 1791
	= **Polishing marble**	Samuel Mullikin	Mar 11, 1791
	= **Raising nap on cloth**	Samuel Mullikin	Mar 11, 1791

America's first patent, issued to Samuel Hopkins of Vermont, was for a process for manufacturing potash, or potassium carbonate, which was used in such industries as glass-, gunpowder-, and soap-making. For every ton produced, an acre of trees was cut down and burned, and the potash extracted from the resulting ashes. This group of pioneer patentees was followed in 1791 by others with devices reflecting the diversity of American inventiveness, and included improvements in making nails and bedsteads, manufacturing boats, and propelling boats by cattle-power.

▼ **Trading Places**
With one computer for every 10 people in the world, the workplace has undergone a transformation, although the true "paperless office" remains a rarity.

TOP 10 COUNTRIES WITH THE HIGHEST PROPORTION OF COMPUTER USERS

	COUNTRY	COMPUTERS (2001) TOTAL	PER 100 INHABITANTS
1	**US**	178,000,000	62.25
2	**Sweden**	5,000,000	56.12
3	**Australia**	10,000,000	51.71
4	**Luxembourg**	230,000	51.45
5	**Singapore**	2,100,000	50.83
6	**Norway**	2,300,000	50.80
7	**Switzerland**	3,600,000	49.97
8	**Denmark**	2,300,000	43.15
9	**Netherlands**	6,900,000	42.85
10	**Finland**	2,200,000	42.35
	Canada	*12,000,000*	*39.02*
	World	*455,366,000*	*7.74*

Source: *International Telecommunication Union*, World Telecommunication Development Report, 2002

THE 10 LATEST WINNERS OF THE NOBEL PRIZE FOR ECONOMIC SCIENCES

	WINNERS/COUNTRY	YEAR
1	= **Daniel Kahneman,** US and Israel	2002
	= **Vernon L. Smith,** US	2002
3	= **George A. Akerlof,** US	2001
	= **A. Michael Spence,** US	2001
	= **Joseph E. Stiglitz,** US	2001
6	= **James J. Heckman,** US	2000
	= **Daniel L. McFadden,** US	2000
8	**Robert A. Mundell,** Canada	1999
9	**Amartya Sen,** India	1998
10	= **Robert C. Merton,** US	1997
	= **Myron S. Scholes,** US	1997

For international business dealings, multinational companies have benefited from the research done by these economists, notably the analytical work by Robert Mundell, credited as integral to the concept of the Euro.

TOP 10 MOST VALUABLE TECHNOLOGY BRANDS*

	BRAND NAME/COUNTRY	BRAND VALUE (2002) (US$)
1	**Microsoft,** US	64,091,000,000
2	**IBM,** US	51,188,000,000
3	**Intel,** US	30,861,000,000
4	**Nokia,** Finland	29,970,000,000
5	**Hewlett-Packard,** US	16,780,000,000
6	**Cisco,** US	16,220,000,000
7	**AT&T,** US	16,060,000,000
8	**Sony,** Japan	13,900,000,000
9	**Oracle,** US	11,510,000,000
10	**Compaq,** US	9,800,000,000

* *Includes computer, telecommunications, and consumer electronics brands*

Source: *Interbrand/BusinessWeek*

Brand consultants Interbrand uses a method of estimating value that takes account of the profitability of individual brands within an industry (rather than that of the parent company), as well as such factors as their potential for growth.

TOP 10 COUNTRIES REGISTERING THE MOST PATENTS

	COUNTRY	PATENTS REGISTERED (2000)
1	**US**	157,496
2	**Japan**	125,880
3	**Germany**	41,585
4	**France**	36,404
5	**South Korea**	34,956
6	**UK**	33,756
7	**Italy**	19,652
8	**Russia**	17,592
9	**Netherlands**	17,052
10	**Spain**	15,809

source: *World Intellectual Property Organization*

World Wide Web

TOP 10 MOST WIRED CITIES, 2001

	CITY/COUNTRY	COUNTRIES CONNECTED IN 2001*	INTERNATIONAL INTERNET BANDWIDTH IN 2001 (MBPS)#
1	**London,** UK	61	237,389.2
2	**Paris,** France	48	179,064.8
3	**New York,** US	71	173,098.6
4	**Amsterdam,** Netherlands	27	170,371.8
5	**Frankfurt,** Germany	28	160,459.0
6	**Brussels,** Belgium	17	76,246.4
7	**Stockholm,** Sweden	18	60,349.0
8	**Copenhagen,** Denmark	13	43,456.0
9	**Milan,** Italy	15	29,701.8
10	**Toronto,** Canada	6	24,942.3

* *Refers to the number of physical direct cable connections that a country has to others*

\# *Mbps are millions of bits or megabits per second, a measure of bandwidth (the total information flow over a given time) over the available telecommunications medium*

Source: *TeleGeography*

THE 10 INTERNET FRAUDS

	CATEGORY	PERCENTAGE OF ALL COMPLAINTS*
1	**Online auctions**	87
2	**General merchandise**	6
3	**Nigerian money offers**	5
4	**Computer equipment/software**	1
5	**Work-at-home plans**	0.5
6	**Internet access services**	0.4
7	**Information/adult services**	0.2
8	= **Advance-fee loans**	0.05
	= **Travel/vacations**	0.05
10	**Prizes/sweepstakes**	0.04

* *January–June 2002*

Source: *National Fraud Information Center, National Consumers League*

The overall loss in the US to Internet fraud in the first half of 2002 was US$7,209,196, with an average loss (per victim of Internet fraud) of US$484.

TOP 10 COUNTRIES WITH THE MOST INTERNET USERS

	COUNTRY	INTERNET USERS*
1	US	168,600,000
2	Japan	56,000,000
3	China	45,800,000
4	Germany	41,800,000
5	UK	30,400,000
6	Italy	25,300,000
7	France	23,000,000
8	Brazil	19,700,000
9	Spain	17,000,000
10	Canada	16,840,000
	World total	*580,000,000*

* *Estimate, as of March 14, 2003*

Source: *CyberAtlas/Nielsen/NetRatings*

Cyber Café

The arrival of Internet cafés in 1984 heralded a new era of communications and information-gathering for people on the move, those lacking personal Internet access, or as a social activity.

TOP 10 COUNTRIES WITH HIGHEST DENSITY OF INTERNET HOSTS 2001

	COUNTRY	INTERNET HOSTS PER 1,000 PEOPLE (2001)
1	US	371.40
2	Tonga	209.00
3	Iceland	190.48
4	Finland	170.72
5	Netherlands	163.47
6	Australia	118.34
7	New Zealand	104.95
8	Denmark	104.53
9	Canada	93.19
10	Sweden	82.51

Source: *International Telecommunication Union, World Telecommunciation Development Report, 2002*

An Internet host is a computer system connected to the Internet—either a single terminal directly connected, or a computer that allows multiple users to access network services through it. The ratio of hosts to population is a crude measure of how "wired" a country is.

TOP 10 RETAIL SITES VISITED BY CANADIANS AT HOME AND WORK

	WEBSITE	UNIQUE VISITORS*
1	eBay	5,580,000
2	Amazon sites#	5,422,000
3	Yahoo! Shopping	2,865,000
4	Columbia House sites#	2,386,000
5	Best Buy sites#	1,735,000
6	MSN Shopping	1,714,000
7	AmericanGreetings.com	1,459,000
8	Sears.ca	1,426,000
9	Theuseful.com	1,385,000
10	Hewlett Packard	1,330,000

* *Total number of unique visitors during December 2002*

\# *Includes all sites associated with the client property, such as .ca, .com, .fr, .co.uk, .de*

Source: *comScore Media Metrix Canada,* Total Canada at All Locations (Home/Work Combined), *December 2002*

According to Statistics Canada, an estimated 2.2 million households spent almost $2 billion purchasing good and services on the Internet in 2001.

WORLD WIDE WORDS

FIRST FACT

BOTH THE INTERNET and its language have evolved over the past 40 years. "Hypertext" was first proposed as early as 1965 by Ted Nelson. Ray Tomlinson pioneered and named email in 1971 and the following year advocated the use of the "@" sign. The first "smiley" [:-)]or emoticon was used by Scott E. Fahlman on a Carnegie Mellon University (CMU) bulletin board in 1982, the same year that novelist William Gibson invented the term "cyberspace" in his novel *Neuromancer*. The world wide web, and its name, were devised by Tim Berners-Lee in 1990, and the description "surfing the Internet" was coined in 1992 by Jean Armour Polly.

TOP 10 USES OF THE INTERNET IN CANADA, 2001

	USE	PERCENTAGE OF HOUSEHOLDS*
1	E-mail	94.7
2	General browsing	91.0
3	Medical/health information	61.8
4	Travel information/arrangements	56.3
5	View the news	53.8
6	Government information	52.5
7	Playing games	50.1
8	Obtaining/downloading music	47.9
9	Formal education/training	47.0
10	Financial information	46.8

* *Regular home-use households*

Source: *Statistics Canada*

TOP 10 SEARCH ENGINES IN THE US

	SEARCH ENGINE	US AUDIENCE REACH (PERCENTAGE)*
1	Google	29.5
2	Yahoo!	28.9
3	MSN	27.6
4	AOL	18.4
5	Ask Jeeves	9.9
6	Overture	4.8
7	InfoSpace	4.5
8	Netscape	4.4
9	AltaVista	4.0
10	Lycos	2.4

* *Based on a sample of 60,000 US web surfers, January 2003; percentage of surfers who visit the search engine site each month*

Source: *Nielsen/NetRatings/SearchEngineWatch.com*

Keep in Touch

▲ **Syncom IV (LEASAT) Satellite**

Since the mid-1960s, satellites launched into geostationary orbit have enabled international telecommunications to become one of the fastest growing industries on Earth—and beyond.

TOP 10 COUNTRIES MAKING THE MOST INTERNATIONAL PHONE CALLS

	COUNTRY	MINUTES PER HEAD 2000	TOTAL MINUTES OUTGOING CALLS 2000
1	US	125.9	34,640,700,000
2	Germany	112.1	9,223,000,000
3	UK	133.5	7,981,000,000
4	Canada	234.9	7,224,000,000
5	France	84.1	4,952,000,000
6	Hong Kong	466.8	3,142,400,000
7	Netherlands	177.0	2,830,000,000
8	Italy	47.8	2,740,000,000
9	Japan	20.3	2,575,000,000
10	Spain	64.1	2,570,000,000

Source: *International Telecommunication Union,* World Telecommunication Development Report, 2002

If this Top 10 list were ranked by total minutes per head, Bermuda would lead with 944.1 minutes.

TOP 10 INTERNATIONAL TELECOMMUNICATIONS CARRIERS

	COMPANY/ORIGIN COUNTRY	OUTGOING TRAFFIC (MINUTES) IN 2001
1	**AT&T Corp.**, US	12,006,800,000
2	**WorldCom,** US	11,454,700,000
3	**Sprint,** US	5,384,400,000
4	**Deutsche Telekom,** Germany	5,025,100,000
5	**France Télécom,** France	4,592,000,000
6	**BT,** UK	4,233,500,000
7	**Cable & Wireless,** UK	3,113,800,000
8	**Telefónica,** Spain	3,084,800,000
9	**Telecom Italia,** Italy	3,042,000,000
10	**China Telecom,** China	2,600,000,000

Source: *TeleGeography*

In 2001, the Top 10 and other international telecommunications carriers handled an estimated total of 144 billion minutes of outgoing traffic—the equivalent of more than 23 minutes for every person on the planet.

TOP 10 COUNTRIES WITH THE MOST POST OFFICES

	COUNTRY	POST OFFICES (2001)* AVG NO. OF PEOPLE SERVED PER OFFICE	TOTAL
1	India	6,568	154,919
2	China	22,490	57,135
3	Russia	3,546	41,052
4	US	7,471	38,123
5	Japan	5,143	24,760
6	Indonesia	10,806	19,881
7	UK	3,377	17,633
8	France	3,469	17,067
9	Ukraine	3,282	14,963
10	Italy	4,203	13,788

* *Or latest year for which data available*

Source: *Universal Postal Union*

There are some 770,000 post offices worldwide, ranging from major city post offices offering a wide range of services to small establishments providing only basic services, such as the sale of stamps.

TOP 10 LETTER-MAILING COUNTRIES

	COUNTRY	AVERAGE NO. OF LETTER POST ITEMS MAILED PER INHABITANT (2001)*
1	Vatican City	6,500.00
2	US	706.11
3	Norway	561.72
4	Liechtenstein	556.00
5	Austria	467.10
6	Luxembourg	449.21
7	France	447.57
8	Finland	344.58
9	Belgium	344.05
10	Slovenia	272.74

* *Or latest year for which data available*

Source: *Universal Postal Union*

Vatican City's statistics are partly explained by the number of official missives dispatched via the Holy See's post office and its 32 mailboxes, but mainly because Rome's inhabitants have discovered that mail posted there and bearing Vatican stamps is treated as priority.

TOP 10 COUNTRIES WITH MOST TELEPHONES PER 100 PEOPLE, 2000

	COUNTRY	TOTAL	TELEPHONE LINES PER 100 INHABITANTS
1	**Luxembourg**	330,988	75.0
2	**Switzerland**	5,235,000	72.6
3	**Denmark**	3,835,000	71.9
4	**Iceland**	196,984	70.1
5	**US**	192,519,000	69.9
6	**Sweden**	6,057,000	68.2
7	**Canada**	20,803,000	67.6
8	**Cyprus**	440,091	64.7
9	**Netherlands**	9,879,000	61.7
10	**Germany**	50,220,000	61.0

Source: *International Telecommunications Union*, Yearbook of Statistics

TOP 10 COUNTRIES WITH THE HIGHEST RATIO OF CELLULAR MOBILE PHONE USERS

	COUNTRY	SUBSCRIBERS 2001	CELL PHONES PER 100 INHABITANTS 2001
1	**Luxembourg**	432,400	96.73
2	**Taiwan**	21,633,000	96.55
3	**Hong Kong**	5,701,700	84.35
4	**Italy**	48,698,000	83.94
5	**Norway**	3,737,000	82.53
6	**Iceland**	235,400	82.02
7	**Israel**	5,260,000	80.82
8	**Austria**	6,565,900	80.66
9	**UK**	47,026,000	78.28
10	**Finland**	4,044,000	77.84
	Canada	*9,923,900*	*32.00*

Source: *International Telecommunications Union*, World Telecommunication Development Report, *2002*

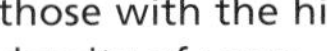

Phone Home
The adoption of cell phones has revolutionized telecommunications worldwide, with Scandinavian countries standing out among those with the highest density of users.

THE 10 FIRST CITIES AND COUNTRIES TO ISSUE POSTAGE STAMPS

	CITY/COUNTRY	DATE ISSUED
1	**UK**	May 1840
2	**New York,** US	Feb 1842
3	**Zurich,** Switzerland	Mar 1843
4	**Brazil**	Aug 1843
5	**Geneva,** Switzerland	Oct 1843
6	**Basle,** Switzerland	July 1845
7	**US**	July 1847
8	**Mauritius**	Sept 1847
9	**Bermuda**	Unknown 1848
10	**France**	Jan 1849

The first adhesive postage stamp issued in the UK—and the world—was the Penny Black, which went on sale May 1, 1840. The first issued in Canada, on April 23, 1851, was the Three-Pence Beaver for domestic mail. It was designed by Sir Sandford Fleming, a Scot, who defied the hitherto unbroken tradition of portraying the reigning monarch on a postage stamp (although the VR monogram of Queen Victoria was included).

Food Favorites

TOP 10 BAKED BEAN CONSUMERS

	COUNTRY	EST. CONSUMPTION PER CAPITA (2004) (LB)	(OZ)	(KG)
1	Ireland	12	5	5.6
2	UK	10	9	4.8
3	New Zealand	5	1	2.3
4	US	4	6	2.0
5	Australia	4	3	1.9
6	= France	3	8	1.6
	= Saudi Arabia	3	8	1.6
8	Switzerland	3	5	1.5
9	Ukraine	2	13	1.3
10	= Canada	2	10	1.2
	= Mexico	2	10	1.2

Source: *Euromonitor*

Canned baked beans originated in New England. Brand leader Heinz's baked beans were test-marketed in the North of England in 1901. They were imported from the US up to 1928, when they were first canned in the UK.

TOP 10 FROZEN FOOD CONSUMERS

	COUNTRY	EST. CONSUMPTION PER CAPITA (2004) (LB)	(OZ)	(KG)
1	Denmark	104	7	47.4
2	Norway	76	15	34.9
3	Sweden	54	7	24.7
4	Finland	51	12	23.5
5	UK	49	2	22.3
6	Ireland	45	3	20.5
7	Switzerland	36	9	16.6
8	Israel	36	2	16.4
9	New Zealand	34	6	15.6
10	US	31	4	14.2

Source: *Euromonitor*

Having studied Eskimos' methods of preserving food by freezing, Clarence Birdseye established the first frozen food company in 1924 in Gloucester, Massachusetts. The Birds Eye company sold its first individual frozen meals—chicken fricassée and steak—in 1939.

TOP 10 POTATO CHIP CONSUMERS

	COUNTRY	EST. CONSUMPTION PER CAPITA (2004) (LB)	(OZ)	(KG)
1	UK	6	9	3.0
2	= Australia	5	15	2.7
	= Ireland	5	15	2.7
4	New Zealand	5	12	2.6
5	= Norway	4	14	2.4
	= US	4	14	2.4
7	Finland	4	10	2.1
8	Sweden	3	15	1.8
9	Israel	3	11	1.7
10	Canada	3	8	1.6

Source: *Euromonitor*

◀ **Full of Beans**
Although originating in the US, baked beans have been adopted as a staple dish by the people of the British Isles, who have become the world's foremost consumers.

TOP 10 MEAT CONSUMERS

	COUNTRY	ANNUAL CONSUMPTION PER CAPITA (2000) (LB)	(OZ)	(KG)
1	US	269	10	122.3
2	Denmark	253	1	114.8
3	Spain	250	14	113.8
4	Australia	243	6	110.4
5	New Zealand	235	7	106.8
6	Austria	235	0	106.6
7	Cyprus	234	2	106.2
8	Mongolia	228	9	103.7
9	France	220	3	99.9
10	Canada	220	0	99.8
	World	*83*	*15*	*38.1*

Source: *Food and Agriculture Organization of the United Nations*

Worldwide, meat consumption ranges from 99.8 kg (220 lb) or more for countries in the Top 10, to less than 5.4 kg (12 lb) per head in countries such as India.

TOP 10 VEGETABLE CONSUMERS

	COUNTRY	CONSUMPTION PER CAPITA (2000) (LB)	(OZ)	(KG)
1	**United Arab Emirates**	694	0	314.8
2	**Lebanon**	679	0	308.0
3	**Greece**	646	2	293.1
4	**Israel**	527	12	239.4
5	**South Korea**	511	14	232.2
6	**Turkey**	463	3	210.1
7	**Macedonia**	461	10	209.4
8	**Libya**	456	5	207.0
9	**Albania**	451	8	204.8
10	**China**	448	10	203.5
	World	*224*	*10*	*101.9*
	Canada	*264*	*1*	*119.8*

Source: *Food and Agriculture Organization of the United Nations*

TOP 10 MAJOR FOOD ITEMS CONSUMED IN CANADA*

	PRODUCT	ANNUAL CONSUMPTION PER CAPITA (2001) (LB)	(OZ)	(KG)
1	**Fresh vegetables**	317	1	143.86
2	**Cereal products**	195	5	88.66
3	**Fresh fruit**	139	8	63.42
4	**Red meat**	138	6	62.86
5	**Dairy products**#	135	4	61.35
6	**Sugar and syrup**	86	8	39.38
7	**Poultry**	79	8	36.20
8	**Oils and fats** (includes butter)	70	2	31.86
9	**Eggs**	24	0	10.88
10	**Legumes and nuts**	21	5	9.73

* *Available for consumption rather than actual quantities consumed. The difference is accounted for by losses in stores, restaurants, private institutions, and the home*

\# *Includes milk solid equivalents, cheese, ice cream, and yogurt*

Source: *Statistics Canada,* Food Consumption in Canada, *2001*

TOP 10 FAST FOOD COMPANIES

	COMPANY/COUNTRY	FAST FOOD MARKET SHARE % (1999)
1	**McDonald's Corporation,** US	21.9
2	**Tricon Global Restaurants, Inc.,** US	10.7
3	**Diageo plc,** UK	7.1
4	**Wendy's International, Inc.,** US	3.8
5 =	**Allied Domecq plc,** UK	2.3
=	**Doctor's Associates, Inc.,** US	2.3
7	**CKE Restaurants, Inc.,** US	2.0
8	**Domino's Pizza, Inc.,** US	1.8
9	**Berkshire Hathaway, Inc.,** US	1.5
10	**Triarc Corporation,** US	1.3

Source: *Euromonitor*

World's leading fast food company McDonald's began in Des Plaines, Illinois, in 1955, with the opening of Ray Kroc's first restaurant. Today, more than 30,000 restaurants serve 46 million people a day in 121 countries, with the one in Pushkin Square, Russia, the busiest of all.

Fruits and Veggies
Although apples, bananas, oranges, melons, and potatoes remain among Canada's favorite produce, the modern shopping basket contains a far more diverse range of products than in the past.

Sweet Success

TOP 10 CONFECTIONERY MANUFACTURERS

	MANUFACTURER/COUNTRY OF ORIGIN	PERCENT SHARE OF CONFECTIONERY MARKET (2001)
1	**Philip Morris Company Inc.,** US	4.5
2	= **Nestlé SA,** Switzerland	4.0
	= **Perfetti Van Melle Group,** Italy/Netherlands	4.0
4	**Hershey Foods Corporation,** US	3.3
5	**Pfizer Inc.,** US	3.1
6	**Cadbury-Schweppes plc,** UK	3.0
7	= **CSM nv,** Netherlands	2.7
	= **Mars Inc.,** US	2.7
9	**August Storck KG,** Germany	2.4
10	**Haribo GmbH & Co. KG,** Germany	2.1

Source: *Euromonitor*

Global sales of confectionery in 2000 were estimated at 12.7 million tonnes, an average of 2 kg (4.4 lb) for everyone on Earth—although per capita consumption in many countries is much higher—with a total value of US$101.2 billion.

TOP 10 CHOCOLATE CONFECTIONERY CONSUMERS

	COUNTRY	CONSUMPTION PER CAPITA (2000) LB	OZ	KG
1	**Switzerland**	25	6	11.5
2	**Liechtenstein**	22	15	10.4
3	**Luxembourg**	22	11	10.3
4	**UK**	21	10	9.8
5	**Belgium**	18	15	8.6
6	**Norway**	17	3	7.8
7	= **Germany**	17	0	7.7
	= **Ireland**	17	0	7.7
9	**Iceland**	16	12	7.6
10	**Austria**	13	14	6.3
	World	*2*	*3*	*1.0*

Source: *Euromonitor*

World chocolate confectionery consumption is around 5.4 million tonnes a year, just under 1 kg (2.2 lb) per capita, with a total value of some US$53 billion.

Taking the Cake
The world's passion for chocolate and sugar-based products grows annually—as do the waistlines of their consumers...

TOP 10 SUGAR-CONSUMING COUNTRIES

	COUNTRY	CONSUMPTION PER CAPITA* (2000) LB	OZ	KG
1	**Macedonia**	162	12	73.8
2	**Belize**	144	6	65.5
3	**Swaziland**	125	8	56.9
4	**Cuba**	124	15	56.6
5	**Trinidad and Tobago**	122	0	55.3
6	**Barbados**	116	4	52.7
7	**Brazil**	114	1	51.7
8	**Costa Rica**	111	8	50.6
9	**New Zealand**	108	9	49.2
10	**St. Kitts and Nevis**	108	0	49.0
	World	*41*	*5*	*18.8*
	Canada	*70*	*5*	*31.9*

* *Refined equivalent*

Source: *Food and Agriculture Organization of the United Nations*

TOP 10 CHEWING GUM CONSUMERS

	COUNTRY	CONSUMPTION PER CAPITA (2000) LB	OZ	G
1	= **Andorra**	2	0	900
	= **Iceland**	2	0	900
	= **Norway**	2	0	900
4	= **Israel**	1	9	700
	= **Liechtenstein**	1	9	700
	= **Switzerland**	1	9	700
	= **US**	1	9	700
8	= **St. Kitts and Nevis**	1	5	600
	= **Spain**	1	5	600
	= **Turkey**	1	5	600
	World	*0*	*3*	*100*
	Canada	*1*	*2*	*500*

Source: *Euromonitor*

Worldwide chewing gum consumption in 2000 was estimated as 795,609.6 tonnes, and that of the US 198,129.8 tonnes, or just under 25 percent of the total.

TOP 10 ICE CREAM CONSUMERS

	COUNTRY	CONSUMPTION PER CAPITA (2000) PINTS	LITERS
1	**Australia**	31.1	17.7
2	**US**	24.1	13.7
3	**New Zealand**	23.4	13.3
4	**Sweden**	20.5	11.7
5	**Ireland**	17.9	10.2
6	= **Denmark**	16.3	9.3
	= **Israel**	16.3	9.3
8	**Canada**	16.0	9.1
9	**Finland**	14.9	8.5
10	**Norway**	14.7	8.4

Source: *Euromonitor*

Just under 4 percent of the world's total expenditure on packaged food is devoted to ice cream, the 10th largest sector in the global market, worth a total of US$43 billion in 2000.

▶ **Knickerbocker Glory**
Invented in the 1930s, this over-the-top concoction was named after Diedrich Knickerbocker, fictitious author of Washington Irving's *History of New York*.

TOP 10 CHOCOLATE CONFECTIONERY COMPANIES IN CANADA*

	MANUFACTURER	MARKET SHARE PERCENTAGE (2001)*
1	**Cadbury Chocolate Canada/ Neilson Cadbury**	18.6
2	**Hershey Canada Inc.**	15.2
3	**Nestlé Canada Inc.**	11.6
4	**Effem Foods Ltd.**	9.8
5	**Ferrero Canada Ltd.**	2.4
6	**Archibald Candy Corp.**	2.1
7	**Quaker Oats of Canada Ltd.**	1.5
8	**Ganong Bros. Ltd.**	1.1
9	**Trebor Allan Inc.**	0.9
10	= **Godiva Chocolates**	0.4
	= **Lindt & Sprüngli Canada Inc.**	0.4

* *Based on $ sales volume of confectionery market*

Source: *Euromonitor*

TOP 10 CHOCOLATE CANDY BARS IN THE US

	BRAND/MANUFACTURER	SALES (US$)*
1	**M&Ms,** Mars	97,404,576
2	**Hershey's Milk Chocolate,** Hershey Chocolate	81,296,784
3	**Reese's Peanut Butter Cups,** Hershey Chocolate	54,391,268
4	**Snickers,** Mars	53,695,428
5	**KitKat,** Hershey Chocolate (under license from Nestlé)	38,168,580
6	**Twix,** Mars	33,174,400
7	**York Peppermint Patty,** York Cone Company	25,494,038
8	**Peter Paul Almond Joy,** Hershey Chocolate	23,721,998
9	**Butterfinger,** Nestlé	22,804,380
10	**Three Musketeers,** Mars	19,834,244
	Total (including those not in Top 10)	773,904,832

* *100 g (3.5 oz) candy bars only; 52 weeks to January 27, 2002*

Source: *Information Resources, Inc.*

Drink Up

TOP 10 CARBONATED SOFT DRINK CONSUMERS

	COUNTRY	CONSUMPTION PER CAPITA IN 2000 GALLONS	LITERS
1	US	42.7	161.8
2	Mexico	30.2	114.2
3	Norway	26.9	102.0
4	Canada	22.6	85.6
5	Australia	21.7	82.3
6	Belgium	21.1	79.8
7	Chile	21.0	79.5
8	Argentina	19.2	72.8
9	UK	19.2	72.7
10	Saudi Arabia	19.0	72.2

Source: *Euromonitor*

◄ **Café Society**
The world's most enthusiastic coffee drinkers are all Europeans—led by the Scandinavians, who consume two or more cups each a day.

TOP 10 BOTTLED WATER DRINKERS

	COUNTRY	CONSUMPTION PER CAPITA IN 2000 GALLONS	LITERS
1	France	34.3	130.0
2	Italy	30.6	115.7
3	Spain	24.6	93.1
4	Belgium	22.4	84.8
5	Germany	19.8	74.7
6	Switzerland	18.0	68.0
7	Austria	16.2	61.2
8	Czech Republic	16.0	60.4
9	Slovakia	10.5	39.6
10	Poland	9.1	34.6
	Canada	7.6	28.8

Source: *Euromonitor*

French bottled mineral water consumption began in the 19th century. Leading sources such as Evian, Perrier, and Vittel supply the domestic market as well as exporting billions of bottles annually to the rest of the world.

TOP 10 ALCOHOL-PURCHASING PROVINCES AND TERRITORIES

	PROVINCE/ TERRITORY	ANNUAL LITERS PER CAPITA* LITERS
1	Yukon	175.3
2	Quebec	112.6
3	Alberta	109.6
4	Newfoundland and Labrador	105.5
5	Ontario	101.9
6	British Columbia	99.8
7	Northwest Territories and Nunavut	96.4
8	Nova Scotia	94.3
9	Manitoba	92.9
10	New Brunswick	92.6

* *In 2000–2001; Canadians aged over 15 purchasing beer, wine, and spirits. Alcohol consumption—which would include duty-free sales, plus homemade and smuggled goods—is not indicated in these figures.*

Source: *Statistics Canada*

CARBONATED DRINKS

FIRST FACT

THE FIRST ARTIFICIAL mineral water—"soda water"—was made by English chemist Joseph Priestley in 1767. His process, which he called "Impregnating Water with Fixed Air," was improved by others. Various manufacturers, including Jacob Schweppe in Europe, began bottling water, while in Philadelphia, Pennsylvania, Townsend Speakman supplied carbonated water to a local doctor, Philip Syng Physick, who administered it to his patients as a medicine. In 1807, Speakman mixed fruit juice with it to create the first flavored carbonated drink, to which he gave the name "Nephite Julep."

TOP 10 COFFEE-DRINKING COUNTRIES

	COUNTRY	CONSUMPTION PER HEAD (2001) LB	OZ	KG	CUPS*
1	**Finland**	24	4	11.01	1,652
2	**Denmark**	21	9	9.79	1,469
3	**Norway**	20	13	9.46	1,419
4	**Sweden**	18	13	8.55	1,283
5	**Austria**	15	9	7.08	1,062
6	**Germany**	15	3	6.90	1,035
7	**Switzerland**	14	15	6.80	1,020
8	**Netherlands**	13	15	6.34	951
9	**Belgium and Luxembourg**	12	3	5.53	830
10	**Italy**	11	15	5.44	816

* *Based on 150 cups per kg (2 lb 3 oz)*

Source: *International Coffee Organization*

TOP 10 TEA-DRINKING COUNTRIES

	COUNTRY	ANNUAL CONSUMPTION PER CAPITA* LB	OZ	KG	CUPS#
1	**Ireland**	5	15	2.71	1,192
2	**Libya**	5	13	2.65	1,166
3	**Kuwait**	5	1	2.29	1,007
4	**UK**	5	0	2.28	1,003
5	**Qatar**	4	14	2.23	981
6	**Iraq**	4	13	2.20	968
7	**Turkey**	4	12	2.17	954
8	**Iran**	3	2	1.43	629
9	**Hong Kong**	3	0	1.36	598
10	**Morocco**	2	15	1.34	589
	Canada	*1*	*4*	*0.59*	*259*

* *1999–2001*

\# *Based on 440 cups per kg (2 lb 3 oz)*

Source: *International Tea Committee Ltd., London*

TOP 10 WINE-PRODUCING COUNTRIES

	COUNTRY	PRODUCTION 1999 GALLONS	LITERS
1	**France**	1,340,375,000	6,093,500,000
2	**Italy**	1,278,237,500	5,811,000,000
3	**Spain**	809,525,000	3,680,200,000
4	**US**	455,137,500	2,069,100,000
5	**Argentina**	349,487,500	1,588,800,000
6	**Germany**	269,325,000	1,224,400,000
7	**Australia**	187,212,500	851,100,000
8	**South Africa**	175,262,500	796,800,000
9	**Portugal**	171,700,000	780,600,000
10	**Romania**	143,062,500	650,400,000
	Canada	*7,698,913*	*35,000,000*

Source: *Commission for Distilled Spirits*

▶ Wine Lovers
Each of the top five wine-drinking countries consumes the equivalent of a bottle of wine per capita every week.

TRANSPORT & TOURISM

On the Road

TOP 10 BEST-SELLING CARS OF ALL TIME

	MANUFACTURER/ MODEL	YEARS IN PRODUCTION	EST. NO. MADE*
1	**Toyota Corolla**	1966–	29,000,000
2	**Volkswagen Golf**	1974–	21,517,415#
3	**Volkswagen Beetle**	1937–†	21,517,414#
4	**Lada Riva**	1972–97	19,000,000
5	**Ford Model T**	1908–27	16,536,075
6	**Honda Civic**	1972–	14,920,000
7	**Nissan Sunny/Pulsar**	1966–94	13,571,100
8	**Honda Accord**	1976–	12,520,000
9	**Ford Escort/Orion**	1967–2000	12,000,000
10	**Chevrolet Impala/Caprice**	1959–	11,509,165

* *To January 1, 2003, except where otherwise indicated*

\# *To June 2002*

† *Still produced in Mexico*

Estimates of manufacturers' output of their best-selling models vary from the vague to the unusually precise 16,536,075 of the Model T Ford, with 15,007,033 produced in the US and the rest in Canada and the UK, between 1908 and 1927. It should be noted that while some of the models listed remained distinctive throughout their life span, others have undergone such major design overhauls that while they remain members of the same family, they may be considered distant relatives of the vehicles with which the model was launched.

TOP 10 BEST-SELLING VEHICLES IN CANADA*

	MANUFACTURER/MODEL	NO. SOLD, 2002
1	**Dodge Caravan**	83,588
2	**GM Silverado/Sierra**	81,695
3	**Honda Civic**	70,074
4	**Ford F-Series**	67,809
5	**GM Venture/Montana/Silhouette**	63,533
6	**Chevrolet Cavalier**	53,614
7	**Mazda Protege**	48,872
8	**Pontiac Sunfire**	46,036
9	**Toyota Corolla**	44,790
10	**Ford Focus**	40,228

* *Includes cars and trucks*

Source: Canadian Auto World *and* World of Wheels

Truck classification comprises pickups, minivans, and sport-utility vehicles (SUVs), plus a number of "crossover vehicles" (car-SUV hybrids).

TOP 10 PRODUCTION CARS WITH THE FASTEST 0–60 MPH TIMES

	MODEL*	COUNTRY	SECONDS TAKEN#
1	**Bugatti 16/4 Veyron**	Italy	3.0
2	**Caterham 7 Superlight R500**	UK	3.4
3	**Westfield 317 FW400**	UK	3.5
4	**Lamborghini Murcielago**	Italy	3.7
5	**TVR Tuscan 4.5**	UK	3.8
6	= **Noble M12 GTO3**	UK	3.9
	= **Dodge Viper SRT-10**	US	3.9
8	**AC Cobra 3.5**	UK	4.0
9	**Porsche 911 GT2**	Germany	4.1
10	**Ferrari 575M**	Italy	4.2

* *Currently in production; highest achiever per make*

\# *May vary according to specification modifications to meet national legal requirements*

Acceleration from a standing start to 97 km/h (60 mph) is widely used to compare the performance of fast cars, some of which are also capable of 0–161 km/h (0–100 mph) in under 8 seconds.

The Road Ahead

For better or for worse, in barely 100 years the coming of the automobile has changed the landscape of vast areas of our planet.

THE FIRST 200 MPH CAR

FIRST FACT

SUPERCARS CAPABLE OF 200 MPH (322 KM/H) are rare even today, so it is remarkable to consider that the first car to break this barrier did so as long ago as 1927. The vehicle was a British-built Sunbeam, powered by two 22.5-liter, 12-cylinder aero engines capable of delivering a total of 1,000 horsepower. On March 29 of that year in Daytona Beach, Florida, in front of a crowd of over 30,000, the US-born British racer Major Henry Segrave (1896–1930) took the car on two runs at an average speed of 203.79 mph (327.97 km/h), establishing a new land-speed record. Segrave was knighted for his achievement, but in 1930 he was killed making an attempt at the water-speed record.

TOP 10 MOTOR VEHICLE MANUFACTURERS

	MANUFACTURER	MOTOR VEHICLE PRODUCTION, 2001*
1	General Motors	7,582,561
2	Ford	6,575,491
3	Toyota-Daihatsu-Hino	6,054,968
4	Volkswagen Group	5,108,982
5	DaimlerChrysler	4,364,492
6	PSA Peugeot Citroën	3,102,449
7	Honda	2,673,671
8	Hyundai-Kia	2,578,443
9	Nissan-Nissan diesel	2,558,979
10	Fiat-Iveco	2,409,016

* *Includes cars, light trucks, heavy trucks, and buses*

Source: *OICA Correspondents Survey*

TOP 10 COUNTRIES WITH THE LONGEST ROAD NETWORKS

	COUNTRY	LENGTH MILES	KM
1	US	3,958,191	6,370,031
2	India	2,062,731	3,319,644
3	Brazil	1,230,315	1,980,000
4	China	869,919	1,400,000
5	Japan	715,948	1,152,207
6	Russia	591,545	952,000
7	Australia	567,312	913,000
8	Canada	560,416	901,902
9	France	554,822	892,900
10	Italy	415,491	668,669

Source: *Central Intelligence Agency*

THE 10 WORST MOTOR VEHICLE AND ROAD DISASTERS

	LOCATION/DATE	NO. KILLED
1	**Afghanistan,** November 3, 1982 Following a collision with a Soviet army truck, a fuel tanker exploded in the 2.7-km- (1.7-mile-) long Salang Tunnel. Some authorities have put the death toll from the explosion, fire, and fumes as high as 3,000.	over 2,000
2	**Colombia,** August 7, 1956 Seven army ammunition trucks exploded at night in the center of Cali, destroying eight city blocks, including a barracks where 500 soldiers were sleeping.	1,200
3	**Thailand,** February 15, 1990 A dynamite truck exploded.	over 150
4	**Nigeria,** November 4, 2000 A fuel tanker collided with a line of parked cars on the Ile-Ife-Ibadan Expressway, with the ensuing explosion burning many to death. Some 96 bodies were recovered, but some estimates put the final toll as high as 200.	150
5	**Nepal,** November 23, 1974 Hindu pilgrims were killed when a suspension bridge over the Mahahali River collapsed.	148
6	**Egypt,** August 9, 1973 A bus drove into an irrigation canal.	127
7	**Togo,** December 6, 1965 Two trucks collided with dancers during a festival in Sotouboua.	125
8	**Spain,** July 11, 1978 A liquid gas tanker exploded at a camping site in San Carlos de la Rapita.	120
9	**South Korea,** April 28, 1995 An underground explosion destroyed vehicles and caused about 100 cars and buses to plunge into the pit it created.	110
10	**Kenya,** early December 1992 A bus carrying 112 passengers skidded, hit a bridge, and plunged into a river.	106

The worst-ever motor racing accident occurred on June 13, 1955, in Le Mans, France, when, in attempting to avoid other cars, French driver Pierre Levegh lost control of his Mercedes-Benz 300 SLR. It then hit a wall and exploded in midair, showering wreckage into the crowd and killing a total of 82. The worst single US highway disaster occurred on December 15, 1967, when the Silver Bridge (spanning the Ohio River from Kanauga, Ohio, to Point Pleasant, West Virginia) collapsed during heavy pre-Christmas afternoon rush hour traffic. The collapse plunged some 60 vehicles into the river, resulting in 46 deaths and many injuries. It is believed that the worst-ever accident involving a single car occurred on December 17, 1956, when eight adults and four children were killed as the overcrowded car in which they were traveling was hit by a train near Phoenix, Arizona, US. Although injured, 20-month-old Crucita Alires survived after being hurled into a tree by the force of the impact.

Track Records

TOP 10 FASTEST RAIL JOURNEYS*

	JOURNEY/COUNTRY	TRAIN	DISTANCE MILES	KM	SPEED MPH	KM/H
1	**Hiroshima–Kokura,** Japan	15 Nozomi	119.3	192.0	162.7	261.8
2	**Valence–Avignon,** France	TGV 5102	80.6	129.7	161.2	259.4
3	**Brussels–Valence,** Belgium/France	ThalysSoleil	516.5	831.3	150.4	242.1
4	**Madrid–Seville,** Spain	5 AVE	292.4	470.5	129.9	209.1
5	**Stendal–Wolfsburg,** Germany	2 ICE	47.3	76.2	118.3	190.4
6	**York–Stevenage,** UK	Tees Tyne Pullman	160.3	258	113.6	182.8
7	**Skövde–Södertälje,** Sweden	X2000 436	172.1	277.0	107.6	173.1
8	**Rome–Florence,** Italy	ES 9548	162.2	261.0	103.5	166.6
9	**Baltimore–Wilmington,** US	9 Acela Express	68.4	110.1	102.6	165.1
10	**Salo–Karjaa,** Finland	Pandollno S126	33.0	53.1	94.3	151.7

* *Fastest journey for each country; all those in the Top 10 have other similarly or equally fast services*

Source: *Railway Gazette International*

Bullet Train
The Shinkansen "bullet trains" were introduced in Japan in 1964 and have been constantly improved: the Nozomi 500 is capable of 300 km/h (186 mph).

TOP 10 LONGEST UNDERGROUND RAILROAD NETWORKS

	CITY	OPENED	STATIONS	TOTAL TRACK LENGTH MILES	KM
1	**London,** UK	1863	267	244	392
2	**New York,** US	1904	468	231	371
3	**Moscow,** Russia	1935	160	163	262
4	**Paris,** France*	1900	297	125	201
5	= **Tokyo,** Japan#	1927	164	111	178
	= **Mexico City,** Mexico	1969	154	111	178
7	**Chicago,** US	1943	140	107	173
8	**Copenhagen,** Denmark†	1934	80	106	170
9	= **Seoul,** South Korea	1974	114	89	144
	= **Berlin,** Germany	1902	170	89	144

* *Metro and RER*

\# *Through-running extensions raise total to 683 km (391 miles), with 502 stations*

† *Only partly underground*

Source: *Tony Pattison, Center for Environmental Initiatives Researcher*

THE 10 OLDEST UNDERGROUND RAILROAD SYSTEMS

	CITY	OPENED
1	**London,** UK	1863
2	**Budapest,** Hungary	1896
=	**Glasgow,** UK	1896
4	**Boston,** US	1897
5	**Paris,** France	1900
6	**Berlin,** Germay	1902
7	**New York,** US	1904
8	**Philadelphia,** US	1907
9	**Hamburg,** Germany	1912
10	**Buenos Aires,** Argentina	1913

The Metropolitan Line, opened in London on January 10, 1863, and the Circle Line, completed in 1884, operated with steam trains equipped with a device to absorb smoke so that passengers did not suffocate in their gaslit carriages. The service could not be electrified until all necessary inventions came together during the 1890s, prompting the construction of underground networks worldwide. Canada's first subway system was opened in Toronto on March 30, 1954.

TOP 10 LONGEST RAILROAD NETWORKS

	LOCATION	TOTAL RAIL LENGTH MILES	KM
1	**US**	132,000	212,433
2	**Russia**	54,157	87,157
3	**China**	41,957	67,524
4	**India**	39,576	63,693
5	**Germany**	25,368	44,000
6	**Canada**	22,440	36,114
7	**Australia**	21,014	33,819
8	**Argentina**	20,967	33,744
9	**France**	19,846	31,939
10	**Japan**	14,698	23,654

Source: *Central Intelligence Agency*

The total of all world networks is today estimated to be 1,201,337 km (746,476 miles). Of this, some 190,000 to 195,000 km (118,061 to 121,167 miles) is electrified.

THE 10 WORST RAIL DISASTERS

	LOCATION/DATE/INCIDENT	NO. KILLED
1	**Bagmati River,** India, June 6, 1981 The cars of a train traveling from Samastipur to Banmukhi in Bihar plunged off a bridge over the Bagmati River near Mansi when the driver braked, apparently to avoid hitting a sacred cow. Although the official death toll was said to have been 268, many authorities have claimed that the train was so massively overcrowded that the actual figure was in excess of 800, making it probably the worst rail disaster of all time.	c.800
2	**Chelyabinsk,** Russia, June 3, 1989 Two passenger trains, laden with vacationers heading to and from Black Sea resorts, were destroyed when liquid gas from a nearby pipeline exploded.	up to 800
3	**Guadalajara,** Mexico, January 18, 1915 A train derailed on a steep incline, but political strife in the country meant that full details of the disaster were suppressed.	over 600
4	**Modane,** France, December 12, 1917 A troop-carrying train ran out of control and was derailed. It has been claimed that it was overloaded and that as many as 1,000 may have died.	573
5	**Balvano,** Italy, March 2, 1944 A heavily-laden train stalled in the Armi Tunnel, and many passengers were asphyxiated. Like the disaster at Torre (No. 6), wartime secrecy prevented full details from being published.	521
6	**Torre,** Spain, January 3, 1944 A double collision and fire in a tunnel resulted in many deaths—some have put the total as high as 800.	over 500
7	**Awash,** Ethiopia, January 13, 1985 A derailment hurled a train laden with some 1,000 passengers into a ravine.	428
8	**Cireau,** Romania, January 7, 1917 An overcrowded passenger train crashed into a military train and was derailed.	374
9	**Reqa al-Gharbiya,** Egypt, February 20, 2002 A fire on the Cairo–Luxor train engulfed the carriages. The driver, unaware of the catastrophe, continued on while passengers were burned or leaped from the train to their deaths.	372
10	**Quipungo**, Angola, May 31, 1993 A trail was derailed by UNITA guerrilla action.	355

Casualty figures for rail accidents are often extremely imprecise, especially during wartime—and no fewer than half of the 10 worst disasters occurred during the two world wars. Further vague incidents, such as one in Kalish, Poland, in December 1914 with "400 dead," one in November 1918 in Norrköpping, Sweden, alleged to have killed 300, and certain other similarly uncertain cases have been omitted from this list.

First Stop
London's Baker Street was one of the stations on the world's first ever underground railroad system.

Water Ways

TOP 10 LONGEST SHIP CANALS

	CANAL	COUNTRY	OPENED	LENGTH MILES	KM
1	**Grand Canal**	China	AD 283*	1,114	1,795
2	**Erie Canal**	US	1825	363	584
3	**Göta Canal**	Sweden	1832	240	386
4	**St. Lawrence Seaway**	Canada/US	1959	180	290
5	**Canal du Midi**	France	1692	149	240
6	**Main-Danube**	Germany	1992	106	171
7	**Suez**	Egypt	1869	101	162
8	= **Albert**	Belgium	1939	80	129
	= **Moscow-Volga**	Russia	1937	80	129
10	**Kiel**	Germany	1895	62	99

* *Extended from* AD *605 to 610 and rebuilt between 1958 and 1972*

THE 10 LARGEST PASSENGER SHIPS EVER SUNK

	SHIP	LOCATION	DATE	TONNAGE
1	**Seawise University***	Hong Kong	Jan 9, 1972	83,763
2	**Titanic**	Off Canada	Apr 14, 1912	46,328
3	**Paris**	Le Havre, France	Apr 19, 1939	34,569
4	**Lusitania**	Off Ireland	May 7, 1915	31,550
5	**Andrea Doria**	Off US	July 25, 1956	29,083
6	**Angelina**	Pacific	Sept 24, 1979	24,377
7	**Lakonia**	Atlantic	Dec 29, 1963	20,314
8	**Mikhail Lermontov**	Off New Zealand	Feb 16, 1986	20,027
9	**Rasa Sayang**	Kynosoura, Greece	Aug 27, 1980	18,739
10	**Bianca C.**	Off Grenada	Oct 22, 1961	18,427

* *Formerly* Queen Elizabeth

Suez Canal
The strategically and economically important Suez Canal, connecting the Mediterranean with the Red Sea, was built over the course of 10 years, from 1859 to 1869.

TOP 10 LARGEST CRUISE SHIPS

	SHIP/COUNTRY BUILT/YEAR	PASSENGER CAPACITY	GROSS TONNAGE
1	**Queen Mary 2,** France, 2004*	2,800	142,200
2	**Explorer of the Seas,** Finland, 2000	3,840	137,308
3	= **Voyager of the Seas,** Finland, 1999	3,840	137,276
	= **Mariner of the Seas,** Finland, 2003*	3,840	137,276
	= **Navigator of the Seas,** Finland, 2002	3,807	137,276
	= **Adventure of the Seas,** Finland, 2001	3,840	137,276
7	= **Diamond Princess,** Japan, 2004*	2,600	113,000
	= **Sapphire Princess,** Japan, 2004*	3,100	113,000
9	= **Carnival Conquest,** Italy, 2002	3,783	110,239
10	= **Carnival Glory,** Italy, 2003*	3,783	110,000
	= **Carnival Valor,** Italy, 2004*	3,783	110,000
	= **Crown Princess,** Italy, 2004*	3,100	110,000

* *Still under construction as at January 14, 2003*

Source: *Lloyd's Register-Fairplay Ltd. at www.lrfairplay.com*

Like her predecessor *Queen Mary* (1934), the latest addition to the Cunard fleet, the 345-m- (1,132-ft-) long *Queen Mary 2*, scheduled to make her maiden voyage in 2004, will be the longest, tallest, and widest cruise ship in the world at the time of launch.

TOP 10 LARGEST OIL TANKERS*

	TANKER/COUNTRY BUILT/YEAR	GROSS TONNAGE#	DEADWEIGHT TONNAGE†
1	**Jahre Viking,** Japan, 1976	260,851	564,650
2	**Sea Giant,** France, 1979	261,453	555,051
3	**Sea World,** Sweden, 1978	237,768	491,120
4	**Arctic Blue,** Japan, 1975	234,287	484,276
5	**Folk II,** Taiwan, 1978	218,593	457,927
6	**Folk I,** Taiwan, 1977	218,593	457,841
7	= **Hellespont Fairfax,** South Korea, 2002	238,700	442,500
	= **Hellespont Metropolis,** South Korea, 2002	238,700	442,500
	= **Hellespont Tara,** South Korea, 2002	238,700	442,500
10	**Hellespont Alhambra,** South Korea, 2002	235,000	441,893

* *As at January 1, 2003*

The weight of the ship when empty

† *The total weight of the vessel, including cargo, crew, passengers, and supplies*

Source: *Lloyd's Register-Fairplay Ltd. at www.lrfairplay.com*

The 485.45-m- (1,504-ft-) long *Jahre Viking* (formerly called *Happy Giant* and *Seawise Giant*) is the longest vessel ever built—longer than 20 tennis courts end-to-end—and 68.86 m (226 ft) wide. It was extensively damaged during the Iran-Iraq War, but was salvaged, refitted, and relaunched in 1991.

TOP 10 MERCHANT SHIPPING FLEETS (OWNERSHIP)

	COUNTRY OF OWNERSHIP	SHIPS IN FLEET*
1	**Japan**	3,962
2	**Greece**	3,032
3	**Germany**	2,321
4	**China**	1,999
5	**US**	1,963
6	**Russia**	1,872
7	**Norway**	1,458
8	**Singapore**	1,122
9	**Netherlands**	1,016
10	**UK**	957
	All countries	*35,213*

**Ships over 1,000 DWT (deadweight tonnage—total weight of the vessel, including cargo, crew, passengers, and supplies) in service December 2002*

Source: *Lloyd's Register-Fairplay Ltd. at www.lrfairplay.com*

TOP 10 WORST OIL TANKER SPILLS

	TANKER/LOCATION	DATE	APPROX. SPILLAGE (TONNES)
1	**Atlantic Empress** and **Aegean Captain,** Trinidad	July 19, 1979	273,875
2	**Castillio de Bellver,** Cape Town, South Africa	Aug 6, 1983	255,125
3	**Olympic Bravery,** Ushant, France	Jan 24, 1976	250,000
4	**Amoco Cadiz,** Finistère, France	Mar 16, 1978	223,275
5	**Odyssey,** Atlantic, off Canada	Nov 10, 1988	140,075
6	**Haven,** off Genoa, Italy	Apr 11, 1991	136,500
7	**Torrey Canyon,** Scilly Isles, UK	Mar 18, 1967	124,150
8	**Sea Star,** Gulf of Oman	Dec 19, 1972	123,175
9	**Irenes Serenade,** Pilos, Greece	Feb 23, 1980	118,950
10	**Texaco Denmark,** North Sea, off Belgium	Dec 7, 1971	102,375

Source: *Environmental Technology Center,* Oil Spill Intelligence Report

In addition to these major slicks, it is estimated that an average of 2,000,000 tonnes of oil is spilled into the world's seas every year. The accidents that resulted in this additional spillage were all caused by collision, grounding, fire, or explosion. However, worse tanker oil spills have been caused by military action: in 1991, during the Gulf War, various tankers were sunk in the Persian Gulf, spilling a total of more than 1,000,000 tonnes of oil.

TOP 10 BIGGEST AIRSHIPS EVER BUILT

	AIRSHIP	COUNTRY	YEAR	VOLUME (CU FT)	VOLUME (CU M)	LENGTH (FT)	LENGTH (M)
1	= **Hindenburg**	Germany	1936	7,062,934	200,000	804	245
	= **Graf Zeppelin II**	Germany	1938	7,062,934	200,000	804	245
3	= **Akron**	US	1931	6,500,000	184,060	785	239
	= **Macon**	US	1933	6,500,000	184,060	785	239
5	**R101**	UK	1930	5,500,000	155,744	777	237
6	**Graf Zeppelin**	Germany	1928	3,708,040	105,000	776	237
7	**L72**	Germany	1920	2,419,055	68,500	743	226
8	**R100**	UK	1929	5,500,000	155,744	709	216
9	**R38**	UK*	1921	2,724,000	77,136	699	213
10	= **L70**	Germany	1918	2,418,700	62,200	694	212
	= **L71**	Germany	1918	2,418,700	62,200	694	212

** UK-built, but sold to US Navy*

Although several of the giant airships in this list traveled long distances carrying thousands of passengers, they all ultimately suffered unfortunate fates: six (the *Hindenburg*, *Akron*, *Macon*, *R101*, *L72*, and *R38*) crashed with the loss of many lives; the *L70* was shot down; and the *L71*, both *Graf Zeppelins*, and the *R100* were broken up for scrap. The *Hindenburg* was the victim of one of the most spectacular of all aviation disasters when, after several successful transatlantic crossings, it flew from Frankfurt, Germany, to Lakehurst, New Jersey, arriving on May 6, 1937. As she moored, she caught fire and turned into an inferno, the last moments of which remain among the most haunting sights ever captured on newsreel, with commentator Herb Morrison describing the horrific scene through floods of tears. Amazingly, 61 of the 97 on board survived, but the day of the airship was over.

THE 10 FIRST ROCKET AND JET AIRCRAFT

	AIRCRAFT	COUNTRY	FIRST FLIGHT
1	**Heinkel He 176***	Germany	June 20, 1939
2	**Heinkel He 178**	Germany	Aug 27, 1939
3	**DFS 194***	Germany	Aug 1940#
4	**Caproni-Campini N-1**	Italy	Aug 28, 1940
5	**Heinkel He 280V-1**	Germany	Apr 2, 1941
6	**Gloster E.28/39**	UK	May 15, 1941
7	**Messerschmitt Me 163 Komet***	Germany	Aug 13, 1941
8	**Messerschmitt Me 262V-3**	Germany	July 18, 1942
9	**Bell XP-59A Airacomet**	US	Oct 1, 1942
10	**Gloster Meteor F Mk 1**	UK	Mar 5, 1943

** Rocket-powered*

 # Precise date unknown

▼ Graf Zeppelin

When built, the *Graf Zeppelin* was the biggest airship in the world. It was the first to circumnavigate the globe, and carried a total of 16,000 passengers before being broken up in 1940.

THE 10 FIRST PEOPLE TO FLY IN HEAVIER-THAN-AIR AIRCRAFT

	PILOT/DATES/NATIONALITY	AIRCRAFT	DATE
1	**Orville Wright** (1871–1948/US)	Wright Flyer I	Dec 17, 1903
2	**Wilbur Wright** (1867–1912/US)	Wright Flyer I	Dec 17, 1903
3	**Alberto Santos-Dumont** (1873–1932/Brazil)	No. 14-bis	Oct 23, 1906
4	**Charles Voisin** (1882–1912/France)	Voisin-Delagrange I	Mar 30, 1907
5	**Henri Farman** (1874–1958/UK, later France)	Voisin-Farman I-bis	Oct 7, 1907
6	**Léon Delagrange** (1873–1910/France)	Voisin-Delagrange I	Nov 5, 1907
7	**Robert Esnault-Pelterie** (1881–1957/France)	REP No.1	Nov 16, 1907
8	**Charles W. Furnas*** (1880–1941/US)	Wright Flyer III	May 14, 1908
9	**Louis Blériot** (1872–1936/France)	Blériot VIII	June 29, 1908
10	**Glenn Hammond Curtiss** (1878–1930/US)	AEA June Bug	July 4, 1908

* *Furnas was a passenger in a plane piloted by Wilbur Wright*

While most of the fliers listed flew on numerous subsequent occasions and broke their first-time records, most other "flights" of the 1906–1908 period, other than those of the Wright Brothers, were uncontrolled or no more than short hops of a few seconds' duration. Meanwhile, the Wrights were so far in advance of their competitors that they were flying under full control for more than an hour and over distances of 80 km (50 miles).

▲ **The First to Fly**
In 1903, Orville Wright became the first person ever to fly a powered aircraft, followed by his brother Wilbur 45 minutes later.

THE 10 FIRST AROUND-THE-WORLD FLIGHTS

	PILOT(S)/AIRCRAFT	ROUTE (START/END LOCATION)	TOTAL DISTANCE (MILES)	(KM)	DATES
1	**Lt. Lowell H. Smith/Lt. Leslie P. Arnold** (US) Douglas World Cruiser *Chicago*	Seattle, WA	26,345	42,398	Apr 6–Sept 28, 1924
=	**Lt. Erik H. Nelson/Lt. John Harding Jr.** (US) Douglas World Cruiser *New Orleans*	Seattle, WA	27,553	44,342	Apr 6–Sept 28, 1924
3	**Dr. Hugo Eckener, Ernst Lehmann, and crew** (Germany) Airship *Graf Zeppelin*	Lakehurst, NJ	20,373	37,787	Apr 8–29, 1929
4	**Wiley Post and Harold Gatty** (US) Lockheed Vega *Winne Mae*	Roosevelt Field, Long Island, NY	15,474	24,903	June 23–July 1, 1931
5	**Wiley Post** (US) Lockheed Vega *Winne Mae* (first solo)	Floyd Bennett Field, NY	15,596	25,093	July 15–22, 1933
6	**Howard Hughes, Lt. Thomas Thurlow, Henry P. McClean Conner, Richard Stoddart, Eddie Lund** (US) Lockheed 14 *New York World's Fair 1939*	Floyd Bennett Field, NY	14,672	23,612	July 10–14, 1938
7 =	**Clifford Evans** (US) Piper PA-12 *City of Washington*	Teterboro, NJ	25,162	40,493	Aug 9 –Dec 10, 1947
=	**George Truman** (US) Piper PA-12 *City of the Angels*	Teterboro, NJ	25,162	40,493	Aug 9 –Dec 10, 1947
9	**Capt. James Gallagher and crew of 13** (US) Boeing B-50A *Lucky Lady II* (first nonstop with in-flight refueling)	Fort Worth, TX	23,452	37,742	Feb 26–Mar 2, 1949
10	**Peter Mack** (US) Bonanza A35 *Friendship Flame*	Springfield, IL	33,789	54,378	Oct 7, 1951–Apr 19, 1952

Air Ways

TOP 10 BUSIEST INTERNATIONAL AIRPORTS

	AIRPORT	LOCATION	INTERNATIONAL PASSENGERS 2001
1	**London Heathrow**	London, UK	53,796,000
2	**Charles de Gaulle**	Paris, France	43,352,000
3	**Frankfurt**	Frankfurt, Germany	39,975,000
4	**Schiphol**	Amsterdam, Netherlands	39,167,000
5	**Hong Kong International**	Hong Kong, China	32,027,000
6	**London Gatwick**	Gatwick, UK	28,114,000
7	**Singapore Changi**	Singapore	26,542,000
8	**Narita International**	Tokyo, Japan	22,241,000
9	**Don Muang International**	Bangkok, Thailand	21,394,000
10	**Kloten**	Zurich, Switzerland	19,968,000

Source: *Air Transport Intelligence at www.rati.com*

Chicago's O'Hare International Airport is the busiest international airport in North America: almost 9.5 million international passengers passed through it in 2001.

Flying Start

Despite recent fluctuations in response to safety and economic concerns, worldwide passenger numbers in 2002 remained stable, at around 1.6 billion.

TOP 10 BUSIEST DOMESTIC AIR ROUTES IN CANADA

	MARKET	DAILY SEATS 2001*
1	**Montreal–Toronto**	3,956
2	**Toronto–Vancouver**	3,053
3	**Calgary–Vancouver**	2,716
4	**Ottawa–Toronto**	2,595
5	**Calgary–Edmonton**	1,957
6	**Calgary–Toronto**	1,656
7	**Edmonton–Vancouver**	1,484
8	**Halifax–Toronto**	1,361
9	**Toronto–Winnipeg**	1,228
10	**Vancouver–Victoria**	1,074

* *The average number of seats offered on non-stop flights in each direction*

Source: *Transport Canada,* Transportation in Canada, 2001 Annual Report. *Reproduced with the permission of the Minister of Public Works and Government Services, 2003.*

HEATHROW'S FIRST FLIGHTS

FIRST FACT

ON JANUARY 1, 1946, a BSAA (British South American Airways) Lancastrian took off from London's Heathrow Airport en route for Buenos Aires, Argentina. What was to become the world's busiest airport was officially opened on May 31. The following day, a Pan Am Constellation became the first transatlantic airliner to land there. At this stage, the former RAF air base was no more than a field with wooden duckboards to keep passengers out of the mud and a check-in that had seen service as a military tent.

TOP 10 LARGEST AIRLINERS

	AIRCRAFT MODEL*	MAXIMUM NO. OF PASSENGERS
1	**Boeing B-747-300**	660
2	**Airbus A-380-800**	656
3	**Boeing B-777-300**	550
4	**Airbus A340-600**	485
5	**Airbus A330-300**	440
6	**Boeing MD-11**	410
7	**Lockheed L-1011 TriStar**	400
8	**McDonnell Douglas DC-10-10**	380
9 =	**Boeing 767-400ER**	375
=	**Ilyushin Il-96**	375

* *Largest of each type listed*

Source: *Air Transport Intelligence at www.rati.com*

TOP 10 AIRLINES WITH THE MOST AIRCRAFT

	AIRLINE/COUNTRY*	FLEET SIZE (2001)
1	**American Airlines**	834
2	**United Airlines**	554
3	**Delta Airlines**	551
4	**Northwest Airlines**	437
5	**Continental Airlines**	370
6	**Southwest Airlines**	367
7	**US Airways**	295
8	**Air France,** France	247
9	**British Airways,** UK	236
10	**Air Canada,** Canada	224

* *From the US unless otherwise stated*

Source: *Airline Business/Air Transport Intelligence at www.rati.com*

TOP 10 AIRLINES WITH THE MOST PASSENGER TRAFFIC

	AIRLINE/COUNTRY	PASSENGER MILES FLOWN, 2001*
1	**United Airlines,** US	116,643,800,200
2	**American Airlines,** US	108,359,679,465
3	**Delta Airlines,** US	101,758,853,300
4	**Northwest Airlines,** US	73,155,894,575
5	**British Airways,** UK	66,033,116,600
6	**Continental Airlines,** US	61,126,148,300
7	**Air France,** France	58,923,387,400
8	**Lufthansa German Airlines,** Germany	53,869,775,500
9	**Japan Airlines,** Japan	49,313,881,930
10	**US Airways,** US	45,997,623,875

* *Total distance traveled by aircraft of these airlines multiplied by number of passengers carried*

Source: *Airline Business/Air Transport Intelligence at www.rati.com*

World Tourism

TOP 10 TOURIST DESTINATIONS

	COUNTRY	INTERNATIONAL VISITORS (2001)
1	France	76,500,000
2	Spain	49,500,000
3	US	45,500,000
4	Italy	39,000,000
5	China	33,200,000
6	UK	23,400,000
7	Russia	21,200,000*
8	Mexico	19,800,000
9	Canada	19,700,000
10	Austria	18,200,000

** 2000 data*

Source: *World Tourism Organization*

The World Tourism Organization's estimate for 2001 puts the total number of international tourists at just under 693 million, down more than five million on the record high of 698 million set in the previous year.

TOP 10 COUNTRIES OF ORIGIN OF VISITORS TO CANADA*

	COUNTRY	VISITORS (2001)	(2002)
1	UK	849,048	749,659
2	Japan	418,445	436,510
3	France	360,661	313,987
4	Germany	341,118	295,715
5	Mexico	150,292	161,843
6	Australia	165,208	157,610
7	South Korea	142,843	151,476
8	Hong Kong	126,929	119,449
9	Netherlands	115,936	107,769
10	Italy	90,972	97,313

** Excluding the US*

Source: *Canadian Tourism Commission*

In 2002, the number of Americans visiting Canada reached 16,152,100.

TOP 10 COUNTRIES WITH GREATEST EARNINGS FROM TOURISM

	COUNTRY	INTERNATIONAL TOURISM RECEIPTS IN 2001 (US$)
1	US	72,300,000,000
2	Spain	32,900,000,000
3	France	29,600,000,000
4	Italy	25,900,000,000
5	China	17,800,000,000
6	Germany	17,200,000,000
7	UK	15,900,000,000
8	Austria	12,000,000,000
9	Canada	10,700,000,000*
10	Greece	9,200,000,000*

** 2000 data* Source: *World Tourism Organization*

Super Duper Roller Coaster
Built at a cost of US$20 million, Superman the Escape held the record as the world's fastest and highest thrill ride.

TOP 10 WORLDWIDE AMUSEMENT AND THEME PARKS

	PARK/LOCATION	ATTENDANCE IN 2002*
1	**The Magic Kingdom at Walt Disney World,** Lake Buena Vista, Florida, US	14,044,800
2	**Tokyo Disneyland,** Tokyo, Japan	13,000,000
3	**Disneyland,** Anaheim, California, US	12,720,500
4	**Disneysea,** Tokyo, Japan	12,000,000
5	**Disneyland Paris,** Marne-La-Vallée, France	10,300,000
6	**Everland,** Kyonggi-Do, South Korea	9,335,000
7	**Lotte World,** Seoul, South Korea	9,100,000
8	**Epcot at Walt Disney World,** Lake Buena Vista, Florida, US	8,289,000
9	**Disney-MGM Studios at Walt Disney World,** Lake Buena Vista, Florida, US	8,031,360
10	**Universal Studios Japan,** Osaka, Japan	8,010,000

* *Estimated*

Source: *Amusement Business*

Canada has 21 amusement parks. In 2001, the annual attendance totalled 12.6 million for all Canadian amusement parks, generating approximately $521 million (US$366 million) in revenue—an average expenditure of more than $41 per attendee. Canada's Wonderland in Vaughan, Ontario, attracted 3 million visitors in 2001.

TOP 10 MOST VISITED CITIES IN CANADA, 2001

	CITY/PROVINCE	VISITORS*
1	**Toronto,** ON	3,733,000
2	**Vancouver,** BC	3,033,000
3	**Montreal,** QC	2,243,000
4	**St. Catharines–Niagara,** ON	2,080,000
5	**Quebec,** QC	1,009,000
6	**Victoria,** BC	905,000
7	**Ottawa–Hull,** ON/QC	803,000
8	**Calgary,** AB	659,000
9	**Edmonton,** AB	445,000
10	**Halifax,** NS	313,000

* *Estimate based on US and overseas residents making overnight visits*

Source: *Canadian Tourism Commission and Statistics Canada*

TOP 10 FASTEST ROLLER COASTERS

	ROLLER COASTER/LOCATION	YEAR OPENED	SPEED MPH	SPEED KM/H
1	**Top Thrill Dragster,** Cedar Point, Sandusky Ohio, US	2003	120	193
2	**Dodonpa,** Fuji-Q Highlands, ShinNishihara, FujiYoshida-shi, Yamanashi, Japan	2001	106.9	172
3	= **Superman the Escape,** Six Flags Magic Mountain, Valencia, California, US	1997	100	161
	= **Tower of Terror,** Dreamworld, Coomera, Queensland, Australia	1997	100	161
5	**Steel Dragon 2000,** Nagshima Spa Land, Nagshima, Mie, Japan	2000	95	153
6	**Millennium Force,** Cedar Point, Sandusky, Ohio, US	2000	93	149
7	= **Goliath,** Six Flags Magic Mountain, Valencia, California, US	2000	85	137
	= **Titan,** Six Flags Over Texas, Arlington, Texas, US	2001	85	137
9	= **Phantom's Revenge,** Kennywood Park, West Mifflin, Pennsylvania, US	2001	82	132
	= **Xcelerator,** Knott's Berry Farm, Buena Park, California, US	2002	82	132

The newly constructed Top Thrill Dragster breaks all previous roller coaster records, with a length of 853 m (2,800 ft), a height of 128 m (420 ft), and a drop of 122 m (400 ft). It can also accelerate from 0 to 193 km/h (0 to 120 mph) in approximately 4 seconds.

TOP 10 MOST VISITED NATIONAL PARKS IN CANADA

	PARK/PROVINCE	PERSON-VISITS* 2001–2002
1	**Banff,** AB	4,687,378
2	**Jasper,** AB	1,947,286
3	**Kootenay,** BC	1,590,596
4	**Yoho,** BC	1,371,105
5	**Prince Edward Island,** PEI	927,625
6	**Pacific Rim Reserve,** BC	644,841
7	**Mount Revelstoke and Glacier,** BC	566,679
8	**Saguenay–St. Lawrence,** QC	442,182
9	**Fathom Five,** ON	435,794
10	**Waterton Lakes,** AB	413,515

* *A person entering onto lands or marine areas within a reporting unit for recreational, educational, or cultural purposes during operating hours. Persons re-entering on the same day, and persons staying overnight in a reporting unit, do not constitute new person-visits.*

Source: *Parks Canada*

SPORTS & LEISURE

Summer Olympics

THE 10 FIRST ATHLETES TO WIN GOLD IN THE SAME EVENT AT FOUR SUMMER OLYMPICS

	INDIVIDUAL/COUNTRY	SPORT	EVENT	YEARS
1	= **Aladár Gerevich*,** Hungary	Fencing	Team saber	1932–52
	= **Pál Kovács,** Hungary	Fencing	Team saber	1932–52
3	**Paul Elvstrøm,** Denmark	Sailing	Finn	1948–60
4	**Edoardo Mangiarotti,** Italy	Fencing	Team epee	1936–60
5	**Rudolf Kárpáti,** Hungary	Fencing	Team saber	1948–60
6	**Al Oerter,** US	Track & field	Discus	1956–68
7	**Hans-Günther Winkler,** Germany	Show jumping	Team	1956–72
8	**Reiner Klimke#,** West Germany	Dressage	Team	1964–84
9	**Carl Lewis,** US	Track & field	Long jump	1984–96
10	**Teresa Edwards,** US	Basketball	Women's	1984–2000

** Also won gold in the same event in 1956 and 1960*

 # Also won gold in the same event in 1988

Few Olympic competitors have succeeded in attaining gold over a span of 16 years or more. When, after becoming the first person to do so, 50-year-old Aladár Gerevich was refused a place on the Hungarian fencing squad at the 1960 Games; he promptly challenged the entire team, defeating them all.

TOP 10 COUNTRIES WITH THE MOST SUMMER OLYMPICS MEDALS, 1896–2000

		MEDALS			
	COUNTRY	GOLD	SILVER	BRONZE	TOTAL
1	**US**	872	659	581	2,112
2	**USSR***	485	395	354	1,234
3	**UK**	188	245	232	665
4	**France**	189	195	217	601
5	**Germany#**	165	198	210	573
6	**Italy**	179	144	155	478
7	**Sweden**	138	157	176	471
8	**Hungary**	150	134	158	442
9	**East Germany**	153	130	127	410
10	**Australia**	103	110	139	352

** Includes Unified Team of 1992; does not include Russia since then*

 # Not including West/East Germany 1968–88

The host nations at the first two Modern Olympics—Greece in 1896 and France in 1900—both led the medal table, the US achieving its first commanding total of 72 medals at the 1904 St. Louis Games. Canada has excelled at swimming and athletics in summer Olympic games, with a total of 89 medals in these two events.

Carl Lewis
Long jump, at the Atlanta Olympic Games, 1996.

TOP 10 MEDAL WINNERS IN A SUMMER OLYMPICS CAREER

	WINNER/COUNTRY	SPORT	YEARS	MEDALS GOLD	SILVER	BRONZE	TOTAL
1	**Larissa Latynina,** USSR	Gymnastics	1956–64	9	5	4	18
2	**Nikolay Andrianov,** USSR	Gymnastics	1972–80	7	5	3	15
3	= **Edoardo Mangiarotti,** Italy	Fencing	1936–60	6	5	2	13
	= **Takashi Ono,** Japan	Gymnastics	1952–64	5	4	4	13
	= **Boris Shakhlin,** USSR	Gymnastics	1956–64	7	4	2	13
6	= **Sawao Kato,** Japan	Gymnastics	1968–76	8	3	1	12
	= **Paavo Nurmi,** Finland	Track & field	1920–28	9	3	0	12
8	= **Viktor Chukarin,** USSR	Gymnastics	1952–56	7	3	1	11
	= **Vera Cáslavská,** Czechoslovakia	Gymnastics	1964–68	7	4	0	11
	= **Carl Osburn,** US	Shooting	1912–24	5	4	2	11
	= **Mark Spitz,** US	Swimming	1968–72	9	1	1	11
	= **Matt Biondi,** US	Swimming	1984–92	8	2	1	11

Larissa Latynina won 6 medals at each of the three Games held between 1956 and 1964. The only discipline at which she did not win a medal was on the beam in 1956. The only Winter Games competitor who would be eligible for this list is Björn Dählie of Norway, who won a total of 12 medals (8 gold and 4 silver) for Nordic skiing at the Olympics held between 1992 and 1998.

TOP 10 MEDAL-WINNING COUNTRIES AT THE SUMMER PARALYMPICS*

	COUNTRY	MEDALS GOLD	SILVER	BRONZE	TOTAL
1	**US**	576	523	522	1,621
2	**UK**	389	401	387	1,177
3	**Germany/ West Germany**	404	385	361	1,150
4	**Canada**	311	250	262	823
5	**France**	279	264	241	784
6	**Australia**	240	248	228	716
7	**Netherlands**	219	179	153	551
8	**Poland**	194	184	148	526
9	**Sweden**	197	190	135	522
10	**Spain**	156	137	152	445

* *Excluding medals won at the 1960 Rome and 1968 Tel Aviv Games—the International Paralympic Committee has not kept records of medals won at these Games*

The first international games for the disabled were at Stoke Mandeville, England, in 1952, when 130 athletes from the UK and the Netherlands competed.

TOP 10 MOST SUCCESSFUL COUNTRIES AT ONE SUMMER OLYMPICS

	COUNTRY	VENUE	YEAR	MEDALS GOLD	SILVER	BRONZE	TOTAL
1	**US**	St. Louis	1904	80	84	76	242
2	**USSR**	Moscow	1980	80	69	46	195
3	**US**	Los Angeles	1984	83	61	30	174
4	**Great Britain**	London	1908	56	50	39	145
5	**USSR**	Seoul	1988	55	31	46	132
6	**East Germany**	Moscow	1980	47	37	42	126
7	**USSR**	Montreal	1976	49	41	35	125
8	**EUN***	Barcelona	1992	45	38	29	112
9	**US**	Barcelona	1992	37	34	37	108
10	**US**	Mexico City	1968	45	28	34	107

* *Unified Team representing the Commonwealth of Independent States (former Soviet republics), formed in 1991*

The Soviet Union's total at Seoul in 1988 is the highest by a country not competing on home soil. East Germany's 126 in 1980 is the highest total of a country not heading the medal list, although the US boycotted the Games that year, enabling Eastern Bloc countries to achieve their greatest-ever medal haul. The only other nations with 100 or more medals at one Games are East Germany (1988, Seoul) with 102, and France (1900, Paris) with 100 exactly. The US gained 97 medals (39 gold, 25 silver, and 33 bronze) at the 2000 Sydney Olympics, the most of any nation.

TOP 10 SPORTS AT WHICH THE MOST GOLD MEDALS HAVE BEEN WON AT THE OLYMPIC GAMES, 1896–2002

	SPORT	GOLD MEDALS
1	**Track & field**	818
2	**Swimming/diving**	527
3	**Wrestling**	340
4	**Gymnastics**	291
5	**Shooting**	229
6	**Boxing**	204
7	**Rowing**	203
8	**Fencing**	179
9	**Cycling**	166
10	**Canoeing**	161

Winter Olympics

▲ **Salt Lake City Celebration**
Olympic medal-winning German, Norwegian, and Swiss ski teams celebrate their respective victories at Salt Lake City, 2002.

TOP 10 MEDAL-WINNING COUNTRIES AT THE 2002 SALT LAKE WINTER OLYMPICS

	COUNTRY	MEDALS GOLD	SILVER	BRONZE	TOTAL
1	**Germany**	12	16	7	35
2	**US**	10	13	11	34
3	**Norway**	11	7	6	24
4	**Canada**	6	3	8	17
5 =	**Austria**	2	4	10	16
=	**Russia**	6	6	4	16
7	**Italy**	4	4	4	12
8 =	**France**	4	5	2	11
=	**Switzerland**	3	2	6	11
10 =	**China**	2	2	4	8
=	**Netherlands**	3	5	0	8

Both Canada's women's and men's hockey teams won gold medals at the Salt Lake City Winter Olympic Games. Canada also won nine medals in speed skating.

TOP 10 GOLD MEDALISTS AT THE WINTER OLYMPICS (MEN)

	MEDALIST/COUNTRY	SPORT	GOLD MEDALS
1	**Bjørn Dählie,** Norway	Nordic skiing	8
2 =	**Eric Heiden,** US	Speed skating	5
=	**Clas Thunberg,** Norway	Speed skating	5
4 =	**Ivar Ballangrud,** Norway	Speed skating	4
=	**Yevgeny Grishin,** Soviet Union	Speed skating	4
=	**Sixten Jernberg,** Sweden	Nordic skiing	4
=	**Johann Olav Koss,** Norway	Speed skating	4
=	**Matti Nykänen,** Finland	Ski jumping	4
=	**Alexander Tikhonov,** Soviet Union	Biathlon	4
=	**Thomas Wassberg,** Sweden	Nordic skiing	4
=	**Nikolai Zimyatov,** Soviet Union	Nordic skiing	4
=	**Gunde Svan,** Sweden	Nordic skiing	4

TOP 10 GOLD MEDALISTS AT THE WINTER OLYMPICS (WOMEN)

	MEDALIST/COUNTRY	SPORT	GOLD MEDALS
1 =	**Lydia Skoblikova,** Soviet Union	Speed skating	6
=	**Lyubov Egorova,** EUN*/Russia	Nordic skiing	6
3 =	**Bonnie Blair,** US	Speed skating	5
=	**Larissa Lazutina,** EUN*/Russia	Nordic skiing	5
5 =	**Galina Kulakova,** Soviet Union	Nordic skiing	4
=	**Lee-Kyung Chun,** South Korea	Short track speed skating	4
=	**Claudia Pechstein,** Germany	Speed skating	4
=	**Raisa Smetanina,** EUN*/Russia	Nordic skiing	4
9 =	**Claudia Boyarskikh,** Soviet Union	Nordic skiing	3
=	**Marja-Liisa Kirvesniemi** (née Hämäläinen), Finland	Nordic skiing	3
=	**Sonja Henie,** Norway	Figure skating	3
=	**Karin Kania** (née Enke), East Germany	Speed skating	3
=	**Gunda Niemann-Stirnemann,** Germany	Speed skating	3
=	**Anfisa Reztsova,** Soviet Union/EUN*	Nordic skiing/biathlon	3
=	**Irina Rodnina,** Soviet Union	Figure skating	3
=	**Vreni Schneider,** Switzerland	Alpine skiing	3
=	**Katja Seizinger,** Germany	Alpine skiing	3
=	**Elena Valbe,** EUN*/Russia	Nordic skiing	3
=	**Yvonne van Gennip,** Netherlands	Speed skating	3

* *Unified Team, Commonwealth of Independent States, 1992*

TOP 10 WINTER OLYMPIC MEDAL-WINNING COUNTRIES, 1924–2002*

	COUNTRY	GOLD	SILVER	BRONZE	TOTAL
1	**Soviet Union**#	113	82	78	273
2	**Norway**	94	93	73	260
3	**US**	70	70	51	191
4	**Austria**	41	57	65	163
5	**Germany**†	54	51	37	142
6	**Finland**	41	51	49	141
7	**East Germany**	39	37	35	111
8	**Sweden**	36	28	38	102
9	**Switzerland**	32	33	36	101
10	**Canada**	30	28	37	95

* *Includes medals won at figure skating and ice hockey included in the Summer Games prior to the launch of the Winter Olympics in 1924*

\# *Includes Unified Team of 1992; excludes Russia since then*

† *Not including East/West Germany 1968–88*

The Winter Olympics have been staged on 19 occasions since the first, with the 20th scheduled for Turin, Italy, February 10–26, 2006. The Soviet Union first competed at the seventh Games in Corina d'Ampezzo, Italy, where it succeeded in leading the medal table with seven gold, three silver, and six bronze medals.

TOP 10 COMPETITOR-ATTENDED WINTER OLYMPICS

	HOST CITY/COUNTRY	YEAR	COMPETITORS
1	**Salt Lake City,** US	2002	2,399
2	**Nagano,** Japan	1998	2,177
3	**Albertville,** France	1992	1,801
4	**Lillehammer,** Norway	1994	1,736
5	**Calgary,** Canada	1988	1,425
6	**Sarajevo,** Yugoslavia	1984	1,274
7	**Grenoble,** France	1968	1,158
8	**Innsbruck,** Austria	1976	1,123
9	**Innsbruck,** Austria	1964	1,091
10	**Lake Placid,** US	1980	1,072

The first Winter Games at Chamonix, France, in 1924 were attended by 258 competitors (of whom 13 were women), representing 16 countries. The second Winter Games, held in 1928 in St. Moritz, Switzerland, saw the number of competitors and countries increase to 464 (including 26 women) and 25 respectively. The third Games in 1932, in Lake Placid, New York, were affected by the Depression, which saw the numbers reduced to 252 competitors (with 21 women) from 17 countries. Since the fourth Games in 1936 in Garmisch-Partenkirchen, Germany (668 competitors, with 80 women, from 28 countries), the number of competitors and countries represented have generally increased: a total of 2,399 competitors (886 women) from 77 countries took part at the 19th Games at Salt Lake City, Utah.

▼ Red Hot Team
The German four-man bobsleigh hurtles to Olympic gold at the 2002 Winter Games.

Winter Sports

TOP 10 ALPINE SNOWBOARDERS (MALE)*

	SNOWBOARDER/COUNTRY	TOTAL POINTS
1	**Tony Albrecht,** Switzerland	2,221.48
2	**Gilles Jaquet,** Switzerland	2,213.60
3	**Cyrill Buehler,** Switzerland	2,194.53
4	**Urs Eiselin,** Switzerland	2,166.30
5	**Simon Schoch,** Switzerland	2,131.04
6	**Philippe Schoch,** Switzerland	2,080.01
7	**Martin Bolt,** Switzerland	1,888.93
8	**Nicolas Wolken,** Switzerland	1,815.41
9	**Roland Haldi,** Switzerland	1,792.86
10	**Antonin Cip,** Czech Republic	1,788,22

* *Ranked by best four results in a 52-week period to January 29, 2003*

Source: *World Snowboarding Federation*

Snowboarding was invented in 1965 by Sherman Poppen of the US, and the sport became an Olympic event in 1998.

TOP 10 ALPINE SNOWBOARDERS (FEMALE)*

	SNOWBOARDER/COUNTRY	TOTAL POINTS
1	**Daniela Meuli,** Switzerland	1,172.30
2	**Perrine Buehler,** Switzerland	1,064.44
3	**Ursula Bruhin,** Switzerland	1,049.06
4	**Blanka Isielonis,** Poland	986.82
5	**Malgorzata Kukcz,** Poland	985.68
6	**Nadia Livers,** Switzerland	913.33
7	**Petra Elsterova,** Czech Republic	911.72
8	**Milena Meisser,** Switzerland	828.13
9	**Fraenzi Kohli,** Switzerland	776.09
10	**Rebekka von Kaenel,** Switzerland	773.97

* *Ranked by best four results in a 52-week period to January 29, 2003*

The World Snowboarding Federation was constituted in 2002 in Munich, Germany, and is now the governing body for the sport internationally.

TOP 10 SKIERS IN THE 2002/03 ALPINE WORLD CUP (FEMALE)

	SKIER/COUNTRY	OVERALL POINTS*
1	**Janica Kostelic,** Croatia	1,570
2	**Karen Putzer,** Italy	1,100
3	**Anja Paerson,** Sweden	1,042
4	**Michaela Dorfmeister,** Austria	972
5	**Martina Ertl,** Germany	922
6	**Carole Montillet,** France	869
7	**Renate Goetschl,** Austria	830
8	**Alexandra Meissnitzer,** Austria	776
9	**Kirsten L. Clark,** US	661
10	**Nicole Hosp,** Austria	558

* *Awarded for performances in slalom, giant slalom, super giant, downhill, and combination disciplines*

Source: *International Ski Federation*

▼ Downhill Racer
Swiss snowboarder Gilles Jaquet is among the world's leading exponents in a sport dominated by his countrymen.

TOP 10 SKI-JUMPERS IN THE 2002/03 SKI-JUMPING WORLD CUP

	SKIER/COUNTRY	OVERALL POINTS
1	**Adam Malysz,** Poland	1,357
2	**Sven Hannawald,** Germany	1,235
3	**Andreas Widhoelzl,** Austria	1,028
4	**Janne Ahonen,** Finland	1,016
5	**Florian Liegl,** Austria	986
6	**Martin Hoellwarth,** Austria	925
7	**Primoz Peterka,** Slovenia	805
8	**Matti Hautamaeki,** Finland	797
9	**Roar Ljoekelsoey,** Norway	757
10	**Sigurd Pettersen,** Norway	747

Source: *International Ski Federation*

A Jump Ahead
German ski-jumper Sven Hannawald gained his fifth World Cup victory at Bad Mittendorf, Austria, but lost out to overall points leader Adam Maylysz.

TOP 10 SKIERS IN THE 2002/03 ALPINE WORLD CUP (MALE)

	SKIER/COUNTRY	OVERALL POINTS*
1	**Stephen Eberharter,** Austria	1,333
2	**Bode Miller,** US	1,100
3	**Kjetil Andre Aamodt,** Norway	940
4	**Kalle Palander,** Finland	718
5	**Didier Cuche,** Switzerland	709
6	**Daron Rahlves,** US	647
7	**Ivica Kostelic,** Croatia	632
8	**Benjamin Raich,** Austria	622
9	**Michael Walchhofer,** Austria	600
10	**Hans Knauss,** Austria	596

* *Awarded for performances in slalom, giant slalom, super giant, downhill, and combination disciplines*

Source: *International Ski Federation*

TOP 10 FASTEST SPEED SKATERS

	SKATER/COUNTRY	LOCATION	DATE	TIME FOR 500 M (SECS)*
1	**Hiroyasu Shimizu,** Japan	Salt Lake City, US	Mar 10, 2001	34.32
2	**Jeremy Wotherspoon,** Canada	Salt Lake City	Jan 11, 2003	34.41
3	**Casey FitzRandolph,** US	Salt Lake City	Feb 11, 2002	34.42
4	**Gerard van Velde,** Netherlands	Calgary, Canada	Jan 18, 2003	34.61
5	**Toyoki Takeda,** Japan	Calgary	Dec 9, 2001	34.62
6	= **Joey Cheek,** US	Salt Lake City	Dec 19, 2001	34.66
	= **Michael Ireland,** Canada	Calgary	Mar 18, 2000	34.66
8	**Kip Carpenter,** US	Salt Lake City	Feb 11, 2002	34.68
9	**Jan Bos,** Netherlands	Salt Lake City	Feb 12, 2002	34.72
10	**Lee Kyu-Hyuk,** South Korea	Salt Lake City	Feb 11, 2002	34.74

* *Only skater's fastest time included*

Source: *International Skating Union*

THE 10 LATEST MARATHON RECORD BREAKERS (MALE)

	ATHLETE/COUNTRY	VENUE	YEAR	TIME
1	**Khalid Khannouchi,** US	London, UK	2002	2:05:38
2	**Khalid Khannouchi,** US	Chicago, US	1999	2:05:42
3	**Ronaldo da Costa,** Brazil	Berlin, Germany	1998	2:06:05
4	**Belayneh Dinsamo,** Ethiopia	Rotterdam, Netherlands	1988	2:06:50
5	**Carlos Lopes,** Portugal	Rotterdam, Netherlands	1985	2:07:12
6	**Steve Jones,** UK	Chicago, US	1984	2:08:05
7	**Rob de Castella,** Australia	Fukuoka, Japan	1981	2:08:18
8	**Derek Clayton,** Australia	Antwerp, Belgium	1969	2:08:34
9	**Derek Clayton,** Australia	Fukuoka, Japan	1967	2:09:36
10	**Abebe Bikila,** Ethiopia	Tokyo, Japan	1964	2:12:11

The marathon commemorates the run of Pheidippides from Marathon to Athens in 490 BC, bringing news of a Greek victory over the invading Persians. The present-day marathon distance of 42.195 km (26 miles 385 yards) was established at the 1908 London Olympics.

THE 10 LATEST MARATHON RECORD BREAKERS (FEMALE)

	ATHLETE/COUNTRY	VENUE	YEAR	TIME
1	**Paula Radcliffe,** UK	London, UK	2003	2:15:25
2	**Paula Radcliffe,** UK	Chicago, US	2002	2:17:18
3	**Catherine Ndereba,** Kenya	Chicago, US	2001	2:18:47
4	**Naoko Takahashi,** Japan	Berlin, Germany	2001	2:19:46
5	**Tegla Loroupe,** Kenya	Berlin, Germany	1999	2:20:43
6	**Tegla Loroupe,** Kenya	Rotterdam, Netherlands	1998	2:20:47
7	**Ingrid Christensen-Kristiansen,** Norway	London, UK	1985	2:21:06
8	**Greta Waitz,** Norway	London, UK	1983	2:25:29
9	**Greta Waitz,** Norway	New York, US	1980	2:25:41
10	**Greta Waitz,** Norway	New York, US	1979	2:27:33

▼ London Marathon
Khalid Khannouchi (No.2) broke his own world record at the 2002 London Marathon. In the past 100 years, the time has been trimmed by more than 50 minutes.

THE 10 LATEST 100-METER RECORD BREAKERS (MALE)

	ATHLETE/COUNTRY	YEAR	TIME
1	**Tim Montgomery,** US	2002	9.78
2	**Maurice Greene,** US	1999	9.79
3	**Donovan Bailey,** Canada	1996	9.84
4	**Leroy Burrell,** US	1994	9.85
5	**Carl Lewis,** US	Aug 1991	9.86
6	**Leroy Burrell,** US	June 1991	9.90
7	**Carl Lewis,** US	1988	9.92
8	**Calvin Smith,** US	July 1983	9.93
9	**Carl Lewis,** US	May 1983	9.97
10	**Silvio Leonard,** Cuba	1977	9.98

In a discipline where the winners and runners-up are separated by hundredths of a second, it is worth noting that the world record time has been cut by more than a second in the past 100 years. The 10.8-second record set by Luther Cary in 1891 remained unbroken until 1906.

▲ **Pole Position**
Russian pole-vaulter and Top 10–ranked female athlete Svetlana Feofanova celebrates winning gold at the 2002 European Championships.

TOP 10 FASTEST WOMEN EVER*

	ATHLETE/COUNTRY	YEAR	TIME
1	**Florence Griffith Joyner,** US	1988	10.49
2	**Marion Jones,** US	1998	10.65
3	**Christine Arron,** France	1998	10.73
4	**Merlene Ottey,** Jamaica	1996	10.74
5	**Evelyn Ashford,** US	1984	10.76
6	**Irina Privalova,** Russia	1994	10.77
7	**Dawn Sowell,** US	1989	10.78
8	= **Xuemei Li,** China	1997	10.79
	= **Inger Miller,** US	1999	10.79
10	**Marlies Oelsner-Göhr,** East Germany	1983	10.81

* *Based on fastest time for the 100 meters*

The late Florence Griffith Joyner's world record for the 100 meters has stood since she set it in Indianapolis on July 16, 1988. In the same year at the Seoul Olympics, she also set the still unbroken 200-meter record (21.34 secs).

TOP 10 FIELD ATHLETES (MALE)

	ATHLETE/COUNTRY	EVENT	SCORE*
1	**Jonathan Edwards,** UK	Triple jump	1,378
2	**Christian Olsson,** Sweden	Triple jump	1,377
3	**Róbert Fazekas,** Hungary	Discus throw	1,362
4	**Adrián Annus,** Hungary	Hammer throw	1,350
5	**Roman Sebrle,** Czech Republic	Decathlon	1,348
6	**Adam Nelson,** US	Shot put	1,346
7	**Jeff Hartwig,** US	Pole vault	1,342
8	**Koji Murofushi,** Japan	Hammer throw	1,341
9	= **Walter Davis,** US	Triple jump	1,334
	= **Sergey Makarov,** Russia	Javelin throw	1,334

* *As at March 10, 2003*

Source: *International Association of Athletics Federations*

These athletes have been ranked by the IAAF, according to their Ranking Score. After each competition, athletes' Performance Scores are calculated, which consist of points awarded for results and placing; athletes are then ranked by taking the average of their top five Performance Scores.

TOP 10 FIELD ATHLETES (FEMALE)

	ATHLETE/COUNTRY	EVENT	SCORE*
1	**Kajsa Bergqvist,** Sweden	High jump	1,363
2	**Tatyana Kotova,** Russia	Long jump	1,345
3	**Hestrie Cloete,** Russia	High jump	1,327
4	**Svetlana Feofanova,** Russia	Pole vault	1,324
5	**Maurren Higa Maggi,** Brazil	Long jump	1,320
6	**Osleidys Menendez,** Cuba	Javelin throw	1,313
7	**Marina Kuptsova,** Russia	High jump	1,305
8	**Ashia Hansen,** UK	Triple jump	1,298
9	**Francoise Mbango Etone,** Cameroon	Long jump, triple jump	1,292
10	**Natalya Sadova,** Russia	Discus throw	1,290

* *As at March 10, 2003*

Source: *International Association of Athletics Federations*

Rankings require a minimum of six performances, four of which must be main events. Result scores take account of wind speed (according to whether it aids or hinders an athlete) and the awarding of a world record, which confers bonus points.

Football

TOP 10 PLAYERS WITH THE MOST CAREER TOUCHDOWNS

	PLAYER	TOUCHDOWNS
1	Jerry Rice*	192
2	Emmitt Smith*	164
3	Marcus Allen	145
4	Cris Carter*	130
5	Jim Brown	126
6	Walter Payton	125
7	Marshall Faulk*	120
8	John Riggins	116
9	Lenny Moore	113
10	Barry Sanders	109

** Still active at end of 2002 season*

Source: *National Football League*

TOP 10 PLAYERS WITH THE MOST CAREER POINTS

	PLAYER	POINTS
1	Gary Anderson*	2,223
2	Morten Andersen*	2,153
3	George Blanda	2,002
4	Norm Johnson	1,736
5	Nick Lowery	1,711
6	Jan Stenerud	1,699
7	Eddie Murray	1,594
8	Al Del Greco	1,584
9	Jim Carney*	1,541
10	Pat Leahy	1,470

** Still active at end of 2002 season*

Source: *National Football League*

TOP 10 PLAYERS WITH THE MOST PASSING YARDS IN A CFL CAREER

	PLAYER	SEASONS	PASSING YARDS
1	Damon Allen	18	58,407
2	Ron Lancaster	19	50,535
3	Matt Dunigan	14	43,857
4	Danny McManus	13	42,528
5	Doug Flutie	8	41,355
6	Tracy Ham	12	40,534
7	Tom Clements	12	39,041
8	Kent Austin	10	36,030
9	Dieter Brock	11	34,830
10	Tom Burgess	10	30,308

Source: *Canadian Football League*

◄ Rice Records
Holder of numerous NFL career records, San Francisco 49ers (1985–2000) and Oakland Raiders (2001–) wide receiver Jerry Rice is considered one of the greatest players of all time.

TOP 10 TEAMS WITH THE MOST GREY CUP WINS

	TEAM	NO. OF GAMES	WINS
1	Toronto Argonauts	20	14
2	Edmonton Eskimos	22	11
3	Winnipeg Blue Bombers	22	10
4	Ottawa Rough Riders	15	9
5	Hamilton Tiger-Cats	18	8
6	Calgary Stampeders	11	5
7	BC Lions	7	4
8	Queen's University	3	3
9	Saskatchewan Roughriders	15	2
10	Baltimore Stallions	2	1

Source: *Canadian Football League*

▲ **Giants Stadium**
The first game played at Giants Stadium was on October 10 ,1976, when the New York Giants were beaten by the Dallas Cowboys 24 to 14.

TOP 10 MOST SUCCESSFUL SUPER BOWL TEAMS

		SUPER BOWL GAMES		
	TEAM	WINS	RUNNERS-UP	POINTS*
1	**Dallas Cowboys**	5	3	13
2	**San Francisco 49ers**	5	0	10
3	**Pittsburgh Steelers**	4	1	10
4 =	**Oakland/Los Angeles Raiders**	3	2	8
=	**Washington Redskins**	3	2	8
6	**Denver Broncos**	2	4	8
7	**Green Bay Packers**	3	1	7
8	**Miami Dolphins**	2	3	7
9	**New York Giants**	2	1	5
10 =	**Buffalo Bills**	0	4	4
=	**Minnesota Vikings**	0	4	4

* *Based on two points for a Super Bowl win, and one for a runner-up; wins take precedence over runners-up in determining ranking*

Source: *National Football League*

TOP 10 LARGEST NFL STADIUMS

	STADIUM	HOME TEAM	CAPACITY
1	**Giants Stadium**	New York Giants/Jets	80,242
2	**FedExField**	Washington Redskins	80,116
3	**Arrowhead Stadium**	Kansas City Chiefs	79,451
4	**Invesco Stadium**	Denver Broncos	76,125
5	**Pro Player Stadium**	Miami Dolphins	75,540
6	**Ralph Wilson Stadium**	Buffalo Bills	73,967
7	**Ericsson Stadium**	Carolina Panthers	73,367
8	**Sun Devil Stadium**	Arizona Cardinals	73,273
9	**Cleveland Browns Stadium**	Cleveland Browns	73,200
10	**Alltel Stadium**	Jacksonville Jaguars	73,000

Source: *National Football League*

The seating capacity of most NFL stadiums varies according to the event. The smallest is the RCA Dome, home of the Indianapolis Colts, with a capacity of 56,127.

Basketball

TOP 10 POINT-SCORERS IN AN NBA CAREER

	PLAYER	TOTAL POINTS*
1	Kareem Abdul-Jabbar	38,387
2	Karl Malone#	36,374
3	Michael Jordan#	32,292
4	Wilt Chamberlain	31,419
5	Moses Malone	27,409
6	Elvin Hayes	27,313
7	Hakeem Olajuwon	26,946
8	Oscar Robertson	26,710
9	Dominique Wilkins	26,668
10	John Havlicek	26,395

* *Regular season games only*

Still active at end of 2002–03 season

Source: *National Basketball Association*

The greatest point-scorer in NBA history, Kareem Abdul-Jabbar was born Lew Alcindor but adopted a new name when he converted to Islam in 1969. He began his career that same year, turning professional with the Milwaukee Bucks, and played 20 seasons before retiring at the end of 1989. Despite scoring an NBA record 38,387 points, he could not emulate Wilt Chamberlain's accomplishment of scoring 100 points in a game, which Chamberlain achieved for Philadelphia against New York at Hershey, Pennsylvania, on March 2, 1962. Chamberlain also scored 70 points in a game six times, a feat Abdul-Jabbar never succeeded in rivaling.

TOP 10 FREE THROW PERCENTAGES

	PLAYER	ATTEMPTS	MADE	%
1	Mark Price	2,362	2,135	.904
2	Rick Barry	4,243	3,818	.900
3	Calvin Murphy	3,864	3,445	.892
4	Scott Skiles	1,741	1,548	.889
5	= Larry Bird	4,471	3,960	.886
	= Reggie Miller*	6,560	5,810	.886
7	Bill Sharman	3,559	3,143	.883
8	Ray Allen*	2,215	1,954	.882
9	Jeff Hornacek	3,390	2,973	.877
10	Ricky Pierce	3,871	3,389	.875

* *Still active 2002–03 season*

Source: *National Basketball Association*

▼ Air Jordan
The holder of numerous basketball records, Michael Jordan has used his astonishing skill to build both a reputation and a personal fortune from the game.

TOP 10 HIGHEST EARNERS IN THE NBA IN 2002–03

	PLAYER/TEAM	EARNINGS (US$)
1	**Kevin Garnett,** Minnesota Timberwolves	25,200,000
2	**Shaquille O'Neal,** Los Angeles Lakers	24,000,000
3	**Alonzo Mourning,** Miami Heat	20,600,000
4	**Juwan Howard,** Denver Nuggets	20,300,000
5	**Scottie Pippen,** Portland Trail Blazers	19,730,000
6	**Karl Malone,** Utah Jazz	19,250,000
7	**Rasheed Wallace,** Portland Trail Blazers	16,185,000
8	**Dikembe Mutombo,** Philadelphia 76ers	16,110,000
9	**Chris Webber,** Sacramento Kings	14,344,000
10	**Allan Houston,** New York Knicks	14,340,000

Source: *InsideHoops.com*

Born in Mauldin, South Carolina, on May 19, 1976, Kevin Garnett turned professional in 1995 after being selected from Chicago's Farragut Career Academy High School, in the draft by the Minnesota Timberwolves (fifth pick in the first round). In 1997, he signed a six-year contract worth over US$126 million. In his seven-year career, he has been selected six times to play on the NBA All Star selection and won the MVP award in 2003. Garnett has twice had 40-point games in his career, but in the time he has been playing for them, the Timberwolves have not enjoyed notable success at team level, failing to get past the first round of the conference playoffs in the seven seasons up to 2001–02. Even with his massive salary of more than US$25 million for the 2002–03 season, Kevin Garnett is still well short of the NBA record of US$33.14 million earned by Michael Jordan in the 1997–98 season.

TOP 10 TEAMS WITH THE MOST NBA TITLES

	TEAM*	TITLES
1	**Boston Celtics**	16
2	**Minneapolis/Los Angeles Lakers**	14
3	**Chicago Bulls**	6
4 =	**Philadelphia/Golden State Warriors**	3
=	**Syracuse Nationals/Philadelphia 76ers**	3
6 =	**Baltimore/Washington Bullets**	2
=	**Detroit Pistons**	2
=	**Houston Rockets**	2
=	**New York Knicks**	2
10 =	**Milwaukee Bucks**	1
=	**Portland Trail Blazers**	1
=	**Rochester Royals#**	1
=	**St. Louis Hawks†**	1
=	**Seattle Supersonics**	1

* *Teams separated by / indicate a change of franchise and denotes that they have won the championship under both names*

\# *Now the Sacramento Kings*

† *Now the Atlanta Hawks*

Source: *National Basketball Association*

TOP 10 PLAYERS WITH THE HIGHEST POINTS AVERAGE

	PLAYER	GAMES PLAYED	POINTS SCORED	POINTS AVERAGE
1 =	**Wilt Chamberlain**	1,045	31,419	30.1
=	**Michael Jordan***	1,072	32,292	30.1
3	**Shaquille O'Neal***	742	20,475	27.6
4	**Elgin Baylor**	846	23,149	27.4
5 =	**Allen Iverson***	487	13,170	27.0
=	**Jerry West**	932	25,192	27.0
7	**Bob Pettit**	792	20,880	26.4
8	**George Gervin**	791	20,708	26.2
9	**Oscar Robertson**	1,040	26,710	25.7
10	**Karl Malone***	1,434	36,374	25.4

* *Still active at end of 2002–03 season*

Source: *National Basketball Association*

TOP 10 BIGGEST NBA ARENAS

	ARENA/CITY	HOME TEAM	CAPACITY
1	**Palace of Auburn Hills,** Auburn Hills	Detroit Pistons	22,076
2	**United Center,** Chicago	Chicago Bulls	21,711
3	**MCI Center,** Washington	Washington Wizards	20,674
4	**Gund Arena,** Cleveland	Cleveland Cavaliers	20,562
5	**First Union Center,** Philadelphia	Philadelphia 76ers	20,444
6	**Continental Airlines Arena,** East Rutherford	New Jersey Nets	20,049
7	**Rose Garden,** Portland	Portland Trail Blazers	19,980
8	**Delta Center,** Salt Lake City	Utah Jazz	19,911
9	**Air Canada Centre,** Toronto	Toronto Raptors	19,800
10	**Madison Square Garden,** New York	New York Knicks	19,763

Source: *National Basketball Association*

Baseball Teams

TOP 10 TEAMS WITH THE MOST WORLD SERIES WINS

	TEAM*	WINS
1	New York Yankees	26
2 =	Philadelphia/Kansas City/Oakland Athletics	9
=	St. Louis Cardinals	9
4	Brooklyn/Los Angeles Dodgers	6
5 =	Boston Red Sox	5
=	Cincinnati Reds	5
=	New York/San Francisco Giants	5
=	Pittsburgh Pirates	5
9	Detroit Tigers	4
10 =	Boston/Milwaukee/Atlanta Braves	3
=	St. Louis/Baltimore Orioles	3
=	Washington Senators/Minnesota Twins	3

** Teams separated by / indicate changes of franchise and are regarded as the same team for major league record purposes*

Source: *Major League Baseball*

Major league baseball started in the US with the formation of the National League in 1876. The rival American League was started in 1901.

THE 10 LATEST WINNERS OF THE WORLD SERIES

YEAR*	WINNER/LEAGUE	CHALLENGER/LEAGUE	SCORE
2002	Anaheim Angels (AL)	San Francisco Giants (NL)	4–3
2001	Arizona Diamondbacks (NL)	New York Yankees (AL)	4–3
2000	New York Yankees (AL)	New York Mets (NL)	4–1
1999	New York Yankees (AL)	Atlanta Braves (NL)	4–0
1998	New York Yankees (AL)	San Diego Padres (NL)	4-0
1997	Florida Marlins (NL)	Cleveland Indians (AL)	4–3
1996	New York Yankees (AL)	Atlanta Braves (NL)	4–2
1995	Atlanta Braves (NL)	Cleveland Indians (AL)	4–2
1993	Toronto Blue Jays (AL)	Philadelphia Phillies (NL)	4–2
1992	Toronto Blue Jays (AL)	Atlanta Braves (NL)	4–2

** The 1994 event was canceled due to a players' strike*

AL = American League

NL = National League

Source: *Major League Baseball*

The Angels won their first World Series in 2002 in dramatic style. They lost the first game to the Giants, then went up two games to one. It was not long before they were trailing three games to two after a 16–4 defeat in Game 5, but the Angels won the last two games to snatch victory from the San Francisco challengers.

TOP 10 TEAMS WITH THE MOST HOME RUNS, 2002

	TEAM	HOME RUN TOTAL
1	Texas Rangers	230
2	New York Yankees	223
3	Chicago White Sox	217
4	Oakland Athletics	205
5	Chicago Cubs	200
6	San Francisco Giants	198
7	Cleveland Indians	191
8	Toronto Blue Jays	187
9	Boston Red Sox	177
10	St. Louis Cardinals	175

Source: *Major League Baseball*

The Rangers also led all MLB teams in 2002 in extra base hits (561) and total bases (2,558). They scored 800-plus runs (843) for the seventh straight season, as well. However, on the other side of the coin, their earned run average of 5.15 was one of the highest in the league. They finished the season in fourth place in the American League (West).

THE 10 TEAMS WITH THE WORST ERA*, 2002

	TEAM	ERA
1	Tampa Bay Devil Rays	5.29
2	Kansas City Royals	5.21
3	Colorado Rockies	5.20
4	Texas Rangers	5.15
5	Detroit Tigers	4.92
6	Cleveland Indians	4.91
7	Toronto Blue Jays	4.80
8	Milwaukee Brewers	4.73
9	San Diego Padres	4.62
10	Chicago White Sox	4.53

** Earned run average*

Source: *Major League Baseball*

The Colorado Rockies are the only team on the list to have had an ERA in excess of 5 in each of the past four seasons: in 2001 it was 5.29, in 2000, 5.27, and in 1999, 6.10. In those years, their only winning season was in 2000, when they had an 82–80 record.

TOP 10 TEAMS WITH THE BEST ERA*, 2002

	TEAM	ERA
1	Atlanta Braves	3.13
2	San Francisco Giants	3.54
3	Oakland Athletics	3.68
4 =	Anaheim Angels	3.69
=	Los Angeles Dodgers	3.69
6	St. Louis Cardinals	3.70
7	Boston Red Sox	3.75
8	New York Yankees	3.87
9	New York Mets	3.89
10	Arizona Diamondbacks	3.92

** Earned run average*

Source: *Major League Baseball*

The Atlanta Braves have had a great record in recent years. They had the best ERA in the National League in three consecutive years—2000, 2001, and 2002—and in that period also topped the MLB list, with the exception of 2001, when they finished tied for second with Oakland behind the leaders, Seattle.

TOP 10 LARGEST MAJOR LEAGUE BALLPARKS*

	STADIUM	HOME TEAM	CAPACITY
1	**Qualcomm Stadium**	San Diego Padres	63,480
2	**Veterans Stadium**	Philadelphia Phillies	62,418
3	**Dodger Stadium**	Los Angeles Dodgers	56,000
4	**Shea Stadium**	New York Mets	55,300
5	**Yankee Stadium**	New York Yankees	55,070
6	**SkyDome**	Toronto Blue Jays	50,516
7	**Coors Field**	Colorado Rockies	50,445
8	**Turner Field**	Atlanta Braves	49,831
9	**Busch Stadium**	St. Louis Cardinals	49,814
10	**Ballpark in Arlington**	Texas Rangers	49,115

* *By capacity*

Source: *Major League Baseball*

Stadium capacities vary constantly, (in some cases from year to year), some being adjusted according to the event: Veterans Stadium, for example, holds fewer people for baseball games than for football games. The first game to take place at SkyDome in Toronto was on June 5, 1989.

TOP 10 BASEBALL TEAM PAYROLLS

	TEAM	TOTAL PAYROLL (2003) US$
1	**New York Yankees**	149,710,995
2	**New York Mets**	116,878,613
3	**Los Angeles Dodgers**	105,897,619
4	**Atlanta Braves**	104,622,210
5	**Texas Rangers**	104,526,470
6	**Boston Red Sox**	96,631,677
7	**Seattle Mariners**	87,184,500
8	**St. Louis Cardinals**	83,150,895
9	**San Francisco Giants**	82,352,167
10	**Chicago Cubs**	80,743,333

* Source: *Associated Press*

Yankees owner George Steinbrenner pushed the team's payroll up to an all-time MLB record in an effort to improve performances on the field, increasing total wages by over US$20 million on 2002. Top earners were Cuban pitcher Jose Contreras and Japanese slugger Hideki Matsui, who signed contracts in December 2002 worth US$32 million over four years and US$21 million over three years, respectively.

TOP 10 LARGEST ATTENDANCE AT TORONTO BLUE JAYS HOME GAMES

	OPPONENT	DATE	ATTENDANCE
1	**Atlanta Braves**	Oct 22, 1992	52,268
2	**Philadelphia Phillies**	Oct 23, 1993	52,195
3	**Atlanta Braves**	Oct 21, 1992	52,090
4	**Philadelphia Phillies**	Oct 17, 1993	52,062
5	**Philadelphia Phillies**	Oct 16, 1993	52,011
6	**Chicago Cubs**	Oct 9, 1993	51,889
7	**Atlanta Braves**	Oct 20, 1992	51,813
8	**Chicago Cubs**	Oct 8, 1993	51,783
9	**Minnesota Twins**	Oct 12, 1991	51,526
10	**Minnesota Twins**	Oct 11, 1991	51,454

Source: *Toronto Blue Jays Baseball Club*

The largest crowd of 52,382 baseball enthusiasts at the SkyDome was actually in the post season, for an all-star game pitting the American League against the National League on July 9, 1991.

TOP 10 NEWEST MAJOR LEAGUE TEAMS

	TEAM	AL/NL	1ST SEASON
1	= **Arizona Diamondbacks**	NL	1998
	= **Tampa Bay Devil Rays**	AL	1998
3	= **Colorado Rockies**	NL	1993
	= **Florida Marlins**	NL	1993
5	= **Seattle Mariners**	AL	1977
	= **Toronto Blue Jays**	AL	1977
7	= **Kansas City Royals**	AL	1969
	= **Montreal Expos**	NL	1969
	= **Seattle Pilots/Milwaukee Brewers**	AL	1969
10	= **Houston Astros**	NL	1962
	= **New York Mets**	NL	1962

AL = American League

NL = National League

Source: *Major League Baseball*

The Arizona Diamondbacks played their first MLB game on March 31, 1998, in front of 50,179 fans at Bank One Ballpark. Andy Benes delivered the Diamondbacks' first pitch, but the new team lost 9–2 to Colorado.

Baseball Stars

PLAYERS WITH THE BIGGEST CONTRACTS

	PLAYER/CLUB	PERIOD OF CONTRACT	TOTAL (US$)
1	**Alex Rodriguez,** Texas Rangers	2001–10	252,000,000
2	**Derek Jeter,** New York Yankees	2001–10	189,000,000
3	**Manny Ramirez,** Boston Red Sox	2001–08	160,000,000
4	**Todd Helton,** Colorado Rockies	2003–11	141,500,000
5	**Mike Hampton,** Colorado Rockies	2001–08	121,000,000
6	**Jason Giambi,** New York Yankees	2002–09	120,000,000
7	**Ken Griffey Jr.,** Cincinnati Reds	2000–08	116,500,000
8	**Kevin Brown,** Los Angeles Dodgers	1999–2005	105,000,000
9	**Mike Piazza,** New York Mets	1999–2005	91,000,000
10 =	**Barry Bonds,** San Francisco Giants	2000–06	90,000,000
=	**Chipper Jones,** Atlanta Braves	2001–06	90,000,000

* Source: *Major League Baseball*

After seven seasons with the Seattle Mariners, New Yorker Alex Rodriguez joined the Texas Rangers in 2001, when his salary went up from US$4,362,500 to US$22,000,000. This is a considerable increase on his first salary of US$442,333 as an 18 year old with the Mariners in 1994. A right-handed batter, Rodriguez's best season was in 1996 when he hit 141 runs and topped the leader board in batting averages, with .358.

PLAYERS WITH THE MOST CONSECUTIVE GAMES PLAYED

	PLAYER	YEARS	GAMES
1	**Cal Ripken Jr.**	1981–2001	2,632
2	**Lou Gehrig**	1923–39	2,130
3	**Everett Scott**	1914–26	1,307
4	**Steve Garvey**	1969–87	1,207
5	**Billy Williams**	1959–76	1,117
6	**Joe Sewell**	1920–33	1,103
7	**Stan Musial**	1941–63	895
8	**Eddie Yost**	1944–62	829
9	**Gus Suhr**	1930–40	822
10	**Nellie Fox**	1947–65	798

Source: *Major League Baseball*

Cal Ripken Jr. took himself out of the starting lineup on September 21, 1998, in a game between the Baltimore Orioles and the New York Yankees, having played in every game since May 30, 1982.

LATEST WINNERS OF THE CY YOUNG AWARD

	AMERICAN LEAGUE PLAYER/TEAM	NATIONAL LEAGUE PLAYER/TEAM
2002	**Barry Zito,** Oakland Athletics	**Randy Johnson,** Arizona Diamondbacks
2001	**Roger Clemens,** New York Yankees	**Randy Johnson,** Arizona Diamondbacks
2000	**Pedro Martínez,** Boston Red Sox	**Randy Johnson,** Arizona Diamondbacks
1999	**Pedro Martínez,** Boston Red Sox	**Randy Johnson,** Arizona Diamondbacks
1998	**Roger Clemens,** Toronto Blue Jays	**Tom Glavine,** Atlanta Braves
1997	**Roger Clemens,** Toronto Blue Jays	**Pedro Martínez,** Montreal Expos
1996	**Pat Hentgen,** Toronto Blue Jays	**John Smoltz,** Atlanta Braves
1995	**Randy Johnson,** Seattle Mariners	**Greg Maddux,** Atlanta Braves
1994	**David Cone,** Kansas City Royals	**Greg Maddux,** Atlanta Braves
1993	**Jack McDowell,** Chicago White Sox	**Greg Maddux,** Atlanta Braves

Source: *Major League Baseball*

At 208 cm (6 ft 10 in), Randy Johnson is the tallest man to play major league baseball, and with the scowl he delivers to batters, he is also one of the most intimidating men in the game. Johnson made his debut with the Montreal Expos in 1988 but was traded to the Seattle Mariners in 1989, and it was then that his true talent emerged. He won the first of four consecutive strikeout titles in 1992, including a Mariners record of 308 in 1993. In 1995, he won the first of five Cy Young Awards, after finishing second to Jack McDowell in 1993 and third behind David Cone and Jimmy Key in 1994. When Johnson won the Cy Young Award in 1999, he became only the third man to do so in both leagues.

PLAYERS WITH THE MOST HOME RUNS IN A CAREER

	PLAYER	YEARS	HOME RUNS
1	**Hank Aaron**	1954–76	755
2	**Babe Ruth**	1914–35	714
3	**Willie Mays**	1951–73	660
4	**Barry Bonds**	1986–*	613
5	**Frank Robinson**	1956–76	586
6	**Mark McGwire**	1986–2001	583
7	**Harmon Killebrew**	1954–75	573
8	**Reggie Jackson**	1967–87	563
9	**Mike Schmidt**	1972–89	548
10	**Mickey Mantle**	1951–68	536

* *Still active in 2002*

Source: *Major League Baseball*

George Herman "Babe" Ruth's career (1914–35) home run record was unbroken until Henry Louis "Hank" Aaron overtook him in 1974. His total of 714 came from 8,399 at-bats, which represents an average of 8.5 percent—considerably better than the next man in the averages, Harmon Killebrew, at 7.0 percent.

THE 10 LATEST PERFECT GAMES

	PLAYER	MATCH	DATE
1	David Cone	New York Yankees vs. Montreal Expos	July 18, 1999
2	David Wells	New York Yankees vs. Minnesota Twins	May 17, 1998
3	Kenny Rogers	Texas Rangers vs. California Angels	July 28, 1994
4	Dennis Martinez	Montreal Expos vs. Los Angeles Dodgers	July 28, 1991
5	Tom Browning	Cincinnati Reds vs. Los Angeles Dodgers	Sept 16, 1988
6	Mike Witt	California Angels vs. Texas Rangers	Sept 30, 1984
7	Len Barker	Cleveland Indians vs. Toronto Blue Jays	May 15, 1981
8	Catfish Hunter	Oakland Athletics vs. Minnesota Twins	May 8, 1968
9	Sandy Koufax	Los Angeles Dodgers vs. Chicago Cubs	Sept 9, 1965
10	Jim Bunning	Philadelphia Phillies vs. New York Mets	June 21, 1964

Source: *Major League Baseball*

Seventeen pitchers have thrown perfect games; that is, they have pitched in all nine innings, dismissing 27 opposing batters, without conceding a run. The first player to pitch a perfect game was Lee Richmond, for Worcester against Cleveland, on June 12, 1880. The first player to pitch a perfect game in American League history was Cy Young in the Boston Red Sox's win over Connie Mack's Philadelphia Athletics on May 5, 1904.

TOP 10 PLAYERS WITH THE MOST CAREER STRIKEOUTS

	PLAYER	YEARS	STRIKEOUTS
1	Nolan Ryan	1966–93	5,714
2	Steve Carlton	1965–88	4,136
3	Roger Clemens	1983–*	3,909
4	Randy Johnson	1985–*	3,746
5	Bert Blyleven	1970–92	3,701
6	Tom Seaver	1967–86	3,640
7	Don Sutton	1966–88	3,574
8	Gaylord Perry	1962–83	3,534
9	Walter Johnson	1907–27	3,508
10	Phil Niekro	1964–87	3,342

* *Still active in 2002*

Source: *Major League Baseball*

Nolan Ryan was known as the "Babe Ruth of strikeout pitchers," pitching faster (a record 162.5 km/h [101 mph]) and longer (27 seasons—1966 and 1968–93) than any previous player. As well as his 5,714 strikeouts, including 383 in one season, he walked 2,795 batters and allowed the fewest hits (6.55) per nine innings.

TOP 10 PITCHERS WITH THE MOST CAREER WINS

	PLAYER	YEARS	WINS
1	Cy Young	1890–1911	511
2	Walter Johnson	1907–27	417
3	= Grover Alexander	1911–30	373
	= Christy Mathewson	1900–16	373
5	Jim Galvin	1875–92	365
6	Warren Spahn	1942–65	363
7	Kid Nichols	1890–1906	361
8	Tim Keefe	1880–93	342
9	Steve Carlton	1965–88	329
10	John Clarkson	1882–94	328

Source: *Major League Baseball*

Denton True "Cy" Young won almost 100 games more than the sport's next-best pitcher, Walter Johnson. Young topped 30 game wins 5 times and 20 game wins 15 times. He was a member of the Boston Red Sox team that played in the first World Series in 1903, winning two games in a 6–3 series win. Born in Gilmore, Ohio, in 1867, Young played for the Cleveland Spiders; St. Louis Perfectos and Cardinals; Boston Americans, Somersets, Pilgrims, Red Sox, and Braves; and the Cleveland Naps (later the Indians). In 1904 he pitched the first perfect game in American League history against the Philadelphia Athletics.

TOP 10 PLAYERS WITH THE HIGHEST CAREER BATTING AVERAGES

	PLAYER	AT BAT	HITS	AVERAGE*
1	Ty Cobb	11,434	4,189	.366
2	Rogers Hornsby	8,173	2,930	.358
3	Joe Jackson	4,981	1,772	.356
4	Ed Delahanty	7,505	2,596	.346
5	Tris Speaker	10,195	3,514	.345
6	= Billy Hamilton	6,269	2,159	.344
	= Ted Williams	7,706	2,654	.344
8	= Dan Brouthers	6,711	2,296	.342
	= Harry Heilmann	7,787	2,660	.342
	= Babe Ruth	8,399	2,873	.342

* *Calculated by dividing the number of hits by the number of times a batter was at bat*

Source: *Major League Baseball*

Second only to the legendary Ty Cobb, Rogers Hornsby stands as the second-best hitter of all time, topping the .400 mark in three seasons. Baseball's greatest right-handed hitter—slugging 20-plus homers on seven occasions—he achieved a career average of .358. Hornsby collected seven batting titles, including six consecutively. Known as "The Rajah," he was the player-manager of the St. Louis Cardinals when they won their first World Series in 1926. He was elected to the Baseball Hall of Fame in 1942.

International Soccer

TOP 10 TRANSFERS IN WORLD SOCCER

	PLAYER/COUNTRY	FROM	TO	YEAR	FEE (US$)*
1	**Zinedine Zidane,** France	Juventus, Italy	Real Madrid, Spain	2001	67,100,000
2	**Luis Figo,** Portugal	Barcelona, Spain	Real Madrid, Spain	2000	56,700,000
3	**Hernan Crespo,** Argentina	Parma, Italy	Lazio, Italy	2000	54,100,000
4	**Rio Ferdinand,** UK	Leeds United, England	Manchester United, England	2001	47,400,000
5	**Gianluigi Buffon,** Italy	Parma, Italy	Juventus, Italy	2002	46,200,000
6	**Gaizka Mendieta,** Spain	Valencia, Spain	Lazio, Italy	2001	40,600,000
7	**Juan Sebastian Veron,** Argentina	Lazio, Italy	Manchester United, England	2001	39,600,000
8	**Rui Costa,** Portugal	Fiorentina, Italy	AC Milan, Italy	2001	39,400,000
9	**Christian Vieri,** Italy	Lazio, Italy	Inter Milan, Italy	1999	38,500,000#
10	**Nicolas Anelka,** France	Arsenal, England	Real Madrid, Spain	1999	37,400,000

* *Figures vary slightly from source to source, depending on whether local taxes, agents' fees, and players' commission are included*

Vieri's transfer was part of a package deal with Nicola Ventola, who was valued at US$11.2 million. Vieri was valued at US$38.5 million

Calculated in UK pounds, the world's first seven-figure transfer was when Giuseppe Savoldi moved from Bologna (Italy) to Napoli (Italy) in 1975 for £1 million (then worth roughly US$2 million); the first £10 million (US$15 million) transfer was Gianluigi Lentini, from Torino (Italy) to AC Milan (Italy), June 1992; and the first to be transferred for £20 million (US$30 million) was Denilson, São Paolo (Brazil) to Real Betis (Spain), 1998.

TOP 10 COUNTRIES THAT HAVE PLAYED THE MOST MATCHES IN THE FINAL STAGES OF THE WORLD CUP

	COUNTRY	TOURNAMENTS	MATCHES PLAYED
1	**Brazil**	17	87
2	**Germany/West Germany**	15	85
3	**Italy**	15	70
4	**Argentina**	13	60
5	**England**	11	50
6	**Spain**	11	45
7	**France**	11	44
8	**Sweden**	10	41
9	**Uruguay**	10	40
10=	**Yugoslavia**	9	37
=	**Russia/USSR**	9	37

Brazil is the only country to appear in the final stages of all 17 competitions.

TOP 10 GOAL-SCORERS IN INTERNATIONAL SOCCER

	PLAYER/COUNTRY	YEARS	GOALS
1	**Ferenc Puskás**, Hungary/Spain	1945–56	84
2	= **Ali Daei,** Iran	1993–2002	77
	= **Pelé,** Brazil	1957–71	77
4	**Sándor Kocsis,** Hungary	1948–56	75
5	**Gerd Müller,** West Germany	1966–74	68
6	**Majed Abdullah,** Saudi Arabia	1978–94	67
7	**Jassem Al-Houwaidi*,** Kuwait	1992–2002	63
8	= **Hossam Hassan*,** Egypt	1985–2002	60
	= **Imre Schlosser,** Hungary	1906–27	60
10	**Kiatisuk Senamuang*,** Thailand	1993–2002	59

* *Still active in 2003*

Source: *Roberto Mamrud, Karel Stokkermans, and RSSSF 1998/2003*

Puskás played for Hungary 84 times, and for Spain on four occasions. For all his exploits, his only international honor with Hungary came in 1952, when he captained his country's team to the Olympic title. He made his international debut against Austria as an 18 year old in 1945, and rose to world prominence when Hungary demolished England 6–3 at Wembley, England, in November 1953.

TOP 10 GOAL-SCORERS IN THE FINAL STAGES OF THE WORLD CUP

	PLAYER/COUNTRY	YEARS	GOALS
1	**Gerd Müller,** West Germany	1970–74	14
2	**Just Fontaine,** France	1958	13
3	= **Ronaldo,** Brazil	1998–2002	12
	= **Pelé,** Brazil	1958–70	12
5	= **Jürgen Klinsman,** Germany	1990–98	11
	= **Sándor Kocsis,** Hungary	1954	11
7	= **Helmut Rahn,** West Germany	1954–58	10
	= **Teófilio Cubillas,** Peru	1970–82	10
	= **Grzegorz Lato,** Poland	1974–82	10
	= **Gary Lineker,** England	1986–90	10
	= **Gabriel Batistuta,** Argentina	1994–2002	10

Source: *Jaroslaw Owsianski and RSSSF 2002*

Gerd Müller scored his first goal in the World Cup finals at Leon, Mexico, on June 3, 1970—just 12 minutes from time—to save West Germany from embarrassment, beating Morocco 2–1 in their opening match. He had already scored 10 goals in the qualifying tournament and added 10 more in the 1970 final stages, including two hat tricks. Just Fontaine's scoring of 13 goals in 1958 is a record for one tournament.

TOP 10 RICHEST SOCCER CLUBS

	CLUB/COUNTRY	TURNOVER (US$)
1	**Manchester United,** England	189,400,000
2	**Real Madrid,** Spain	167,800,000
3	**Bayern Munich,** Germany	148,200,000
4	**AC Milan,** Italy	145,200,000
5	**Juventus,** Italy	143,000,000
6	**SS Lazio,** Italy	128,500,000
7	**Chelsea,** England	124,100,000
8	**Barcelona,** Spain	121,700,000
9	**Inter Milan,** Italy	111,500,000
10	**AS Roma,** Italy	103,700,000

Source: *Deloitte & Touche Sport data*

The latest Deloitte & Touche/SportBusiness International Rich List compares the incomes of the world's top soccer clubs during the 1999–2000 season. It reveals the extent to which soccer has become a major business enterprise, with many clubs generating considerably more revenue from commercial activities, such as the sale of merchandise and income from TV rights, than they receive from admissions to matches.

TOP 10 COUNTRIES WITH THE MOST REGISTERED SOCCER CLUBS

	COUNTRY	REGISTERED CLUBS*
1	**South Africa**	51,944
2	**Russia**	43,700
3	**England**	42,000
4	**Germany**	26,760
5	**France**	21,629
6	**Italy**	20,961
7	**Uzbekistan**	15,000
8	**Japan**	13,047
9	**Brazil**	12,987
10	**Spain**	10,240

* *Registered with FIFA through national associations*

◄ **World Class**
One of the foremost goal-scorers of the World Cup, Ronaldo shows off his skills during the 2002 tournament.

Hockey Highlights

TOP 10 GOAL-SCORING ROOKIES IN THE NHL, 2002–03*

	PLAYER	TEAM	GAMES PLAYED	GOALS
1	Henrik Zetterberg	Detroit Red Wings	79	22
2	Ales Kotalik	Buffalo Sabres	68	21
3	Tyler Atnason	Chicago Blackhawks	82	19
4	Rick Nash	Columbus Blue Jackets	74	17
5	Adam Hall	Nashville Predators	79	16
6	= Jason Chimera	Edmonton Oilers	66	14
	= Alexander Frolov	Los Angeles Kings	79	14
8	= Stanislav Chistov	Mighty Ducks of Anaheim	79	12
	= Branko Radivojevic	Phoenix Coyotes	79	12
10	= Ramzi Abid	Phoenix Coyotes/Pittsburgh Penguins	33	10
	= Dan Snyder	Atlanta Thrashers	36	10

* *Regular season only*

Source: *National Hockey League*

TOP 10 ASSISTS IN AN NHL CAREER*

	PLAYER	SEASONS	ASSISTS
1	Wayne Gretzky	20	1,963
2	Ron Francis#	21	1,222
3	Ray Bourque	26	1,169
4	Mark Messier#	24	1,168
5	Paul Coffey	29	1,135
6	Adam Oates#	20	1,063
7	Gordie Howe	26	1,049
8	Marcel Dionne	18	1,040
9	Mario Lemieux#	15	1,011
10	Steve Yzerman#	20	1,010

* *Regular season only*

\# *Still active at end of 2002–03 season*

Source: *National Hockey League/Hockey Database*

When Gretzky retired in 1999 after a 20-year career, he held 10 NHL scoring titles including those for more goals, assists, and points than anyone in league history.

TOP 10 POINT-SCORERS IN AN NHL CAREER*

	PLAYER	SEASONS	GOALS	ASSISTS	TOTAL POINTS
1	Wayne Gretzky	20	894	1,963	2,857
2	Gordie Howe	26	801	1,049	1,850
3	Mark Messier#	23	676	1,168	1,844
4	Marcel Dionne	18	731	1,040	1,771
5	Ron Francis#	22	536	1,222	1,758
6	Mario Lemieux#	15	682	1,011	1,692
7	Steve Yzerman#	20	660	1,010	1,670
8	Phil Esposito	18	717	873	1,590
9	Ray Bourque	22	410	1,169	1,579
10	Paul Coffey	21	396	1,135	1,531

* *Regular season only*

\# *Still active at start of 2002–03 season*

Wayne Gretzky holds, or jointly holds, 61 official NHL records: 40 for the regular season, 15 for Stanley Cup playoffs, and 6 in the All-Star Game. His point-scoring records include most in a career (2,857); most in a regular season (215 in 1985–86); and most in a season, including playoffs (255 in 1984–5). His final NHL point was an assist scored by Mathieu Schneider for the New York Rangers against the Pittsburgh Penguins on April 18, 1999.

TOP 10 GOAL-SCORERS IN AN NHL CAREER*

	PLAYER	SEASONS	GOALS
1	Wayne Gretzky	20	894
2	Gordie Howe	26	801
3	Marcel Dionne	18	731
4	Phil Esposito	18	717
5	Brett Hull#	18	716
6	Mike Gartner	19	708
7	Mario Lemieux#	15	682
8	Mark Messier#	24	676
9	Steve Yzerman#	20	660
10	Luc Robitaille#	17	631

* *Regular season only*

\# *Still active at end of 2002–03 season*

Source: *National Hockey League*

The first of Wayne Gretzky's 894 goals was against the Vancouver Canucks on October 14, 1979, while his last was against the New York Islanders on March 29, 1999.

TOP 10 BIGGEST NHL ARENAS

	ARENA	HOME TEAM	CAPACITY
1	**Molson Centre,** Montreal, QC	Montreal Canadiens	21,273
2	**United Center,** Chicago, IL	Chicago Blackhawks	20,500
3	**Ice Palace,** Tampa Bay, FL	Detroit Red Wings	19,758
4	**First Union Center,** Philadelphia, PA	Philadelphia Flyers	19,523
5	**National Car Rental Center,** Sunrise, FL	Florida Panthers	19,250
6	**Continental Airlines Arena,** East Rutherford, NJ	New Jersey Devils	19,040
7	**SAVVIS Center,** St. Louis, MO	St. Louis Blues	19,022
8	**Air Canada Centre,** Toronto, ON	Toronto Maple Leafs	18,819
9	**Raleigh Entertainment and Sports Arena,** Raleigh, NC	Carolina Hurricanes	18,730
10	**MCI Center,** Washington, DC	Washington Capitals	18,672

Source: NHL Official Guide & Record Book 2002

TOP 10 GOALIES WITH THE BEST SAVE PERCENTAGES IN THE NHL, 2002–03*

	PLAYER	TEAM	GAMES PLAYED	TOTAL SAVES	SAVES (%)
1	**Marty Turco**	Dallas Stars	55	1,267	0.932
2	**Sean Burke**	Phoenix Coyotes	22	588	0.930
3	**Martin Gerber**	Might Ducks of Anaheim	22	509	0.929
4	**Dwayne Roloson**	Minnesota Wild	50	1,236	0.927
5	= **Manny Legace**	Detroit Red Wings	25	630	0.925
	= **Roman Cechmanek**	Philadelphia Flyers	58	1,266	0.925
7	**Emmanuel Fernandez**	Minnesota Wild	50	898	0.924
8	**Ed Belfour**	Toronto Maple Leafs	62	1,675	0.922
9	= **J. Giguere**	Mighty Ducks of Anaheim	65	1,675	0.920
	= **Patrick Roy**	Columbus Blue Jackets	63	1,586	0.920

* *Minimum qualification 20 games; regular season only*

Source: *National Hockey League*

Born in Sault Ste. Marie, Ontario, on August 13, 1975, Marty Turco enjoyed a highly successful amateur career before turning professional. He holds the record for posting the most wins in National Collegiate Athletic Association (NCAA) history with a 127–28–7 record (.806 winning percentage) for the Michigan Wolverines.

TOP 10 GOAL-SCORERS IN THE NHL, 2002–03*

	PLAYER/TEAM	GOALS
1	**Milan Hejduk,** Columbus Blue Jackets	50
2	**Markus Naslund,** Vancouver Canucks	48
3	**Todd Bertuzzi,** Vancouver Canucks	46
4	**Marian Hossa,** Ottawa Senators	45
5	**Glen Murray,** Boston Bruins	44
6	**Dany Heatley,** Atlanta Thrashers	41
7	**Ilya Kovalchuk,** Atlanta Thrashers	38
8	= **Brett Hull,** Detroit Red Wings	37
	= **Alex Kovalev,** New York Rangers	37
	= **Zigmund Palffy,** Los Angeles Kings	37
	= **Mats Sundin,** Toronto Maple Leafs	37

* *Regular season only*

Source: *National Hockey League*

THE 10 LATEST STANLEY CUP WINNERS

YEAR	WINNER
2002	**Detroit Red Wings**
2001	**Colorado Avalanche**
2000	**New Jersey Devils**
1999	**Dallas Stars**
1998	**Detroit Red Wings**
1997	**Detroit Red Wings**
1996	**Colorado Avalanche**
1995	**New Jersey Devils**
1994	**New York Rangers**
1993	**Montreal Canadiens**

Source: *National Hockey League*

The Stanley Cup is named for Frederick Arthur Stanley, Governor General of Canada (1888–93), who presented a trophy to be contested by the best amateur teams in Canada.

TOP 10 TEAM SALARIES IN THE NHL, 2002–03

	TEAM	SALARY (US$)
1	**Dallas Stars**	71,685,169
2	**New York Rangers**	68,527,085
3	**Detroit Red Wings**	67,510,506
4	**St. Louis Blues**	63,217,000
5	**Colorado Avalanche**	60,470,926
6	**Toronto Maple Leafs**	54,861,600
7	**Philadelphia Flyers**	54,645,833
8	**New Jersey Devils**	52,372,626
9	**Washington Capitals**	51,402,458
10	**Montreal Canadiens**	48,647,360

Source: *National Hockey League Players Association*

The average NHL team payroll for the 2002–03 season was US$42.6 million and the average player's salary was US$1.76 million. The Dallas Stars had 12 players earning more than this figure, with an average salary of US$2.68 million each.

Racket Sports

TOP 10 TABLE TENNIS WORLD CHAMPIONSHIP GOLD MEDAL WINNERS

	COUNTRY	MEN'S	WOMEN'S	TOTAL*
1	**China**	41.5	48	89.5
2	**Hungary**	42	26	68
3	**Japan**	23.5	23.5	47
4	**Czech Republic**	17.5	10.5	28
5	**Romania**	-	17	17
6	= **England**	8	6	14
	= **Sweden**	14	-	14
8	**US**	5	5	10
9	**Austria**	3	3	6
10	**Germany**	1	4	5
	All countries	*161*	*154*	*315*

* *Includes team events, singles, doubles, and mixed; 0.5 golds were possible when doubles pairs could be of different nationalities—today, only players of the same nationality can play in pairs*

Source: *International Table Tennis Federation (ITTF)*

The first World Championships were played in London in 1926, with just nine countries taking part. There are now 140 countries affiliated with the ITTF.

MALE SQUASH PLAYERS

	PLAYER/COUNTRY	AVERAGE POINTS*
1	**Peter Nicol,** England	1,312.500
2	**Jonathon Power,** Canada	1,213.844
3	**David Palmer,** Australia	1,034.375
4	**John White,** Scotland	634.444
5	**Stewart Boswell,** Australia	624.219
6	**Thierry Lincou,** France	474.219
7	**Anthony Ricketts,** Australia	371.094
8	**Ong Beng Hee,** Malaysia	354.688
9	**Lee Beachill,** England	350.781
10	**Martin Heath,** Scotland	294.444

* *As of January 2003*

Source: *Dunlop PSA World Rankings*

The players' rankings have been decided by taking the total points they have scored and dividing it by the number of tournaments in which they have competed. Peter Nicol confirmed his preeminent position by winning the England National Squash Championship in February 2003.

TOP 10 FEMALE SQUASH PLAYERS

	PLAYER/COUNTRY	AVERAGE POINTS*
1	**Sarah Fitz-Gerald,** Australia	1,956.471
2	**Carol Owens,** New Zealand	1,745.278
3	**Natalie Pohrer,** England	1,322.905
4	**Linda Charman-Smith,** England	915.471
5	**Vanessa Atkinson,** Netherlands	876.750
6	**Tania Bailey,** England	860.342
7	**Cassie Campion,** England	848,750
8	**Rachael Grinham,** Australia	833,368
9	**Rebecca Macree,** England	565.095
10	**Fiona Geaves,** England	542.158

* *As of January 2003*

Source: *WISPA World Rankings*

Women's squash has been played at an international level since the 1920s. British players dominated the sport until Australian player Heather McKay played undefeated from 1962 to 1980. Fellow Australian Sarah Fitz-Gerald has been World Open Champion on five occasions (1996–98 and 2001–02).

TABLE TENNIS FIRSTS

FIRST FACT

"INDOOR TENNIS" WAS FIRST played in the early 1880s by British army officers in India and South Africa, using lids from cigar boxes as bats and the rounded part of champagne corks as balls. English athlete James Gibb introduced the use of celluloid balls after 1900, developing the game he called "ping pong," echoing the sound of the ball in play. This was registered in 1901 as a trade name by croquet pioneers John Jacques, and by Parker Brothers in the US. The studded rubber bat surface was invented by E. C. Goode in 1902. The Fédération Internationale de Tennis de Table (International Table Tennis Federation) was founded in 1926, and table tennis first became an Olympic sport in 1988.

TOP 10 COUNTRIES WITH THE MOST WIMBLEDON SINGLES TITLES

	COUNTRY	SINGLES TITLES WOMEN'S	SINGLES TITLES MEN'S	TOTAL
1	**US**	46	33	79
2	**UK**	36	35	71
3	**Australia**	5	20	25
4	**France**	6	7	13
5	**Germany**	8	4	12
6	**Sweden**	-	7	7
7	**Czechoslovakia/ Czech Republic**	3	2	5
8	**New Zealand**	-	4	4
9	**Brazil**	3	-	3
10	**Spain**	1	1	2

Men's singles championships have been held since 1877, and women's since 1884, with breaks during both world wars.

TOP 10 FEMALE TENNIS PLAYERS*

	PLAYER/COUNTRY	WEEKS AT NO. 1
1	**Steffi Graf,** Germany	377
2	**Martina Navratilova,** Czechoslovakia/US	331
3	**Chris Evert,** US	262
4	**Martina Hingis,** Switzerland	209
5	**Monica Seles,** Yugoslavia/US	178
6	**Lindsay Davenport,** US	38
7	**Serena Williams,** US	32
8	**Tracy Austin,** US	22
9	**Jennifer Capriati,** US	17
10	**Arantxa Sanchez-Vicario,** Spain	12

* *Based on weeks at No. 1 in WTA rankings (1973 to 13 January 2003)*

As well as the most weeks in total, Steffi Graf achieved the longest unbroken run at No. 1, with 186 weeks (August 17, 1987, to March 10, 1991). Venus Williams, ranked No. 1 for 11 weeks, is just outside the Top 10.

TOP 10 MALE TENNIS PLAYERS*

	PLAYER/COUNTRY	WEEKS AT NO. 1
1	**Pete Sampras,** US	286
2	**Ivan Lendl,** Czechoslovakia/US	270
3	**Jimmy Connors,** US	268
4	**John McEnroe,** US	170
5	**Björn Borg,** Sweden	109
6	**Andre Agassi,** US	87
7	**Stefan Edberg,** Sweden	72
8	**Lleyton Hewitt,** Australia	65
9	**Jim Courier,** US	58
10	**Gustavo Kuerton,** Brazil	43

* *Based on weeks at No. 1 in ATP rankings (1973 to 13 January 2003)*

Jimmy Connors had the longest unbroken run at No. 1, with a total of 160 weeks, from July 29, 1974 to August 22, 1977. Pete Sampras's longest run was 102 weeks, from April 14, 1996 to March 29, 1998.

For Pete's Sake
Pete Sampras holds more Grand Slam singles titles than any other man in the history of the sport.

Golfing Greats

▶ **Iron Man**
Foremost money winner and youngest-ever winner of the US Masters, Tiger Woods has taken golf by storm since turning pro in 1996.

TOP 10 PLAYERS TO WIN THE MOST MAJORS IN A CAREER

	PLAYER*	TOTAL#
1	**Jack Nicklaus**	18
2	**Walter Hagen**	11
3	= **Ben Hogan**	9
	= **Gary Player,** South Africa	9
5	= **Tom Watson**	8
	= **Tiger Woods**	8
7	= **Bobby Jones**	7
	= **Arnold Palmer**	7
	= **Gene Sarazen**	7
	= **Sam Snead**	7
	= **Harry Vardon,** UK	7

* *All US unless otherwise indicated*

\# *To the end of 2002 season*

The four Majors are the British Open, US Open, US Masters, and US PGA. Of these, the oldest is the British Open, first played in Prestwick, Scotland, in 1860 and won by Willie Park. The first US Open was at the Newport Club, Rhode Island, held in 1895 and won by Horace Rawlins, playing on his home course.

TOP 10 MONEY-WINNING GOLFERS, 2002

	GOLFER*	CAREER WINNINGS (US$)#
1	**Tiger Woods**	35,944,852
2	**Phil Mickelson**	22,709,944
3	**Davis Love III**	21,663,495
4	**Vijay Singh,** Fiji	19,353,024
5	**Ernie Els,** South Africa	17,168,329
6	**Scott Hoch**	17,137,297
7	**Nick Price,** Zimbabwe	17,086,904
8	**David Duval**	16,195,473
9	**Jim Furyk**	15,068,084
10	**Justin Leonard**	14,853,334

* *All US unless otherwise indicated*

\# *As at March 16, 2003*

TOP 10 WINNERS OF WOMEN'S MAJORS

	WINNER*	TOTAL#
1	Patty Berg	16
2	= Louise Suggs	13
	= Mickey Wright	13
4	Babe Zaharias	12
5	Julie Inkster	10
6	Betsy Rawls	8
7	JoAnne Carner	7
8	= Pat Bradley	6
	= Glenna Collett Vare	6
	= Betsy King	6
	= Patty Sheehan	6
	= Karrie Webb	6
	= Kathy Whitworth	6

* *All US* # *To end of 2002 season*

The present-day Majors are the US Open, LPGA Championship, Nabisco Championship, British Open, and the amateur championships of both the US and the UK. Also taken into account in this Top 10 are wins in the former Majors: the Western Open (1937–67), Titleholders Championship (1930–72), and the du Maurier Classic (1977–2000).

THE 10 LATEST WINNERS OF THE MASTERS TOURNAMENT

YEAR	WINNER/COUNTRY	SCORE
2003	**Mike Weir,** Canada	281
2002	**Tiger Woods,** US	276
2001	**Tiger Woods,** US	272
2000	**Vijay Singh,** Fiji	278
1999	**José Maria Olazabal,** Spain	280
1998	**Mark O'Meara,** US	279
1997	**Tiger Woods,** US	270
1996	**Nick Faldo,** UK	276
1995	**Ben Crenshaw,** US	274
1994	**José Maria Olazabal,** Spain	279

On April 13, 2003, Mike Weir became the first Canadian to win the Masters, and the only Canadian man to win a major golf championship. The left-hander is from Bright's Grove, Ontario, near Sarnia.

◄ **Julie Inkster**
Julie Inkster is only the second woman to win all four women's gold Grand Slam tournaments.

THE 10 LATEST WINNERS OF THE CPGA WOMEN'S CHAMPIONSHIP

YEAR	WINNER	SCORE*
2002	Liz Earley	-4
2001	Lorie Kane	-13
2000	Nancy Harvey	-7
1999	Lorie Kane	-10
1998	Lorie Kane	-5
1997	Lorie Kane	-3
1996	Lorie Kane	-2
1995	Nancy Harvey	even
1994	Nancy Harvey	-3
1993	Lanie Cahill	4

* *Based on number of strokes over or under par total for two rounds of the course on date tournament was played*

Source: *Canadian Professional Golfer's Association*

THE 10 LATEST WINNERS OF THE CPGA MEN'S CHAMPIONSHIP

YEAR	WINNER	SCORE*
2002	Arron Oberholser	268
2001	Richard Zokol	271
2000	Chad Wright	268
1999	Scott Petersen	203
1998	Tim Clark	272
1997	Guy Hill	276
1996	Ashley Chinner	205
1995	Trevor Dodds	276
1994	Stuart Hendley	275
1993	Steve Stricker	274

* *Total number of strokes for each player recorded from the tournament, which is comprised of four rounds*

Source: *Canadian Professional Golfer's Association*

THE FIRST GRAND SLAM

FIRST FACT

In 1930, Bobby (Robert Tyre) Jones (1902–71) won the Open and Amateur tournaments in both his native US and the UK, thereby completing the first ever golfing "Grand Slam," previously dismissed as the "impregnable quadrilateral." Jones—who never relinquished his amateur status—remains the only golfer ever to achieve this feat. Considered the greatest player in the history of the game, he was the co-founder of the Augusta National Golf Club and the originator of the US Masters tournament, which has been played there for 70 years.

Water Sports

TOP 10 OLYMPIC ROWING COUNTRIES

	COUNTRY	GOLD	SILVER	BRONZE	TOTAL
1	US	29	29	21	79
2 =	East Germany	33	7	8	48
=	Germany*	21	13	14	48
4	UK	21	16	7	44
5	Soviet Union#	12	20	11	43
6	Italy	14	13	10	37
7 =	Canada	8	12	13	33
=	France	6	14	13	33
9	Romania	15	10	7	32
10	Australia	7	8	10	25

* *Not including West/East Germany 1968–88*

\# *Includes Unified Team of 1992; excludes Russia since then*

Olympic rowing dates from 1900 for men, but as recently as 1976 for women. The total includes several discontinued events. Canada's Marnie McBean and Kathleen Heddle won three gold medals in double sculls at the 1996 Summer Games, and in coxless pairs and eights at the 1992 Games.

TOP 10 OLYMPIC CANOEING COUNTRIES

	COUNTRY	GOLD	SILVER	BRONZE	TOTAL
1	Hungary	14	25	21	60
2 =	Germany*	22	16	15	53
=	Soviet Union#	30	14	9	53
4	Romania	10	10	14	34
5	East Germany	14	7	9	30
6	Sweden	14	11	4	29
7	France	3	7	16	26
8	Bulgaria	4	5	8	17
9	Canada	3	8	5	16
10 =	Poland	0	5	10	15
=	US	5	4	6	15

* *Not including West/East Germany 1968–88*

\# *Includes Unified Team of 1992; excludes Russia since then*

Canoeing has been an official Olympic sport since 1936, although it was first seen as a demonstration sport at the 1924 Paris Olympics.

TOP 10 MEN'S 100M FREESTYLE TIMES IN CANADA

	SWIMMER/AGE	YEAR	TIME SECS
1	**Brent Hayden,** 18	2002	49.53
2	**Yannick Lupien,** 22	2002	49.90
3	**Stephen Clarke,** 24	1997	50.06
4	**Craig Hutchison,** 25	2000	50.07
5	**Michael Mintenko,** 27	2002	50.41
6	**Sandy Goss,** 22	1989	50.45
7	**Rick Say,** 22	2002	50.52
8	**Riley Janes,** 22	2002	50.63
9	**Marcel Gery,** 23	1988	50.68
10	**Steven VanderMeulen,** 21	1990	50.69

* *Of all time, men, 50-m pool*

Source: SwimNews

ACROSS THE CHANNEL

FIRST FACT

ALTHOUGH CHANNEL crossings had previously been made using flotation aids, the first swimmer to do so unaided was a British sailor, Captain Matthew Webb (1848–83), on August 24–25, 1875. Sustained by beef tea, beer, coffee, and an omelette, and despite being stung by a starfish, he landed at Calais after 21 hours, 44 minutes, and 55 seconds in the water. It was not until September 6, 1911, that Thomas William Burgess (UK) became the second man to swim the English Channel. The first woman to make the crossing was Gertrude Ederle (US), on August 6, 1926, and in 1934, Edward Temme (UK) became the first person to swim the Channel in both directions.

TOP 10 FASTEST CROSS-CHANNEL SWIMMERS

	SWIMMER/NATIONALITY	YEAR	TIME HR:MIN
1	**Chad Hundeby,** US	1994	7:17
2	**Penny Lee Dean,** US	1978	7:40
3	**Tamara Bruce,** Australia	1994	7:53
4	**Philip Rush,** New Zealand	1987	7:55
5	**Hans Van Goor,** Netherlands	1995	8:02
6	**Richard Davey,** UK	1988	8:05
7	**Irene van der Laan,** Netherlands	1982	8:06
8 =	**Paul Asmuth,** US	1985	8:12
=	**Gail Rice,** US	1999	8:12
10	**Anita Sood,** India	1987	8:15

Source: *Channel Swimming Association*

An earlier record, of 9 hours 36 minutes, was set in 1973 by Lynne Cox (US), aged 16—the youngest permitted age for solo swimmers—while the current female record has been held since 1978 by another American, Penny Dean, who was aged 23 at the time of her crossing.

TOP 10 MEN'S OLYMPIC 100M FREESTYLE TIMES

	SWIMMER/NATIONALITY	YEAR	TIME SECS
1	**Pieter van den Hoogenband,** Netherlands	2000	47.84
2	**Pieter van den Hoogenband**	2000	48.30
3	**Matt Biondi,** US	1988	48.63
4	**Pieter van den Hoogenband**	2000	48.64
5	**Alexander Popov,** Russia	2000	48.69
6	**Gary Hall Jr.,** US	2000	48.73
7 =	**Alexander Popov**	1996	48.74
=	**Michael Klim,** US	2000	48.74
9	**Michael Klim**	2000	48.80
10	**Gary Hall Jr.**	1996	48.81

Gary Hall Jr. is a member of a family of swimmers: his grandfather, Charles Keating, was an All-America swimmer at the University of Cincinnati; his uncle a member of the 1976 US Olympics team; while his father, Gary Hall Sr., won silver medals at the 1968 and 1972 Olympics, and a bronze in 1976.

TOP 10 WATERSKIERS WITH THE MOST WORLD CUP WINS

	SKIER/NATIONALITY	M/F*	SLALOM	JUMP	TOTAL
1	**Andy Mapple,** UK	M	29	-	29
2	**Emma Sheers,** Australia	F	2	15	17
3	**Jaret Llewellyn,** Canada	M	-	16	16
4	**Toni Neville,** Australia	F	4	7	11
5	**Wade Cox,** US	M	10	-	10
6 =	**Bruce Neville,** Australia	M	-	9	9
=	**Kristi Overton-Johnson (née Overton),** US	F	9	-	9
8	**Freddy Krueger,** US	M	-	8	8
9	**Scot Ellis,** US	M	-	7	7
10 =	**Susi Graham,** Canada	F	6	-	6
=	**Carl Roberge,** US	M	1	5	6

* *Male/female*

Waterskiing was invented in 1922 by 18-year-old Ralph W. Samuelson of Lake City, Minnesota, using two 2.4-m (8-ft) planks and 30 m (100 ft) of sash cord. The first international governing body, the World Water Ski Union, was established in 1946 in Geneva, Switzerland.

THE 10 LATEST WINNERS OF THE AMERICA'S CUP

	WINNING BOAT/SKIPPER/COUNTRY	DEFENDER/COUNTRY	SCORE
2003	**Alinghi,** Russell Coutts, Switzerland	Team New Zealand, New Zealand	5-0
2000	**Team New Zealand,** Russell Coutts, New Zealand	Prada-Luna Rossa, Italy	5-0
1995	**Black Magic,** Russell Coutts, New Zealand	Young America, US	5-0
1992	**America3,** Bill Koch, US	Il Moro di Venezia, Italy	4-1
1988	**Stars and Stripes,** Dennis Conner, US	KZ1, New Zealand	2-0
1987	**Stars and Stripes,** Dennis Conner, US	Kookaburra III, Australia	4-0
1983	**Australia II,** John Bertrand, Australia	Liberty, US	4-3
1980	**Freedom,** Dennis Conner, US	Australia, Australia	4-1
1977	**Courageous,** Ted Turner, US	Australia, Australia	4-0
1974	**Courageous,** Ted Hood, US	Southern Cross, Australia	4-0

One of the costliest and most prestigious of all sporting events, the America's Cup is also historically among the most one-sided, with the New York Yacht Club competitor winning every event from 1851 to 1983.

America's Cup winners
Team New Zealand crosses the finish line off its home country to take the 2000 America's Cup.

Tough Guys

THE 10 LATEST WINNERS OF THE WORLD'S STRONGEST MAN

CONTEST	STRONGMAN/COUNTRY
2002	**Mariusz Pudzianowski,** Poland
2001	**Svend Karlsen,** Norway
2000	**Janne Virtanen,** Finland
1999	**Jouko Ahola,** Finland
1998	**Magnus Samuelsson,** Sweden
1997	**Jouko Ahola,** Finland
1996	**Magnus Ver Magnusson,** Iceland
1995	**Magnus Ver Magnusson,** Iceland
1994	**Magnus Ver Magnusson,** Iceland
1993	**Gary Taylor,** UK

Source: *StrongestMan.com*

Polish Performance
Poland's Mariusz Pudzianowski is the latest winner of a grueling contest that involves such feats as lifting cars and pulling trucks.

TOP 10 OLYMPIC FREESTYLE WRESTLING COUNTRIES

		MEDALS			
	COUNTRY	GOLD	SILVER	BRONZE	TOTAL
1	**US**	44	35	24	103
2	**Soviet Union***	31	17	15	63
3	= **Bulgaria**	7	17	9	33
	= **Japan**	16	9	8	33
	= **Turkey**	16	11	6	33
6	= **Iran**	5	9	12	26
	= **Sweden**	8	10	8	26
8	**Finland**	8	7	10	25
9	**Korea**	4	7	8	19
10	**UK**	3	4	10	17
	Canada	*1*	*5*	*5*	*11*

* *Includes Unified Team of 1992; excludes Russia since then*

Daniel Igali, a native of Nigeria but presently living in British Columbia, won a gold medal at the Sydney 2000 Summer Games, Canada's first in freestyle wrestling.

THE 10 LATEST UNDISPUTED WORLD HEAVYWEIGHT BOXING CHAMPIONS

	FIGHTER*	YEAR
1	**Lennox Lewis,** UK	1999
2	**Riddick Bowe**	1992
3	**Evander Holyfield**	1990
4	**James Buster Douglas**	1990
5	**Mike Tyson**	1987
6	**Leon Spinks**	1978
7	**Muhammad Ali**	1974
8	**George Foreman**	1973
9	**Joe Frazier**	1970
10	**Muhammad Ali**	1967

* *From the US unless otherwise stated*

"Undisputed" champions are those recognized by the main governing bodies (World Boxing Council, World Boxing Association, International Boxing Federation, and World Boxing Organization) at the time of winning their world title. Champions not recognized by all major bodies may coexist with these, so there may be more than one "world champion" in each weight division.

TOP 10 MEDAL-WINNING WEIGHTLIFTERS (WOMEN)

	SENIOR WORLD WEIGHTLIFTER/COUNTRY	CHAMPIONSHIP MEDALS
1	**Maria Takacs,** Hungary	12
2	= **Shu-Chih Chen,** Taipei	8
	= **Milena Tredafilova,** Bulgaria	8
	= **Maria Isabel Urrutia,** Colombia	8*
5	= **Robin Goad-Byrd,** US	7
	= **Nameirakpam Kunjarani,** Indonesia	7
7	= **Maria Christoforidou,** Greece	6
	= **Izabela Dragneva-Rifatova,** Bulgaria	6
9	= **Jui-Lien Chen,** Taipei	5
	= **Nan-Mei Chu,** Taipei	5
	= **Hongyun Li,** China	5
	= **Erika Takacs,** Hungary	5

* *Also won a gold medal in the Olympic Games*

Source: *International Weightlifting Federation*

TOP 10 OLYMPIC JUDO COUNTRIES

	COUNTRY	GOLD	MEDALS SILVER	BRONZE	TOTAL
1	**Japan**	23	12	13	48
2	**France**	10	5	17	32
3	**Korea**	7	10	13	30
4	**Soviet Union***	7	5	15	27
5	**Cuba**	5	7	8	20
6	**UK**	–	7	9	16
7	**Netherlands**	4	–	7	11
8	= **Brazil**	2	3	5	10
	= **China**	4	1	5	10
	= **Germany**#	1	1	8	10
	= **Italy**	2	3	5	10
	Canada	–	2	2	4

* *Includes Unified Team of 1992; excludes Russia since then*

\# *Not including West/East Germany 1968–88*

Judo made its debut, for male competitors only, at the 1964 Tokyo Olympics but then was not included at the next Games in 1968 in Mexico City. It reappeared in 1972, while women's judo was not introduced until the 1992 Barcelona Games.

TOP 10 MEDAL-WINNING WEIGHTLIFTERS (MEN)

	WEIGHTLIFTER/COUNTRY	MEDALS WON, 1891–2001 OLYMPICS	SWC*	TOTAL
1	**Imre Földi,** Hungary	3	10	13
2	= **Waldemar Baszanowski,** Poland	2	10	12
	= **Seresht Mohammad Nasiri,** Iran	3	9	12
4	= **Tamio Kono,** US	3	8	11
	= **Norbert Schemansky,** US	4	7	11
	= **Naim Süleymanoglu,** Turkey	3	8	11
	= **Arkadi Vorobiev,** USSR	3	8	11
	= **Marian Zielinski,** Poland	3	8	11
9	= **Vasili Alexeev,** USSR	2	8	10
	= **Yoshinobu Miyake,** Japan	3	7	10
	= **Nicu Vlad,** Romania	3	7	10

* *SWC = Senior World Championships*

Source: *International Weightlifting Federation*

Hawaii Ironman

The Hawaii Ironman triathlon was first undertaken in 1978 at Waikiki Beach, but since 1981 has been held at Kailua-Kona.

TOP 10 FASTEST WINNING TIMES FOR THE HAWAII IRONMAN

	WINNER/COUNTRY	YEAR	TIME HR:MIN:SEC
1	**Luc Van Lierde,** Belgium	1996	8:04:08
2	**Mark Allen,** US	1993	8:07:45
3	**Mark Allen**	1992	8:09:08
4	**Mark Allen**	1989	8:09:16
5	**Luc Van Lierde**	1999	8:17:17
6	**Mark Allen**	1991	8:18:32
7	**Greg Welch,** Australia	1994	8:20:27
8	**Mark Allen**	1995	8:20:34
9	**Peter Reid,** Canada	2000	8:21:01
10	**Peter Reid**	1998	8:24:20

Perhaps one of the most grueling of all contests, in which competitors engage in a 3.86-km/2.4-mile swim, followed by a 180-km/112-mile cycle race, and finish with a full marathon (42.20 km/26 miles, 385 yards).

Horsing Around

TOP 10 HORSE-RACE BETTING COUNTRIES

	COUNTRY	VALUE (US$)*
1	Japan	35,400,000,000
2	US	17,300,000,000
3	China#	10,610,000,000
4	UK	8,000,000,000
5	Australia	5,800,000,000
6	France	5,700,000,000
7	South Korea	3,400,000,000
8	Italy	2,200,000,000
9	Malaysia	1,400,000,000
10	Canada	1,200,000,000

* *Value of indigenous betting*

\# *Including Hong Kong*

◄ Horse Power
With over 30,000 races held annually in Canada, and more than 120,000 employees involved, the horse industry is estimated to contribute and estimated $3 billion a year to this country's economy.

TOP 10 WOODBINE JOCKEY STANDINGS, 2002

	JOCKEY	WINS	EARNINGS ($)
1	Patrick Husbands	167	9,222,378
2	Todd Kabel	130	8,522,672
3	Emile Ramsammy	122	7,088,188
4	Chantal Sutherland	124	5,751,417
5	Jim McAleney	106	5,747,948
6	Constant Montpellier	98	5,194,901
7	David Clark	69	3,820,339
8	Raymond Sabourin	63	3,520,498
9	Dino Luciani	66	3,440,378
10	Slade Callaghan	54	3,435,971

Source: *Woodbine Entertainment Thoroughbreds*

TOP 10 US JOCKEYS WITH MOST CAREER WINS

	JOCKEY	YEARS RIDING	WINS*
1	**Laffit Pincay Jr.**	39	9,471
2	**Willie Shoemaker**	42	8,833
3	**Pat Day**	30	8,389
4	**Russell Baze**	29	8,075
5	**David Gall**	43	7,396
6	**Chris McCarron**	28	7,339
7	**Angel Cordero Jr.**	35	7,057
8	**Jorge Velasquez**	33	6,795
9	**Sandy Hawley**	31	6,449
10	**Larry Snyder**	35	6,388

* *As of the end of the 2002 season*

Source: *NTRA Communications*

Having broken Bill Shoemaker's record tally on *Irish Nip* at Hollywood Park on December 10, 1999, Panama-born Laffit Pincay Jr. went on to become the only jockey ever to hit a career wins total of 9,000, which he achieved riding *Chicim* at Santa Anita on October 28, 2000.

TOP 10 FASTEST WINNING TIMES OF THE KENTUCKY DERBY

	HORSE	YEAR	TIME MIN:SEC
1	**Secretariat**	1973	1:59.2
2	**Monarchos**	2001	1:59.4
3	**Northern Dancer**	1964	2:00.0
4	**Spend A Buck**	1985	2:00.2
5	**Decidedly**	1962	2:00.4
6	**Proud Clarion**	1967	2:00.6
7	**Grindstone**	1996	2:01.0
8	= **Affirmed**	1978	2:01.2
	= **Fusaichi Pegasus**	2000	2:01.2
	= **Lucky Debonair**	1965	2:01.2
	= **Thunder Gulch**	1995	2:01.2

Source: *The Jockey Club*

The Kentucky Derby is held on the first Saturday in May at Churchill Downs, Louisville, Kentucky. The first leg of the Triple Crown, it was first raced in 1875 over a distance of 1 mile 4 furlongs (2km 415m), but after 1896 was reduced to 1 mile 2 furlongs (2km 12 m).

THE 10 LATEST TRIPLE CROWN WINNING HORSES

	HORSE*	YEAR
1	**Affirmed**	1978
2	**Seattle Slew**	1977
3	**Secretariat**	1973
4	**Citation**	1948
5	**Assault**	1946
6	**Count Fleet**	1943
7	**Whirlaway**	1941
8	**War Admiral**	1937
9	**Omaha**	1935
10	**Gallant Fox**	1930

* *Horses that have won the Kentucky Derby, the Preakness, and Belmont Stakes in the same season*

Since 1875, only 11 horses have won all three races in one season.

THE 10 LATEST HORSES TO WIN THE QUEEN'S PLATE*

YEAR	HORSE	JOCKEY	TIME MIN:SEC#
2002	**T J's Lucky Moon**	Steve Bahen	2:06.9
2001	**Dancethruthedawn**	Gary Boulanger	2:03.8
2000	**Scatter the Gold**	Todd Kabel	2:05.2
1999	**Woodcarver**	Mickey Walls	2:03.0
1998	**Archers Bay**	Kent Desormeaux	2:02.1
1997	**Awesome Again**	A.E. Smith	2:04.1
1996	**Victor Cooley**	Emile Ramsammy	2:03.4
1995	**Regal Discovery**	Todd Kabel	2:03.4
1994	**Basqueian**	Jack Laron	2:03.2
1993	**Peteski**	Craig Perret	2:04.1

* *Held at Toronto's Woodbine Racetrack*

\# *Fractions of a second are in fifths*

Source: *Woodbine Entertainment Thoroughbreds*

TOP 10 OLYMPIC EQUESTRIAN COUNTRIES

		MEDALS			
	COUNTRY	GOLD	SILVER	BRONZE	TOTAL
1	**Germany***	22	13	12	47
2	**US**	9	17	15	41
3	**Sweden**	17	8	14	39
4	**France**	11	12	11	34
5	**West Germany**	11	5	9	25
6	**Italy**	6	10	7	23
7	**Great Britain**	5	8	9	22
8	**Switzerland**	4	10	7	21
9	**Netherlands**	8	9	2	19
10	**Soviet Union#**	6	5	4	15

* *Not including West Germany or East Germany 1968–88*

\# *Includes Unified Team of 1992; excludes Russia since then*

These figures include the medal totals for both individual and team disciplines: Show Jumping, Three-Day Event, and Dressage. German rider Reiner Klimke won eight medals—six gold and two bronze—in Olympic events during the period 1964–88.

On Two Wheels

TOP 10 MOTOCROSS COUNTRIES

	COUNTRY	WORLD CHAMPIONSHIP WINS* 125CC	250CC	500CC	TOTAL
1	**Belgium**	9	13	22	44
2	**Sweden**	0	6	8	14
3	**France**	3	5	0	8
4	= **Italy**	5	1	1	7
	= **UK**	0	1	6	7
	= **US**	3	3	1	7
7	**Finland**	1	1	3	5
8	= **Netherlands**	3	1	0	4
	= **Russia**	0	4	0	4
	= **South Africa**	2	2	0	4

* *To the end of 2002 season*

World Moto Cross Championships have been held since 1947 when the five-man Moto Cross des Nations team championship was launched.

TOP 10 FASTEST AVERAGE WINNING SPEEDS IN THE TOUR DE FRANCE

	WINNER/COUNTRY	YEAR	AVERAGE SPEED MPH	KM/H
1	**Lance Armstrong,** US	1999	25.026	40.276
2	**Lance Armstrong,** US	2001	24.898	40.070
3	**Marco Pantani,** Italy	1998	24.844	39.983
4	**Lance Armstrong,** US	2002	24.804	39.919
5	**Lance Armstrong,** US	2000	24.587	39.570
6	**Miguel Indurain,** Spain	1992	24.546	39.504
7	**Jan Ullrich,** Germany	1997	24.380	39.237
8	**Bjarne Rijs,** Denmark	1996	24.374	39.227
9	**Miguel Indurain,** Spain	1995	24.353	39.193
10	**Bernard Hinault,** France	1981	24.208	38.960

Staged since 1903, the Tour de France did not record a winning speed exceeding 30 km/h (18.6 mph) until 1935.

TOP 10 DOWNHILL RIDERS IN THE UCI MOUNTAIN BIKE WORLD CUP, 2002 (WOMEN)

	RIDER/COUNTRY	POINTS*
1	**Anne Caroline Chausson,** France	1,143
2	**Fionn Griffiths,** UK	1,043
3	**Sabrina Jonnier,** France	1,010
4	**Tracy Moseley,** UK	1,000
5	**Marielle Saner,** Switzerland	960
6	**Celine Gros,** France	801
7	**Vanessa Quin,** New Zealand	779
8	**Kathy Pruitt,** US	696
9	**Nolvenn Le Caer,** France	685
10	**Helen Gaskell,** UK	637

* *Total points scored over a series of eight competitions*

Source: Union Cycliste Internationale (International Cycling Union)

TOP 10 DOWNHILL RIDERS IN THE UCI MOUNTAIN BIKE WORLD CUP, 2002 (MEN)

	RIDER/COUNTRY	POINTS*
1	**Steve Peat,** UK	1,134
2	**Christopher Kovarik,** Australia	1,015
3	**Cedric Gracia,** France	903
4	**Mickael Pascal,** France	799
5	= **Oscar Saiz,** Spain	775
	= **Nicolas Vouilloz,** France	775
7	**Fabien Barel,** France	770
8	**Mick Hannah,** Australia	705
9	**David Vazquez Lopez,** Spain	687
10	**Nathan Rennie,** Australia	635

* *Total points scored over a series of eight competitions*

Source: Union Cycliste Internationale (International Cycling Union)

Riding High

Lance Armstrong's 1999 Tour de France win, the first by an American since Greg LeMond in 1990, set an unbeaten record speed.

TOP 10 FASTEST WINNING SPEEDS OF THE DAYTONA 200

	RIDER*/BIKE	YEAR	AVERAGE SPEED MPH	KM/H
1	**Miguel Duhamel,** Canada, Honda	2003	113.83	183.20
2	**Mat Mladin,** Australia, Suzuki	2000	113.63	182.87
3	**Miguel Duhamel,** Canada, Honda	1999	113.47	182.61
4	**Kenny Roberts,** Yamaha	1984	113.14	182.08
5	**Scott Russell,** Yamaha	1998	111.78	179.89
6	**Kenny Roberts,** Yamaha	1983	110.93	178.52
7	**Scott Russell,** Kawasaki	1992	110.67	178.11
8	**Graeme Crosby,** New Zealand, Yamaha	1982	109.10	175.58
9	**Steve Baker,** Yamaha	1977	108.85	175.18
10	**Miguel Duhamel,** Canada, Honda	1996	108.82	175.13

* *From the US unless otherwise stated*

THE FIRST DAYTONA 200

FIRST FACT

THE BEACH IN DAYTONA, Florida, has long been the venue for speed record attempts and races. It was there on January 24, 1937, that the first ever Daytona 200 event—known in its early years as the "Handlebar Derby"—took place, with 120 entries. It was won by Californian Ed Kretz on an Indian motorcycle at an average speed of 118 km/h (73.34 mph). The original race combined 2.4 km (1.5 miles) of public roads and 2.4 km (1.5 miles) of beach and was carefully timed so that riders did not have to contend with the incoming tide.

TOP 10 MANUFACTURERS WITH THE MOST MOTORCYCLE GRAND PRIX WINS

	MANUFACTURER	FIRST WIN	WINS
1	**Honda**	1961	536
2	**Yamaha**	1963	401
3	**MV Agusta**	1952	275
4	**Suzuki**	1962	153
5	**Aprilia**	1987	140
6	**Kawasaki**	1969	85
7	**Derbi**	1970	81
8	**Kreidler**	1962	65
9	**Garelli**	1982	51
10	**Gilera**	1949	47

* *To the end of 2002 season*

Japanese manufacturer Yamaha was originally a musical instrument maker (hence the crossed tuning fork trademark); it did not make its first motorcycle—a single-cylinder, 125cc two-stroke—until 1954. Yamaha made its first racing bike in 1961 and had its first Grand Prix win in 1963 in Spa, Belgium, when Fumio Ito of Japan won in the 250cc class.

TOP 10 RIDERS WITH THE MOST GRAND PRIX RACE WINS

	RIDER/COUNTRY	YEARS	RACE WINS*
1	**Giacomo Agostini,** Italy	1965–76	122
2	**Angel Nieto,** Spain	1969–85	90
3	**Mike Hailwood,** UK	1959–67	76
4	**Rolf Biland,** Switzerland	1975–90	56
5	**Mick Doohan,** Australia	1990–98	54
6	**Phil Read,** UK	1961–75	52
7	**Valentino Rossi,** Italy	1996–2002	50
8	**Jim Redman,** Southern Rhodesia	1961–66	45
9	**Anton Mang,** West Germany	1976–88	42
10	**Carlo Ubbiali,** Italy	1950–60	39

* *To the end of 2002 season*

All except Biland were solo machine riders. Britain's Barry Sheene won 23 races during his career and is the only person to win Grand Prix races at 50 and 500cc.

Wheels of Fortune
Italian motorcycle maestro Giacomo Agostini won both the first and last of his record 122 Grand Prix races at Nürburgring, Germany.

Auto Racing

TOP 10 CART MONEY WINNERS

	DRIVER/COUNTRY	TOTAL PRIZES (US$)*
1	**Al Unser Jr.**, US	18,828,406
2	**Michael Andretti**#, US	17,928,118
3	**Bobby Rahal**, US	16,344,008
4	**Emerson Fittipaldi**, Brazil	14,293,625
5	**Mario Andretti**, US	11,552,154
6	**Rick Mears**, US	11,050,807
7	**Jimmy Vasser**#, US	10,627,244
8	**Danny Sullivan**, US	8,884,126
9	**Paul Tracy**#, Canada	8,825,270
10	**Arie Luyendyk**, Netherlands	7,732,188

* *As of January 1, 2003*

\# *Still active at end 2002 season*

Source: *Championship Auto Racing Teams*

CART Success
Michael Andretti, one of the most successful CART riders of all time, races toward the finish at the Milwaukee Mile in 1999.

TOP 10 CONSTRUCTORS WITH THE MOST FORMULA ONE GRAND PRIX WINS*

	CONSTRUCTOR/COUNTRY	YEARS	WINS
1	**Ferrari**, Italy	1951–2002	169
2	**McLaren**, UK	1968–2002	135
3	**Williams**, UK	1979–2002	105
4	**Lotus**, UK	1960–87	79
5	**Brabham**, UK	1964–85	35
6	**Benetton**, Italy	1986–97	27
7	**Tyrrell**, UK	1971–83	23
8	**BRM**, UK	1959–72	17
9	**Cooper**, UK	1958–67	16
10	**Renault**, France	1979–83	15

* *To end of 2002 season*

Having finished second in two races (the Monaco Grand Prix and the Italian Grand Prix) in the inaugural World Championship season, Ferrari eventually registered its first win in the fifth race of the 1951 season. The honor went to driver José Froilan Gonzalez of Argentina, at the British Grand Prix at Silverstone on July 14. The only race McLaren did not win in the 1988 season was the Italian Grand Prix in Monza, which was won by Austrian Gerhard Berger in a Ferrari.

THE 10 LATEST WINNING SPEEDS IN THE TORONTO MOLSON INDAY

YEAR	DRIVER/COUNTRY	CAR	SPEED MPH	SPEED KM/H
2002	**Cristiano da Matta**, Brazil	Toyota/ Lola/Bridgestone	93.361	150.246
2001	**Michael Andretti**, US	Honda Reynard H/R/F	108.445	174.521
2000	**Michael Andretti**, US	Havoline Ford Lola-Fd. Cosworth/LT/F	122.922	197.818
1999	**Dario Franchitti**, UK	Honda-RI F	110.102	177.187
1998	**Alex Zanardi**, Italy	Reynard Honda RI Honda F	105.480	169.205
1997	**Mark Blundell**, UK	Mercedes-R971 Mer. F	105.142	169.205
1996	**Adrian Fernandez**, Mexico	Lola LT96-Honda F	109.838	176.762
1995	**Michael Andretti**, US	95 Lola Ford-Cosworth XB/G	109.936	176.920
1994	**Michael Andretti**, US	94 Reynard Ford-Cosworth XB	109.027	175.457
1993	**Paul Tracy**, Canada	PC93 Chevy-V8/Cosworth	109.544	176.289

Source: *Molson Indy*

TOP 10 FASTEST WINNING SPEEDS OF THE INDIANAPOLIS 500

	DRIVER/COUNTRY	CAR	YEAR	SPEED MPH	KM/H
1	**Arie Luyendyk,** Netherlands	Lola-Chevrolet	1990	185.981	299.307
2	**Rick Mears,** US	Chevrolet-Lumina	1991	176.457	283.980
3	**Bobby Rahal,** US	March-Cosworth	1986	170.722	274.750
4	**Juan Pablo Montoya,** Colombia	G Force–Aurora	2000	167.607	269.730
5	**Emerson Fittipaldi,** Brazil	Penske-Chevrolet	1989	167.581	269.695
6	**Helio Castroneves,** Brazil	Dallara-Chevrolet	2002	166.499	267.954
7	**Rick Mears,** US	March-Cosworth	1984	163.612	263.308
8	**Mark Donohue,** US	McLaren-Offenhauser	1972	162.962	262.619
9	**Al Unser,** US	March-Cosworth	1987	162.175	260.995
10	**Tom Sneva,** US	March-Cosworth	1983	162.117	260.902

Because drivers in many US races start on the run and race around oval circuits, consistently higher average lap speeds are achieved there than on most European race circuits. Car racing in the US on specially built circuits dates back to 1909, when Indianapolis Speedway opened. CART (Championship Auto Racing Teams, Inc.) was formed in 1978, and in 1996 the Indy Racing League was established in response to disputes over regulations governing the Indy 500. Indy 500 races have counted for CART points in 1979, 1980, and 1983–95.

TOP 10 FORMULA ONE DRIVERS WITH THE MOST GRAND PRIX WINS

	DRIVER/COUNTRY	CAREER	WINS*
1	**Michael Schumacher,** Germany	1991–	64
2	**Alain Prost,** France	1980–93	51
3	**Ayrton Senna,** Brazil	1984–94	41
4	**Nigel Mansel,** UK	1980–95	31
5	**Jackie Stewart,** UK	1965–73	27
6	= **Jim Clark,** UK	1960–68	25
	= **Niki Lauda,** Austria	1971–85	25
8	**Juan Manual Fangio,** Argentina	1950–58	24
9	**Nelson Piquet,** Brazil	1978–91	23
10	**Damon Hill,** UK	1992–99	22

** As at end 2002 season*

Grand Prix racing is European in origin. From the late 19th century until the formation of Formula One after World War II, caar races had customarily taken place on public roads. This tradition is reflected in the construction of today's circuits, which incorporate chicanes and bends that test drivers' skills to the limit. The first Formula One race was held at Silverstone, England, on May 13, 1950.

"The Maestro"
King of the race track during the 1950s, Juan Manuel Fangio (1911–95) won 24 Grand Prix races and secured a record five world titles.

Sports Media

THE 10 LATEST WINNERS OF THE CANADIAN PRESS "TEAM OF THE YEAR" AWARD

YEAR	WINNER	SPORT
2002	Men's Olympic hockey team	Hockey
2001	Jamie Salé and David Pelletier	Figure skating
2000	Daniel Nestor and Sebastien Lareau	Tennis
1999	Team Canada '72*	Hockey
1998	Sandra Schmirler	Curling
1997	World junior hockey team	Hockey
1996	Canadian 4x100 relay team	Track & field
1995	Canada's world junior hockey team	Hockey
1994	Montreal Expos	Baseball
1993	Toronto Blue Jays	Baseball

* *Named "Team of the Century" as no "Team of the Year" was awarded in 1999*

Source: *Canadian Press*

Canada's men's hockey team beat the US 5–2 in the gold-medal final at the Salt Lake City Winter Olympic Games in February 2002. It was the first time since 1952 that Canada had won the gold in men's hockey. Canada's women's hockey team won the gold medal also when it defeated the US 3–2 a few days earlier.

THE 10 LATEST WINNERS OF THE BOBBIE ROSENFELD AWARD FOR "FEMALE ATHLETE OF THE YEAR"*

YEAR	WINNER	SPORT
2002	Catriona Le May Doan	Speed skating
2001	Catriona Le May Doan	Speed skating
2000	Lorie Kane	Golf
1999	Nancy Greene#	Skiing
1998	Catriona Le May Doan	Speed skating
1997	Lorie Kane	Golf
1996	Alison Sydor	Cyclist
1995	Susan Auch	Speed skating
1994	Myriam Bedard	Biathlon
1993	Kate Pace	Skiing

* *Presented by The Canadian Press and Broadcast News*

Named "Female Athlete of the Century" as no "Female Athlete of the Year" was awarded in 1999

Source: *Canadian Press*

Bobbie Rosenfeld (1904–69) won a gold medal for the 400 meter relay and a silver for the 100 meters at the Amsterdam Olympics in 1928. She was named Canada's "Female Athlete of the Half-Century" in 1950 by a press poll of sportswriters and was among the first athletes to be inducted into Canada's Sports Hall of Fame.

TOP 10 SPORTS FILMS

	FILM	YEAR	SPORT
1	Rocky IV	1985	Boxing
2	Space Jam	1996	Basketball
3	The Waterboy	1998	Football
4	Days of Thunder	1990	Stock-car racing
5	Cool Runnings	1993	Bobsledding
6	A League of Their Own	1992	Baseball
7	Remember the Titans	2000	Football
8	Rocky III	1982	Boxing
9	Rocky V	1990	Boxing
10	Rocky	1976	Boxing

The boxing ring, immortalized in the Sylvester Stallone *Rocky* series, is predominant in Hollywood's most successful sports-based epics (based on worldwide box-office income). All those in the Top 10 have earned at least US$120 million. If *Forrest Gump* (1994) were considered in this category on the grounds that football and table tennis were featured, it would top the list.

THE 10 LATEST WINNERS OF THE LIONEL CONACHER AWARD FOR "MALE ATHLETE OF THE YEAR"

YEAR	WINNER	SPORT
2002	Steve Nash	Basketball
2001	Mike Weir	Golf
2000	Mike Weir	Golf
1999	Wayne Gretzky*	Hockey
1998	Larry Walker	Baseball
1997	Jacques Villeneuve	Auto racing
1996	Donovan Bailey	Track & field
1995	Jacques Villeneuve	Auto racing
1994	Elvis Stojko	Figure skating
1993	Mario Lemieux	Hockey

* *Named "Male Athlete of the Century" as no "Male Athlete of the Year" was awarded in 1999*

Source: *Canadian Press*

Lionel Conacher (1901–54) is considered by many to be Canada's greatest all-around athlete. He played football with the Toronto Argonauts, hockey with the Montreal Maroons and the Chicago Blackhawks, and baseball with the Toronto Maple Leafs, as well as participating in lacrosse, soccer, track and field, and boxing. In 1950, he was voted Canada's "Male Athlete of the Half-Century" by the Canadian Press.

TOP 10 MOST-WATCHED SPORTING EVENTS ON CANADIAN TELEVISION, 2001–02*

	EVENT	NETWORK	VIEWERS
1	**Salt Lake City Winter Olympic Games—Closing Ceremonies**	CBC	4,601,000
2	**Salt Lake City Winter Olympic Games—Opening Ceremonies**	CBC	2,986,000
3	**Grey Cup Game 2001**	CBC	2,390,000
4	**NHL Stanley Cup 2002 Playoffs—Round 3**	CBC	2,362,000
5	**Salt Lake City Winter Olympic Games**	CBC	2,305,000
6	**NHL Stanley Cup 2002 Playoffs—Round 2**	CBC	2,150,000
7	**NHL Stanley Cup 2002 Playoffs—Round 1** (7 pm)	CBC	1,971,000
8	**Stanley Cup 2002 Finals**	CBC	1,733,000
9	**NHL Stanley Cup 2002 Playoffs—Round 1** (3 pm)	CBC	1,628,000
10	**Salt Lake City Winter Olympic Games—Preview**	CBC	1,569,000

* *On English-language networks; sporting event telecasts from September 3, 2001, to September 1, 2002*

TOP 10 MOST EXPENSIVE OLYMPIC GAMES TV RIGHTS

	VENUE	YEAR	RIGHTS (US$)
1	**Athens**	2004	394,000,000
2	**Sydney**	2000	363,000,000
3	**Atlanta**	1996	240,000,000
4	**Torino***	2006	135,000,000
5	**Salt Lake City***	2002	120,000,000
6	**Barcelona**	1994	90,000,000
7	**Nagano***	1998	72,000,000
8	**Seoul**	1988	26,000,000
9	**Lillehammer***	1994	24,000,000
10	**Los Angeles**	1984	19,800,000

* *Winter Games*

▼ A Run for Their Money
As the Olympic Games attract ever-larger international TV audiences, so the costs, levels of sponsorship, and TV rights have escalated to multimillion-dollar levels.

Leisure Pursuits

TOP 10 COUNTRIES SPENDING THE MOST ON CONSOLE AND COMPUTER GAMES PER CAPITA

	COUNTRY	SALES IN 2000 (US$) TOTAL	PER CAPITA
1	Canada	1,724,000,000	56.1
2	US	14,348,000,000	52.1
3	UK	2,648,000,000	44.6
4	Japan	4,155,000,000	32.7
5	Germany	2,648,000,000	21.1
6	South Korea	1,724,000,000	20.9
7	Italy	990,000,000	16.5
8	Sweden	113,000,000	12.7
9	Australia	219,000,000	11.4
10	France	639,000,000	9.7

Source: *Euromonitor*

TOP 10 FAVORITE SPORTS ON TV (MEN)

	SPORT	PERCENTAGE OF MEN WITH A PREFERENCE
1	Soccer	32
2	= Football	9
	= Baseball	9
4	Basketball	8
5	Auto racing	5
6	Boxing	4
7	= Track & field	2
	= Golf	2
	= Tennis	2
10	= Figure skating	1
	= Gymnastics	1
	= Volleyball	1

Source: *Ipsos-Reid*/Screen Digest

This international survey averages out any national enthusiasms, revealing to Canadian audiences the huge global popularity of soccer and the total eclipse of ice hockey. British and Australasian readers may be saddened to see cricket and rugby similarly discounted.

TOP 10 FAVORITE SPORTS ON TV (WOMEN)

	SPORT	PERCENTAGE OF WOMEN WITH A PREFERENCE
1	Soccer	13
2	= Baseball	8
	= Basketball	8
	= Figure skating	8
5	Football	6
6	= Gymnastics	5
	= Tennis	5
8	= Track & field	4
9	= Swimming	3
	= Volleyball	3

Source: *Ipsos-Reid*/Screen Digest

Beyond sports with a long-standing female following, soccer has experienced a particular surge of interest among women, as both participants and spectators. The 2002 World Cup and the film *Bend It Like Beckham* (2002) are credited with initiating the wave of women's enthusiasm for the game, the latter even inspiring the creation of the first women's soccer league in India.

TOP 10 MOST POPULAR TYPES OF TOY

	TOY	MARKET SHARE PERCENTAGE (2000)
1	Video games	23.2
2	Infant/preschool toys	11.6
3	= Activity toys	10.8
	= Other toys	10.8
5	Games/puzzles	10.6
6	Dolls	9.7
7	Toy vehicles	8.2
8	Plush toys	6.5
9	Action figures	4.4
10	Ride-on toys	4.2

Source: *Eurotoys/The NPD Group Worldwide*

This list is based on a survey of toy consumption in the European Union and can be taken as a reliable guide to the most popular types of toy in the developed world.

TOP 10 TOY-BUYING COUNTRIES

	COUNTRY*	SPENDING ON TOYS PER CAPITA IN 2000 (US$)
1	US	126.1
2	UK	90.1
3	Canada	87.9
4	Belgium	73.7
5	Japan	72.4
6	Denmark	58.8
7	France	57.4
8	Ireland	56.1
9	Sweden	51.3
10	Switzerland	50.5

* *Of those covered by survey*

Source: *Euromonitor*

FIRST COMPUTER GAMES

FIRST FACT

THE FIRST ARCADE GAME, the precursor of all modern computer games, was invented by Nolan Bushnell and Ted Dabney and given the name "Computer Space." Described as "a cosmic dogfight between a spaceship and a flying saucer," it went on sale in 1971 but proved too complicated to achieve wide appeal. Undaunted, its creators, along with Al Alcorn, designed Pong, a game launched in 1972 that achieved enormous success. Bushnell then formed a company called Syzygy, later renamed Atari, and in 1975 sold a version of Pong to be played on a TV set, beginning the era of the home computer games console.

TOP 10 CULTURAL ACTIVITIES IN CANADA

	ACTIVITY	NUMBER OF MEN AND WOMEN PARTICIPATING (1998)*
1	Reading a newspaper	19,851,000
2	Listening to cassettes, records, CDs	18,625,000
3	Watching a video	17,690,000
4	Reading a magazine	17,264,000
5	Reading a book	14,881,000
6	Going to a movie	14,340,000
7	Visiting a conservation area or nature park	10,904,000
8	Attending a professional concert or performance	8,391,000
9	Visiting a historical site	7,863,000
10	Visiting a zoo, aquarium, botanical garden, planetarium	7,820,000

* *Aged 15 and older*

Source: *Statistics Canada*, General Social Survey 1998

◀ In the Swim

Ranking fourth in a list of the most popular sporting activities in Canada, swimming also is one of the best routes to all-around fitness.

TOP 10 ITEMS OF RECREATION SPENDING IN THE US

	CATEGORY	TOTAL EXPENDITURE IN 2000 (US$)*
1	Video and audio goods, including musical instruments	72,700,000,000
2	Commercial participant amusements*	69,200,000,000
3	Nondurable toys and sports supplies	64,600,000,000
4	Wheel goods, sports and photographic equipment, boats, and pleasure aircraft	58,300,000,000
5	Magazines, newspapers, sheet music	36,800,000,000
6	Computers, peripherals, and software	34,300,000,000
7	Books and maps	33,900,000,000
8	Spectator amusements#	27,300,000,000
9	Flowers, seeds, and potted plants	17,500,000,000
10	Clubs and fraternal organizations	16,800,000,000

* *Category includes amusement parks, billiards, bowling, dancing, casino gambling, golfing, riding, shooting, skating, swimming, and sightseeing*

\# *Category includes motion pictures, theater, opera, non-profit entertainments, and spectator sports*

Source: *US Bureau of Economic Analysis,* Survey of Current Business, *April 2002*

Further Information

THE UNIVERSE & THE EARTH

Astronauts & Cosmonauts
http://www.worldspaceflight.com/bios Biographies and other data on space travelers

Encyclopedia Astronautica
http://www.astronautix.com Spaceflight news and reference

NASA
http://www.nasa.gov The principal website for the US space program

Nine Planets
http://www.seds.org/nineplanets/nineplanets A multimedia tour of the solar system

Peaklist
http://www.highalpex.com/Peaklist/peaklist.html Lists of the world's tallest mountains

Space.com
http://www.space.com Reports on events in space exploration

United Nations Atlas of the Oceans
http://www.oceansatlas.org/index.jsp An information resource on oceanographic issues

Volcano Live
http://www.volcanolive.com World volcano news and information

Weather Network
http://www.weather.ca Source for Canadian and worldwide weather data

WebElements
http://www.webelements.com Online periodic table

LIFE ON EARTH

Atlas of Canada
http://atlas.gc.ca/site/english/index.html Geographic facts about Canada, including maps and statistics

Convention on International Trade in Endangered Species of Wild Fauna and Flora (CITES)
http://www.cites.org Lists endangered species of flora and fauna

Dinosauria On-Line
http://www.dinosauria.com Information on and pictures of dinosaurs

Electronic Zoo
http://netvet.wustl.edu/e-zoo.htm Links to sites devoted to animals

FishBase
http://www.fishbase.org/home.htm Global information on fish

Food and Agriculture Organization of the United Nations
http://apps.fao.org FAO statistics on agriculture, fisheries, and forestry

International Shark Attack
http://www.flmnh.ufl.edu/fish/sharks/ISAF/ISAF.htm A database of shark attack records

International Union for the Conservation of Nature
http://iucn.org The leading nature conservation site

PetsForum
http://petsforum.com Information about cats, dogs, and other pets

United Nations Environment Programme
http://www.unep.ch Includes the UN's System-wide Earthwatch and its Global Resource Information Database

THE HUMAN WORLD

Canada Health Portal
http://chp-pcs.gc.ca/CHP/index_e.jsp Access to authoritative health information and services

Eponym
http://www.eponym.org Links to personal name websites

Health Canada
http://www.hc-sc.gc.ca/english/index.html Information and links on health for Canadians

International Agency for Research on Cancer
http://www-dep.iarc.fr Statistics on the incidence of cancer worldwide

Inter-Parliamentary Union
http://www.ipu.org Includes data on women in parliaments

Interpol
http://www.interpol.int Worldwide crime statistics

Rulers
http://rulers.org A database of the world's rulers and political leaders

Statistics Canada
http://www.statcan.ca Canada's statistics-gathering agency, profiling the nation's economy and society

United Nations
http://www.un.org The launch site for accessing the UN's many agencies

World Health Organization
http://www.who.int/en World health information

TOWN & COUNTRY

CIA World Factbook
http://www.odci.gov/cia/publications/factbook Detailed country-by-country data

International Commission on Large Dams
http://www.icold-cigb.org A searchable guide to the world's dams

Skyscrapers.com
http://www.skyscrapers.com/re/en A detailed, searchable guide to the world's tallest buildings

Statistics Canada
http://www.statcan.ca

United Nations City
http://www.photius.com/wfb1999/rankings/cities.html City information for capitals and those with 100,000-plus populations

United Nations Population Division
http://www.un.org/esa/population/unpop.htm Worldwide data on population issues

US Census Bureau
http://www.census.gov US and international population statistics

World Bank
http://www.worldbank.org Development and other statistics from around the world

World's Largest Bridges
http://www.struct.kth.se/research/bridges/Bridges.htm The world's longest bridges listed by type

World's Longest Tunnel Page
http://home.no.net/lotsberg A database of the longest rail, road, and canal tunnels

CULTURE & LEARNING

The Art Newspaper
http://www.theartnewspaper.com News and views on the art world

Canada Council for the Arts
http://www.canadacouncil.ca/home-e.asp Presenter of awards to artists, authors, and scholars

Canadian Library Association
http://www.cla.ca Information on Canadian libraries and book awards

Culture Canada
http://culturecanada.gc.ca A portal to Canadian history, language, music, arts, sports, and education sites

Dorling Kindersley
http://cn.dk.com The Canadian website of the publisher of this book

Global Reach
http://www.glreach.com Facts and figures on online languages

Library of Congress
http://www.loc.gov An online gateway to one of the world's greatest collections of words and pictures

Nobel Prizes
http://www.nobel.se A searchable database of all Nobel Prize winners

Pulitzer Prizes
http://www.pulitzer.org A searchable guide to the prestigious US literary prize

United Nations Educational, Scientific and Cultural Organization (UNESCO)
http://www.unesco.org Comparative international statistics on all aspects of education and culture

MUSIC & MUSICIANS

All Music Guide
http://www.allmusic.com A comprehensive guide to all genres of music

Billboard
http://www.billboard.com US music news and charts data

Canadian Recording Industry Association
http://www.cria.ca The CRIA provides industry sales statistics, and gold, platinum, and diamond certifications

ClassicalUSA.com
http://classicalusa.com An online guide to classical music in the US

Grammy Awards
http://www.naras.org The official site for the US music awards

Juno Awards
http://www.juno-awards.ca Information on winners and artists' summaries

MTV
http://www.mtv.com Online site for the TV music channel

MuchMusic
http://www.muchmusic.com A Canadian television network dedicated to promoting popular music

Rock and Roll Hall of Fame
http://www.rockhall.com The museum of the history of rock

Rolling Stone magazine
http://www.rollingstone.com Website of the popular rock magazine

STAGE & SCREEN

Academy of Canadian Cinema & Television
http://www.academy.ca Information on Genie and Gemini awards

Academy of Motion Picture Arts and Sciences
http://www.oscars.org The official Oscars website

Golden Globe Awards
http://hfpa.org/html Site for the Hollywood Foreign Press Association, which presents these awards

Hollywood.com
http://www.hollywood.com A general US movie website with details on new releases

Internet Movie Database
http://www.imdb.com One of the best of many publicly accessible film websites

Internet Theatre Database
http://www.theatredb.com A Broadway-focused searchable stage site

London Theatre Guide
http://www.londontheatre.co.uk A comprehensive guide to West End theater productions

Theatre Canada
http://www.theatrecanada.org/english/default.htm Information about theater in Canada, including the Dora Awards

Variety
http://www.variety.com Extensive entertainment information (some features are available only with a subscription)

Yahoo! Movies
http://movies.yahoo.com Features and links to the latest movie releases

THE COMMERCIAL WORLD

Forbes magazine
http://www.forbes.com "Rich lists" and other business information

Fortune magazine
http://www.fortune.com/fortune Information on global companies

International Currency Converter
http://www.oanda.com/convert Daily exchange rates for 164 currencies, 1990–present

International Labor Organization
http://www.ilo.org Facts and figures on the world's workers

International Telecommunications Union
http://www.itu.int Worldwide telecommunications statistics

Organization of Economic Co-operation and Development
http://www.oecd.org World economic and social statistics

SMARTRISK
http://www.smartrisk.ca A non-profit organization dedicated to preventing injuries and saving lives

Statistics Canada: Labour
http://www.statcan.ca/english/Pgdb/labour.htm Canadian labor and employment figures

United Nations Development Program
http://www.undp.org Country gross domestic product and other development data

World Bank
http://www.worldbank.org World development and labor statistics

TRANSPORT & TOURISM

AirDisaster.com
http://www.airdisaster.com Reports on aviation disasters

Canadian Tourism Commission
http://www.canadatourism.com A source of Canadian tourism statistics, both provincial and regional

International Registry of Sunken Ships
http://users.accesscomm.ca/shipwreck A database of the world's wrecked and lost ships

International Road Federation
http://www.irfnet.org Facts and figures on the world's roads

Light Rail Transit Association
http://www.lrta.org/world/worldind.html A guide to the world's light railways and tram systems

Parks Canada
http://www.parkscanada.gc.ca A portal to websites about national parks, historic sites, and marine conservation areas in Canada

Railway Gazette International
http://www.railwaygazette.com A website studying the world's railroad business in depth

Roller Coaster DataBase
http://www.rcdb.com A searchable database of some 1,600 world roller coasters

Tourism Offices Worldwide Directory
http://www.towd.com Contact details for tourism offices for countries around the world

World Tourism Organization
http://www.world-tourism.org The world's principal travel and tourism organization

SPORTS & LEISURE

International Association of Athletics Federations
http://www.iaaf.org The statistics and rankings of the world's top athletes

International Olympic Committee
http://www.olympic.org The official website of the Olympic movement, with a searchable database

International Paralympic Committee
http://www.paralympic.org The official website of the International Paralympic Committee

Major League Baseball
http://www.mlb.com The official website of the MLB

National Basketball Association
http://www.nba.com The official website of the NBA

National Football League
http://www.nfl.com The official website of the NFL

National Hockey League
http://www.nhl.com The official website of the NHL

Professional Golfers' Association (PGA) Tour
http://www.pgatour.com

The Sports Network
http://www.tsn.ca Comprehensive site for Canadian sports information

Yahoo! Sports
http://dir.yahoo.com/recreation/sports The directory of entries at Yahoo! covering all aspects of sports

Index

A

B

C

G

I

J

L

M

N

O

Index

Z

Acknowledgments

Special US research: Dafydd Rees
Sport consultant: Ian Morrison
Special Canadian music research: Nanda Lwin, Music Data Research

Alexander Ash; Caroline Ash; Nicholas Ash; David B. Barrett; Nathalie Benoit; Richard Braddish; David Bray; Chuck Breckenridge; Thomas Brinkoff; Pete Compton; Joanna Corcoran-Wunsch; Luke Crampton; Sidney S. Culbert; Anthony D'Aprile; Alain P. Dornic; Lisa Eaton; Philip Eden; Bonnie Fantasia; Christopher Forbes; Cullen Geiselman; Russell E. Gough; Monica Grady; Stan Greenberg; Brad Hackley; Duncan Hislop; Eric Holmes; Andreas Hörstemeier; Richard Hurley; Alan Jeffreys; Todd M. Johnson; Tessa Kale; Larry Kilman; Robert Lamb; Jo LaVerde; Dr. Benjamin Lucas; Catherine McGravey; John Malam; Roberto Mamrud; Dr. Gregg Marland; Chris Mead; Dr. William T. O'Hara; Roberto Ortiz de Zarate; Tony Pattison; Lisa Prenol; Christiaan Rees; Linda Rees; Julia Roles; Adrian Room; Bill Rudman; Michael Seidelman, William Shields; Robert Senior; Karel Stockkermans; Thomas Tranter; Alexis Tregenza; Anita Vanderdonk; Lucy T. Verma; Tony Waltham; Nigel Wilcockson

Academy of Canadian Cinema and Television (Genie and Gemini Awards); Academy of Motion Picture Arts and Sciences (AMPAS)—Oscar statuette is the registered trademark and copyrighted property of the Academy of Motion Picture Arts and Sciences; ACNielsen MMS; *Ad Age Global; Advertising Age; Airline Business;* Air Transport Intelligence; American Film Institute (AFI); American Forestry Association; American Jewish Association; American Library Association (ALA); American Motorcyclist Association (AMA); American Pet Products Manufacturers Association (APPMA); American Religious Identity Survey (ARIS); American Theater Wing (Tony awards); America's Cup; Amnesty International; *Amusement Business;* The Ark Trust; *The Art Newspaper;* Art Sales Index; Association of Workers' Compensation Boards of Canada; Associated Press; Association of Tennis Professionals (ATP); Audit Bureau of Circulations; Bat Conservation International; BC Injury Research & Prevention Unit; BC Ministry of Forests; *Billboard;* Bonham Group; Booker Prize; *BP Statistical Review of World Energy 2002;* British Cave Research Association; British Columbia Register of Big Trees; British Columbia Vital Statistics Agency; *Business Week;* Canada Council for the Arts; Canadian Association of Broadcasters; Canadian Association of Research Libraries; Canadian Cat Association; Canadian Centre for Justice Statistics; Canadian Council of Fire Marshals and Fire Commissioners; Canadian Council on Animal Care; Canadian Football League; Canadian Kennel Club; Canadian Newspaper Association; Canadian Press; Canadian Professional Golfers Association; Canadian Tourism Commission; Cannes Film Festival; CBC Radio Archives; CBC Research; Center for Disease Control (CDC); Central Intelligence Agency (CIA); Centre for Environmental Initiatives, UK; Championship Auto Racing Teams (CART); Channel Swimming Association; Christian Research, UK; Christie's; *Classical Music; The Columbia Granger's Index to Poetry in Anthologies;* Columbia University (Pulitzer Prizes); Commission for Distilled Spirits; comScore Media Metrix Canada; Council of Administrators of Large Urban Public Libraries; Crain Communications; CyberAtlas; Deloitte & Touche Sport; *The Economist; Editor & Publisher Yearbook;* Electoral Reform Society; Elephant Trade Information System (ETIS); Energy Information Administration (EIA); Environmental Technology Center; Euromonitor; Eurotoys; *FBI Uniform Crime Reports;* Federal Bureau of Prisons; Federal Emergency Management Agency; Fédération Equestre Internationale (FEI); Fédération Internationale de Football Association (FIFA); The Financial Times Ltd; Florida Museum of Natural History; Food and Agriculture Organization of the United Nations (FAO); *Forbes; Fortune;* Gemstone Publishing, Inc; Geographical Names Board of Canada, Natural Resources Canada; Geological Survey of Canada, Continental Geoscience Division; Global Reach; *Globe and Mail;* Golden Raspberry Award Foundation; Helpard Publishing; Hennessy & Bray Communications; Hockey Database; Hollywood Foreign Press Association (Golden Globe Awards); Imperial War Museum, IMS Health Canada; Information Resources, Inc; InsideHoops.com; Interbrand; International Agency for Research on Cancer; International Association of Athletics Federations (IAAF); International Atomic Energy Agency; International Coffee Organisation ; International Intellectual Property Alliance (IIPA); International Labor Organization (ILO); International Olympic Committee (IOC); International Paralympic Committee; International Shark Attack File; International Skating Union (ISU); International Ski Federation (FIS); International Table Tennis Federation (ITTF); International Tea Committee Ltd; International Telecommunication Union (ITU); International Trade Administration (ITA); International Union for the Conservation of Nature (IUCN); International Water Ski Federation (IWSF); International Weightlifting Federation (IWF); Inter-Parliamentary Union; Interpol; Ipsos-Reid; Jockey Club; Jockey Club of Canada; Jupiter Media Metrix; League of American Theaters and Producers; Library of Congress; Lloyds Register-Fairplay Ltd; McDonald's; Magazine Publishers of America; Major League Baseball; MastheadOnline.com; Metropolitan Museum of Art; Metropolitan Opera; *Mobile Beat magazine;* Montreal Museum of Fine Arts; Motion Picture Theatre Associations of Canada; MTV; MuchMusic; Music Information Database; National Academy of Popular Music; National Academy of Recording Arts and Sciences (NARAS); National Academy of Television Arts and Sciences (Emmy Awards); National Aeronautics and Space Administration (NASA); National Archives of Canada; National Association of Broadcasters (NAB); National Association of Stock Car Auto Racing, Inc (NASCAR); National Basketball Association (NBA); National Book Foundation; National Center for Education Statistics (NCES); National Center for Health Statistics (NCHS); National Center for Injury Prevention and Control; National Council on Pet Population Study and Policy (NCPPSP); National Fire Data Center (NFDC); National Football League (NFL); National Fraud Information Center, National Consumers League; National Gallery, Washington, DC; National Hockey League (NHL; National Hockey League Players Association (NHLPA); National Park Service; *National Post Business;* National Sporting Goods Association; National Thoroughbred Racing Association (NTRA); Natural History Museum, UK; NetRatings Audience Measurement Service; New York Drama Desk; Nielsen; Nielsen Media Research; Nielsen Media Research Canada; Nobel Foundation; The NPD Group Worldwide; Office of Critical Infrastructure Protection and Emergency Preparedness (OCIPEP); Office of Travel and Tourism Industries; *OperaGlass;* Organisation Internationale des Constructeurs d'Automobiles (OICA); *The Overstreet Comic Book Price Guide;* Parks Canada; Penguin Books; Phobics Society; The Poetry Poll; Pollstar; Professional Golfers' Association (PGA); Professional Squash Association (PSA); Public Library Association ; *Publishers Weekly; Railway Gazette International;* Recording Industry Association of America (RIAA); Rogers Video; Royal Brompton National Heart and Lung Hospital, UK; RSSSF ; Russell Reynolds Associates; Ryder Cup; *Screen Digest;* SearchEngineWatch.com; Sotheby's; *Sports Illustrated; Statistical Abstract of the United States;* Statistics Canada; *Stores;* Students for the Exploration and Development of Space (SEDS); Swimnews Publishing; Swiss Re; Taylor Nelson Sofre; TeleGeography; Toronto Blue Jays Baseball Club; Toronto Stock Exchange; Toronto Theatre Alliance (Dora Mavor Moore Awards); Tour de France; Tourism Industries, International Trade Administration; Transport Canada; UK Home Office; Union Cycliste Internationale (UCI); United Nations (UN); United Nations Educational, Scientific and Cultural Organization (UNESCO); United Nations Environment Programme (UNEP); United Nations Population Division (UNPD); United Nations System-wide Earthwatch; Universal Postal Union; US Bureau of Economic Analysis; US Bureau of Labor Statistics; US Census Bureau ; US Department of Agriculture; US Department of Commerce; US Department of Justice; US Department of Labor; US Fire Administration; US Geological Survey; US Patent and Trademark Office; *Variety;* Verifone; VH1; *Video Business;* VSDA VidTrac; Ward's AutoInfoBank; WebElements; Weddings Canada; Westbridge Publications; Woodbine Entertainment Thoroughbreds; Women's International Squash Players Association (WISPA); Women's Tennis Association (WTA); World Association of Newspapers (WAN); *World Atlas of Coral Reefs;* World Bank; *World Christian Trends;* World Conservation Monitoring Centre (WCMC); World Health Organization (WHO); World Intellectual Property Organization (WIPO); World Motocross Championships; *World of Learning;* World Snowboarding Federation (WSF); World's Strongest Man Contest; World Tourism Organization (WTO); Yellow Pages Integrated Media Association; Zurich World Rankings.

Statistics Canada information is used with the permission of the Minister of Industry, as Minister responsible for Statistics Canada. Information on the availability of the wide range of data from Statistics Canada can be obtained from Statistics Canada's Regional Offices, its World Wide Web site at http://www.statcan.ca, and its toll-free access number 1-800-263-1136.

Picture Credits

The publisher would like to thank the following for their kind permission to reproduce their images: (Position key: c=centre, b=bottom, r=right, l=left, t=top)

1: Getty Images/Alan Klehr (b); Getty Images/Alan Thornton (t); **2–3**: Corbis/Alan Schein Photography (t), **2–3**: Image Quest 3-D/Scott Tuason (b); **4**: Pa Photos (b); **5**: Getty Images/Sylvaine Achernar; **6–7**: Corbis/Rick Doyle; **8–9**: Corbis/Paul Hudson; **10**: NASA; **11**: NASA; **12**: NASA; **13**: Science Photo Library/NASA; **14–15**: Corbis/Brandon D. Cole; **17**: Getty Images/Sylvaine Achernar; **18–19**: Corbis/Galen Rowell; **23**: Science Photo Library/ArSciMed; **24–25**: Popperfoto/Reuters; **27**: Rex Features/El Tiempo; **28–29**: Image Quest 3-D/Scott Tuason; **43**: Corbis/Yann Arthus-Bertrand; **44**: Photodisc; **45**: Photodisc; **47**: Photodisc; **48–49**: Corbis/Gavriel Jecan; **50**: Foodpix; **52**: Corbis/Peter Turnley; **54**: Corbis/Wolfgang Kaehler; **55**: Corbis/Lindsay Hebberd; **57**: Getty Images/Luc Beziat; **60–61**: ImageState/Pictor/Jurgen Magg Photography; **63**: Press Association Picture Library/EPA; **64**: Getty Images/Tony Garcia; **67**: Getty Images/Paul Edmondson; **69**: Hulton Archive/Getty Images; **70**: Corbis/Steve Kaufman; **71**: Corbis/Galen Rowell; **74–75**: Getty Images/Austin Brown; **82**: Panos Pictures/Jean-Léo Dugast; **84**: Press Association Picture Library/EPA; **85**: Corbis/Bettmann; **86–87**: Axiom/Jim Holmes; **88–89**: Getty Images/Ron Chapple; **90**: Getty Images/China Tourism Press; **94**: Panos Pictures/Jeremy Hartley; **97**: Camera Press/Tom Wargacki; **98**: P A Photos/Matthew Fearn; **101**: Getty Images/Derek P. Redfearn; **102–103**: DK Picture Library/Alistair Duncan; **105**: Courtesy of Sotheby's Picture Library, London; **106**: Retna Pictures Ltd/Michael Putland; **108–109**: Getty Images/Darrell Gulin; **110**: P A Photos/EPA; **112**: Kobal Collection/Paramount; **113**: Redferns/Michael Ochs Archives; **114**: Redferns/Nicky J. Sims; **115**: Redferns/George Chin; **117**: Redferns/James Dittiger; **119**: Redferns/John Gumon; **120**: Redferns/David Redfern; **122**: Corbis/Lynn Goldsmith; **123**: Redferns; **124**: Rex Features/Alex Oliveira; **125**: Rex Features/ Matt Baron/BEI; **127**: Pa Photos; 128: Redferns/Martin Philbey; 129: Redferns/John Gunion; **130**: Kobal Collection/Paramount; **132–133**: Corbis/Alan Schein photography; **134**: Pa Photos/Jordan Peter Jordan; **135**: Rex Features/Donald Cooper; **136**: Album/Lucus Films LTD & TM/Keith Hamshere; **138**: Dinodia Picture Agency; **139**: Aquarius Library/Miramax; **140**: Kobal Collection/Columbia/Marvel; **141**: Kobal Collection/Wing Nut Films/Pierre Vinet.; **143**: Rex Features/Dreamworks/ Everett (EVT); **145**: Kobal Collection/Miramax/ David James; **146**: Rex Features/Miramax/ Everett (EVT); **148**: Kobal Collection/ Paramount/Miramax/Clive Coote; **150**: Kobal Collection/Focus Features/ Studio Canal/Guy Ferrandis; **152**: Kobal Collection/Universal/Vivian Zink; **154**: Kobal Collection/ Paramount; **156**: Kobal Collection/20th Century Fox; **157**: Rex Features/Warner Br/Everett (EVT); **159**: Kobal Collection/Warner Bros/Bob Marshak; **160**: DK Picture Library/Magnus Rew; **162**: Getty Images/Don Smetzer; **164–165**: Getty Images/Alan Klehr; **166**: Corbis/SABA/Keith Dannemiller; **169**: Corbis/David Samuel Robbins; **170**: Getty Images/David Seed Photography; **172**: Getty Images/Bruce Hands; **174–175**: Corbis/David Samuel Robbins; **176**: Corbis/SABA/Mark Peterson; **177**: Rex Features; **178**: Corbis/Mark E. Gibson; **179**: Corbis/Francesca Muntada; **180–181**: Getty Images/Yellow Dog Productions; **182**: Rex Features; **184**: NASA; **192–193**: Getty Images; **195**: Getty Images/VCL (tr); **196**: Pa Photos/EPA; **198**: Corbis; **200**: Hulton Archive/Getty Images/American Stock/Archive Photos; **201**: Hulton Archive/Getty Images; **202–203**: alamy.com/Charlie Newham; **203**: Getty Images/VCL (tr); **204**: Rex Features; **206–207**: Getty Images/Alan Thornton; **208**: Empics Ltd/Aubrey Washington; **210**: Empics Ltd/Tony Marshall; **211**: Empics Ltd/Tony Marshall; **212**: Getty Images/Al Bello/Allsport; **213**: Getty Images/Agence Zoom; **214**: Empics Ltd/Adam Davy; **215**: Empics Ltd/Tony Marshall; **216**: Action Plus; **217**: Action Plus; **218**: P A Photos/EPA; **225**: Topham Picturepoint/John Babb/Pro Sport; **229**: Empics Ltd/Tony Marshall; **230**: Empics Ltd; **231**: Getty Images/David Cannon; **233**: Empics Ltd/Fotopress Photographer Phil Walter; **234**: Empics Ltd/Forum Press; **235**: Corbis/Rick Doyle; **236**: Getty Images/David Norton; **238**: Empics Ltd/DPA Photographer Gero Breloer; **239**: Empics Ltd/Sport and General; **240**: Empics Ltd/John Marsh; **241**: Empics Ltd/Steve Etherington; **243**: Corbis/Wally McNamee; **256**: Album/Lucus Films LTD & TM/Keith Hamshere.

For further information see: **www.dkimages.com**

Publisher's acknowledgments
Dorling Kindersley would like to thank the following for their contributions: Editorial Sharon Lucas; Design Marianne Markham, Design Revolution; Picture Research Franziska Marking, Cynthia Frazer, Marie Osborn; Picture Library Hayley Smith, Richard Dabb, Claire Bowers

Index
Ursula Caffrey

Packager's acknowledgments
The Bridgewater Book Company would like to thank Susie Behar, Alison Bolus, Stephanie Horner, and Tom Kitch for editorial assistance, and Richard Constable, Chris Morris, Warrick Sears, and Barbara Theisen for their design work.